Smarter Cities
for a Bright Sustainable Future: A Global Perspective

ALAN R. SHARK

SYLVIANE TOPORKOFF

SÉBASTIEN LÉVY

Public Technology Institute and ITEMS International • Publishers

Washington, DC • Paris, France

Library of Congress Cataloging-Publication-Data
Shark, Alan; Toporkoff, Sylviane; Lévy, Sébastien
Smarter Cities for a Bright Sustainable Future: A Global Perspective
p. cm.
ISBN-13: 9781497339453
ISBN-10: 1497339456

1. Cities and towns–History. 2. City Planning–Technological innovations. 3. Regional planning–Technological innovations. 4. Information technology 5. Public administration I.Title

Public Technology Institute
1420 Prince Street, Suite 2
Alexandria Virginia 22314

www.pti.org

Other Books Published by PTI and Items International

eHealth-A Global Perspective (2010)

Beyond eGovernment-Measuring Performance: A Global Perspective (2010)

Beyond e-Government & e-Democracy: A Global Perspective (2008)

Preface

Why are we all spending time talking about smart cities and counties? Experts predict that by end of next year, 70% of the world's population will be living in cities. According to the United Nations, 84% of a projected world population of 10.8 billion will be city dwellers by the year 2100.

These are startling projections. These statistics mean that we, as local leaders, need to continually discuss and visualize options for meeting the challenges and changing dynamics of a growing number of residents, businesses, visitors, and infrastructure.

The truly smart city embraces:

- Effective leadership
- New types of governance
- An engaged public
- Innovative policy development
- Investments in human capital (education, training)
- Investments in and traditional and modern infrastructure
- Sustainable and green practices
- Resiliency
- A high quality of life for all citizens
- Effective use of technology

Notice that last word: Technology. Technology courses through all the elements cited above. This is why I am so pleased that the Public Technology Institute, in partnership with Items International, has published this book to provide a practical guide for local officials who are interested in pursuing a path towards becoming a smarter city.

The chapters in this book provide examples of Smart Cities policies, practices, decisions and programs that have been deployed in communities within the United States and across the world. The chapters have been written by actual practitioners and private sector experts who have embraced this and embarked on this journey.

Smart cities do not just happen; this is an emerging area and we are all seeking collaborative approaches to find the right answers. As local leaders we need to be engaged and be aggressive and progressive in the Smart

Cities movement. As local leaders we need to be committed and visionary to ensure that our communities are on the forefront of this movement.

I am personally proud to be a part of this Smart Cities discussion and I am pleased that my organization, the National League of Cities, is taking a leadership role in promoting resources, like this book, and educating our audience about the opportunities that this movement provides.

CLARENCE ANTHONY *is the Executive Director of the National League of Cities. The NLC is dedicated to helping city leaders build better communities. Working in partnership with the 49 state municipal leagues, NLC serves as a resource to and an advocate for the more than 19,000 cities, villages and towns it represents.*

Mr. Anthony served as the Mayor of South Bay, FL for 24 years. He is known as a creative and thoughtful leader in his community. He is considered an expert in citizen engagement and techniques that build a "sense of community" within cities. Mr. Anthony has been on the forefront of politics in the United States and internationally for the past 20 years, culminating with productive presidencies of the Florida League of Cities and the NLC, respectively.

He holds a Masters Degree in Public Administration with specialization in City Growth Management policy from Florida Atlantic University.

Introduction

Ancient Rome and Athens were once considered by every indication, great cities! European cities have endured a number of long wars that nearly destroyed them permanently. In the U.S., the City of San Francisco was nearly wiped out by the earthquake of 1906 and in 1871 the City of Chicago was nearly destroyed by fire. In nearly every case, these major cities were able to recover, rebuild, transform, making them stronger and more resilient. Today the so-called "smart cities" movement is based in part on the confluence of new technologies, economic growth, a re-evaluation of quality of life factors, as well as the resurgence of interest in cities across the globe. For example, only recently have we witnessed the trend towards urban growth in American cities. Today the outward migration has reversed itself after decades of residents moving to the suburbs or further out to rural parts of the country. Now, people are returning to our cities, or have decided not to leave as their forefathers had before them. This reinforces the need to re-think and to act differently when it comes to urban planning and maintaining sustainable cities.

Even the smartest of cities can not rest on their past success. Smart cities require a constant process of vision, execution, and renewal, which makes it more a journey than a destination. There are many elements that comprise a smart or intelligent city. This book was created to further explore those elements and the pathways towards becoming and maintaining a smart city.

This book is a collection of works from thought-leaders across the globe, with authors currently residing in no less than 10 countries including France, Spain, Italy, Belgium, South Africa, Japan, Saudi Arabia, Singapore, Estonia, and Russia, in addition to the United States. The twenty-seven chapters reveal that there is far more in common than not, as each author shares their research and insights, all aimed at helping the reader better understand and appreciate the contemporary smart city movement.

As the smart cities movement gains attention, some have been critical—going as far to say that this is only a passing fad or a relabeling of current events. Whether this is a fad or not, one thing is crystal clear, cities are growing and are here to stay. It is an undeniable fact that growing populations place an enormous strain on our cities in terms of transportation, infrastructure, public safety, health, education, and the quality of natural resources such as water and air. Finally there is the issue of energy and sustainability from an environmental perspective.

The fall of ancient Rome may not have happened in a day, but its decline and those of other, once great, cities provide both lessons and warnings that are instructive. These lessons remind us that in the end cities are a profound collection of citizens, and without their meaningful engagement we may be left with cities that are no longer smart.

About the Executive Editors

DR. ALAN R. SHARK currently serves as the Public Technology Institute's executive director/CEO. He also serves as Associate Professor of Practice at Rutgers University's School of Public Affairs and Administration where he also serves as the Director of the Center for Technology Leadership. As an author, lecturer, and speaker on technology developments and applications for most of his distinguished career, He is a Fellow of the National Academy for Public Administration, and was the recipient of the prestigious 2012 National Technology Champion Award from the National Association of State Chief Information Officers. He is the author of the book *Seven Trends that Will Transform Local Government Through Technology*.

DR. SYLVIANE TOPORKOFF is partner and founder of ITEMS International, a company specialized on strategic ICT consulting, and full Professor at the University of Paris 8, Institute of European Studies, in France. She obtained her doctorate in Economics from the University of Paris I Pantheon Sorbonne. Dr. Toporkoff is specialized on international (Europe, USA and worldwide) research and consulting in the area of the Information Society; public policy; economic and strategic international partnerships for industrialists, operators and local authorities; marketing on issues related to e-Business; e-Gov; e-health; local, regional and international development through the use of ICT; e-Democracy; and telecommunications industry regulation. Dr. Toporkoff is President and founder of the Global Forum/Shaping the Future, a think tank on ICT, which annually assembles international top-level managers of leading companies and organizations, cities and regions since 1992.

SEBASTIEN LÉVY is senior consultant and associate partner of ITEMS International, a strategic consulting company with a core focus on ICT. As expert consultant and ICT advisor, he has worked for a large number local governments in France and the European Commission. Mr. Lévy collaborated to a wide range of studies at the strategic and policy level. Being involved in different national and European smart cities projects, he contributed to the development and deployment of smart cities strategies in several European cities. Sebastien Lévy is also vice-president of the Global Forum/Shaping the Future—an annual international high-profile Think Tank, bringing together senior government officials, policymakers and industry leaders from across the world. Mr. Lévy is expert in the Open Innovation Strategy and Policy Group (OISPG) initiated by the European Commission and actively contributed to the development of the European Commission's Living Lab strategy. Sebastien Lévy is "Chevallier de l'Ordre National du Mérite".

Acknowledgements

This book is the fourth in a series by the Public Technology Institute (PTI) and Items International. As with each of the books published in our Global Perspective series, this book is aimed at providing a forum that reaches out to a rather unique universe of practitioners, academics, researchers, and government thought leaders on the significance of smarter cities.

We want to thank our 39 contributing authors for taking the time from their busy schedules in order to write 27 outstanding chapters. The strength of this type of a book is found in its rich diversity of opinion, style, and perspective. Some may find the varying writing styles (which we maintained) to be somewhat of a distraction, but we wanted to preserve the essence of the message as it was told by the author to near original form. This was intentional, and hopefully most readers will be appreciate what we strived to maintain and achieve.

We are also grateful to the PTI's production team, which includes, our copy editor, Patti Tom Watt who is an award-winning, multi-platform writer, editor and manager with more than a decade of experience. She excels in creating engaging and accurate content through various mediums, and as importantly, delivering on deadline. Sally Hoffmaster is also an award-winner who once again served as our excellent and talented graphic designer who designed the cover and the physical layout for each page of the manuscript. Both devoted many long hours accompanied by many obstacles and challenges along the way.

About The Global Forum & Items International

Items International is headquartered in Issy-les-Moulineaux Cedex, France; with additional offices in select cities around the world. The Global Forum is part of Items International that for over twenty years meets once a year—rotating among various cities across the globe. The Global Forum is an internationally recognized think-tank for exchange and networking among governments at national, regional & local levels, private & public organizations, as well as research & development experts. The Global Forum is an independent, high-profile, international, non-for-profit annual event dedicated to business and policy issues affecting the successful evolution of the Digital Society. The Global Forum brings each year in a different city around the world more than 300 key policy-makers and public/private stakeholders from more than 30 countries from all continents, it is often considered as the Davos for ICT.

For more information, see: http://globalforum.items-int.com/

About PTI

Located in the greater Washington DC area, PTI was founded in 1971 and continues to actively support technology leadership for local government executives and elected officials through research, education, executive-level consulting services, training and development programs, and national recognition programs. As the only technology organization created by and for cities and counties, PTI works with a core network of leading local officials—the PTI membership—to identify research opportunities, share solutions, recognize member achievements and address the many technology issues that impact local government. PTI also offers online educational programs throughout the year and maintains a strong strategic partnership with Rutgers University's School of Public Affairs & Administration.

For more information, see: www.pti.org

Contents

1

What Makes Smart Cities Smart?

Dr. Alan R. Shark

No mayor wants to be the leader of a "dumb" city. To the contrary, mayors enjoy being able to promote how great and "smart" their cities are. Most definitions of smart include "showing intelligence or good judgment." Yet there are many ways to explain what a smart city is and looks like.

Popular descriptors for smart cities include: sustainable, intelligent, connected, livable, resilient and innovative, to name a few. These terms all share a common theme in describing how adopting and intelligently using technologies and coordinated systems in key areas improves the quality of life in cities (let us not forget counties, townships and villages, too).

Cities simply do not become smart by accident or without thoughts regarding sustainability. The corporate world has invested substantial resources in promoting its vision of smart cities. Information management companies such as IBM, Cisco, Siemens and Microsoft, for instance, are attracted to this type of initiative because of the opportunities to provide solutions to an entire municipality instead of knocking on each and every individual government department's door Thus, smart cities need to be viewed as a comprehensive composite of a city's various systems.

However, whether becoming a smart city is a goal or a destination remains to be seen. Cities, always vying for No. 1 status in at least one positive category, have visions and plans that are often driven by leaders in various departments and divisions. Public managers, for example, are always seeking ways to bolster their economic development strategies and plans aimed at increasing revenues while adding quality of life-type factors. Meanwhile, cities strive to attract new businesses and seek ways to retain the businesses that they have. Cities also face business development challenges to address citizens' growing quality of life issues.

With an increasingly mobile population, if a city's crime rate becomes unlivable, or traffic and transportation become unbearable, people will move to another city where things appear to be better. The citizens that move tend to be the ones with the highest incomes and who are able to pay the cost to move. This places pressure on cities that cannot afford to lose some of their largest taxpayers and spenders.

The need for smarter cities is growing. This is especially true because for the first time in nearly 50 years, the population growth rate in American cities is greater than the growth rate in suburban and rural areas. More than 82 percent of Americans live in a city, and some predict that number will climb to 90 percent by 2050. For a variety of quality of life issues, people are moving back to cities where they seek employment opportunities, as well as improved transportation systems, healthcare, education, and sports and cultural activities.

Cities consume two-thirds of the nation's energy, consume 60 percent of water resources, and produce 70 percent of greenhouse gas emissions. Cities looking to meet the challenges of a growing population must also face aging infrastructure—both the physical and the digital—challenges. Consequently, for many urban planners and senior public managers, creating a smart city is somewhat of an elusive dream. They see themselves faced with tremendous pressure to do so much more with so less against a backdrop of a growing population with rising expectations and declining revenues.

Understanding Smart Cities

To better understand smart cities, it might be useful to look at a smart home. There is no single distinguishing factor that makes a smart home. Instead, a smart home implements attributes, such as a clean and appealing exterior design, lighting that adjusts to ambient surroundings, and uses natural sunlight when possible. The lighting usually consumes less energy than a typical dwelling. Heating and cooling systems also are designed to work in concert with the building structure to use natural sunlight and heat, or to reflect radiant external heat away from the skin of the building. Cooling systems can rely on natural below-earth tanks. Solar panels may be mounted on the roof to generate and store electricity. And water can be heated and rain water collected from roofs and stored for a sunny day. Thermostats often are remote and programmable so temperature can be adjusted when no one is home. Entertainment systems often are found throughout the dwelling and connected wirelessly through ultra-fast WiFi. A smart home's layout should be designed more efficiently so that living, dining, storage and sleeping areas are maximized for usage and livability. Ultimately, a smart home is sustainable and energy-efficient. Smart homes are rather simplistic compared to smart cities. Nevertheless, smart buildings are a key subset of smart cities where components and systems cooperate.

Building a Smart City

Building a smart city begins with a vision, goal or a statement of principal. The difficultly then lies in the details and mustering the necessary financial resources and senior management talent. Finding the right people who will collaborate department and agency-wide can be as large a stumbling block as finding financial resources to build a smart city. Cities employ municipal workers who comprise a number of common ecosystems that traditionally have operated as independent authorities in which the various heads would have little incentive to build relationships from the top down or across to the various bureaucratic boundaries. Many long-standing silos and stovepipes will be challenged in their historic culture of autonomous influence and control.

In addition to managerial challenges, there are technical challenges to building a smart city, which has many moving parts.

Cities are comprised of citizens and visitors who depend on services, as well as business and commerce. The explosive growth of technology and the ability to better store and retrieve information, and to do so in a relatively inexpensive manner, is also pushing cities to modernize. The cost of both computing power and storage capacity has increased in complexity and functionality, while the price has remained constant or decreased. Because of technological advancements, smart cities often incorporate data-driven decision-making. This is the ability to take structured and unstructured data, and develop information that leads to better decision-making and planning. Numerous thought-leaders have written about or have identified the many elements of a smart city. Such elements include: energy and utilities; traffic control; water management along with water reuse; clean air; social services; communications; education; public safety; economic development; abundant green space; retail and business support; intelligent transportation; as well as data and information technology systems and infrastructure, to name a few.

Much of this can be reduced to the following set of six components that are found in most smart cities.

1. Smarter Transportation (Bus, Car, Train, Planes, Boats)

People need to move about freely and safely, let alone conveniently. Urban transportation is no longer focused on cars, trains, buses, planes and ferryboats. There is a growing blur between private and public transportation, and the two systems have become inseparable. Private cars rely on public thoroughfares and, through taxes, help pay for road and bridge maintenance. Today, smart cities are embracing ride-sharing or short-term car rentals. Bike sharing also has become popular in most major U.S.

cities. To be successful, many of these initiatives require public-private partnerships to maintain incentives for private businesses and to provide the infrastructure and spaces.

Parking in cities is always a challenge. Today we see the growth of more innovative technologies that include apps to alert citizens as to where open parking spaces are available in real-time. Smart parking meters in which a citizen who has paid for a parking meter using his or her smart device can be notified when the meter is about to expire, and be given the option to add money to the meter without having to physically going to the meter itself. This allows citizens to enjoy greater flexibility, and the city benefits by generating greater revenue through the smart metering process.

High occupancy vehicle (HOV) and high occupancy toll (HOT) lanes that control traffic flow during peak and nonpeak hours are often features of smart cities. Most urban traffic planners agree that the nation's road infrastructure cannot keep pace with the population growth. Unless better technologies and economic incentives are deployed, citizens face the prospect of urban gridlock.

Urban planners also agree that cities need better incentives and technologies to encourage greater use of all forms of public transportation. Bus systems used to be notorious for their inability to coordinate their many routes with neighboring transportation systems and the city's own subway system. Everything often operates independently without a standard fare card system. In the Washington, D.C., metro area, there are no less than 17 commuter bus systems and three rail systems, and until recently they did not accept a common fare card system, which made it difficult for commuters and tourists to get around the region.

Cities are getting better at coordinating transportation scheduling and pricing. Yet a smart city requires a responsive, understandable and affordable system. Ridership increases when citizens can look at a bus stop sign (or app) and know in real-time when the next bus is arriving, that the bus is clean and at a comfortable climate; possibly offers WiFi, and adheres to schedules that conform to an active lifestyle. Cities today are experimenting with light rail projects, special commuter bus routes with accompanying incentives, and even the use of ferryboats where it makes sense. Some communities are assigning different transportation services based on need, using smaller vehicles for non-peak hours and larger vehicles during peak hours. Many cities are linking in airports with public transportation to bring passengers directly into the city. And smart municipalities are at the forefront of using alternative fuels (electric power, natural gas, etc.) for public transportation vehicles. Ultimately, a smart city looks at the demographic data from its citizens and uses the data wisely to better serve the community with direct routing and scheduling of transportation options.

Meanwhile, the federal government is playing a vital role in promoting intelligent transportation. For instance, it has been active partner in the adoption of alternative fuels, better highway mileage standards for cars and trucks, and the adoption of emission requirements for a cleaner and healthier environment. The government has invested in smart signage projects, special time-metered hot lanes and the use of electric cars.

Public Transportation Dislikes

- *Poorly designed schedules*
- *Wrong stops*
- *Dirty buses or trains*
- *Complicated schedules requiring transfers*
- *Complicated fare structures*
- *Fares that are perceived as being too high*
- *Unpredictable lateness*
- *Over-crowded*
- *Unprotected stations and stops*
- *Uncomfortable seats*
- *Complicated maps*
- *Poor lighting*
- *Poor climate control*
- *Poor maintenance*
- *Safety issues*

Future smart city initiatives might include self-driving cars, interactive trip planning tools on smart phones and tablets, more time-based fares on public transportation systems, WiFi on public transportation systems, ubiquitous parking and fare card systems, and the ability to pay for fares and services by merely swiping their smart device. Future smart city initiatives also might include real-time vehicle location on maps, and the ability to view hundreds, if not thousands of camera feeds along any chosen route.

The key to intelligent urban transportation planning lies in the ability for planners to use the latest technologies and take a holistic approach toward a city's transportation needs.

2. Smarter Digital Infrastructure

Cities require a robust and powerful digital infrastructure that not only has a rich mixture of fiber and wireless communications, but it also must provide for a variety of strategic sensors and monitors that measure the flow of human and physical events. Simply put, a smart city needs to insure that there is ample broadband availability, affordability and accessibility throughout a given region. This requires that buildings, transportation, utilities and public safety, as well as its citizens, are all connected in various ways with multiple devices. Broadband is the new conduit that makes smart cities possible and serves as the backbone of all other smart city initiatives. Cities need not necessarily build the broadband infrastructure systems themselves, but they must play an active leadership role in making sure that the city's needs are being met. Cities can provide incentives such as zoning, one-dig plan requirements, right-of-way easements, public-private partnerships, as well as economic incentives, to name a few.

3. Citizen Engagement

Citizens need to feel connected and informed to enjoy a sense of community. When addressing the issue of smart and sustainable cities, citizen engagement often has been left out. Reliable and high-speed broadband access is a fundamental element of smart cities to help foster that sense of community. Because citizens increasingly are using smart devices everywhere they go, smart devices, which rely on broadband technology, have become social and economic enablers.

Studies show that citizens want to be engaged with their friends and family and, to a growing extent, their cities. Thus, smart cities increasingly are engaging citizens and building that feeling of community through web applications, smart phone apps, and other forms of social and civic communications. City websites and related apps allow citizens to get the latest information about business, government, services and culture. This channel of communications also allows citizens to submit online forms and pictures, and receive a timely response from the city. For instance, apps are allowing citizens to report potholes, abandoned cars, uncollected garbage, housing violations, and more. With community-driven data, smart cities can better pinpoint citizen needs, better deploy resources and more easily resolve problems. Even as citizens are mobile, handheld devices will serve as a central communication hub that places hundreds of government and community programs and services at their fingertips.

With smart technology, the public will not only be able to solicit information and identify government resources, but it also will be able to engage with government. Citizens will have the capacity to develop content about their communities that might include pictures, data, information, and experiences that can be shared. With shared citizen information, the public will be able to more easily evaluate a community's transportation, public safety, healthcare, education, social services, and cultural opportunities and offerings This will influence how citizens navigate their governments' services and offerings. This also will influence where citizens deem the best places to live and work. From a citizen-centric point of view, smart devices should allow cities to be more livable, more enjoyable, and to create sustainable programs that meet the public's needs.

4. Smart and Big Data

Cities have always been awash in data like rain that is plentiful but not collected. In the past few years, cities and public managers have begun to realize the potential of not only collecting data, but also of analyzing data so that it creates useful information. Smart data and big data, both structured and unstructured, have gained importance as technology tools allow public managers to delve deeper into this ocean of data. For instance, there is also a growing and renewed performance measurement movement that focuses on taking data and placing it within a system that provides the necessary tools to analyze and to better understand how the needs of citizens are being articulated. Such a system also provides the tools necessary to compare data among internal and external city operations.

With the advent of smart data comes predictive analytics. Predictive analytics has the ability to take real-time data so that it can be used to predict current and future events. A good example is crime prevention. If with data law enforcement can identify a particular crime that occurs repetitively at a particular time and in a particular area, it becomes easier to project when the next crime might occur. Smart data, big data and predictive analytics thus are being used to better understand the workings of the city, its span of operations, its citizens and visitors.

It is not enough to collect data independently, however. Successful cities need to collect and analyze data, as well as share and collaborate. For the citizen this might mean that instead of filling out multiple forms over the years for various city services, there will be one record that is more accurate and maintained across city agencies and departments.

Unstructured data that is not necessarily associated with any specific individual, also can be useful in better understanding the overall habits and usage of city services. Today, health officials can measure intelligent maps where illnesses can be plotted from the moment they are reported to the moment they are cured. Traffic pattern measurements can be used to identify which roads are used most heavily, at what time of the day, how well our transportation systems are coping with demand, and how well transportation systems are being used at any given moment. Mashing up data sets from one database to another provides public managers with new insights to better manage scarce resources.

Cities such as New York, Chicago, Philadelphia, and San Francisco have created open data sites on their websites. These initiatives make it possible for citizens, businesses, nonprofits and entrepreneurs who intake structured and unstructured data to create new forms of applications and understanding. Like smart cities, smart data is a combination of structured and unstructured data sets that provide public managers with the tools necessary to be only better informed, as well as to make better decisions in a time when resources are scarce.

5. Data Visualization

City leaders and citizens need to be able to visualize what has been planned in their neighborhoods, such as new buildings, transportation routes, and other improvements that lend themselves to maps accompanied by solid visual data. However, not all visualized data has to be directly associated with maps. Information normally presented in spreadsheets can now be shown in brilliant color with three-dimensional charts that can better illustrate trends, patterns, and comparisons by time of day, day of month.

Enterprise geospatial systems are becoming essential tools that can take location-based data and plot tit on interactive maps. This allows urban planners to draw upon hundreds of layers of data to help public managers better see the present as well as envision the future. New structures—buildings or infrastructure such as streets and roadways—can be modeled to see how they can best be positioned and built. Geospatial systems can enable planners to predict trends, monitor real-time scenarios, and literally "see" the future without wasting time and resources. Citizens, too, can serve as "volunteer sensors" that feed into data systems that are generated from smart phones and other mobile devices.. Through geospatial systems, city managers will be better equipped to know what, when, where, why and how to take action. They will have the tools and unsurpassed ability to integrate information and discover relationships between objects and people.

6. Leadership & Vision

Smart cities and smart technology require strong leadership to see and envision the big picture. The necessary leadership is not just about the qualities of a mayor or city manager, or their immediate staff. Leadership must involve many division and departmental senior public managers, too. Running a city is much like conducting a symphony where each section has its own expertise, but someone needs to lead and coordinate the movement to ensure everyone is reading the same music sheet. In a smart city, leadership develops a vision and then systems are built around shared acceptance of that vision. There is room for improvisation on some levels, but smart cities need to coordinate key services.

To succeed in creating a smart city, it must be more than an election slogan. There is every indication that cities will continue to grow in population and demand for services will increase because of the growth.

Municipal leaders need to make decisions that address how to best utilize technology to maintain and improve quality of life for citizens. This is especially true when cities are challenged with doing so much more with far fewer resources. Cities will grow regardless of how well they are planned. Some will merely grow, while others that understand the characteristics of expansion and plan how the sum of its parts can better work together will grow smartly. The smart city ecosystem will serve as the economic engine for a brighter and sustainable future.

DR. ALAN R. SHARK *is the executive director and CEO of the Public Technology Institute (PTI). He is a noted author and sought-after speaker focusing on mobile and e-government, technology trends in government, and thought-leadership professional development issues for IT executives and public managers. He is an associate professor of practice at Rutgers University, where he teaches a masters-level course on technology and public administration. He also serves as the director for The Center for Technology Leadership.*

Shark is the recipient of the 2012 National Technology Champion Award from the National Association of State Chief Information Officers. He also is a fellow of the National Academy for Public Administration and serves on the U.S. steering committee for the Global Forum.

2

The City as a Platform

Sylviane Toporkoff and Hervé Rannou

Smart Cities are going to introduce dramatic changes in the relationship between cities, public utilities and citizens. The increasing amount of data we generate today drastically fosters the emergence of new services for citizens and new tools to local governments. City as a Platform proposes an approach based on the compelling compromise for both Strategic Governance and Infrastructures & Services Management within an innovative Smart City.

Smart City gathers different technologies and services which are going to change the relationship between the city, the citizen and the organizations in charge of services provisioning: the utilities.

1. Digital technologies for utilities: a history of "positive" silos

The digital technologies have introduced fundamental changes concerning utilities. Their impact can be measured at different levels: real time systems included in infrastructures, technical operations including internal technical processes, services provisioning, billing and customers care, organizations processes and management.

In the end, the digital technologies have improved:

- the way the infrastructure works,
- the way the utilities operate,
- the way companies interact with the citizen.

Each domain can get an advantage from the technologies developed for specific needs within the cities. It means that each of them has) rolled out advanced architectures including its own sensors, meters, real time systems, IT systems and software.

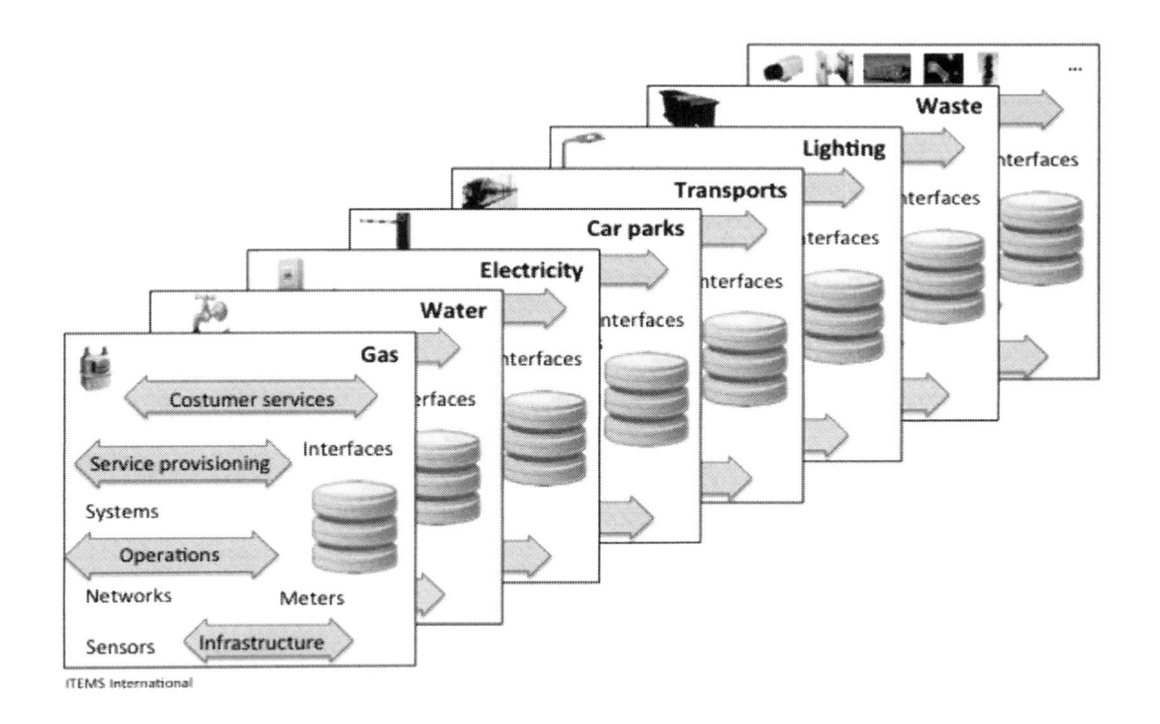

Figure 1. *Digital layout for public utilities.*

It is frequent to present public entities as silos. This representation actually highlights the fact that the different utilities have always been operating independently. Several objective reasons can explain and justify this situation. Firstly, the public utilities used to request strong and specialized expertise. Secondly, the budget management and control imply to identify assets and operations.

Generally, the introduction of Digital Technologies in each of these sectors is not generally due to central decisions. It results from the specific added value applied to a specific domain, for instance electricity, telecom, transports, water ...

The concept of Smart Cities offers the opportunity of a new global approach, which could allow cities to manage public utilities within a coherent perspective. Positive presentations are promoted and emphasized by vendors. But it is not enough. The main purpose of Smart City is not to build a global umbrella that would be imposed by a global IT system. It has to deliver real added value to both the city ensuring better efficiency, more transparency and making it more attractive for investors, and the citizens improving the quality of services.

2. The data access shift

The relationship between city administrations and utilities—particularly when they are private bodies—is one of the crucial issues of Smart Cities.

Historically, cities have given a high priority to the management of the budget dedicated to public infrastructures. Cities have many requirements.

Knowledge

Local infrastructures are numerous and complex. This issue is particularly tricky for the underground infrastructures: cities do not have the information when they have to deliver authorizations for urban engineering works or when they have to face an emergency crisis (gas explosion, water damage, ...)

Today, local governments wish to get data concerning their public infrastructures, so they can feed their own GIS (Geographical Information System).

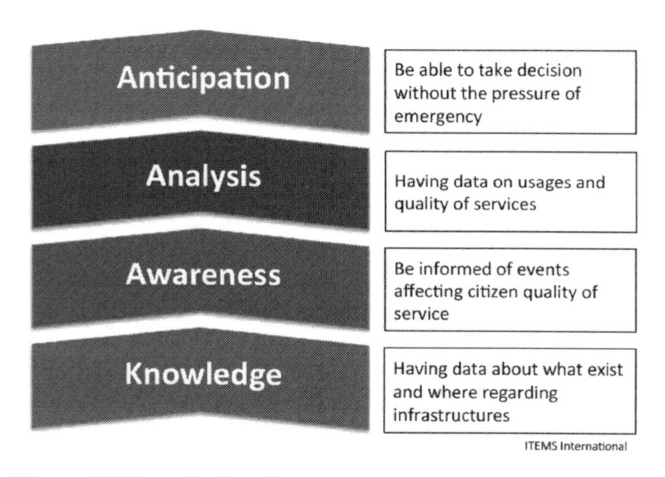

Figure 2. *Knowledge, Awareness, Analysis, Anticipation*

Awareness

Cities wish to be informed in real-time when significant events occur. Leaders do not accept anymore to be informed by the media the day after.

Analysis

Cities are in charge of public investments, which include infrastructures. Relevant data could allow them to better measure and anticipate the impact of their decisions. These data would provide information about traffic, energy consumption ...

Based on the result of the analysis of these data (traffic, consumption, ...), local governments can take actions on the short term and prepare medium and long term plan of actions.

Anticipation

Local governments shape the future of cities through investments.

This requires criteria that are addressing different categories of issues. Part of them is extremely sensitive regarding privacy (e.g. data regarding citizens) or confidentiality in the case of business (e.g. strategic data for a private utility).

All of these requirements are legitimate in the case the city owns and operates the infrastructures for water, traffic lights, sewers ... when the infrastructures are operated by a private utility, this is another story.

Electricity is a good example. The development of Smart Metering in electric infrastructure has raised many questions about the access to data. Debates have been opened on that topic by governments (US in 2010[1], UK in 2011[2], European Commission in 2011[3], ...)

Regulation regarding data's access recognizes the right of the users on one side and of the operators managing the data on the other side. Many questions have been raised regarding access to data and the role of DSOs[4]. However, there is no specific access right, which allows local governments to access these data.

This situation is paradoxical when we consider that local governments are those who mainly invest in public infrastructures. If they have chosen to operate infrastructures by themselves, they have immediate access to any data. If they have decided to delegate and make a contract with a private company, it then becomes a black box: they do not have any right. Private companies can argue from the fact that data are confidential or can refer to private and confidential business information.

As a matter of fact, there are different kinds of potential needs in data access which could be summarized as follows (see Figure 3, next page).

All parties have specific and legitimate needs and requests. It is a serious shift for utilities, which are not prepared for this evolution. Some of them have taken the initiative of proposing data access to users with the "Green Button"[5].

Local governments can introduce obligations in agreements with private utilities. However, due to the duration of the contracts, most of local governments are facing concrete barriers to data access. This is different when local governments own the utilities. In fact, it is not obvious at all for city administrations to get data from its own utilities.

---

[1] http://energy.gov/gc/downloads/department-energy-data-access-and-privacy-issues-related-smart-grid-technologies

[2] https://www.gov.uk/government/uploads/system/uploads/attachment_data/file/43046/7225-gov-resp-sm-data-access-privacy.pdf

[3] http://ec.europa.eu/energy/gas_electricity/smartgrids/doc/expert_group2.pdf

[4] http://www.eui.eu/Projects/THINK/Documents/Thinktopic/Topic12digital.pdf

[5] http://www.greenbuttondata.org/

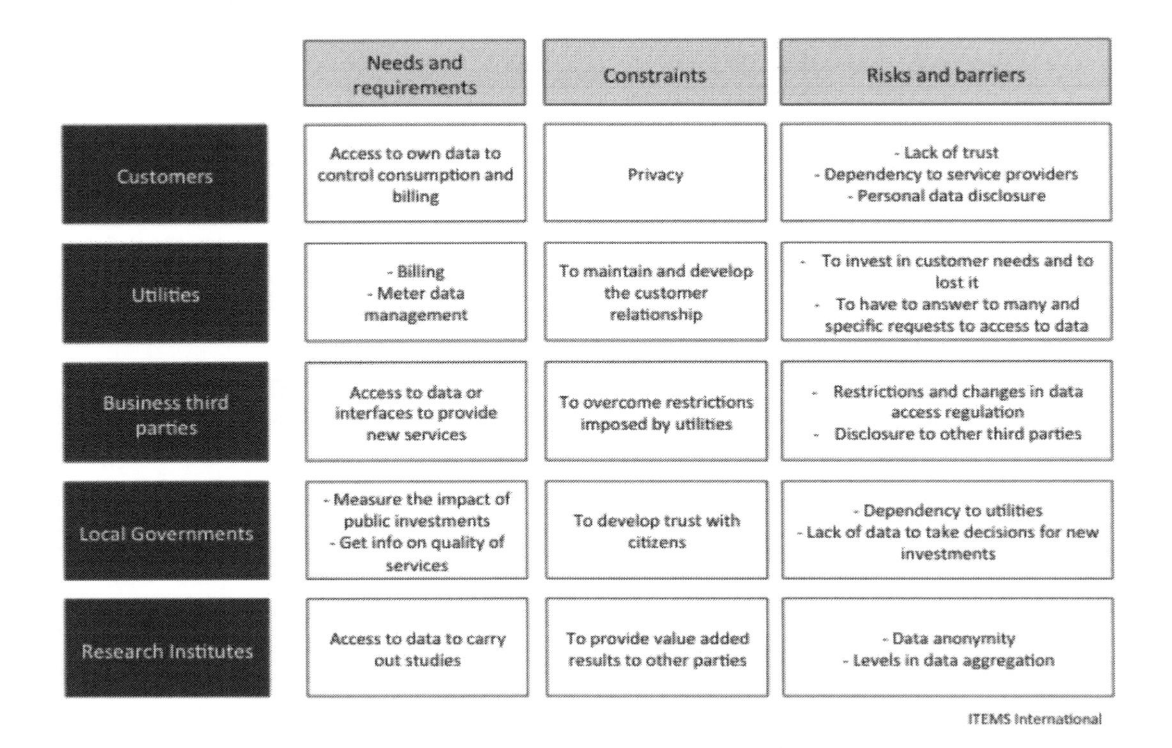

	Needs and requirements	Constraints	Risks and barriers
Customers	Access to own data to control consumption and billing	Privacy	- Lack of trust - Dependency to service providers - Personal data disclosure
Utilities	- Billing - Meter data management	To maintain and develop the customer relationship	- To invest in customer needs and to lost it - To have to answer to many and specific requests to access to data
Business third parties	Access to data or interfaces to provide new services	To overcome restrictions imposed by utilities	- Restrictions and changes in data access regulation - Disclosure to other third parties
Local Governments	- Measure the impact of public investments - Get info on quality of services	To develop trust with citizens	- Dependency to utilities - Lack of data to take decisions for new investments
Research Institutes	Access to data to carry out studies	To provide value added results to other parties	- Data anonymity - Levels in data aggregation

ITEMS International

Figure 3. *Data access needs in cities.*

However difficult is the access to data, it does not change the strength of the trend: **Data will become the fuel of cities.**

More and more data are going to be opened when some of them have to be protected to ensure privacy or confidentiality.

This layout is becoming more and more complex due to the diversification of the categories of data and the increasing sectors covered by cities. It requests coherent approach and architecture to allow cities keeping the control of what is happening now without overwhelming costs.

It is tempting to consider that new technologies are a tool for cities. The question is how can we manage these new technologies in order to avoid them getting out of control or to see their vendors imposing decisions and choices. Cities will have to protect themselves and their citizens.

3. Interoperability: an undeniable challenge for cities

The challenges of interoperability are:

- To open markets to competition,
- To allow interactions between systems (in particular in data access),

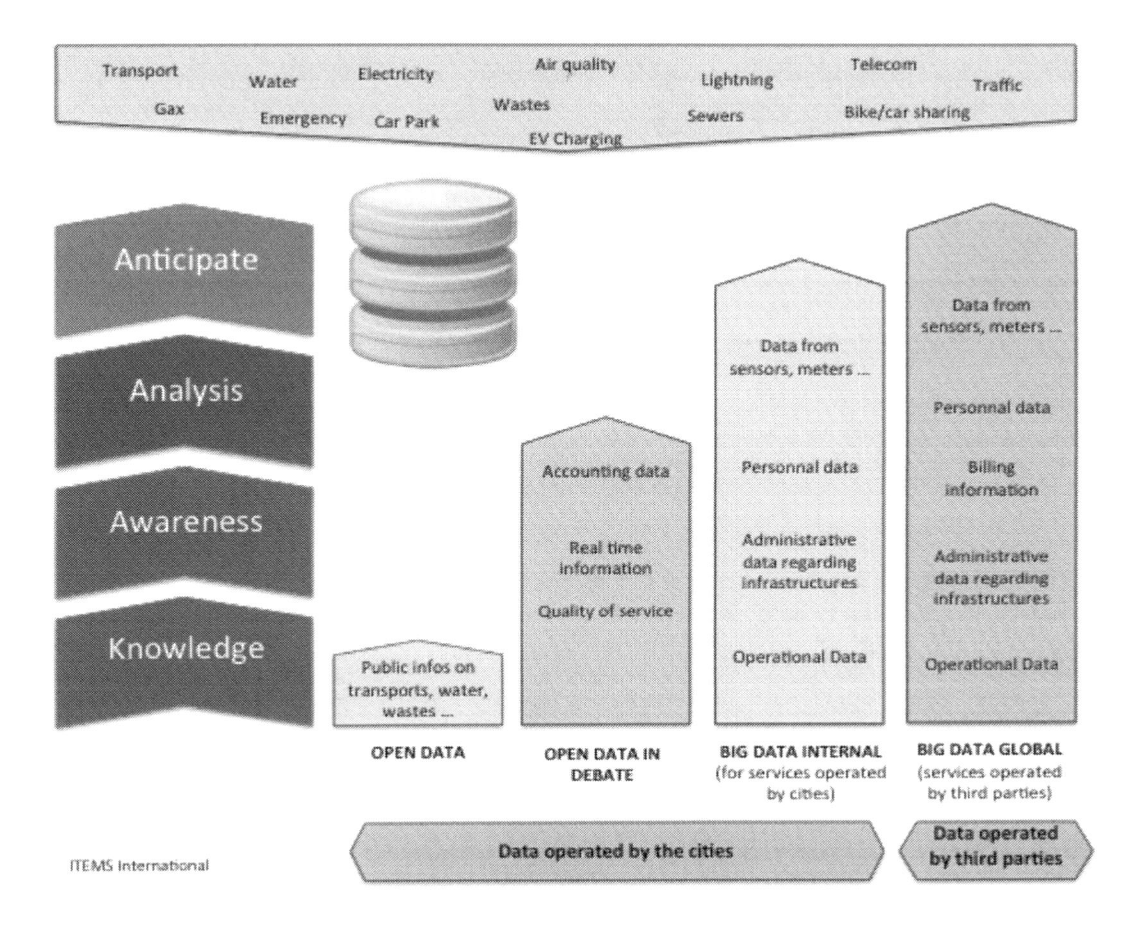

Figure 4. *From open data to big data in cities.*

- To favor the openness of systems in developing new infrastructures, new features, new services,
- To control costs.

The management of Interoperability does not imply to choose the technology itself or to understand how it works. It needs to have a good overview of for four elements: networks, components and subsystems, interfaces, data.

Networks

Networks used to be a key challenge. With the generalization of broadband and IP standards in land and mobile networks, they are now everywhere. They still represent a barrier and a factor of disparities regarding data access for citizens and companies. Current challenges for interoperability in communication infrastructures mainly concerns M2M for which competition between standards is still strong.

Technological subsystems and components

Usually, equipments, systems or devices are made of different subsystems, which are made of technological components (more or less complex pieces of software or/and hardware). The technology used by a vendor to develop components is under his responsibility and can refer to patents or intellectual property rights. Vendors can decide to open it by using free software, open source, open hardware ... In any case; it depends on his own choice.

Interfaces

Interfaces allow components to interact together, what ever it is a Service Interface—for exchanges between components within a system, an equipment (e.g. an application having access to the web)—or a Protocol Interface—for exchanges between components from one system and equivalent components from another system (e.g. two smartphones in communication or exchanging data).

The pieces of code, which allow access to an interface of an IT system, is an API (Application Program Interface). Who ever controls the API can control the real standards either they are open or not. Google is the first company who has really understood the role of API when others focused mainly on systems and software. Google does not care. Its objective is to control the API. Beyond the technology, Google is the best friend of the communities of developers all over the world.

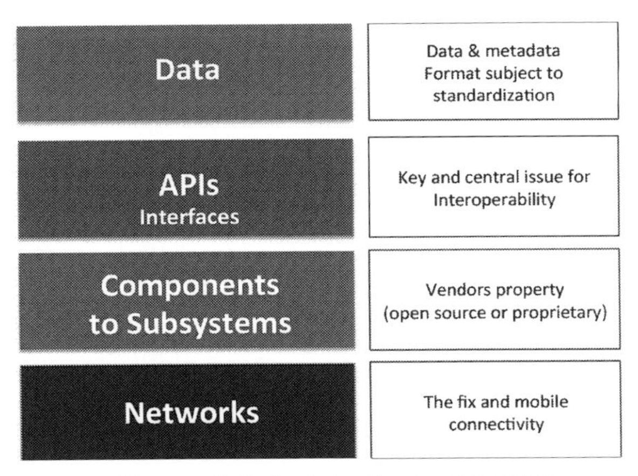

Figure 5. ***Data, interfaces et blocks.***

Data

Data is the fuel and the result of what produces digital technologies. The access to data—including the standardization process in data formatting—has become a key issue in IT management. Open Data and Big data trends are boosting this tendency.

In the past, systems were more or less independent. The interoperability was not a key issue regarding as each system was dedicated to one specific function. The increasing need of exchanges between systems and to access data is going to change the rules.

Let's try to take a comparison with a car, which gathers different technical subsystems: the core of the engine, the carburetor or the electric system ... Car companies used to assemble these subsystems without having to provide any data on how the car was functioning. Interoperability requirements did not existed. This is the reason why, the State of California has decided in 1985 to issue a standard OBD[6] to allow central diagnostics. In a first time, the vendors disagreed with this decision taken by politicians. However, after the second release, ODB-II became an obligation in California in 1996. Thane It had been rapidly adopted by the federal government[7]. It became an obligation in Europe in 2002 (E-OBD[8]).

The requirements are similar within a city: the diagnostic and control justify the needs of interoperability based on standards. Vendors are often unhappy about this kind of decisions but they can become competitive advantages over time.

As mentioned before, standards refer to Interfaces and format of data. A standard is generally considered as "open" (vs "de facto standard") when it is adopted by Standard Development Organizations (SDO) such as ETSI, W3C, IEEE, IETF, ITU ... The open standards can be free of charge or submitted to patents depending on each SDO policy.

Technical components are not directly concerned by standards. This is the business of the vendors. Considering that these rules are too complex, some public or private organizations—including cities and governments—request open source in tenders based on royalty-free standards. This point is subject to discussions. Some vendors argue that this is in contradiction with commercial legal frameworks. Public authorities can legally overcome this constraint, however they can face legal procedures.

It can be an illusion to consider that a city is going to solve all problems in IT with open source code. Often, Open-source software only switches the dependency from software vendors to software service companies.

---

[6] http://www.arb.ca.gov/msprog/obdprog/obdprog.htm

[7] http://www.epa.gov/obd/

[8] http://eur-lex.europa.eu/LexUriServ/LexUriServ.do?uri=CONSLEG:1998L0069:19981228:FR:PDF

4. Scenarios for convergence within cities

As mentioned previously, there are convergences in the utilities architectures. They have their own infrastructures, including sensors, meters and control operation devices and systems. Other components could be developed in theory. They are based on IT systems, software and data networks. In the end, we could imagine global IT platforms and networks, which could control different utilities. Is this going to happen?

We can think of different scenarii:

Projective scenario

In this scenario, each utility develops itself intelligent infrastructures and services:

- The infrastructures include more sensors and real time based systems. Transports vehicles, transports ticketing, water, gas, sewers, car parks ... All utilities have been facing for many years the increasing role of digital technologies within the core of their own systems and services,
- The citizen's relationship has been evolving in the recent years. Users have more requirements in particular regarding the quality of services and billing. Most of utilities have developed CRM[9] systems and advanced billing systems,
- Utilities manage complex and secured IT systems including database. They have to face requirements for Open Data and Big Data that come either from the cities themselves either from third parties,
- Utilities have developed online services for customers. All of them provide services on Internet and have developed or plan to develop mobile apps for smartphones and tablets.

It is interesting to notice that the city administration itself has faced the same evolution with e-Administration. And there are similar challenges regarding systems, applications, open data/big data, citizen's relationships ... After all, It remains unclear how can we precisely define what is a utility vs an administrative service.

We can imagine a future in which all these entities, formerly utilities of administrative services, would work independently from each other. Some of these entities could share IT services and in some cases common systems. But fundamentally, the silo organization would remain, as it exists today. Nothing would be really shared except scoreboard.

[9] Customer Relationship Management

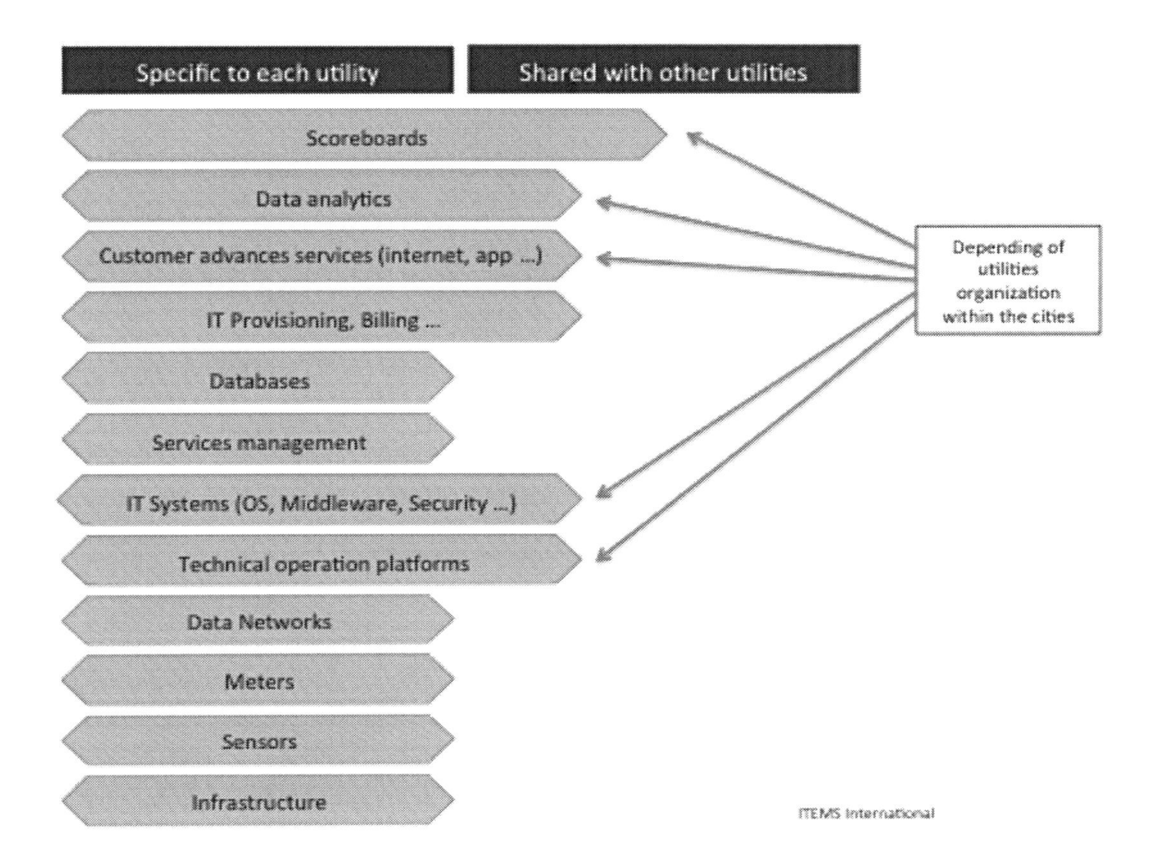

Figure 6. *Specific and shared investments in projective scenario.*

This scenario implies that an organization in which the central CIO has enough power to see his recommendation adopted in all cities. That said, this would require a strong coordination between the city administration and the utilities.

Three major drawbacks can be identified regarding this scenario:

a) Costs: in the past, the technologies used to be specific for each sector, in consequence, independent investments were not considered as a problem. Today, many investments can be shared with digital technologies,

b) Barriers for cross-sectorial applications: the need of these applications comes from two reasons.

- The first is the increasing requirements of the cities, which are summarized by the KAAA model. For example: cities need to get geographical data and to insert them in their GIS system. If it is possible to manage many GIS systems, it is a waste of time, a waste of money and a dissemination of expertise within cities.

- The second reason is that applications need to interoperate with different sectors. For example, new generation of Traffic Management applications have to deal with road and streets works, traffic lights systems, car park management, quality of air, emergency systems, electric vehicle charging stations ...

c) Lost of control: Independency of silos combined to the increasing complexity of IT systems encourage managers to ask third parties independent providers to provide global services. If this trend is normal, it depends how it is managed. In particular, how the city keeps the control in the perspective of complying requirements mentioned in point b).

The scenario of the global integration

This scenario considers that all IT systems and networks are going to run on an integrated architecture, including common methodologies, rules and processes when they are not specific to an infrastructure.

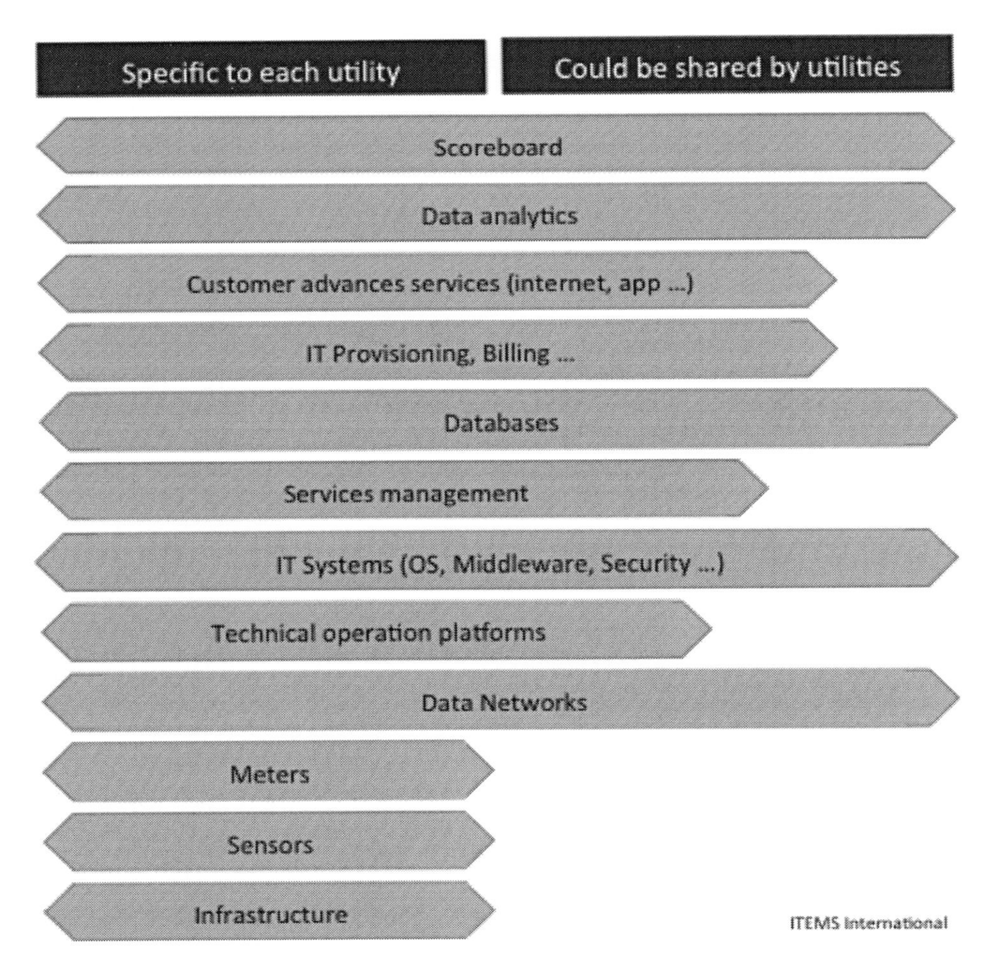

Figure 7. *Specific and shared investments in the scenario of global integration.*

The scenario is favored by a trend that privileges the pressure on common investments and common services.

In the end, common architectures and technical choices aim at rationalizing IT Systems and software, including data networks.

This is a situation a CIO or an IT company could dream about. There is no doubt that the increasing role of IT and data networks could encourage cities to consider this scenario.

However, there are some drawbacks, which have to be taken in consideration.

a) **Organization:** The systems cannot decide for the organization. They have to be adapted to the diversity of organizations. About utilities, some can be managed by the cities when others can be operated by third parties. The cities have to keep in mind that the most appropriate organizations and Integrated IT Systems can represent a barrier,

b) **Independence of third parties:** following the previous point, there is no reason for the city to decide of the technical IT systems that a third party operator would have to use,

c) **Reactivity:** Each sector has to be very reactive regarding user needs, quality of services or technical innovations. An integrated architecture would have an effect on that reactivity because any technical choice would have to meet global specifications. It could represent a major risk for innovation,

d) **Lost of control:** in the end, the risk in this scenario is to lead city administration manager to entrust one IT group only to provide a global and homogeneous architecture. The advantage of this option is to have an IT third party that could resolve all problems coming from the heterogeneity of the systems. The inconvenient is to give the control of the intelligence of the city to one vendor and to become dependent of it.

The scenario of the global interoperability

The third scenario is not only a compromise between the two previous versions: it can take advantage of the convergences between the technologies and can be adapted to decentralization of decision-making processes in utilities management.

With interoperability, the point for users is not necessarily to share or to use the same systems but to give them the ability to exchange data and to make them understandable by their respective systems.

Internet is a booster of the interoperability by itself, and as such has played an important role in Interoperability in IT Systems.

In the early years of its development, Internet standards (adopted by W3C) have been progressively adopted in Data Networks. At that time, the architectures proposed in IT Systems by vendors were not complying with

Internet standards. Today, this situation has changed for accessing applications (HTML) or and partially for exchanges between applications (web-services). Other families of standards based over W3C standards for exchanges between applications have been adopted. This is for instance the case in e-Government in OASIS [10].

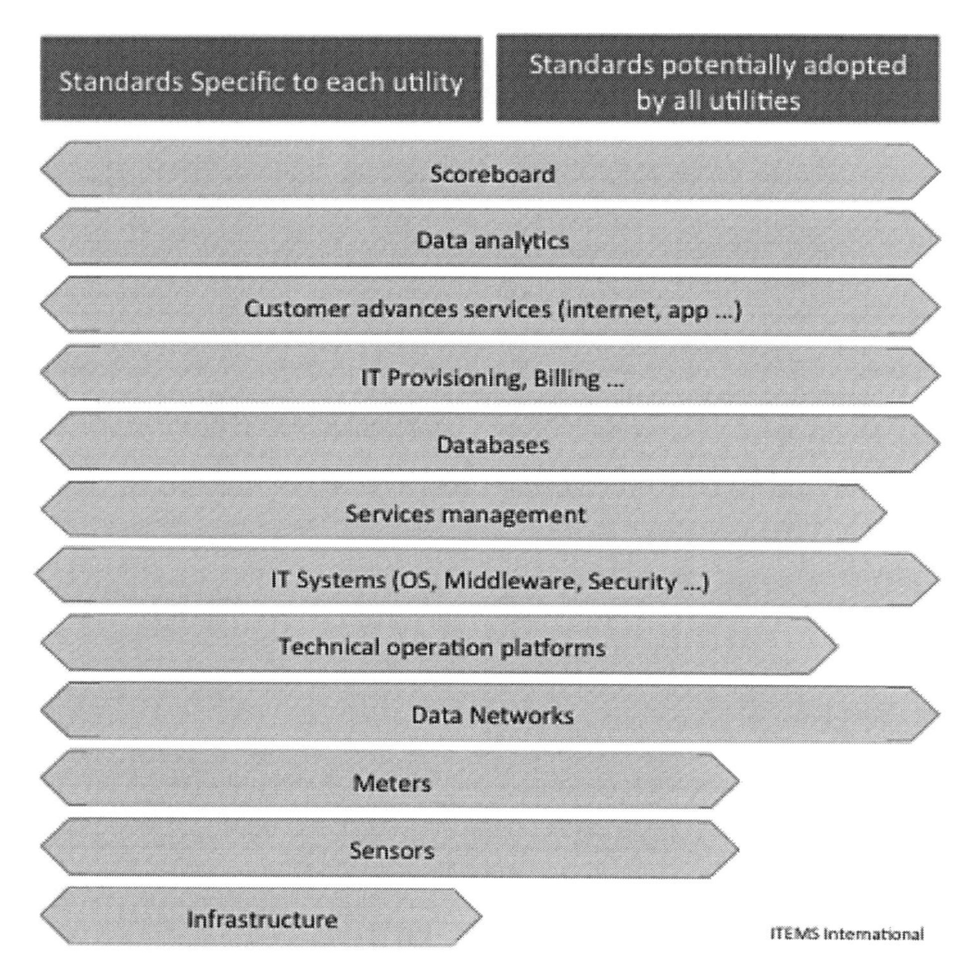

Figure 8. *Specific and shared standards in the scenario of global interoperability.*

However, there are a lot of barriers for Interoperability objectives:

a) Standardization processes are very complex and look like a global battlefield between vendors. There are many organizations that work on standards and they are generally competing,

[10] https://www.oasis-open.org/committees/tc_home.php?wg_abbrev=egov

b) Because of this complexity, some vendors may prefer to setup ad-hoc groups, alliances, consortia or any kind of organizations, which could develop new standards. This is for example the case of the Open Geospatial Consortium (OGC) for standardization in geo-location,

c) There is no guarantee that major vendors would accept to adapt their own systems or services to adopted standards. Example: Google has its own specification for geo-location and even if they have not been through a standardization process, there are de facto considered as standards,

d) Data and metadata can be considered as a mess for standardization. Many initiatives have been taken by OASIS, Dublin Core ... to improve standardization. But Data is going to become the new Eldorado of Tech markets[11]. The competition is fierce and big players are reluctant to work on such an issue without a clear understanding of the value added of the standardization for themselves ...

e) Interoperability in utilities is a long process. Transports and electricity are probably the most complex sectors due to the fact that they refer to the merge of two families of standards: transports + ICT (Intelligent Transport Systems/ITS), electricity + ICT (Smart Grids). The chart below shows up how this landscape is fragmented in electric Smart Grids.

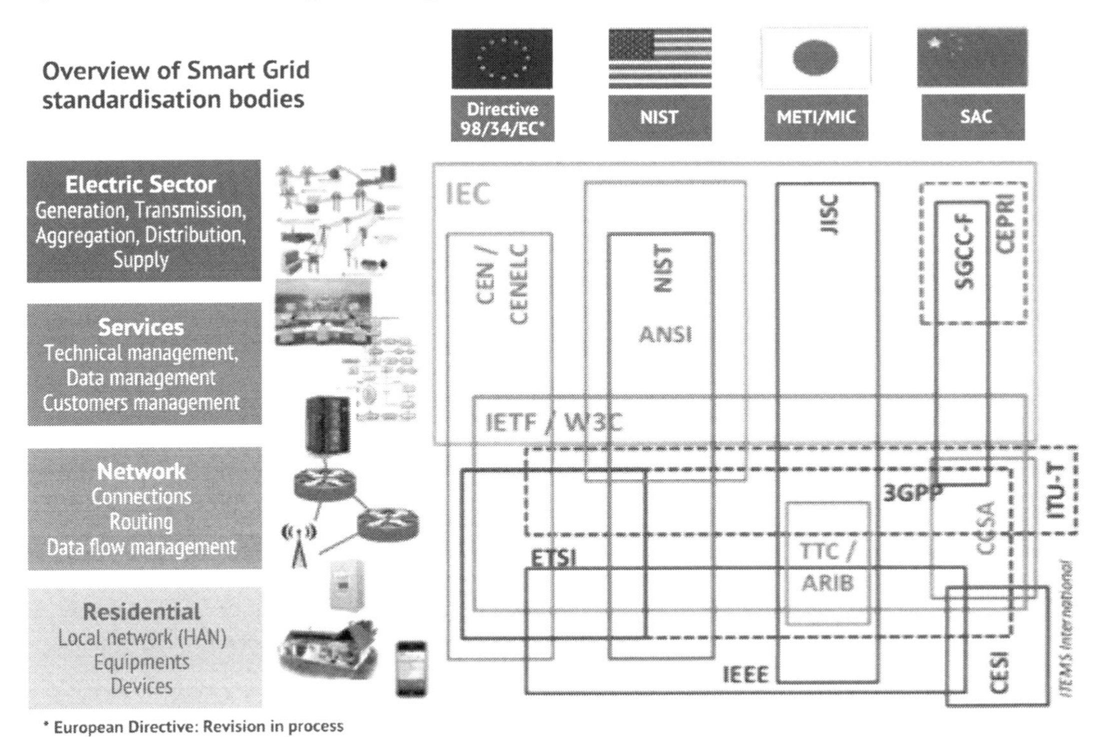

Figure 9. *Fragmentation of standards organizations in Smart Grids.*

[11]http://wikibon.org/wiki/v/Big_Data_Vendor_Revenue_and_Market_Forecast_2012-2017

Interoperability is a clear objective but as a result of the reality cities are becoming more pragmatic. Sometimes, it can be advantageous to ask to one vendor to deal with standardization issues... with its own standards. It is very risky for the independency of future investments and it is an illusion within smart cities, which has the objective to make different sectors, different cultures working together.

5. City as a platform

Considering the need for interoperability on one side, and the difficulties to address this objective, the point is to define an approach based on key standards principles, which are promoted within the cities.

Discussions about interoperability issues have pointed out the role of components or subsystems, Interfaces and data. It is interesting to notice that, in the past, the most critical issue was the control of the technology. Interfaces were generally related to the technologies themselves and data were considered as specific and closed.

Today, the panorama is completely different. The priorities are now interfaces and Data.

- **Interfaces:** because it is the key point for the development of interoperability and to built up a strong and scalable architecture for the future. The most important argument is how APIs favor the development of communities of developers and users.
- **We can come back to the example of Google with Google maps:** Geographical systems used to be very complex and reserved to experts. Today, for most common uses except very specialized usages, nobody cares about the technology used by Google. Users have adopted Google Maps APIs.
- **Data:** because that is the fuel of services and who controls the fuel ... is going to control the services. Cities are going to face a tsunami of data[12]: sensors, video, geographical and multidimensional systems, smart meters ... Utilities, waste Management, Transports are among the sectors that are going to have an increasing amount of objects connected, which are going to produce data[13]. Cities are going to face the challenge to get value from this amount of data[14]. For the city itself and for citizens, Big Data is changing the world[15].

[12] http://arxiv.org/ftp/arxiv/papers/1301/1301.0159.pdf

[13] http://www.mckinsey.com/~/media/McKinsey/dotcom/Insights%20and%20pubs/MGI/Research/Technology%20and%20Innovation/Big%20Data/MGI_big_data_full_report.ashx

[14] http://arxiv.org/ftp/arxiv/papers/1301/1301.0159.pdf

[15] http://www.bbc.co.uk/news/technology-23253949

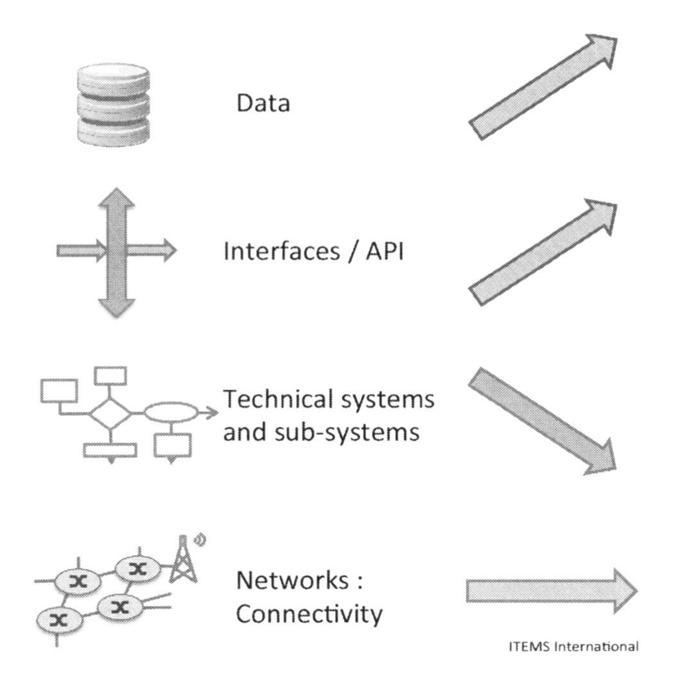

Figure 10. *Moving priorities in Smart Cities design.*

Systems with technological components and networks remain important regarding disparity in access. But they do not represent a challenge in interoperability except in M2M communications.

Cloud Computing and Big Data are a total illustration of this trend: the system architecture is no more a barrier. Welcome to the cloud architecture for which the Prism revelations could favor hybrid clouds[16]. And welcome to competition on APIs and the Big Data.

Regarding the question of interoperability, it is an illusion to standardize all data formats. It is too complex and it is a headache to try to convince all people (developers, IT designers, organization structure) to adopt a common standard. The best compromise is to have applications interfaces that can give access to data. In the end, the interoperability in data is again a question of APIs.

As mentioned previously, big companies like Google have understood the key role of APIs. The accidental post written by Steve Yegge in 2011[17] illustrates this trend. This paper that seems to be a technical digression on software design is a strong analysis on the industry trend that emphasizes the APIs vision. Beyond the APIs, Steve Yegge points out the concept of platforms.

---

[16] http://www.wired.com/insights/2013/08/what-next-for-cloud-computing-after-prism/, http://money.msn.com/technology-investment/post--will-prism-break-our-cloud-addiction

[17] http://upalc.com/google-amazon.php

This concept is ambiguous and unclear. It can refer to a system or to a whole set of software. The concept has moved and refers today to:

- An internet service or application that is used by large range of people,
- A way to create a third party developers community who creates additional services for all users

In the former model, the owner of an original application or service could refuse this. In the new Internet world, he considers everything that makes its community increase. That is the reason why industry players propose APIs to access to their applications and services. The more developers the players have access to, the more users use their APIs. As a consequence, developers create more content, which develops new services and new businesses.

This is what really is beyond the concept of platform, which is clearly well understood by companies like Facebook, eBay ... And it inspires others such as newspapers like the Guardian which intends to become such a platform[18].

Cities are experimenting this approach with Open Data. For many local governments, Open Data is a change of paradigm both from a technical and cultural point of view. Cities are not used to leave external people or organizations access to their own data. Even data produced by government can be considered as a public asset. Most administrations consider that it is their property. However, the trend in favor of Open Data is on its way and many cities in the world offer a set of APIs to allow developers to access to their data. In addition, many governments (local, regional or national) propose open platforms of APIs to access Open Data sets. In these platforms, the point is not to standardize all formats of data but to provide the access to data, including the description of their own format. Among the most interesting initiatives we can mention Helsinki[19], which is one of the cities, which have understood the role of developers in economic development and for the promotion of the city. Philadelphia[20] also dedicates a website to APIs with more than just Open Data.

Moreover, it is an illusion to think that there will be standards for everything. As a more realistic approach, APIs gives the cities the possibility of adaptation to standards when they will exist, to specific technologies, to innovations when they appear on the market. APIs introduces dynamic approach in IT design that aims to share these APIs with the largest community of developers. By doing that, the interoperability does not depend of

---

[18] http://www.theguardian.com/open-platform

[19] http://dev.hel.fi

[20] http://phlapi.com

any international organization but gives the ability to communities of developers to share the same interfaces.

Many cities have developed such approaches with Open Sources communities. However, Open Source requires strong internal expertise and the city can become dependent of its own technical developments. "City as a platform" can include open source or not. The key is the development of communities on APIs.

We can see with interest initiatives like the Open 311 Platform[21]—adopted by cities in the US—CitySDK[22] and OpenDAI[23]—in Europe. In this last example, the objective is precisely to "renew public administration's information systems toward an open model and Service Oriented Architecture. This, in order to overcome the monolithic and closed models and facilitate software maintenance of existing silos".

We do not know the future of such initiatives. What we can strongly express is that the Smart Cities will fail without interoperability and that the future of Interoperability is APIs and open platforms. This represents a cultural change for which Open Data is just a warm up of the "City as a platform" challenge.

DR.SYLVIANE TOPORKOFF *Founder & Partner and* ***HERVÉ RANNOU*** *Founder and President Items International, France and CEO of Cityzen Data.*

[21] http://open311.org

[22] http://www.citysdk.eu

[23] http://www.open-dai.eu

3

A Smart City Maturity Model: A Roadmap for Assessment and Action on the Path to Maturity

Ruthbea Clark

Cities today are facing a perfect storm of economic, environmental and demographic challenges in which rising urban populations are exacerbating urban problems and straining resources in the context of uncertain economic times. Citizens' high expectations for services delivery and the need for sustained tourism and business development are pressing cities to consider the opportunities afforded by emerging technologies.

What is a Smart City?

The concept of the smart city is a model for technology-enabled local government transformation. Transformation, which implies a large-scale change, is a long-term and complex process, and so is the transformation of cities today into the smart cities of the future.

Smart cities arise from the shift that is occurring in the information and communication technology (ICT) industry to a new technology platform for growth and innovation. This new platform is built on mobile devices and apps, cloud services, mobile broadband networks, big data and analytics, and social media technologies. This has given rise to an explosion of new products and smart city solutions.

A smart city or smart city project uses devices, ICT, and instrumentation to achieve the explicit goals of improving the quality of life of citizens and sustainable economic development. These goals are achieved via improved service delivery, more efficient use of resources (human, infrastructure and natural), and financially and environmentally sustainable practices.

The vision of a smart city is to provide more inclusive, secure, efficient and effective services to citizens, thus ensuring the livability and sustainability of the wider city community. As cities operate in a globally competitive environment—for workers, tourists and businesses—the goal of smart city initiatives is to attract businesses and citizens for a vibrant city economy. To do this, cities must tackle urban challenges through coordinated and focused investment.

Smart City and Smart Project Characteristics

There are some basic differences between a smart project/initiative and a traditional city project. Among them:

- **Smart city leaders see themselves as part of a movement that is working toward social and behavioral change.** These leaders often see their city as a force for change in the global community. For example, smart city leaders look to meeting sustainability targets by enabling long-term behavior change in citizens, encouraging them to drive less , conserve energy and engage more directly with government.

- **There is a focus on outcomes not transactions.** A traditional city may focus on transactions as performance measures. For example, the city might track a law enforcement officer by how many speeding violations and traffic stops she can make. A smart city initiative would be framed by the outcome of reducing car accidents.

- **Smart cities leverage their city resources differently than traditional cities.** Smart cities look at the relationships and resources they have within their cities as true partners in finding solutions to urban challenges. These cities actively seek to engage citizens, businesses, community groups and academia in the process of innovation and change.

- **Smart projects have certain technological and process characteristics.** Smart projects are typically event-driven, end-to-end processes that rest on pervasive broadband communications infrastructure. Smart projects gather data from a multitude of sources, including citizens and other parts of government; process and analyze that data; visualize and display the data in an actionable format; and have parameters for an optimal response. This response could be enacted by a machine, for example, when tolling congestion charges automatically increase, or by workers, for example, when there is a traffic accident and emergency services need to be deployed and traffic rerouted across several municipalities.

- **Smart cities integrate smart projects.** A smart city integrates many smart projects in a systematic and systemic way. This integration is flexible; organizations within a city retain their autonomy as part of a system of systems that shares resources and works toward a citywide vision.

Why Smart Cities Are Important

Cities traditionally operate in a highly fragmented state with budgets, governance, decision-making, IT platforms and information handled by individual departments. The result is that IT strategy, investment and the processes that support services delivery are inefficient when viewed in a citywide operational context. Multiple data sets and applications exist in different departments, relevant information is not shared, and operations are not coordinated beyond emergency protocols or when required for special events. Despite the desire by many city workers to improve and change, it is difficult for cities to overcome risk-averse cultures and procurement processes that make experimentation and innovation a challenge.

Demographic and technology trends are creating a pressing need for cities to rethink how they use and leverage IT and existing infrastructure, as well as resources such as government workers, citizens, and community and business groups. City infrastructure is strained, and services delivery cannot keep pace with need. The financial woes of many central governments also are affecting cities as funding for local projects is reduced. To make matters worse, the expectations of businesses and citizens are rising to include anywhere, anytime mobile access to information and services, and the ability to interact directly with government via apps and social media. These factors, coupled with the opportunities that emerging technologies like big data, analytics, the Internet of things and machine-to-machine communications, geographic information systems (GIS), and social media afford, are pushing cities to adopt smart city models of transformation and IT investment.

There are an overwhelming number of issues city leaders must address, and it can be difficult to know where or how to begin. Many city leaders ask common questions as they research smart city solutions, such as:

- How do I begin a smart city transformation? Where is a good place to start?
- What is the process for change?
- How do we assess ourselves and plan our future strategy for IT investment?
- Can I look to other cities as examples, or is my city unique in the challenges we face?

A Smart City Maturity Model provides a roadmap for assessing progress and a planning tool for adopting smart city technologies and practices.

How To Begin Creating a Smart City

The maturity model rests on the belief that cities have common problems, challenges and goals—despite unique populations, geography, regulations and culture. In researching and discussing smart city strategies with vendors, mayors, chief information officers and other government leaders involved in urban innovation, it is clear that while the details may vary, most city leaders are concerned about the same issues (traffic and crime reduction, energy resource management, job creation and economic development are common priorities). Most cities face similar challenges in managing aging, outdated or undeveloped technology infrastructures, siloed information and processes, and many bureaucratic and cultural factors that influence progress. The same questions arise in Beijing or Boston as cities consider how to grow and keep pace with technology and the expectations of their citizens and businesses.

A maturity model provides a common path for smart city development that helps city leaders to assess their situation and determine the critical capabilities needed to enable a smart city. The model helps to define the key technology- and non-technology-related areas for assessment. This Smart City Maturity Model is a framework of stages, critical measures, outcomes and actions required for organizations to effectively advance along the successive stages of competency toward data- and event-driven decision-making. A Smart City Maturity Model will enable a city to:

- Begin to assess its smart city current competency and maturity;
- Define short- and long-term goals, and plan improvements;
- Prioritize technology, partnership, staffing and other related investment decisions; and
- Uncover maturity gaps among departments and business units, or between functional and IT groups.

The Maturity Model

This Smart City Maturity Model describes five common stages through which cities progress as they work to create a smart city system. Cities can use the model to assess coordination and integration across departments and agencies for the city system as a whole, or to assess a single department. Typically, different departments or agencies within a city will be at different levels of maturity in terms of their processes and operations.

Table 1. *An Overview of the Maturity Model.*

	Phase 1: Ad Hoc	Phase 2: Opportunistic	Phase 3: Repeatable	Phase 4: Managed	Phase 5: Optimized
Key Characteristic	Siloed	Intentional	Integrated	Operationalized	Sustainable
Goal	Tactical Services Delivery	Stakeholder Buy-In	Improved Outcomes	Prediction and Prevention	Competitive Differentiation
Outcome	Proof of concept and business case development via ROI from pilot projects	Cross-organization deployments and development of foundational strategy and governance	Replicable success in project process and outcomes across multiple organizations	Enterprise-wide strategy, process, data, etc., bring improved service-delivery via adaptive sense-and-respond systems	Agility, innovation and continuous improvement in service delivery bring competitive advantage

The Five Stages of Maturity

The Ad Hoc Phase: This first stage is the traditional modus operandi for city government with initiatives formed in an ad hoc manner with department-based planning and funding, and discrete smart projects that are implemented independent of each other. The goal of the ad hoc stage is to begin to prove the value of the smart city concept and develop the business case via demonstrated return on investment (ROI) from pilot projects. Once this is achieved, cities progress to the next phase. Ad hoc projects typically focus on areas of need in focused city functions that are easier to address and often are the responsibility of one department, such as smart water or smart parking.

Opportunistic: In the second stage, opportunistic project deployments result in proactive collaboration within and between departments. Key stakeholders start to align around developing strategy, a common language, and identify barriers to adoption. The goal at the opportunistic stage is to engage stakeholders and get their buy-in and participation as the strategy and road map for smart city initiatives are developed. Stakeholders can include the mayor's office, city council members, IT leaders from different city agencies, local business and community leaders, and partners from local colleges or universities.

Repeatable: In the repeatable stage, recurring projects, events and processes are identified for integration and replication. Formal committees are assigned and begin to document defined strategies, processes and technology investment needs with stakeholders. Sustainable funding models for larger initiatives and governance issues become a focus.

The goal of the repeatable stage of maturity is improved outcomes and service delivery as a result of repeatable standard processes for smart city projects and their coordination beyond the department level. More formalized processes develop measures of both outputs and outcomes to determine success of the initiatives. Specific initiatives begin to be scaled and integration begins. Better use of information and the processes in place to respond to events drives improved outcomes and service delivery.

Managed: In the managed stage, formal systems for work/data flows and leveraging technology assets are in place and standards emerge. Performance management based on outcomes shift culture, budgets, IT investment and governance structure to a broader city context. The goal of the managed stage of maturity is for cities to be able to predict the needs of their residents and businesses, and provide preventative services before problems arise.

Optimized: In the final stage of maturity, a sustainable citywide platform is in place. Agile strategy, IT and governance structures allow for departmental autonomy within an integrated system of systems, and the focus is on continuous improvements. At this level, cities show superior outcomes and services delivery that delivers differentiation from other cities.

The ultimate goal of the optimized smart city is competitive differentiation that drives sustainable economic development or revitalization by creating jobs and attracting investment. Mature smart cities will attract business investments, visitors, tourists and citizens because they provide high-quality citizen services, are easy to do business with, and offer a higher quality of life.

Key Measures for Assessment

There are key dimensions, or measures, that need to be addressed to make the smart city concept operational. Many of these are not technology-related measures because the largest challenges that cities face are related to people and process. Entrenched culture, siloed budgeting processes, local bylaws and governance structures, and outdated ways of measuring success must change to fulfill a smart city vision.

The following measures and corresponding attributes are key to the Smart City Maturity Model:

Strategy: The smart city strategy defines the city's intent and vision for the city, including sustainability and economic development goals, and how each city plans to capitalize on its strengths and unique qualities while addressing its weaknesses. Part of any smart city strategy should include a systemic and coordinated future vision for city operations. Also included in strategy is the development of the business case for smart city initiatives and the identification of lead sponsors of smart city projects who move smart city strategy forward along the stages. These leaders typically include mayors, CIOs and/or community and business leaders.

Culture: Culture refers to the culture of innovation and citizen engagement within a city. Cities tend to be risk averse, not only because their resources typically are very scarce but also because failure can have big career implications and impact citizens. One aspect of this measure assesses how cities can become more experimental and innovative to solve long-standing problems.

Citizens (including community and business leaders) offer an untapped source of talent and ideas. Citizen sourcing for mobile app development, crowd-sourced operational information, and new ideas are now possible using social networks and mobile devices. The culture measure also considers how a city will capitalize on its citizens' resources.

Process: Process measures two key enablers of successful change: governance and partnerships. Governance measures the structure for implementing change at the city level, including organizational structures, budgeting processes, and how performance is measured and success is defined. Partnerships are important to smart city development because collaborations with ICT vendors, academia, private industry and citizen groups are necessary to deploy smart solutions, as well as to create innovation ecosystems that continue to push new ideas, new uses of technology and new partnership models for financing smart city projects.

Technology: Technology measures the adoption and penetration of ICT infrastructure and related technologies, as well as the development of smart city enterprise architecture. Smart cities function on an IP-enabled backbone, and a robust telecom infrastructure is required. Often, cities have unequal broadband penetration with underserved neighborhoods. Additionally, advanced and intelligent sensors, cameras, and other devices are needed as data collection points to help create more efficiencies via (M2M) and automation, as well as to provide the data for advanced analytics. The performance and function of these technologies in the context of legacy systems and legacy-enterprise architectures are important as technology assets need to be shared and integrated across the city for better government service delivery.

Data: Open data is a big component of the smart city movement, and citizens are expecting more government transparency. Open data is also a strategy for crowdsourcing skills, particularly in areas such as mobile app development, as well as supporting the creation of start-ups that leverage this data. Smart cities also rest on using big data and analytics to mine data for predictive and preventative responses. These solutions rely on clean and accurate data. Cities have a wealth of data in their current systems, as well as a flood of new data coming into systems every day. It is imperative that this data is cleansed, processed, integrated and analyzed so it can be used optimally. Real-time data must be displayed using dashboards, GIS and other visualization tools to improve decision-making.

Table 2. *The Development of Measures Across the Five Stages.*

	Ad Hoc	Opportunistic	Repeatable	Managed	Optimized
Strategic intent (Vision, Business case, Leadership)	• No strategy or vision exists • Business case undefined • Leadership targets discrete areas for investment	• Strategy is at the department level • Business case developed via demonstrated ROI from pilot projects • Desired outcomes and goals defined • Leadership engages stakeholders	• Strategy spans and involves multiple organizations • Business case applied across multiple projects or initiatives • Formal documentation defines Smart City goals and outcomes • Leadership and key stakeholders invest in projects with vision of long-term scalability	• Strategy is accepted citywide • Business case applied citywide with widely accepted tools and processes for investment, ROI, and outcomes measurement • Leadership provides budgeted and ad hoc funding	• Strategy is optimized and evolves based on continuous feedback • Continuous progress on KPIs against mission-based performance • Leadership is vested in holistic and broad-scale transformation of processes, culture, and operations
Culture (Innovation, Citizen engagement)	• Government has no formal process to engage those with new ideas inside or outside of government • Pockets of innovation exist within risk-averse culture	• Government experiments with citizen participation via social networks and mobile apps as a new channel • Opportunistic innovation where there is department-level support	• Government proactively engages citizens though partially personalized direct communications • Innovation culture supported by processes that allow risk • Chief innovation officers or innovation groups are hired or formed • New projects that capitalize on 3rd platform technologies are funded	• Government uses multiple channels to engage citizens based on their needs (web, social media, in person meetings, mobile apps) • Innovation is systematic to leverage ideas from citizens, government workers, and groups outside of government	• Government has cultivated engagement models that are inclusive, personalized, and multi-directional on-going collaborations • Innovation is institutionalized and managed within the whole city paradigm

continued on next page

continued from previous page

	Ad Hoc	Opportunistic	Repeatable	Managed	Optimized
Process (Partnerships, Governance)	• Traditional client-provider-supplier relationships managed by separate departments • Governance is characterized siloed budgeting and decentralized decision-making	• Government begins to test new models of engagement with partners • Some multi-department budgets and decision-making based on projects	• Partnerships models evolve to include gain sharing, co-development, performance contracting • There are stable, joint committees that bring together high-level officials to address smart city needs • Sustainable funding for initiatives is a focus area, and there is reorganization of departments/budgets	• Partnerships aligned with long-term vision and multiple stakeholders coordinated • Annual multi-year planning and budgeting for common programs, services, and infrastructures	• Partner ecosystem evolves to shared outcomes • New combinations of programs are created based on optimal services provisioning • Budgets allocated based on impact on the whole city
Technology (Architecture, Adoption)	• Architecture is decentralized and transaction-based with duplication • Inconsistent broadband/wireless infrastructure adoption • Basic levels of instrumentation in strategic localized areas	• Service-oriented architecture (SOA) is achieved via consolidation of systems • Adoption and buildout of wireless broadband, sensors, cameras and advanced devices to meet specific project goals	• SOA is used pervasively as an open platform in development • Focus is on decrease service time/maintenance costs with investment tied clearly to missions • Broadband coverage and instrumentation is leveraged for multiple projects and goals across organizations	• SOA principles are complemented by event-driven architectures that are interoperable and agile • Ubiquitous broadband coverage and instrumentation of physical city assets leads to real-time dynamic data outputs	• Open platforms, SOA, leverages technology investments across entire enterprise • Intuitive infrastructure predicts and adapts for improved outcomes and services delivery

	Ad Hoc	Opportunistic	Repeatable	Managed	Optimized
Data (Use, Access)	• Data is underutilized and housed in disparate systems • Access is limited to single organizations because of issues with data integrity, privacy/security and integration	• Data integrity is more fully addressed as data is used in big data and advanced analytics projects • Some data sets are opened to public • Data becomes more widely shared across departments	• Data use is focused on maintaining quality for big data and analytics use cases • Progress is made in accuracy and semantic consistency • Open data becomes strategic to leverage skills and ideas from many organizations and citizen/community groups	• Data is used to provide actionable information to further smart city goals • Advanced data analysis done for multiple purposes • Data is all inclusive with fully operational data sharing among organizations and individuals inside and outside of government	• Data is used for predictive models for improved services; real-time data collection allows faster response for non-predictable events • Information is ubiquitous, open, personalized, and proactively delivered as desired

Challenges to Address

The path to the Optimized Smart City Maturity Model is a long-term effort that will take years, rather than months, to achieve. Today there is sporadic adoption of smart city solutions across cities, with only a handful of cities worldwide actively in the opportunistic or repeatable implementation stage. Most cities are focused on researching and evaluating use cases and vendor capabilities along with defining their vision of a smart city and identifying barriers to adoption.

It is worth pointing out (as in Figure 1, see next page) that it is not a steady and consistent march from one stage to the next. The move from ad hoc to opportunistic takes less time and effort than the progression from opportunistic to repeatable, which requires significant effort to address how to scale and fund projects. Similarly, moving from repeatable to managed is a longer process, with process issues at the forefront. However, going from managed to optimized may take less time because all of the foundational strategic, process and cultural issues will have been largely resolved.

People often ask, "which are the smartest" cities? Or, which cities are smart cities?" At this early stage, cities in the optimized stage do not exist. Most cities are in the ad hoc stage and are either researching or evaluating smart city solutions or testing the waters with pilot projects. The most developed cities are in the repeatable stage, but typically only in one or two focused areas within the city, not across the entire city system. Examples or cities in the repeatable stage include: San Francisco with regard to smart

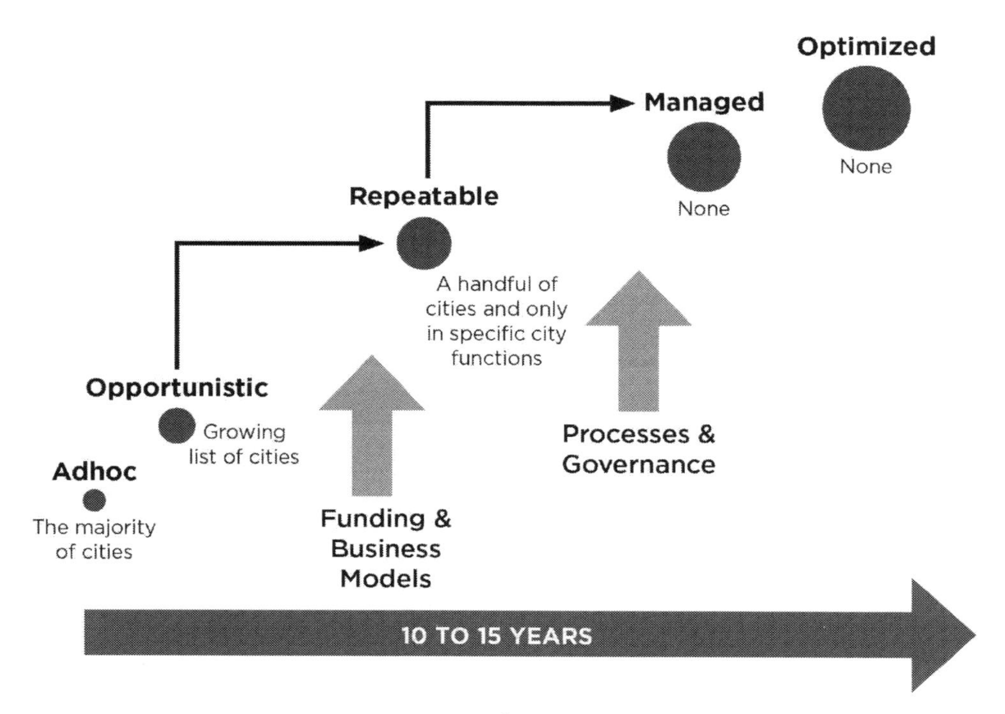

Figure 1.

parking and open data; Singapore for intelligent transportation systems, Stockholm in congestion charging; and Boston for civic innovation.

At this point, much of the smart city discussion is around the business model of solutions and how to sustain funding for projects. Many of these new projects have been at least partially funded via grants from central or international governments or foundations. After this money is used, the question remains as to how these new ICT and staffing investments will be sustained. How will the technology be maintained, supported and upgraded? Some smart projects provide better revenue and fee collections, as seen with smart parking solutions, advanced tolling or road charging systems, or permitting and licensing upgrades. These systems allow for better tracking of payments, as well as easier payment options from citizens. This increased revenue can then support the new systems.

In other cases, like smart water solutions, there can be significant cost-savings. Sensors can detect water leakages faster, for example, and reduce water costs. The savings then can be used for other smart projects.

Even with these cases, the business models for smart cities are still developing and need to mature to get more cities to the repeatable stage. New partnership models, from co-investment to co-development of solutions to performance contracting, will provide some answers. For smaller-scale initiatives, crowd-funding may suffice. Open data also has potential as a way to citizen-source app development, spur start-up creation, and engage more closely with universities to build services without significant government investment.

Eventually, these issues bleed into process and governance issues, particularly around budgeting and procurement. To reach a managed level of maturity, departments need to be considered for consolidation or shared budgeting, and departmental leaders will need to communicate amongst each other for citywide decision-making on budget allocations and procurement processes.

Actions to Consider

To progress along the stages of the Smart City Maturity Model":

- Use the model to socialize the idea of smart city transformations to those leaders that are open to innovation and are change agents within the city.
- Focus on each of the five measures of the model and ensure that there is a coordinated progression along all of the five measures, as opposed to becoming much more mature in one area, which inhibits overall progress.
- Use a set of KPIs or performance measures to define the success of each stage.

The following guidelines set to specific timelines maximize the benefits of the Smart City Maturity Model:

- ***Now:*** Assess the business and IT smart city "as is" situation. Identify opportunities to use existing data, technology, workers and citizens in new ways. Explore opportunities to use new low-cost public cloud and open source options as they emerge, including citizen-sourcing of app development. Identify relevant innovation, leadership, technology, and analytics skills among existing staff and vendors. Experiment with proof-of-concept and prototype projects.
- ***In the next one—to two years (the next budget cycle):*** Use early quantifiable wins to demonstrate potential and justify budget allocations. Evaluate the existing technology and its shortcomings. Assess skills gaps and plan to hire and/or externally source professional services. Identify business sponsors and champions that will support and promote smart city projects. Expand projects and begin to define architectural standards. Begin governance and performance management discussions.

Table 3. *Guidance for Actions to Take at Each Stage of Maturity.*

STAGE	GUIDANCE
AD HOC **Outcome:** Proof of smart city concept and business case development via demonstrated ROI from pilot projects	• Invest in pilot/experimentation projects in a specific domain that will provide a monetary ROI either from revenues or cost savings. • Engage LOBs and city leaders for executive support for initial projects and to begin strategy discussions across departments and agencies. • Identify change agents and innovators within government and the community for future innovation and engagement activities. • Identify barriers to adoption, such as inconsistent broadband infrastructure or a lack of available skills sets. • Use social media and mobile apps to engage with citizens and community groups
OPPORTUNISTIC **Outcome:** Cross-organizational deployments and development of foundational strategy and governance	• Look to invest in build-out of pilot projects across departments or organizations. Identify high-priority areas that will continue to bring measurable and public results. Use data scientists to uncover new insights from pilots. • Start to document long-term desired outcomes and goals with multiple stakeholders. • Redefine the purpose of IT to include innovation and establish an innovation team/organization (from previously identified change agents) to coordinate efforts. • Take an inventory of existing infrastructure across organizations to develop a plan for leveraging these assets and sharing information. • Begin to research and evaluate enterprise architectures that will support mission. • Open data sets to the public and foster data use by holding hackathons and contests for new ideas and mobile app development.
REPEATABLE **Outcome:** Repeatable success in project process and outcomes across multiple organizations	• Formalize collaboration by creating cross-departmental work groups for services delivery beyond emergencies, events, and disaster management. Hold in-person and online meetings to discuss new project ideas and ways to leverage existing data and systems. • Document processes and define specific outcomes. Define how successful outcomes will be measured. • Move beyond one-off contests to engage citizens on a continuous basis via personalized apps, direct communication via social media, and using gamification models. • Data integrity must be a priority as information sharing across organizations becomes a reality. Continue to expand the availability of and to integrate internal multi-structured data sources. Be aware that data governance policies and procedures will be difficult to implement at single-business-unit level. • Budget for scaling out of projects. Perform costs-benefit analysis for Smart City projects to determine resource allocation. Begin serious discussions with partners on business models. Define what return partners will get by putting "skin in the game." • Develop a skills pipeline. Work with academic institutions to use students to intern on projects to augment staff but also to mentor potential new hires.

MANAGED **Outcome:** Enterprise-wide strategy, process, data, and technology bring improved service delivery via adaptive and sense-and-respond systems	• Assign an executive-level leader to coordinate the development of a cross-business-unit smart city strategy and to work regularly with partners and other stakeholders, like educational institutions. • Create a centralized smart city team that provides support for decentralized staff within business groups and that works consistently on citizen engagement. • Monitor outcomes-focused metrics by which processes, staff, and outcomes are measured to ensure goals are being met. • Deploy fit-for-purpose and workload-optimized technology. Incorporate predictive analytics into technology performance monitoring and management processes. • Enable broad technology adoption by ensuring that an appropriate technology pricing structure is negotiated with IT vendors.
OPTIMIZED **Outcome:** Agility, innovation, and continuous improvement in service delivery bring competitive advantage	• Make available information about all data sources for users with business units. The centralized smart city team should take charge of continuous improvements in process and to refine and improve on methodology for governance and measurements. • Employ decision management techniques to enable continuous process improvement and integration of innovation and citizen engagement into business processes. • Reorganize departments and agencies in accordance with outcomes and service delivery goals and match budgeting process to fund new organizations. • Regularly provide training to all the technology, analytics, and business staff to ensure everyone continues to work toward a common vision and outcomes, even as they are adjusted and refined. • Ensure that open data continues to be used to support the growth of new business and services by a continuous refresh of available data as well as tools that have been successful in fostering their use (Open APIs, contests, etc). • Continue, or further develop, applied smart city R&D initiatives with academic and private partners.

Smart cities are going to be a significant force of investment for the future. The Smart City Maturity model is a place to begin for city leaders. At this very early stage in smart city development, it is important to use this model to develop a clear vision, common language, and a strategic road map with key leaders and innovators in the city ecosystem.

RUTHBEA YESNER CLARKE *is research director of the global* Smart Cities Strategies *program at IDC. In this program, Ms. Clarke discusses strategies and execution of relevant Smart City technologies and services implementations with a focus on local government administration, economic development, partnership models, sustainable growth in public works, transportation, and public safety, and innovations in citizen engagement, Open Data, mobility and social business.*

Ms. Clarke holds a BA from Wesleyan University, and graduated Summa Cum Laude from Boston College with an MBA and MSW joint degree.

It Takes a Smart City to Become an Intelligent Community

Robert Bell

What is the difference between a city being *smart* and being *intelligent*? It sounds like a riddle—but the difference is far more important. For more than a decade, the Intelligent Community Forum (ICF) has studied that unique place where technology intersects with people at the local level. The organization wants to understand and share widely with others how cities and regions turn broadband and information technology into economic value, social value and cultural value. Those three values are the foundation of places all people like to live: places of inclusive prosperity, with a strong sense of local identity and hopes for a better future.

From that study, the foundation has taken away one lesson relevant to smart cities. Not every smart city is intelligent, but every one of the 120 intelligent communities studied is smart.

The Smart City Surge

Since the words "smart" and "city" were first put together by Cisco in 2005 in response to a challenge from former U.S. President Bill Clinton, the smart city surge has been accelerating down the runway for takeoff. IBM jumped into the game in 2008 with its Smarter Planet program, based on work with Madrid and New York on crime control, with Stockholm on a congestion fee system, and on a pioneering project to build an emergency operations center for the city of Rio de Janeiro. Rio suffers from landslides, brought on by heavy rains, in its vast slums called *favellas*. Using data from an array of new weather sensors, the center was able to predict where there was a high risk of landslides 24 hours in advance and coordinate city resources to prepare for and respond to emergencies[1]. The operations center

[1]"IBM, Cisco and the Business of Smart Cities" by Pete Swabey, *Information Age*, Feb. 23, 2012.

cost Rio US$14 million.[2] From that project came IBM's Smarter Planet product, the Integrated Operations Center.

Meanwhile, in 2010, when Cisco's pledge to the Clinton Foundation expired, it launched its Smart + Connected Communities division to commercialize the products and services it had developed in work with San Francisco, Amsterdam, Seoul and other cities.[3] Cisco's most recent project is a pilot for the French city of Nice, which is testing multiple applications such as smart parking, waste disposal, lighting and environmental monitoring along the 800-yard Victor Hugo Boulevard.[4]

The smart city technology market is forecast to grow from $1.6 billion in 2012 to more than $20 billion in 2020, according to GI Research. In this year alone, 70 percent of spending on smart city projects will focus on energy, transportation and public safety, and 90 percent will be at least partially funded by government. As the number of people living in cities grows from 3.6 billion today to 6.3 billion in 2050, dozens of megacities with more than 10 million people are expected to arise, each bursting with problems that smart city technology can solve.[5]

Meanwhile, the European Commission sees the smart city idea as a path to meeting its environmental commitments (on which, like most of the industrialized world, it has made largely negative progress). The European Initiative on Smart Cities will support cities and regions investing in greenhouse gas (GHG) emissions reduction through sustainable use and energy production. The goal is to prime the pump sufficiently in terms of energy-efficient and low-carbon technologies to trigger private-sector investment in the market. Investment is sorely needed: The Europen Union seeks a 40 percent reduction in GHG emissions by 2020 from 1990 levels through programs in smart grid, alternative-fuel vehicles and new building standards.[6]

Smart City Pathways

With dozens of smart city projects and governmental support programs around the world, two paths are emerging. One involves cities that

---

[2] "Mission Control, Built for Cities" by Natasha Singer, *The New York Times*, March 3, 2012.

[3] "IBM, Cisco and the Business of Smart Cities."

[4] "Cisco and Nice Say Bonjour to a Smarter City" by Heather Clancy, *Greenbiz.com*, June 25, 2013.

[5] "Smart City Technology Market to Reach $20.2 Billion in 2020: Top 20 Predictions for 2013," GI Research, Feb. 6, 2013.

[6] "European Initiative on Smart Cities," European Commission, http://setis.ec.europa.eu

already exist, and the installation of systems, software and services to improve how they work. The second path uses smart systems to create new cities.

Smart city has become a popular term, with the top tech companies packaging solutions for municipal customers. Yet fundamentally, there is nothing revolutionary about making an existing city smart. Manufacturing facilities throughout the industrialized world have done it before by. automating factories and deploying information and communications technology (ICT) that enabled them to do more with less. The same principles govern the automating of a city. In one end goes a lot of specialized ICT—sensors, actuators and servers run by sophisticated software developed and installed by engineers. Out the other end comes better, faster and cheaper performance. Once-murky processes become visible and measurable, turnaround becomes faster and more reliable. Additionally, costs fall permanently because cities are more efficient and need fewer people to run things. That is a "win" for a manufacturer. However, the results are more ambiguous for a city, where every headcount reduction means a citizen has lost a job.

From its success in Rio, IBM went on to analyze "fuel poverty" in Glasgow, Scotland, and the challenge that low-income households face in paying high heating fuel prices. The analysis revealed that exhaust heat from nearby industry facilities could be cost-effectively redirected to warm people's homes.[7]

Cisco's Nice pilot is designed to identify cost-saving opportunities that could be deployed citywide. Tests of smart parking services aim to help residents and visitors find parking more quickly and easily; early results suggest the potential for a 30 percent reduction in traffic congestion. By equipping streetlights with sensors that adjust brightness based on traffic activity or weather, the city hopes to reduce electricity costs for lighting from 20 percent to 80 percent.[8]

An American company called PredPol offers a predictive policing system that analyzes crime reporting in real time, as well as historical trends and weather data to make predictions about where to deploy police officers. Crime, like infectious disease, forms patterns in time and space. A burglary in a peaceful neighborhood raises the risk for adjoining properties, but that threat rapidly diminishes if no further burglaries take place. Within six months of the start of a PredPol pilot in the Los Angeles foothills in late 2011, property crimes fell 12 percent compared with the prior year, while in neighboring areas they rose 0.5 percent.[9]

---

[7] "IBM, Cisco and the Business of Smart Cities."

[8] "Cisco and Nice Say Bonjour to a Smarter City."

[9] "Don't Even Think About It," *The Economist*, July 20, 2013

Shake 'n Bake

Shake 'n Bake is used with chicken parts or pork chops: put them in a plastic bag with the product, shake it thoroughly to coat the meat, then bakd it. The result is a breaded entrée that tastes pretty good.

Shake 'n Bake comes to mind in a smart city project called Tokyo Teleport Town. When the Japanese government privatized the state-owned telephone company in 1985, it offered part of the proceeds to city governments in the form of interest-free loans to build what are now called smart city districts. In Tokyo, the money went to build two large artificial islands in Tokyo Bay with fiber-to-the-premise everywhere, a district control center, automated waste disposal through a system of chutes, and a new bridge and transit system run entirely by computers. The project was designed as a mixed-use development that would catapult Tokyo into the 21st Century for a cost of US$3 billion just for the islands and infrastructure. It opened in 1994 and, six years later, a city official confessed that the project had turned out to be an enormous white elephant on which the city would be lucky to get payback in 30 years. He said that because residential and business development on the islands was so slow, Tokyo Teleport Town had become best- known as a place where young lovers could go for some private time away from the crowd and noise of downtown.

Tokyo Teleport Town represented an early version of the second pathway for smart cities: the greenfield development of a city or district where none existed before. The Japanese smart city surge of the '80s spurred Malaysia's government to announce the Multimedia Supercorridor, a 1996 plan to create a high-tech corridor 15 kilometers (km) wide and 50 km long where only rubber plantations then existed. The government downsized the plan several times, leaving a corridor that exists largely in name only.

Nevertheless, two Shake 'n Bake cities emerged. Putrajaya is the Malaysian Brasilia: a city created to house Malaysia's national government when it evicted itself from Kuala Lumpur. Cyberjaya is a technology park where global companies can go to find the industrialized-world infrastructure to which they are accustomed.

Today's contenders in the super smart city category include such famous projects as Masdar City in Abu Dhabi and Sejong City in South Korea. In 2007, the government of Abu Dhabi, which controls 8 percent of the world's oil reserves, announced it would build the world's first zero-carbon city, called Masdar. Through innovative design and ubiquitous smart systems, it would use half the energy of a city of comparable size—generated 100 percent from renewable sources—and would produce zero waste. The city would also be home to a university dedicated to sustainability studies, which would help the city attract the best companies in clean tech from around the world.

According to a *Time* magazine article, reality has not kept pace with the dream of Masdar. The financial crisis, which hit the United Arab Emirates hard, delayed development. The 2015 target date for completion was pushed back indefinitely. The goal of a zero-carbon city proved out of reach with available technologies. Keeping energy use low has turned out to require some old-fashioned social engineering: monitoring electricity use in every room in the city and nagging residents to keep air-conditioning set to 77 degrees F. (25 degrees C.) in a country where rooms are normally cooled to 60 degrees F. (15.5 degrees C.). The Masdar Institute of Science and Technology is open, but it is "not clear" that clean tech companies will find the city a magnet, according to the *Time* reporter.[10]

Sejong City also was scheduled for completion in 2015 but officially opened in 2012. Originally intended as the site of a new capital, the US$19.6 billion city was later re-envisioned as a place to house 36 government ministries and agencies, another variation on the Brasilia story. The state Board of Audit and Inspection has expressed doubt about the government's target of bringing in a half a million residents by 2030. "People will not live there from the beginning," a professor of architecture told the Korea Herald, "and only fathers of families will commute every day or maybe during the weekend because the rest of the family will live in Seoul."[11]

The Soul of the City

There is nothing new about very large infrastructure development projects facing severe challenges. From Boston's "Big Dig" and Hong Kong's Chek Lap Kok airport to the Channel Tunnel and the Øresund Bridge between Sweden and Denmark, large-scale projects take longer, prove more complicated and cost enormously more than anyone expects. Cities keep doing them, however, because they also deliver enormous benefits across the generations, long after the aggravation and financial losses are forgotten.

The question is whether it makes sense to think of entire cities as big infrastructure projects. We have the ingenuity to lay out streets, master-plan properties and design utility and transportation networks. We can use ICT to build greater flexibility, usability and responsiveness into that infrastructure, and to run it with less energy, less maintenance and lower costs. However, we cannot, as part of design, give the city a soul.

---

[10] "Masdar City: The World's Greenest City?" by Bryan Walsh, *Time*, Jan. 25, 2011.

[11] "Do Planned Cities Work?" *The Korea Herald*, July 30, 2012.

Design alone cannot give cities that special something that makes Tokyo into Tokyo, Rio into Rio, Nice into Nice, or the place you were born into a distinct spot on the map with a personality of its own that attracts other people. These things take time. They take the confluence of geography with human dreams and human interaction. They take love, without which no place becomes a home.

Shake 'n Bake cities will continue to amaze and inspire by their sheer scale and daring. As infrastructure projects, they may ultimately deliver value across generations—although many people would prefer not to invest any of their money into such projects considering how often the original investors in big infrastructure lose their shirts. Yet all of the "smarts" cannot make cities. To have any legitimacy, that is a title that must be bestowed by the people who live there. And that is the reason why not every smart city is intelligent, but all intelligent communities are smart.

Intelligent communities tend to be rich in the same software, systems and services that define a smart city, but they approach development from the other end. They use ICT not just to gain efficiencies or to reduce costs by 10 percent to 15 percent. Rather, they use ICT to create new competitive advantages for the local economy, to solve big, hairy social problems, and to extend and enrich the value of local culture. Instead of trying to do more with less, the goal is to do more with more: to generate more economic energy in the form of new employment from new employers. The aim is to use ICT to break down social and cultural barriers that hold back part of the population, so that they can participate in the knowledge-based digital economy. They also aim to turn local culture into a product for the global economy, and to preserve treasured languages, histories and ways of life that give life meaning. ICT, properly applied, creates efficiencies, so intelligent communities also get better, faster and cheaper performance. And that is a side effect of far more meaningful change.

There is a potent word that comes to us from finance: leverage. Anyone who has borrowed money to finance a home, car or education has used it. A home mortgage lets people live in a nice place where a family can prosper and children can receive a great education even when they don't have cash to buy that home. Leverage is generally a powerful force for good. However, pushed to excess, as it was in the global financial crisis, it can have a very dark side. But it is generally a powerful force for good.

Being a smart city is about squeezing more out of existing or planned assets by measuring better and responding better. Being an intelligent community is about using ICT to leverage a better future for a town, city or region so that it can have more and do more of all the things that make life rewarding. It is about a particular place choosing to seize a new and greater destiny.

On the Waterfront

The list of today's "green" smart city developments would not be complete without Waterfront Toronto (WT). Built on a Brownfield site, the Waterfront development is a US$8.45 billion public-private effort to redevelop 800 hectares of formerly industrial land along Toronto's shoreline into 40,000 residential units and 1 million square meters of commercial space. Toronto (an ICF Top7 Intelligent Community in 2013) will host the 2014 Pan American Games, and that has driven parts of the development plan at breakneck speed. A total of US$3.48 billion has already gone into the ground, making WT home to the single largest concentration of construction cranes in North America.

When it comes to smart city features, WT has all the bells and whistles. It is constructing a 1 gigabit per second fiber-to-the-premise network, operated by a private, well-established fiber-optic network provider called Beanfield. The network will be the backbone for a WiFi cloud that will spread across all public areas, as well as service interactive information kiosks throughout WT. The city will have solar- and wind-powered streetlights , smart buildings, tele-health and tele-education. Aggressive green building requirements will make the Waterfront one of the most energy-efficient urban districts in Canada.

WT, however, is more than a smart city; t is an intelligent community. Instead of having architects and property builders in the driver's seat, the project is led by community builders, WT President John Campbell foremost among them. Given the high value of waterfront property, WT could easily become a gated community for the uber-rich. Instead, it seeks to transform the entire city in its image. Rather than having to invent a soul, WT aims to translate what is best about the existing city into 21st century terms.

The development team believes that public trust is the project's greatest asset and has spent years gathering ideas, explaining decisions and reporting progress to citizens and local business. Twenty percent of all housing is reserved for low-income residents—and they will not be tucked away into one low-rent corner of the waterfront but spread across its length. The master plan devotes three-eighths of the total land to public parks. WT forbids the construction of a "wall of condos" blocking the water view and takes such a sustainable approach to building that it has actually sparked an increase in the number of fish species in Lake Ontario.

WT's ultra-broadband network is funded by fees paid by every developer leasing property for construction. Residential developers will bundle broadband service into condominium fees to encourage ubiquitous use, while low-income residents will receive it free. The network is beginning to deliver on one of the waterfront's key goals: to attract digital media and information technology companies back to downtown.

Like many large cities, Toronto has lost many of its fastest-growing companies to the suburbs that ring the city, because its aging transportation network and high costs imposed such a burden on employers and employees. Toronto's Board of Trade has identified gridlock as the greatest threat to economic prosperity in the region—a problem estimated to cost the economy US$5.64 billion annually—and estimates that commuters in the region experience longer round trips than any other city in the world.

While the construction cranes are still on the move, the waterfront has already become home to a state-of-the-art Center for Health Sciences for George Brown Community College and the headquarters and production center of Corus Entertainment, a fast-growing owner of radio and TV stations across Canada, which consolidated 10 locations and 1,100 employees scattered across Toronto into one of the first major buildings in the Waterfront zone.

Beanfield, the network operator, is being besieged by building owners outside the waterfront zone to be hooked up. This is in contrast to a few years ago, when building owners demanded that Beanfield pay them rent for access. By creating demand for the highest speed broadband services, WT expects its network to drive demand for massive bandwidth across the city.

The Mechanical Kingdom

Taichung City in central Taiwan is not on anyone's list of smart cities, but it probably should be. ICF's "2013 Intelligent Community of the Year," Taichung has overlaid an ICT infrastructure on an existing port city that is also the center of the greater Taichung Technology corridor, home to 1,500 precision manufacturers in more than a dozen science and technology parks. The city's legacy in precision manufacturing gave it the nickname "The Mechanical Kingdom." The city collaborates with communications carriers to deploy overlapping 4G, WiMAX and fiber networks toward a goal of ubiquitous coverage at 100 megabits per second, with 20 to 50 Mbps already broadly available. The government uses this network to run such smart city applications as an operations command-and-control system, video surveillance network, traffic management system, and a georgraphic information system (GIS)-based 3D model of the city for urban planning and construction management. A radio frequency identification (RFID)-based system at the port automates the clearing of shipping containers for exit, slashing the time trucks spend idling at the gate. The city, universities and tech parks have collaborated on developing a shared, cloud-based enterprise resource planning (ERP) system for the city's small to midsize manufacturers that sharply improved their competitiveness compared with global players.

All of this development, however, takes place in a living, breathing city that aims to diversify its economy and make the community a crossroads for global culture. The city's popular mayor, Jason Hu, likes to say that "a grassy field can transform an entire city" and lavishes his attention on the aspects of Taichung that make special.

Taichung is home to the most famous temple in Taiwan dedicated to worship of a Chinese sea deity called Mazu. To support the 5 million visitors who come to the annual Mazu festival, the city coordinates global positioning systems (GPS) and Internet technologies that direct synchronized pilgrimages for nearly 750,000 people. The city is also renowned for its pastries, and the city tied a traditional cultural festival to a "pastry carnival" that helped drive a 20-times increase in sales from 2001 to 2011. The Taichung International Floral Tapestry and Sea of Flower Festival generates more than US$43 million in economic output. The city marked a cultural milestone when director Ang Lee chose to film his *Life of Pi* in Taichung, where an old terminal building at Shuinan Airport was converted into a sound stage.

City of Arts and Culture

Toronto and Taichung are big cities, each with about 2.6 million people, as well as centers of economic regions. But size is no requirement for municipal intelligence. Take, for example, Riverside, Calif., a city of 306,000 located 60 miles east of Los Angeles. Home to the University of California Riverside, it had an economy based on agriculture, logistics and was a bedroom community for Los Angeles until it launched a successful drive to get its share of California's ICT industries. The financial crisis struck a major blow to its booming housing sector, from which the city struggles to recover. Meanwhile, the ciy's knowledge-based economy has prospered, giving rise to multiple incubators that leverage the university's emerging talent.

Smart city-type innovation has become central to how the city operates. Riverside used to have a big problem with graffiti left by gangs, who like to "tag" their territory. Graffiti matters as much as broken windows and boarded-up storefronts because they signal to both law-abiding and law-breaking citizens that things are out of control. They tend to breed fear on the one hand and crime on the other.

So to combat graffiti, the city built an innovative system connecting multiple departments. Now, city workers or ordinary citizens take photos of graffiti with a smartphone app that transmits the picture along with GPS data to the system. Pattern recognition software matches the image in an ever-growing database of images. In most cases, police can identify the "tagger" based on past examples of his work. The system generates work orders for removal of the graffiti while simultaneously preparing criminal complaints by the city attorney. Since its introduction, successful prosecutions have generated $200,000 in restitution, which helps to remove a lot of gang tags.

However, technology is the foundation for a much more profound change in Riverside. A public-private SmartRiverside organization operates a Digital Inclusion Center that gets technology and training into the hands of low-income families. The technology comes from a collaboration between a computer services company that collects e-waste, and a gang prevention program called Project Bridge. The company hires and trains former gang members recruited by Project Bridge to refurbish used computers. Equipment that cannot be refurbished is sold to a certified local recycler. Working equipment other than PCs is refurbished and sold on eBay, and this revenue helps to pay for the program. Additionally, former gang members gain marketable job skills while knowing that they are contributing to their community. And, like graffiti removal, the program returns revenue to cover its costs.

SmartRiverside is not a technology solution to a public-sector problem. Rather, it is an illustration of technology leaching into government operations, the business environment, educational system and civic culture. It is like the outcome of the first Internet revolution, which was supposed to doom brick-and-mortar businesses to obsolescence. Instead, brick-and-mortar businesses embraced the technology and allowed it to transform the way they work.

The smart city industry promises design, engineering and technology fixes for urban challenges, many of them based on big data analytics that reveal formerly hidden patterns that open avenues for design, engineering and technology solutions. Whether they will deliver on their potential or fall prey to the overwhelming complexity and exploding costs of most big infrastructure projects remains to be seen. In either case, however, they are just scratching the surface of what the ICT revolution can mean to cities and regions—the chance to transform how people live, how they govern themselves, and how businesses and institutions can contribute to the local economy and achieve greater success..

To him who holds a hammer, everything looks like a nail. To her with a full box of tools, the problems are more diverse and subtle, and the solutions infinitely more rewarding.

__ROBERT BELL__ is co-founder of the Intelligent Community Forum, which studies and promotes the best practices of the world's intelligent Ccommunities as they adapt to demands and seize opportunities presented by information and communications technology (ICT). The ICF Foundation consists of 119 cities and regions that ICF has designated as intelligent communities, and which participate in an ongoing global dialogue to strengthen local economies. For more information, go to www.intelligentcommunity.org.

5

Becoming a Smarter City: A Getting Started Guide for Smaller Cities

Theresa A. Pardo, Donna S. Canestraro and Meghan E. Cook

Cities the world over are embracing the idea of using technology and information to become "smarter." The desirable status of being "smart" is an outcome sought by the public and city officials alike. As a result, increasing attention is being paid to city governments that are successful in transforming their cities through smart city initiatives. Many studies of successful smart city efforts and much of the attention being paid to ways cities are becoming smarter are focused on larger cities. However, most of the world's population spends its time in small- to medium-sized cities. These cities, particularly small-sized cities throughout the United States, lack the policy, management and technology capabilities necessary to realize the transformations underway in the larger and more technologically and organizationally advanced cities.

However, projects underway in two small cities in New York are on building the capabilities necessary to transform themselves through information and technology innovation.

Seeking to Be Smart

The phrase "smart city" is being used more regularly by elected officials, civil society, the private sector and academia. Regardless of this increasing use, there is no agreed-upon description of what "smart" implies in the context of a city (Chourabi et al, 2012). A review of the literature makes the case that "smart city" is broadly understood as improvements in: city infrastructure, including information and communication infrastructures; physical infrastructures, such as roads, bridges, and buildings, services such as utilities, social services, and transportation; and a variety of resources such as natural resources, financial resources, cultural resources, and human capital (Nam and Pardo 2012). Calling a city smart or seeking to be a smarter city however, is often a normative claim. People, including government officials, want the cities they live in and are responsible for to be smarter; they want to close the gap between their current status and their expectations. As a result, increasing attention is being paid to city governments that are successful in transforming their cities through smart city initiatives.

Award programs and ranking efforts are emerging, and societies and research communities are coming together worldwide to envision the city of the future; to develop strategies to achieve those visions; to identify and award those who are successful; and to develop new understanding of these efforts and their impact on the lives of the people and organizations who live and do business there.

Large cities such as New York and Seoul have consistently viewed technology innovation as critical to their efforts to provide citizens with a quality of life and to grow their economies. As early as 2002 under the leadership of Mayor Michael Bloomberg, New York received top rankings nationally by surveys such as the Digital Cities Survey; tying for 2nd place with Seattle in 2002, and winning best of the web awards even earlier in 2001 for its efforts to improve the lives of its citizens through innovations in information and communications technology. Mayor Rudy Giuliani, who preceded Mayor Bloomberg, also was a technology enthusiast and sought ways to support innovations that would improve the lives of citizens. He created innovative programs such as the city's first release of restaurant inspection data[1]. And Mayor Bloomberg is building on that foundation, taking New York to a completely new level of technology innovation and service delivery through a range of programs including the city's award winning NYC311 program[2].

Equally impressive and ahead of the curve, is Seoul. Like New York, Seoul has consistently and successfully invested in technology innovation in the interests of becoming a smarter city[3]. Seoul also has earned recognition for its efforts, securing top honors in formal evaluations and ranking first for four years in a row from the 100 Cities e-Government Survey[4].

Smart and Small

Recent studies of smart cities emphasize smartness of government, administration and public management as core factors in creating a smart

---

[1] http://www.gothamgazette.com/index.php/open-government/2144-e-government-in-nyc

[2] http://www.accenture.com/us-en/company/overview/awards/Pages/nyc-311-wins-un-public-service-award-solutions.aspx

[3] http://www.itu.int/net/itunews/issues/2010/04/40.aspx

[4] http://www.unpan.org/PublicAdministrationNews/tabid/651/mctl/ArticleView/ModuleID/1555/articleId/22366/Default.aspx

city (Chourabi et al 2012, Nam & Pardo 2011a & 2011b). Many such studies of the factors that influence success are focused on larger cities. However, most of the world's population lives in small- to medium-sized cities[5], and thus it is critical that we understand the differences between small and large cities with respect to innovation capability.

Moreover, new knowledge about how local context interacts with the characteristics of various smart city initiatives is needed. Such new knowledge, paired with leadership commitment and a range of policy, management and technology capabilities, may tip the balance for small cities in favor of becoming smarter cities.

Today, hundreds of small-sized cities (population under 100,000) throughout the United States lack the policy, management and technology capabilities necessary to match the progress being seen in the larger and more technologically and organizationally advanced cities. Large cities such as San Francisco and New have information technology enterprises that are second-to-none. Within these enterprises, they benefit from a new class of city government official; those specifically focused on advancing innovations in the creation, management and use of information and technology. Chief information officers have been joined by chief technology officers, chief data officers and even chief innovation officers. In 2010, New York's Mayor Bloomberg appointed a chief digital officer[6] reporting directly to him with responsibility "to help the city use technology to better serve citizens"[7].

These new roles and the people who fill them are changing the ways cities around the world think about and use technology. However, for every one of these innovative leaders and cutting-edge models, hundreds of cities are wrestling with the gap between their vision of using technology to better serve citizens with new understanding of their cities and their citizens made possible by insights generated through data newly available to inform public policy and program decision-making.

Smaller-Sized Standouts

In two small cities in New York State, Schenectady[8] and Binghamton[9], you would expect to find deep appreciation for the potential of technology innovation and some capability for engaging in such efforts. Schenectady is the birthplace of General Electric. Endicott, N.Y., just outside of

[5] http://www.unfpa.org/pds/urbanization.htm.

[6] http://www.nyc.gov/html/media/html/news/cto_announcement.shtml

[7] http://www.huffingtonpost.com/2011/01/24/rachel-sterne-named-citys_n_813154.html

[8] http://www.cityofschenectady.com/

[9] http://www.binghamton-ny.gov/

Binghamton, is where Harlow Bundy, a Binghamton native, launched IBM's predecessor, ITG. Even with such auspicious claims, these cities have struggled to become 21st century cities and to deliver on the promises of technology and data. Yet through two separate projects carried out in partnership with these cities, the Center for Technology in Government (CTG) examined the challenges facing each city as they worked to become smarter. In both cases, CTG partnered with teams from Schenectady and Binghamton to explore a particular problem. Schenectady faced a lack of readily accessible and shareable code enforcement data; Binghamton lacked a 21st century management structure for information technology.

Once problems were identified, an outline to address the problems and develop a vision statement to design new capability was created. Work meetings to design the outline included workflow modeling and gap analysis sessions, as well as management, policy and technology context reviews. Background research was conducted in both cases to understand and document relevant data, resources and policies. Based on those case studies, a set of recommendations for small cities seeking to create the capability necessary to become smarter has developed.

Creating a 21st Century IT Enterprise in the City of Binghamton.

Binghamton[10] is the county seat of Broome County and lies in the southern tier of state on the border with Pennsylvania. It is home to about 47,000 people. The structure of government in Binghamton is comprised of a mayor and a seven-member, unicameral city council serving single member districts. Both the mayor and city council members are subject to term limits of two consecutive four-year terms. Mayor Matthew Ryan will complete his second and final term at the end of 2013.

Consistent with similar cities in New York, Binghamton experienced steady growth and prosperity through the 19th and 20th centuries, largely due to the confluence of transportation networks such as extensions of the Erie Canal and major railroads. Being well-situated as a hub of commerce spurred manufacturing through the WWII era. Although the city experienced the same post-war outmigration to the suburbs as other U.S. cities, the regional strength of its defense-related industries buffered the negative impact of a declining population. However, with the close of the Cold War, the underbelly of Binghamton's economic reliance on a single sector was exposed. Binghamton, like many other small cities in the United States, is wrestling with economic shortfalls and a shifting economic base.

As home to one of the four University campuses of the State University of New York, Binghamton has prime proximity to a highly regarded

[10] http://en.wikipedia.org/wiki/Binghamton,_New_York

institution, graduating thousands of would-be residents each year. Despite the prospect of approximately 17,000 students, the city and region is unable to capture this population for permanent residency, primarily due to the lack of a diversified and vibrant economy.

The Problem. Historically, information management systems within small cities focus on specific transactions or operations. This focus is typical of most municipalities in which information technology arose as a function within the finance department to assist in automating accounting books and producing payroll checks. These back-office minicomputer or mainframe systems required a dedicated "data processing" staff to manage. As desktop computing expanded, individual departments independently acquired software and hardware. Departments began hiring IT staff to meet their own needs, and resources were assigned to solving problems and building systems that met the specific needs of those departments.

In the past 15 years, with support from the city council and the mayor's office, smart reform has been a priority for Binghamton. The city has invested in hardware and software to modernize its IT operations. This included consolidating and sharing services with the county of Broome, deploying new workstation computers with a uniform operating system and productivity software, consolidating to a single network environment, deploying new servers, and streamlining many internal processes. All of these changes were in response to and anticipation of demands brought upon the city by a changing world and the changing role of IT.

However, while smart reform efforts invested in modernization, the investments were at the department level in the form of computer hardware and large-scale systems, rather than an enterprise system with capability to respond to the shift toward enterprise software services and cloud-based solutions, and to the increasing role of data as a tool for policy and program decision-making at the city level, as well as within programs.

Individual departments now are struggling to keep up with service-demands, and therefore run the risk of wasting time and money. In the short term, departments may be able to meet their service demands, but in the long term, the city as a whole is unable to harness the power that a citywide (or 'enterprise') perspective provides to information management, decision-making and the ability to quickly address outside reporting demands.

As other cities win awards for leveraging data assets from across the enterprise in the interest of policy and planning, Binghamton finds itself still committed to innovation but ill-prepared to operate as an integrated and cohesive organization.

The Vision. In his 2012 State of the City address, Mayor Matthew Ryan outlined his goal for the city: "If we want Binghamton to thrive in the 21st

Century, we need a City Hall to function as a cohesive organization with 21st Century tools." This address made it clear the mayor was committed to embracing a new set of tools—policy, management and technology tools that would enable the city to operate in a more integrated and cohesive way. Through several executive visioning workshops conducted during the project, department leadership from across the city agreed on a set of characteristics for an ideal city government. The ideal characteristics list (see Table 1), developed and vetted by city leaders, set the stage for the development of a city roadmap. Many department heads envisioned having more information about what data is collected by other department and saw such information as enabling thinking beyond their own department to a citywide perspective, both programmatically and in terms of overall service delivery.

Table 1. *Characteristics of an Ideal City Government.*

Ideal Characteristic	Description
Increase Organizational Capacity	• Improve organizational efficiency and effectiveness through education and training, documentation of standard procedures and protocols. • Encourage staff who are dedicated not only to the ongoing maintenance of the infrastructure but who are looking ahead to the strategic use of information to support the city's strategic goals.
Use Information Management as a Strategic Asset	• Create a citywide (enterprise) approach to information management. • Create a governance structure that helps institutionalize the policies and procedures for information management and enterprise governance. • Embed this into the overall executive management of the city so that all decision making for any IT expenditure is considered across the enterprise as opposed to departmentalized budgets or procedures.
Improve Access to Data and Information	• Build workforce capability to access and use data. • Provide data in useable format for both internal and external users. • Allow for 24-7 access to data and government services because citizens expect access online and outside of the normal 8 a.m. to 5 p.m. workday.
Institutionalize Data Management Processes and Procedures	• Create an understanding of the importance of professional management of data. • Create the protocols and procedures to protect data, but also "free" the data from departmental isolation
Cultivate a Culture of Access	• Make information available and useable in ways that embody an "inclusive" culture. • Establish a "concierge" or coach to help guide personnel, the public, and employees through the process of accessing and using the data. • Create an educational component through hosting a "Frequently Asked Questions" to maximize access. • Create or empower city employees to understand department functions across all departments that would help cultivate this new culture of information sharing.
Optimize Organizational Performance and Perception	• Create a mechanism where performance data is used to monitor effectiveness. • Promote the city as a vibrant, active, and engaged partner that is attractive for new economic development. The "Restoring the Pride" campaign could easily be adapted to this "Smarter Binghamton" perspective.

Challenges to Binghamton's Vision. Mayor Ryan faces predominantly five challenges to his vision of a "cohesive and coherent" Binghamton. (See Table 2). First, City IT staff resources are limited and typically not able to keep up with increasing demands or to coordinate technological concerns from a citywide perspective. A few staff with IT skills work across organizational units when they can to support all the departments within the city—managing systems for hundreds of users with dozens of different software packages and hundreds of different devices, and at the same time performing their own departmental duties. Regardless of staffefforts to work across organizational units as much as possible, the needs of the individual departments end up dictating IT decisions within the city. Individual departments have taken on the burden (or in some cases, are unable to take on the burden) of acquiring and supporting their individual departmental systems.

Second, the lack of a centralized IT department means that in many cases, departments must fend for themselves. It also means there is no citywide strategy or department that is charged with coordinating information and technology management efforts to make the desired coherency possible.

Third, the lack of an executive with responsibility for leading information and technology management citywide creates a gap in capability required for innovation and change.

Fourth, isolated departmental systems are creating department-level repositories of information. These disparate data sets take a variety of forms: electronic, paper, checklists and emails, all contained primarily within personal or departmental filing systems. Staff members are unable to find the information they need to carry out their assigned responsibilities. In applications serving a single department, such as police or fire, data or information often is not shared outside of these departments. This isolated view has negative implications across the enterprise and may, if unresolved hamper the city's ability to respond quickly and efficiently to current and emerging demands for service.

Fifth, the lack of a governing framework charged with coordinating action across the silos and driving enterprise versus departmental decision making on IT has resulted in a number of. The ideal characteristics presented in Table 1 reiterate this point. Current information and technology resources are managed in silos, and as a consequence, there is limited opportunity to leverage investments across departments. For example, the return on investments in education and training and documentation of standard procedures and protocols, is limited, as there is no formal entity charged with the coordination of activity across the silos.

Table 2. *Five Challenges to Realizing Binghamton's Vision for a Smarter City.*

1. IT staff is limited in number and assigned to specific departments.
2. No department is charged with responsibility for information and technology management citywide.
3. No executive is charged with leading information and technology management citywide.
4. Department level depositories of information hamper search and access efforts.
5. There is a lack of a governing framework to coordinate actions across silos and to drive enterprise versus departmental decision-making.

Smarter Cities through Regional Data Sharing

Schenectady, with a population of about 66,000, is the county seat of Schenectady County and lies within the same metropolitan area as Albany, New York's capital. The city is linked with Albany and Troy to form the "Tri-City," or Capital District region of upstate New York, where the Mohawk and Hudson Rivers meet. Schenectady is governed by a mayor serving four-year terms[11] and a seven-member city council elected at-large to four-year terms. The mayor, Gary McCarthy, was first appointed by the city council as acting mayor in April 2011 and was subsequently elected to his first full term in November 2011.[12] While the mayor largely maintains oversight of separate city departments, the council appoints the city clerk and certain commission and board members. The council determines policy, approves contracts and agreements, sets salaries, and approves contracts for goods and services.

Schenectady has an extensive and significant past, both historically and economically. It was first settled in 1661 by the Dutch and is one of the oldest establishments in the nation, with strategic significance during the French and Indian War and Revolutionary War. Although already an established trading post, like many cities dotting the Mohawk River, Schenectady gained increased economic strength through the establishment of the Erie Canal in 1825, which opened a strategic trade route between New York and the Great Lakes. Soon after in 1831, the Albany & Schenectady Railroad went into service, which was the first rail line in New York and one of the first in the United States. In short order, two major transportation innovations positioned the city and region as a commercial hub. Throughout the 19th and 20th centuries, Schenectady became a manufacturing center known as, "The City that Lights and Hauls the World," which referenced the creation of Edison Electric Co. (now known as General Electric) and American Locomotive Co. (ALCO) The population of Schenectady

[11] http://cityofschenectady.com/city_council.htm

[12] http://cityofschenectady.com/mayor.html

peaked in 1930 with 95,000,and experienced fluctuations during the next three decades until a continual decline began in the 1960s resulting in one-third of the population to leave. With post-WWII production levels falling, so did the employment numbers of General Electric and ALCO, the two major employers. With the demise of ALCO in 1979, downsizing of General Electric throughout the post-war era, and significant outmigration, Schenectady was confronted with a diminishing tax base and a city built to serve a much larger population.[13]

The Problem. Schenectady, like many cities of its size and demographic and economic footprint, is wrestling with "problem properties". These properties become problems over time through neglect, fraud and a host of social and economic challenges facing property owners and renters. The factors that feed the downward cycle from a rented building to an abandoned property, which then contribute to a range of other social and economic issues within the city, are well understood. Intervening in the process, however, is almost impossible due to a lack of information about the status of any single property and the ability to connect one property to another and ideally, to the property owner. The city does not have access to the data it needs to identify and address problems at the property level, let alone to create new understanding about how a set of properties in such condition contributes to citywide problems and the related expenses caused by systematic fraud, abuse and neglect.

Code enforcement covers building, zoning, housing, environmental, nuisance and other codes and ordinances. Code enforcement processes are used to record and track code violations, updated inspections, hazardous structures, occupied/unoccupied housing, site conditions and land-use. The city, with its current systems, cannot respond to queries from investors or residents on the status of properties with respect to their compliance with code, let alone launch proactive intervention strategies. The lack of electronic access, mobile or otherwise, to code enforcement data increases the risk taken by first responders who are present at a property to fight a fire or help a citizen. Human services interventions also do not benefit from data that might make city officials more effective in responding to a complaints or taking action on behalf of a child living in one of these properties. Even basic services provided by water departments are impacted. For example, the city's water department has the responsibility to alert code enforcement officers and police and fire departments of water shut-offs at specific locations. They have to make multiple calls to the code enforcement, police and fire departments to share that information. This information may be recorded in one department, but it is typically not

[13] http://en.wikipedia.org/wiki/Schenectady,_New_York

connected to any other information another department might have about the property. This creates a data tracking and information dissemination problem.

The Vision. Code enforcement officers use various processes to record and track code violations, update inspections, report hazardous structures, determine occupied/unoccupied housing, and document site conditions and land-use. An excess of violations can lead to unsafe and undesirable properties, and many times entire blocks and neighborhoods within a city. Careful management and use of code enforcement data within a single city is critical to good management practices in that city. Schenectady's Mayor McCarty has a vision for a regional code enforcement approach that would make it possible for code enforcement data to be used as a tool to support the full range of government programs and services within his city and across the capital region. Proactive and coordinated use of code enforcement data beyond a single government entity has, according to the Mayor, the potential to create regional impact as well in terms of crime rate and property values, and more generally to the overall health, safety and general welfare of citizens at a regional level. He sees code enforcement, like a number of other responsibilities carried out by city governments, as fundamental to sustainable growth, economic development, enhanced service delivery and greater citizen participation in the process of governing. The impact potential at both the city and the regional level is substantial. At the city level, he imagines all emergency and public safety professionals, as well as human service and even pet control workers, would have access to information on the structures they are entering to deliver services—before they enter those structures.

Creating a regional code enforcement shared service will support the resolution of a number of recurring issues such as landlord violations that plague multiple governments within the region. Investigations into chronic violators and recurrent fraudulent activities could draw on data from across the region. And future investments in economic development, community safety and security programs could benefit from the insight gained by looking both within the city and across the region. In addition, the mayor sees that data within such a repository could be used to promote urban initiatives through improvement of regional communication, and increased partnerships among government agencies and research institutions.

Challenges to Schenectady's Vision. Mayor McCarthy faces three main challenges to his vision (see Table 3, next page). First, legacy systems and process plague enforcement code processes. Code data in Schenectady is collected by hand during a property inspection, returned to city hall on paper and then entered manually into the system. This fact alone characterizes the legacy environment challenging city efforts to become smarter.

Second, challenges presented by the legacy environment are further compounded by the lack of an entity or department charged with citywide information and technology management. Such a department would be responsible for addressing, at an enterprise level, such legacy issues.

Third, the lack of a citywide or region-wide coordinating entity for data challenges the mayor's vision to integrate code data, once it is available in digital form, with data from a range of other programs throughout the city. The cities and counties of New York's Capital Region recognize the interdependencies among their individual public safety, economic growth and community goals, and the potential value of a regional approach to achieve those goals. They also recognize that code enforcement information is a critical part of reaching those goals. However, Schenectady and other cities within the Capital Region cannot maximize the use of this data because they lack the infrastructure needed to collect, share and use data. They have not developed the capability to share code enforcement data or to integrate it with other critical internal decision-making systems. In some cases, this is because the data is not available in electronic form. In others cases, it is because the systems in use are not integrated or designed in a way that that is standard and would allow for easy data sharing. New capability for coordinated action will be required to ensure that these disparate processes are newly informed by the availability of code data.

Fourth, in terms of the regional repository, the lack of a standardized code form for local government will increase the coordination effort required to reconcile the different approaches used by municipalities within the region and to create a standard or strategy for sharing that is acceptable to all involved.

Table 3. *Four Challenges to Realizing Schenectady's Vision.*

Challenges
1. Legacy systems and processes plague enforcement code processes.
2. Legacy issues further compounded by the lack of entity or department charged with city-wide information and technology management.
3. No executive charged with leading information and technology management city-wide.
4. Lack of a city-wide coordinating entity for data challenges the Mayor's vision to integrate code data, once it is available in digital form, with data from a range of other programs throughout the city.
5. The lack of a standardized code form for local government will increase the coordination effort.

Helping Small Cities to Become Smarter

Both Binghamton and Schenectady strive to be 21st century cities. They want to be smarter and more efficient; they want to engage citizens and leverage data to refine and evaluate programs and services. Yet, they face major institutional, organizational and technical challenges to achieve their respective visions.

Their focus is different: Binghamton wants to create to enterprise capability to manage information and technology across the city, and Schenectady wants to build both city-level and regional capability to share code enforcement information. Nevertheless, their challenges are quite similar. They are both encumbered with legacy technologies and challenged by legacy institutional and organizational arrangements. Their combined 10 challenges require them and others like them to think beyond the vision of being a smarter city and to look closely at the capabilities required to successfully deliver on those visions.

Three common challenges seem to rise above the others as threshold issues to address in the two cities. The first is the deeply entrenched model of information as the purview of individual departments, rather than as a citywide asset. This is not to say that the city officials are committed to this model—they are very committed to the idea that data should flow freely and be made readily available for use. This is in large part what drives them toward the concepts of a smarter city. The second common challenge is the lack of a roadmap to guide the cities toward a shared vision of a smarter city that is based on an information-centric view of city operations with a full understanding of the investments in new capability necessary to leverage technology and organizational innovation toward realizing that vision. The third common challenge across the two cities is the lack of an executive with citywide responsibility for IT and the information assets of the city. Whether a CIO or another executive, someone must be charged with leading the transition from a legacy infrastructure to a city with the capability necessary to envisions what “smart” means for that city and to deliver on that vision.

Following are five recommendations to help similar small cities get started in their efforts to create the capability necessary to set their own vision of a smart city and to deliver on it. These recommendations don’t require large infusions of resources and technologies—they rely on new ways of thinking and acting.

First, develop a roadmap that captures and communicates the vision that is right for the city. Use that roadmap to guide the long- and short-term policy, management and technology changes required. Such a roadmap can be used to inform changes to the day-to-day operations within individual departments and as a touchstone for city leadership as they make decisions about more strategic and long-term changes. Such a roadmap is necessary as seeds of change in the information culture of the city.

Second, establish an accountable executive with responsibility for addressing the operational and strategic issues of information and technology management. This person is the owner and champion of the roadmap and should participate as part of the city's executive team. This executive must have the same status as that of other department heads, although it might be some time before there is an IT department for this person to lead. This may be a new position or it may be a new responsibility assigned to a person in full or in part. Many smaller cities are now considering establishing and hiring chief information officers. In many cases, this is not possible. Yet whether through a new person or a new responsibility assigned, someone must have responsibility if real change in how the city sees itself and operates is to begin.

Third, begin to change the way data is viewed and managed. The shift to a view that data is a city-level asset rather than a departmental asset, or worse yet, a process-level asset, can begin simply by laying such a perspective out as part of the roadmap document and changing the way information-related issues are considered and resolved. This is a long process that will lead to new technologies and policies. It must, however, start with a new perspective.

Fourth, establish an organized governance model for IT to communicate the criticality of information and IT in realizing the vision of a smarter city, regardless of whether the vision leads a city to be more like New York or simply to ensure that basic city processes have access to necessary data in real-time. Such a body is necessary to create the conditions for sharing information across the boundaries of departments and other governments as imagined in Schenectady. Such bodies can be charged understanding which investments will best support a city in its efforts to respond to pressing problems facing that city.

Fifth, adopt a project portfolio model that requires information and technology projects be evaluated systematically by the governance body and from multiple perspectives, including within the context of the roadmap. Reviewing each project with a common set of questions about how each initiative contributes to the roadmap and is reflective of or adheres to previous decisions about standards and guidelines ensures that the information management structure will remain consistent with the agreed-upon policies and priorities as communicated through the roadmap.

Getting started on the road to becoming a smarter small city begins with the development of a locally relevant smart city model. The award-winning stories and the articles about emerging technologies and how they are transforming cities throughout the world are incentivizing. But they can also lead a city to make investments in strategies or solutions before the capability to be successful is in place or under development. Can Binghamton and Schenectady create the same smart city found in NYC and Seoul, San Francisco and Barcelona? Maybe, but the first step is to develop a vision that fits with their city and their context.

What does a smarter Binghamton and smarter Schenectady look like? And "what changes to a city's institutional and organizational arrangements are necessary for it to leverage technology and new tools for using data on behalf of the city?

The case vignettes presented here and the recommendations drawn from them are provided to support the smart city efforts of small but committed cities like Binghamton and Schenectady that are hampered with pre-21st century legacy environments. Hhundreds, maybe thousands of cities like them are trying to catch-up to the era of smart cities, as well. They see larger and richer cities leverage emerging technologies to provide increasing public value to their citizens. What they must also see is how those cities, particularly those most recognized for their efforts, have invested in the development of citywide technology plans and leadership positions and identified priority initiatives such as enterprise data governance. Such foundations and capabilities are necessary for any city seeking to become smarter, regardless of the vision or the size.

THERESA A. PARDO, *Center Director,* ***DONNA S. CANESTRARO,*** *Program Director, and* ***MEGHAN E. COOK,*** *Program Director; Center for Technology in Government (CTG), State University of New York at Albany. CTG is an applied research center devoted to improving government and public services through policy, management, and technology innovation.*

REFERENCES

1. Chourabi, H., Nam, T., Walker, S., Gil-Garcia, J. R., Mellouli, S., Nahon, K., Pardo, T. A., and Scholl, H. J. (2012). Understanding smart cities: An integrative framework. In Proceedings of the 45th Hawaii International Conference on System Sciences (pp. 2289–2297), January 4–7, Maui, Hawaii, USA.
2. Nam, T. and Pardo, T. A. (2011a). Conceptualizing smart city with dimensions of technology, people, and institutions. In Proceedings of the 12th Annual International Conference on Digital Government Research (pp. 282–291), June 12–15, College Park, MA, USA.
3. Nam, T. and Pardo, T. A. (2011b). Smart city as urban innovation: Focusing on management, policy, and context. In Proceedings of the 5th International Conference on Theory and Practice of Electronic Governance (pp. 185–194), September 26–28, Tallinn, Estonia.

6

Innovating Through Public Technology: Taking Data Democratization to the Next Level in Philadelphia

Andrew Buss, Adel Ebeid, and Mark Headd

Technology has the potential to make cities better places to live Within the past five years, significant national and local initiatives have focused on making technology more available and relevant to the public.

At the federal level, President Barak Obama's administration has attempted to address both data transparency and technology access and adoption by initiating an open data policy; launching an open data portal referred to as Data.gov; and funding the Broadband Technology Opportunities Program (BTOP). At the local level, many municipal governments are including technology in their policy agendas and looking for ways to make it more meaningful for residents. One common theme across these municipal technology initiatives is the focus on engaging local communities around technology issues and building a citizen-centric group of stakeholders to help drive programs. Largely because of this citizen-engagement approach to public technology, the public mindset about how government can and should interact with technology is changing.

Communities have an opportunity to create a healthy ecosystem around public technology. For instance, the city of Philadelphia linked two seemingly disparate communities—the government and residents—to develop best practices in harnessing technology for both.

The Data Democratization Movement

Data democratization is typically defined as releasing government data for public consumption and allowing non-governmental entities to process and present it (Ingram, 2012; Nasri, 2013). When Vivek Kundra was appointed chief information officer for the United States in 2009, one of his first actions was to make public as much government data as possible so that the private sector could use it for innovation (Ingram, 2012).

Municipal governments are increasingly following the federal direction and releasing previously inaccessible data about government services and information to the. Referred to as "open data," data democratization efforts are well underway in several large cities, including New York, Chicago, Boston, Philadelphia and San Francisco. These municipal open data efforts focus largely on targeting high-value data sets and releasing them to the public in highly usable formats. Efforts often include a centralized clearinghouse for public data, the creation of a municipal open data policy, and possibly appointing a chief data officer to drive the initiative.

Early municipal data democratization efforts have shown promising results. Publicly accessible data storehouses are in place in several cities, and a growing community of open-source software developers has generated numerous examples of citizen-driven applications built from recently released government data. Hackathons, scheduled events where software developers gather to collaborate on software projects, have become common and allow rapid prototyping of new applications from the newly available trove of public data.

The municipal data democratization efforts are beneficial in several ways. First, municipalities establish transparency and accountability with their citizens by releasing the data that illustrates government workings. Secondly, wide-ranging government data that provides information about everything including transit schedules, crime incidents and restaurant inspections allows government entities, businesses and nonprofits to create new uses for the data. Third, data democratization may enable governments to become more efficient by permitting third-party analysis of previously inaccessible data. Through data analytics, current conditions and trends can be identified so that more effective programs and policies can be developed. Finally, making data more accessible engages the software developer community in the workings of government and results in application development that benefits the public-at-large (see Figure 1 on next page). Before municipal governments began making data democratization a key aspect of governance, the local software developer community had fewer reasons to interact with municipal government; they didn't have access to much government data and therefore couldn't use it for innovative purposes.

Technology Access Challenges

Like data democratization, municipal efforts centered on digital inclusion have grown in the past five years, particularly after the Obama

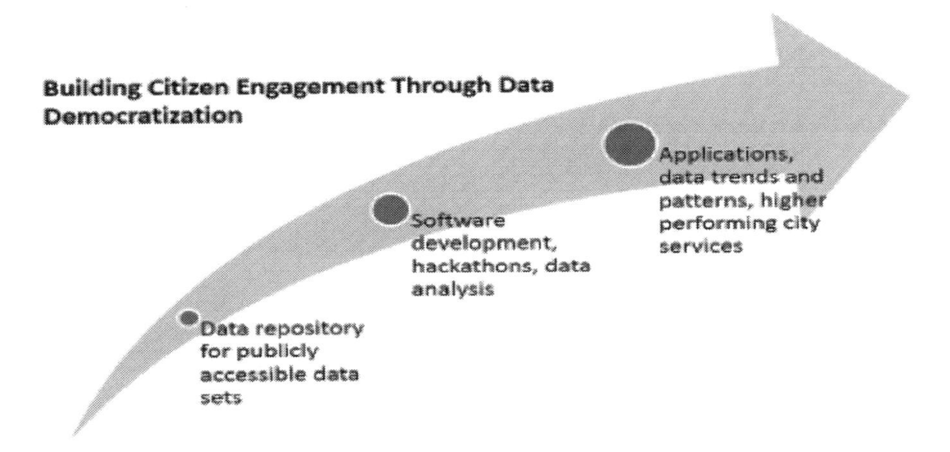

Figure 1. *Data Democratization Pathway.*

Administration initiated BTOP to address growing inequalities in technology access and adoption. After several municipally driven, largely unsuccessful efforts to provide in-home wireless service, BTOP focused instead on issuing competitive grants to enhance broadband infrastructure, make technology and the Internet accessible via public computing centers, and address the significant gap in technology adoption in many urban neighborhoods through training programs. Many cities have used these awards to implement technology access and adoption projects so that urban residents can fully participate in an increasingly digitally driven society.

Digital inclusion is generally defined as incorporating information technology into a community to improve quality of life and education (PC Magazine, 2013) To improve the quality of life and education, however, individuals and groups must be able to access and effectively use that technology (Webjunction, 2013). Digital inclusion is particularly challenging in urban neighborhoods. A nationwide survey in 2010 found that approximately 40 percent of households lacked a broadband connection, and this statistic is exacerbated in many impoverished, inner-city neighborhoods where up to 60 percent of households lack broadband connectivity (Dunbar, 2012). This trend is clearly visible in a large city such as Philadelphia, where broadband connectivity is less than 40 percent in many neighborhoods see Figure 2).

Like municipal open data undertakings, BTOP-funded programs frequently rely on the participation of community-based organizations to increase technology access and adoption.. Although many of these BTOP programs are managed and coordinated by municipal government, they were acutely informed during inception and implementation by communities and residents (see Figure 3). While data democratization efforts engage local software developer communities, these digital inclusion programs typically involve and activate another community—with different needs and interests—outside of city governments.

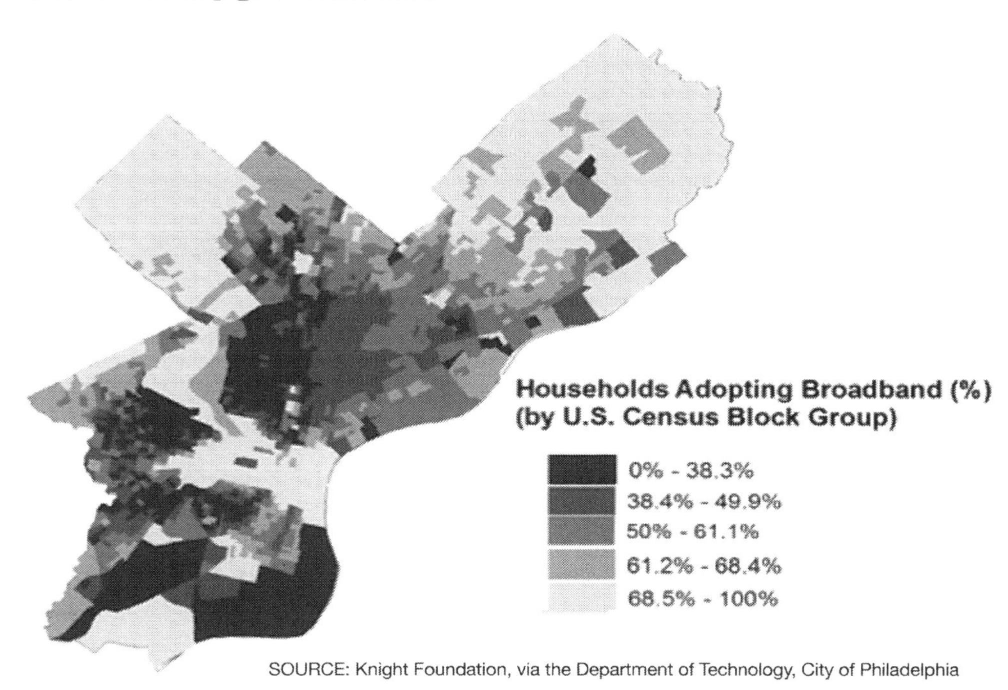

Figure 2. *Philadelphia Household Broadband Connectivity (Kaylor, 2012)*

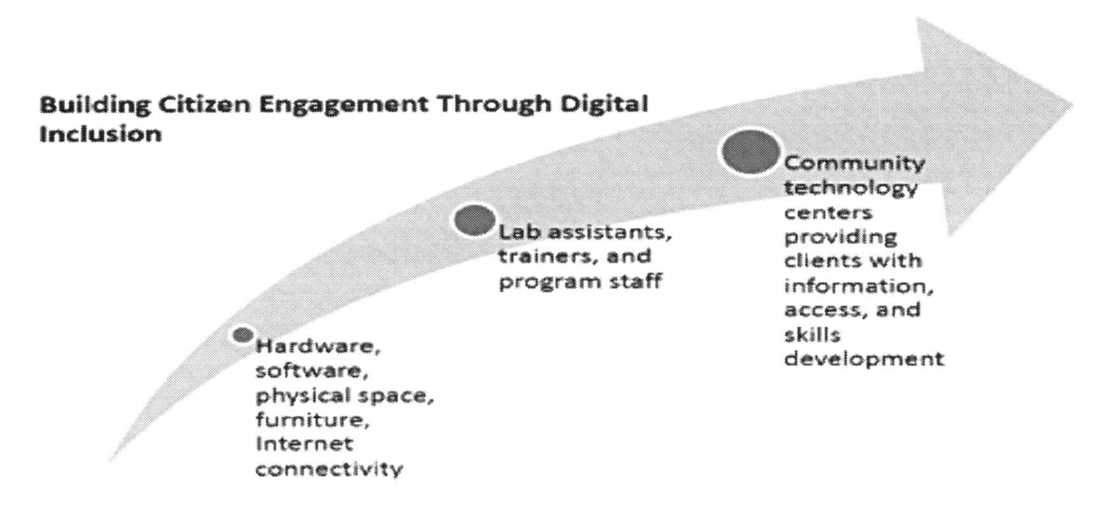

Figure 3. *Digital Inclusion Pathway.*

Bridging Communities

Open data initiatives are actively proceeding in several major cities and in the past two to three years have demonstrated the value of making previously inaccessible, government data available to diverse urban communities.

Boston's data democratization effort, for instance, yielded a partnership with Code for America and eventually the AdoptAHydrant application (http://adoptahydrant.org). AdoptAHydrant allows residents to assume responsibility for shoveling out the fire hydrant nearest to them following a snowstorm.

In Honolulu, developers used a similar programming code and data about tsunami siren locations to create Adopt-a-Siren, an application that allows residents to monitor functionality of the tsunami siren closest to them. Closely following this and other data releases, the Hawaii, in 2013, adopted an open data law requiring the release of data sets from Executive Branch departments (http://hawaiiopendata.com).

In Chicago, which has an open data policy, the release of vacant property data inspired a vacant building finder application that provides citizens, property developers and city staff with spatial tools to identify neighborhoods and blocks showing high rates of vacancy (http://chicagobuildings.org).

And in Baltimore, a public data catalog called OpenBaltimore contains a data set of location-based parking citations that inspired the creation of SpotAgent, a mobile application that calculates for prospective parkers their chances of getting a parking ticket in a location by using a green/yellow/red scale (http://spotagent.com) (Badger, 2013).

Recent municipal digital inclusion initiatives also have been successful at increasing the public's access to technology and making it meaningful to their daily lives. Chicago's city government collaborated with the Local Initiatives Support Corp. on a marketing campaign using personal stories to illustrate the value of broadband adoption. A subsequent citywide study found noticeable increases in broadband subscribership, particularly in low-income neighborhoods targeted by the program (National Telecommunications and Information Association, 2013).

Similarly, the city of Tampa Bay used BTOP funding to establish Internet access in all of its 3,500 public housing units, and an on-call squad was deployed to help residents with technology questions (National Telecommunications and Information Association, 2013).

Considering the recent success of many data democratization and digital inclusion initiatives, what is the benefit, if any, of municipal government pursuing both? Perhaps a better way to consider this question is to examine what is lost by pursuing one without the other. Data democratization gives the public access to government data and helps residents use it in meaningful ways. For software developers, data access provides an opportunity to develop new applications that deliver previously inaccessible information in creative ways. For other residents with personal access to technology who have fully adopted its use through personal computers or mobile devices, data democratization allows them to engage more fully with government by consuming new applications.

However, if residents cannot afford personal technology or lack awareness about how to use technology, then they cannot avail themselves to the benefits of improved access to government data and services resulting from open data. Access to useful and potentially empowering information remains confined only to residents with the means and skills to consume it. Ultimately, municipal governments that fail to address challenges of technology access and adoption alongside data democratization efforts likely miss an opportunity to reach a large proportion of city residents.

Similarly, public technology portfolios that focus solely on digital inclusion without an equal effort to democratize data miss the opportunity to engage citizens with their government. Key to digital inclusion is providing access to technology and using it to improve quality of life by providing information and services that are meaningful on a personal level. Because one goal of data democratization efforts is to provide opportunities for residents to engage with their government by accessing its data, municipalities without an open data effort lose this opportunity. Even municipalities with high rates of technology access and adoption lose the chance to help residents understand that government is intended to work for and with the public.

Only by coordinating a municipal data democratization effort with an equally strong initiative focusing on digital inclusion can open data movements reach their fullest potential and influence the broadest spectrum of residents. This focused approach on reaching the "last mile" of data democratization is well underway in Philadelphia.

Philadelphia's Model

Philadelphia's effort to maximize its data democratization initiative hinged on developing a coordinated portfolio of public technology initiatives within the newly formed Innovation Management group in the city's Office of Innovation and Technology (OIT). Developing and managing public technology initiatives was a new role for this office, which had traditionally provided information technology infrastructure and operations support for city agencies. OIT's attention to public technology began with two individual initiatives, seemingly unrelated except that both relied largely on using civic engagement to achieve their outcomes.

In 2010, Philadelphia won a competitive $6.4 million BTOP grant to implement a citywide network of technology-enabled community centers. The city's intent was to address on a broad scale its challenges around universal technology access and adoption.

Also in 2010, OIT was selected as a participant in the initial year of the Code for America program, a nonprofit focused on using technology to engage communities and make government more transparent. The city's engagement with Code for America lasted two years and produced numerous publicly accessible, open source software applications. Most notably from Code for America arose Textizen, an application that provides residents the capability to interact with government about public interest matters via text messaging (https://www.textizen.com).

Another lasting impact of the Philadelphia's participation with Code for America was a growing community of open-source software developers that began to actively participate with the municipal government around application development and data. This collaboration coincided with the inception of Open Data Philly, a repository of publicly accessible government and non-government data, and the progenitor of the city's open data effort (http://opendataphilly.org).

Data democratization efforts in Philadelphia continued with a Mayoral Executive Order, calling for the creation of an open data policy and the naming of a Chief Data Officer. Subsequent efforts have so far led to the release of more than 50 city data sets and the development of numerous publicly focused applications using that data. The local community of software developers remains active, collaborating often with the Chief Data Officer and staging frequent hackathons. Because of its open data work, Philadelphia has realized the benefits of releasing data to the public by engaging residents and activating the local community of software developers.

Proceeding in parallel to Philadelphia's open data effort was the grant implementation for technology-enabled community centers. The grant application process, as well as implementation of the work, was collaborative and cultivated real community stakeholders committed to the mission of digital inclusion. Because of this civic engagement, the city and its partners had by the middle of 2012 implemented 80 centers (branded as Keyspots) and was providing technology and Internet access to thousands of Philadelphians who were otherwise without it.

Because of the community-based focus, participating organizations provided technology services close to where people lived, and in safe, pleasant spaces that were conducive to social learning. Anecdotal evidence seems to indicate that the community of technology users has grown in Philadelphia, particularly in some underserved neighborhoods, as a result of the centers. Moreover, whether residents end up accessing technology in public centers or in their homes, it is also a reasonable assumption that more Philadelphia residents now access municipal data and services, or benefit from software applications, that were developed from the city's parallel open data initiative.

Portfolio Evolution

Philadelphia's approach to public technology innovation continues to evolve. To expand the data democratization effort, the city has added to the Innovation Management group a Director of Civic Technology, who is exploring applications that allow residents to more easily interact with government services. One example is the Actual Value Initiative (AVI) calculator, available in six languages and functional on multiple devices, that allows residents to calculate their property tax liability after a recent citywide reassessment. Coupled with open data work around property records, this AVI calculator provides an excellent example of how publicly accessible data can become even more meaningful to residents when it is intentionally used to make interacting with government easier for the average resident. Although property owners do not look forward to paying property taxes, they can at least more easily calculate the amount they must pay.

Development and deployment of the AVI calculator illustrates the value of linking an open data initiative with a complementary one tackling digital access. Making municipal data publicly accessible, in this instance property data, and then presenting it in a meaningful way with the AVI calculator could not have been accomplished without an active data democratization effort. Additionally, ensuring access to that data and subsequent use of the AVI application required that equal attention be paid to digital inclusion. Philadelphia's implementation of a citywide network of community technology centers provided residents without in-home technology the ability to participate in a critical government function; calculating property tax liability. As a result, these complementary initiatives have enabled larger numbers of Philadelphia residents to access property tax information, including those in traditionally underserved neighborhoods.

Philadelphia's strategy around public technology innovation also includes developing data standards in collaboration with other municipalities that will enable a comparative measurement of service performance between one city and another. The G7, an informal working group of seven large city Chief Innovation/Information Officers (including Philadelphia's Chief Innovation Officer), has embarked on an initiative to create a multi-city open data platform (Douglas, 2012). This publicly available platform will house standardized data from G7 members and provide a foundation for multi-city applications and performance metrics. As a result, one municipality will be able to compare its performance at providing government services with other participating cities. This effort to standardize performance measurement data across cities provides another example of how an open data initiative can benefit underserved neighborhoods; cross-municipality data standards enable a comparative analysis of service performance and can lead to improvement in providing critical social services.

Another key ingredient in a comprehensive public technology portfolio is the use of geographic information systems (GIS) that enable people to visualize, analyze and interpret data made available through an open data program. This ability to display data spatially is critical to identifying patterns and relationships between different data sets. In Philadelphia, an initiative promoting access to healthy food from corner stores and farmers' markets was linked to open data to produce an application allowing residents to search by address for the healthy food option closest to their neighborhood (http://www.phila.gov/map#id=0ff0c6a19df44ac5a86275bc393b8d50). By displaying healthy food data visually in a way that the average citizen can understand, residents and communities can find important information and services that might otherwise remain inaccessible. This example of using spatial data to identify healthy food locations again illustrates how closely open data and digital access are linked; residents unaccustomed to using technology can consume and understand large amounts of data when it is presented visually.

One future direction for Philadelphia's public technology portfolio is to use its open data work to inform and shape other city programs. The advent of using newly accessible data for data analytics provides an opportunity for municipalities to predict problems and focus resources more efficiently in underserved neighborhoods. One community-centric program that lends itself well to data analytics is PhillyRising. The PhillyRising Collaborative addresses crime and quality of life challenges in underserved neighborhoods by coordinating and convening community groups, streamlining city services, and supporting residents so that they can build a shared vision for their community. With data now publicly available through the city's open data work, Philadelphia can work closely with PhillyRising to create newly engaged communities. As communities take part in interpreting data and making it relevant to their residents, open data again becomes an important method for making technology meaningful in underserved communities.

Philadelphia and other large cities have an ideal chemistry for open data movements: lots of data plus significant urban challenges. Cities are fertile ground for data democratization efforts because a strategic opportunity exists to use data assets to remediate the challenges faced by municipalities and their governments. Not all data must be used to solve intractable urban problems, but data access can contribute to quality of life and make cities more appealing places to live. Data, for example, can help people find parking spots, check the cleanliness of restaurants, or locate recreational trails.

One challenge that many cities face is the large percentage of residents that lack access to basic technology. As a result, access to public data and the beneficial applications generated from it will remain limited to residents who can access and use technology. Only by linking data democratization initiatives with concurrent efforts around digital inclusion can municipal governments fully realize the potential for engaging residents and making them true stakeholders in civic governance. Philadelphia's comprehensive and coordinated public technology portfolio provides an effective roadmap for reaching the "last mile" of data democratization.

***ANDREW BUSS,** Director of Innovation Management at Office of Innovation & International Data CorporationTechnology, **ADEL EBEID,** Chief Innovation Officer, **MARK HEADD,** Chief Data Officer; City of Philadelphia.*

REFERENCES

Badger, E. (2013). The Best Parking App We've Ever Seen. Retrieved July 23, 2013 fromhttp://www.theatlanticcities.com/commute/2013/02/best-parking-app-weve-ever-seen/4762/.

Douglas, M. (2012). Gang of 7 Big-City CIOs Forges Ahead Despite Turnover. Retrieved July 31, 2013 from http://www.govtech.com/pcio/Gang-of-7-Big-City-CIOs-Forges-Ahead-Despite-Turnover.html.

Dunbar, J. (2012). Poverty Stretches the Digital Divide. Retrieved July 22, 2013 from http://investigativereportingworkshop.org/investigations/broadband-adoption/story/poverty-stretches-digital-divide/.

Ingram, M. (2012). Kundra: Democratizing Means a Fundamental Shift in Power. Retrieved July 23, 2013 from http://gigaom.com/2012/06/21/kundra-democratizing-data-means-a-fundamental-shift-in-power/).

Kaylor, C. (2012). Whither Freedom Rings: Evaluating Progress and Leveraging the Partnership. Unpublished report.

Nasri, G. (2013). Power to the People: How Data Democratization is Enabling Consumers and Businesses to Make More Informed Decisions. Retrieved July 23, 2013 from http://www.huffingtonpost.com/grace-nasri/data-democratization_b_3279778.html.

National Telecommunications and Information Administration. (2013). NTIA Broadband Adoption Toolkit.

PC Magazine. (2013). Definition of digital inclusion. Retrieved July 24, 2013 from http://www.pcmag.com/encyclopedia/term/41336/digital-inclusion).

Webjunction. (2013). Definition of Digital Inclusion. Retrieved July 24, 2013 from http://www.webjunction.org/explore-topics/digital-inclusion.html.

7

The City Protocol: Building the Cities of the Future

Manel Sanromà and Vicente Guallart

Cities are one of the most successful technological developments of humankind. Their longevity is the best demonstration of their success: While living beings and human organizations have a limited time scope, very few cities die once they are born. It is no surprise that these places, where more humans tend to develop their lives and that have long lifespans, are influenced and shaped by big technological revolutions.

In fact, the first technological wave, namely agriculture, was the very same driving force in the appearance of cities. The second wave, industry, shaped cities' current framework. The third technological revolution, that of the information technologies, has not changed our cities much—yet.

The changes that cities are going to experience, that many include under the paradigm of smart cities, go way beyond technology. The changes will delineate a future in which cities will no longer be passive actors of the changes they experiment but will become protagonists of a new world.

Cities acquired a relevant role at the end of the Agricultural Era, but when society entered the Industrial Age, the new and powerful states that shaped the world during the past centuries superseded them. Politics (the ordering of the Polis, the city) has been more a question of identities, nations and states than of citizens, humans living in cities. This is about to change. With weapons of mass construction (smart phones and intelligent gadgets) in the pockets of almost every citizen, cities will again become the places where worldwide politics is created.

This is the new paradigm that is at stake when talking about smart cities.

Cities of smart citizens will no longer beat the end of a top down hierarchy (nation-region-city-citizen). Instead, they will be at the base of a new bottom up paradigm where citizens and cities are protagonists in shaping a new world. In this new flat world, cities will share their leadership with other stakeholders that adopt a city-centred view of their activities. Industry will produce and spread the technology needed by citizens and cities for a better living. Academia will adopt the city as a new laboratory and basic measurement unit for research. Organizations will be interested in deepening different aspects of life in cities. All of the sectors must partner to build and shape the future of cities, the places where most humans will live.

The internet and mobile devices are the tip of the iceberg of this third technological wave, and they represent the technology that has had a more rapid socialization in history. The success of the internet, the network of networks that has changed the world in the past two decades, is based on the introduction of communication standards amongst computers: what is known as the internet protocol (IP) suite. One of the less-known but most important secrets of this success is the way these protocols are built: in an open, collaborative and evolving way.

The IP is open because anyone can contribute to it and because it is accessible to anyone for free. The IP is collaborative because it is built in a bottom up process by consensus among those who contribute to it. And the IP is evolving because there is no law that compels its use, but its practical functioning. Rough consensus and running code is the motto of those who build the IP suite.

The Internet's Lessons

The process of the internet's creation and governance is one of the less known yet most important technological/political architectures of the modern world. Three organizations constitute the core of it all, namely the Internet Engineering Task Force (IETF), Internet Society (ISOC) and World Wide Web Consortium (W3C)

The IETF: is the main body that determines the standards that allow the internet to be created and to evolve. IETF runs under the auspices of the ISOC. The IETF operates through working groups to deal with specific technical issues. There are currently more than 100 working groups in eight areas. The IETF has no formal constitution and, in fact, preceded ISOC. The later was created as a formal organization that could act as an umbrella of the IETF. The ISOC formally owns the standards created by the IETF.

The IETF (www.ietf.org) defines itself as a large open international community of network designers, operators, vendors, and researchers concerned with the evolution of the internet architecture and the smooth operation of the internet. The IETF is open to any interested individual. The work of the IETF is performed mainly over the internet, and it holds meetings three times per year. Technical standards problems are suggested by members and, if there is enough interest, a working group is formed, with a defined terms of reference. Each working group has either an elected or self-designated chair. The working group deliverable is a document called request for comments (RFC). After a well-defined process, RFCs become the de facto standards on which the internet is built.

The IETF process is called "rough consensus," and the task force was a pioneer in this. Consensus as a concept does not have a formal definition. IETF working groups make decisions by rough consensus that does not require that all participants agree although it, of course, is preferred. In general, the dominant view of the working group prevails. Consensus can be determined by a show of hands, humming or any other means by which the the working group forms a rough consensus. Note that 51 percent of the working group does not qualify as rough consensus, and 99 percent is better than rough; It is up to the chair to determine if rough consensus has been reached.

The ISOC: The Internet Society is the parent corporation of the IETF. As such, all IETF RFCs, including those that describe "internet standards," are copyrighted by the ISOC. (ISOC documents are available to anyone, including non-members, at no charge). The ISOC grew out of the IETF to support those functions that require a corporate form rather than the ad hoc IETF approach. In reality, the ISOC was formed because the IETF Secretariat, which had been operated under (NSF) contract by staff at the Corporation for National Research Initiatives (CNRI), was not going to be supported beyond 1991. The then Internet Activities Board sought to create a nonprofit institution that could provide financial support for the IETF Secretariat, among other things. Thus, CNRI served as the first host for ISOC's operation.

ISOC has more than 55,000 members, more than 100 chapters worldwide and more than 130 organization members. Members work with a range of partners from nonprofit agencies, local and global NGOs, academia, technologists, local councils, federal policy and decision-makers, business, and more, to ensure an harmonic development of the internet.

The W3C: To provide order when improving standards for the world wide web, its creator, Tim Berners-Lee, founded the World Wide Web Consortium (W3C) in 1994. W3C's mission is "To lead the world wide web to its full potential by developing protocols and guidelines that ensure long-term growth for the web."

Housed at the Massachusetts Institute of Technology (MIT) Laboratory for Computer Science, the W3C was supported by both (DARPA) and the European Commission, making it an international NGO. Unlike the IETF where members are individuals, W3C members are organizations primarily from the private sector. W3C describes itself as "industry consortium dedicated to building consensus around web technologies". The way W3C develops standards is similar to IETF, with Areas and Working Groups functioning in an open and collaborative but also a directed way.

As an example of the IETF, ISOC and W3C, a group of people in and around Barcelona came up with the idea of applying the same principles and methodologies to the deployment of technology in cities. The working methodology would be that of the IETF and W3C, with an open, collaborative, rough consensus approach. Governance would be structured similar to the ISOC and W3C, with formal membership by organizations, supervision and ownership of the city protocol (CP), and a board elected by constituencies.

From Internet of People to Internet of Cities

The internet was conceived so that different networks of computers could communicate with each other and thus make it possible for information to flow smoothly between computers. Almost all of this information had been created and/or captured by humans. So in that sense, we can talk of the net as the "internet of people." But by the end of past century, it was conceived that inanimate objects and things could gather much more information without any help from people, and that information could be used to track and count everything, helping to reduce waste, loss and cost. During the past decade, technologies such as radio frequency identification (RFID) or implementations of new IP versions literally allow anything to have an IP address. This has made the "internet of things" a reality. In fact, the term internet of Everything (IoE) has been coined to talk about the internet that connects people, things, processes and information.

With this new IoE paradigm, a new approach can be envisioned: the internet of cities. Using this term sheds more light on how technology add value to cities than the popular term smart cities does, the latter of which was introduced with a marketing orientation. Cities are complex systems of systems made up of environment, infrastructures, public space, nodes, people and information. These six systems each fall into some of the four categories of the IoE.

The natural environment existed before any civilization and is the physical basis, with the natural resources, on which cities are built and developed. The network of infrastructures provides the framework through which cities transform natural resources that will be consumed by the city. These infrastructures fall into six categories: information, water cycle, energy, matter cycle, mobility and nature. Overlying of all these infrastructures creates public space, which is where social interaction occurs and that fixes the character of cities.

The activities in a city occur on functional nodes that have the form of objects, of buildings or of complexes in increasing order of services that they provide to people. There are different (logarithmic) scales from 1 (individual), 10 (house), 100 (building), 1000 (block), 10000 (neighborhood), 100000 (district), 1000000 (city), 10000000 (metropolis) and so on up to countries, continents and the whole earth (the terms are only approximations because you could call a city any system between some thousands to some millions). The different objects also apply to these categories. Thus, a book corresponds to an individual, while a bookshelf is associated with a house, a library a neighbourhood, city, and so on. In the same manner, a light bulb is associated with individuals, solar panels with buildings and power plants with cities or metropolitan scales. The multi-scaled nodes and their interactions allow citizens to analyze urban activities in terms of services and/or physical structures. Thus, societies have education/schools, health/hospitals, commerce/shops, culture/museums, and so on.

Finally, people do activities at different scales and with relations that form the social organization of a city: families, companies, associations and organizations. All these categories generate information that flow among them and that constitute the raw material for the construction of intelligent cities.

With this framework or basic anatomy of any city in mind, it is possible to build a CP, a scientific approach (and thus independent of the observer) for cities that allows for an assessment of their performance in terms of, for instance, resilience, self-sufficiency, competitiveness, efficiency, creativity, etc. (See Figure 1 on next page).

The City Protocol

The concept and name of the CP has been inspired by the existence and process of creating the IP or IP suite. A protocol is commonly defined as “a set of conventions governing the treatment and formatting of data in a communication system,” and also as “the records that show the agreements arrived at by a group of negotiators.” Building a protocol that allows all types of computers and networks to communicate with each other, and the collaborative and consensus process in which it has been built, is one of the big successes of our era. However, there also could be a protocol that represents the agreement arrived at by the community of those stakeholders interested in the harmonic development of cities, the places where human beings live and work

To accomplish this, an open task force of individuals should do the work to achieve rough consensus in all those matters in which cities are alike; a formal city protocol society (CPS), made up of all the constituencies (cities, industry, academia and organizations), should constitute the

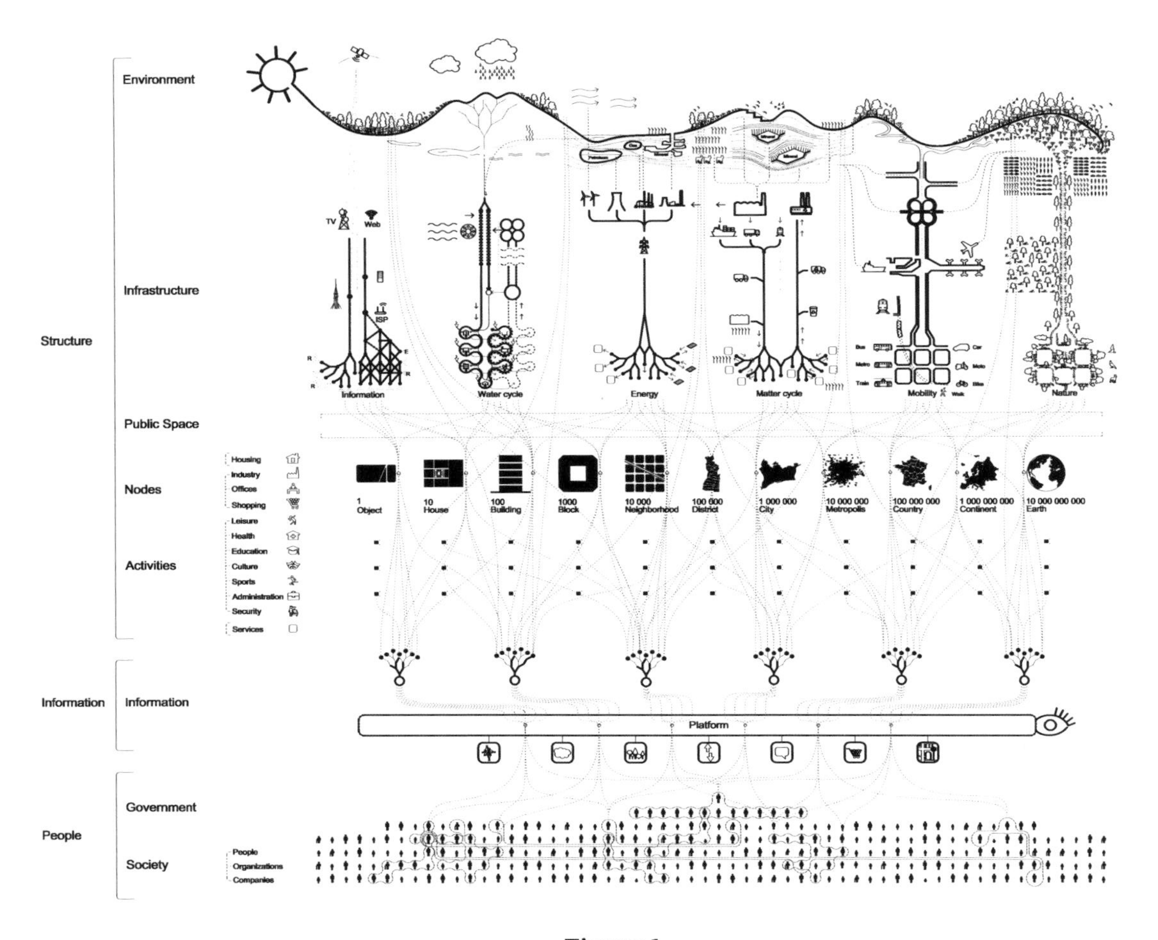

Figure 1.

formal covering of these activities and at the same time foster the CP so that it is openly available for every city to use.

The CP must be understood as a system to rationalize, under the shared basis of the city protocol framework (CPF), the responsible transformation of cities to benefit all urban communities worldwide. The CPF encompasses city anatomy (i.e., the structure of the natural and built environments), technology and people, as well as an approach to facilitate the evaluation of city performance (self-sufficiency, resilience, etc.). These four elements delineate the thematic areas where task-and-finish teams (TAFTs) focus their work.

TAFTs are typically small, delivery-focused teams with a well-defined set of objectives and milestones meant to address a particular transformational challenge to cities. A schedule of milestones and deliverables is used to gauge the progress of each TAFT. When a team has completed its milestones, it may disband or propose a revised charter with new schedule and milestones. Each TAFT is aligned and integrated within a thematic area, although it may also have secondary (communication rather than oversight) relationships with other areas.

The City Protocol Society and its Chapters

The CPS, much as the internet society is for the IETF work, is conceived as the umbrella organization that will foster the development of the CP to ensure that it is open and available to everyone. The CPS is conceived as a trusted community of cities, companies, academia and other organizations that leverages knowledge and experience in cities worldwide to accelerate sustainable transformation. It will accomplish this by offering curated guidance and collaborative action so that cities do not have to navigate their transformation journeys alone.

The current (July 2013) proposed bylaws of the CPS establishes its two main objectives:

1) To develop the CP as a system to rationalize, under a shared basis, city transformation, captured in the form of a series of recommendation documents that may guide and accelerate city-to-city learning. In turn, this will facilitate the responsible adaptation and transformation of cities for the benefit of all urban communities worldwide.

2) Advance an economy of urban innovation to foster the definition of standards, platform integration and the development of technologies aimed at urban solutions that promote resource-use efficiency, self-sufficiency, and social and economic progress in cities.

For that purpose, the CPS will foster the following activities:

1) Build and maintain a repository of documents describing projects, policies and recommended practices that may be tested in cities working and learning together to tackle their common transformational challenges, with the support of commercial and nonprofit organizations, academic and research institutions, and other relevant stakeholders. To this end, the society will support working teams formed by cities and members from the rest of their constituencies.

2) Establish the basis for the evaluation and accreditation of standards and recommendation documents for city transformations that will guide the development of the CP and its continuous improvement.

3) Become an organization that creates and maintains city-related knowledge continuously. To this end, it shall create and maintain, or adopt from other organizations, a network and/or platform for education and knowledge sharing among all members. This networking activity will

include the temporary joining of cities involved in similar challenges so that they can share methods, tools, expertise and insights. It will also include protocols and tools to assist cities with documentation results and conclusions of their work using clear communication and the repository of documents to facilitate learning by others.

Global organizations with diverse stakeholders, as is the case with the CPS, should have an instrument to address those many issues (political, economic, cultural, societal, etc.) that are local by nature. Therefore, the existence of local or regional chapters is a necessary ingredient for the organization's success. The purpose of local chapters is to complement and support the work of the global CPS and that of stakeholders within a specific geographic region. They can cover important activities such as communicating the value of CPS locally, exploiting the value of core CPS projects, creating and promoting local projects, recruiting new member organizations, and organizing local and thematic events among others.

Local chapters may be formed by a team of at least one CPS member from each of the member categories: the basic combination of cities, industry and organizations from civil society should be mimicked by chapters. However, chapters also may include organizations that are not yet CPS members. They also may encourage individuals to become members. Chapters will typically be oriented around a lead city or group of cities in a region, which are actively involved in the development and deployment of the CP. Only CPS organizational members may lead chapters, but they are encouraged to include institutions that are not yet formal CPS members. This flexibility can be particularly useful to get small cities and/or companies involved in the development of the CP without having to assume a formal membership in the global society. The society will approve a local chapter as a CPS member after examination of its charter. This charter will be in practice a contract between a chapter and the CPS to collaborate in the development and dissemination of the CP and to foster participation in CP development through CPS membership.

To date, the CPS is about to be formally constituted: some dozen cities, companies, universities and organizations from around the world have already shown their willingness to participate in its creation, and the initial bylaws of the CPS have been circulated and approved upon by all of them. Some preliminary CP working groups have been initiated on several topics, although the board of directors of the newly constituted CPS to organize these groups and/or incorporate others that already may exist. The CP should be inclusive and not duplicate efforts already in the making by other organizations, groups or individuals.

The CP is a long-term endeavour that will be measured both by the implication of many and varied worldwide stakeholders and for the deliverables that they produce. The internet of cities, part of the Internet of Everything, will be based on its success.

MANEL SANROMÀ *is the CIO for the Barcelona City Council and Professor at the Universitat Roviera I Virgili.* ***VICENTE GUALLART*** *is Chief Architect for the Barcelona City Council.*

Acknowledgements: The city protocol is a global initiative that only makes sense if it is adopted by a wide community. Many individuals have contributed to the first documents (see www.cityprotocol.org), and also to the efforts to constitute the City Protocol Society. Particular credit goes to Antoni Vives, deputy major of Barcelona. His leadership has been key to the implication of Barcelona as the initial seed and trigger to make the CP possible. Graham Coulclough (Capgemini), Charlie Catlett (Argonne National Laboratory) and Michael Mulquin (city of Derby, UK) also have been early adopters and have provided much work and insight in the first developments of the idea. Tribute also should be paid to volunteer members of the interim steering committee that was constituted after a first CP workshop in Barcelona in July 2012. Alan Shark, executive director and CEO of the Public Technology Institute, suggested writing this article. Cisco and Gas de France Suez are two companies that have supported CP work from onset. And Francesc Giralt and Helena Ricomà assumed the daily work of the secretariat. They are the pioneers that must be credited for the short, yet very important, history of the CP. Daniela Frogheri and Fernando Meneses of the Institut d'Arquitectura Avançada de Catalunya should receive credit for the graphics.

8

San Francisco: Building a Smart City in the Innovation Capital of the World

Peter Hirshberg and Jay Nath with assistance from Timothy Popandreou and Jake Levitas

It did not take long after San Francisco (SF) first opened its data five years ago to realize that it had started a movement. On Oct. 21, 2009, then Mayor Gavin Newsom made his open data announcement with an aspiration:

"By bringing city data and San Francisco's entrepreneurs together, we can effectively leverage existing resources to stimulate industry, create jobs and highlight San Francisco's creative culture and attractiveness as a place to live and work."

Within a year communities had formed around the use of SF data to address issues as diverse as transit use, crime patterns, and the lack of access to healthy foods in disadvantaged neighborhoods.

Practically every weekend, civic organizations, nonprofits, and technology companies came together in "hack-a-thons," initially to visualize city data and then to become makers and attack problems. Something as seemingly technical as application program interfaces (APIs) had become a powerful invitation to civic engagement. The ability to read and write to city data has led to *read-write urbanism*—where any citizen might participate in the civic sphere, prototype improvements to the city, and shine light on what is and is not working.

Today, the city has more than 524 machine-readable datasets at its open data portal: data.sfgov.org. This has created large-scale public benefit, enhancing government transparency and supporting cost-effective development of new applications and civic tools.

In 2013, San Francisco passed landmark legislation requiring each city department to ensure that data under its control is open and shared, consistent with privacy guidelines. San Francisco also has established a chief

Figure 1.

data officer to coordinate these activities and set its vision and direction in this arena.

The initial open data experience helped define San Francisco's overall innovation strategy. San Francisco learned that:

- The smartest city is the one that best engages the creativity and contributions of all its citizens;
- That the best ideas often come from outside government; and
- That government governs best when it is challenged with new ideas and with "competition" from its citizens.

The city has also learned that the innovation process is often messy—that lots of experiments (many of which might not be successful) are often the best way to make a city smarter and faster. Many of these new approaches suggest alternatives to traditional government structures, and the city is learning every day the challenges of making these new connections work.

While the open data strategy is a new one, it is deeply rooted in San Francisco's culture and heritage. We talk about San Francisco as the innovation capital of the world. It is blessed with the world's greatest technology companies, startups, and entrepreneurs eager to make a difference. The city has an equally strong tradition of activism and social innovation (Think: the beat movement, free speech movement, environmental movement, leadership in gay rights, etc.) Together, these create the conditions for one of the world's greatest civic laboratories.

One high profile San Francisco project,is the Urban Prototyping movement, an ongoing series of projects that bring together a wide range of citizens, nonprofit organizations and government, to experiment on and improve the city via emerging technology and place-making. Moreover, San Francisco is formalizing the innovation process through mechanisms such as Living Innovation Zones and an Entrepreneur in Residence program. Additionally, two departments, Public Health and Transportation, have adopted new technologies to become smarter and more responsive to citizen needs.

> *"We are working to improve the relationship between residents and government, and to increase collaboration, because, oftentimes, the best ideas come from outside of City Hall. Incorporating lessons from the private sector, we are making government more user-friendly and taking new, and sometimes risky, approaches to providing better services for residents and business owners. We are collaborating with the private and social sectors, engaging volunteers, designers and developers in thousands of hours of community service through hackathons, design charrettes, and new forms of civic participation. By opening up city data and creating new channels for residents to voice their concerns and share their ideas, we are also making government more transparent and accessible."*
>
> **– MAYOR ED LEE**

Building a Civic Innovation Movement

San Francisco's open data activates stimulate citizen and tech community experimentation, but it also raises many questions from city departments and elected officials around the applications and value of open data. Among officials' questions are: How will open data make the city work better? How will it help meet the needs of citizens who aren't part of the tech economy? And how will all this get us re-elected?

To help answer these questions, The Mayor's Office of Civic Innovation teamed with the Gray Area Foundation for the Arts (GAFFTA), the city's leading digital arts nonprofit organization on an initiative known as Summer of Smart that was designed to bring together innovative thinking, open data, and rapid application creation to solve some of the city's most pressing problems. The project (now known as Urban Prototyping (UP) became a three-month-long celebration of urban innovation that capitalized on the 2011 San Francisco mayor's race. The project engaged the entire field of 16 mayoral candidates, a dozen department heads and top bureaucrats, and more than 250 developers, journalists, urbanists and design professionals.

With so many ideas and proposals underway, civic innovation became an ongoing theme during campaign season. We knew that when one candidate offered a new idea about parking, transportation, housing or other key issues, every other candidate would likely respond within days with his or her own suggestions for improvement. Consequently, GAFFTA constructed Summer of Smart to be a font of fresh ideas, crafted to engage candidates and their future constituents. GAFFTA invited the candidates to take part in debates on open data and civic innovation, attend urban hackathon weekends and serve on panels responsible for deciding which festival-generated urban applications merited further development resources.

"Our goal was to transform ideas conceived during urban development weekends into issues candidates could debate during the campaign," says Josette Melchor, GAFFTA's executive director. "By becoming a source for innovation, we raised the level of political discourse."

With a tip of the hat to the TED conference, famous for its moniker "ideas worth spreading," the Summer of Smart set out to produce "ideas worth stealing". In the words of candidate Phil Ting, it was "policy entrepreneurship ... as candidates running for office we were always looking for the best new ideas and approaches. The Summer of Smart kept producing great ideas. It was a form of policy entrepreneurship and education for us."

"The candidates became our clients," adds Jake Levitas, at the time GAFFTA's research director and now a mayoral innovation fellow. "Attendees learned from the candidates, and the candidates learned from the attendees."

The festival's innovation weekends generated wide ranges of ideas. Unlike a traditional hackathon, which conjures up images of geeks focused on specific coding challenges for a company, the Summer of Smart's hackathons were about diversity and inclusion. More than 48 hours, designers, coders, planners, policymakers, journalists, artists and city employees worked together to prototype solutions to civic issues. While all this was going on, city officials and community leaders listened, gave advice and taught the citizen teams.

Figure 2.

Ultimately, the Summer of Smart captured hundreds of ideas to improve San Francisco. Using open data, participants engineered 23 civic projects around the topics of community development and public art, food nutrition and health, and transportation and sustainable buildings. Five hundred people participated and collectively donated more than 10,000 hours of their time. GAFFTA nurtured the winning teams by connecting them with government officials and other resources. Eventually, the city implemented several of the winning projects at very little cost.

Figure 3.

SMARTmuni

SMARTmuni was typical of a project that addressed a city problem and taught the city about the innovation process. During one of the hackathons, Emily Drennen, an intern from the public transit agency Muni, observed that the city did a great job opening real-time transit data, but that same information was not available to Muni employees. Many apps helped citizens find out when a bus is arriving so they do not have to wait at a bus stop. However, if a bus has an operational problem, the process of locating it, assigning a repair crew and prioritizing the problem were manual operations. Passengers knew more about bus locations and schedule delays than transit supervisors did.

Drennen led a field trip to a Muni operations center and then put together a team to address the problem. The team created SMARTmuni, a location-aware iPad app that solves data flow problems for San Francisco's transit system, accessing and compiling real-time vehicle location information to avoid delays and help operators to run Muni more efficiently. The team presented the prototype to the mayoral candidates and it won enthusiasm, with unanimous campaign promises that if elected mayor, the idea would be implemented.

After the election, Mayor Lee turned to SFciti, an alliance of San Francisco technology companies, to fund a full-scale pilot deployed by Muni to its repair force. That project illuminated on one of the key challenges of citizen-led urbanism: How does a municipal agency, used to acquiring technology from established vendors, do business with a self-forming team of problem-solvers who solve a problem before the city does? The solution, which involved embedding the SMARTmuni team with the transit agency, is one of many forms of civic incubation the city is adopting.

Figure 4.

Creative Currency

Summer of Smart taught San Francisco that there is great capacity among citizens to bring fresh approaches to city problems. But the city also learned that scaling those efforts require a design process that brings those with a deep knowledge of urban problems together with developer enthusiasm and ingenuity. San Francisco needed to develop an incubation processes that identifies high-potential ideas, and then provide sufficient time to test them.

In May 2013, a partnership between the Mayor's Office of Civic Innovation, GAFFTA, Hub Bay Area and American Express launched Creative Currency. This project turned its attention to imagining new forms of trade, credit and currency exchange for one of San Francisco's most economically challenged neighborhoods—Central Market and the Tenderloin.

San Francisco challenged its citizen's to ask what innovation looks like in a part of town defined by homelessness, poverty and an informal economy based on bartering and the absence of bank financing.

Much of technology innovation in the San Francisco Bay Area is already focused on the sharing economy. Companies like Airbnb (apartment and home sharing); Lyft and Sidecar (auto sharing); and TaskRabbit (skill sharing) are all examples of finding informal mechanisms that unleash economic value. San Francisco wanted to match that kind of expertise to solve its most pressing urban problems.

In its mission statement, Creative Currency asked, "How can financial data empower low-income residents? How can local currencies support local businesses and community organizations? How can the city tailor sharing platforms to fit the needs of under-served communities? How can tools like crowdfunding and microcredit be put to work for social service organization and individuals alike?"

San Francisco attracted 200 participants and set the stage for the rapid prototyping of 12 community-centered projects around new economic principles of exchange. The projects ranged from alternative finance to time banking. Over the course of four months, four winning projects received continued mentorship, acceleration and $15,000 in seed funding. To ensure that the outcomes of Creative Currency were grounded in existing community efforts and relationships, we spent weeks interviewing local organizations and compiled our findings into a Community Brief to inform the project. The full Creative Currency community brief that includes the result of one-on-one interviews with more than 20 local organizations in the Mid-Market area is available at: http://creative-currency.org/community/community-brief/.

Creative Currency consisted of four stages that foster a balance between rapid prototyping, sustained impact and community input. This program model has become the basis for many of San Francisco's ongoing efforts, and of civic innovation programs nationwide.

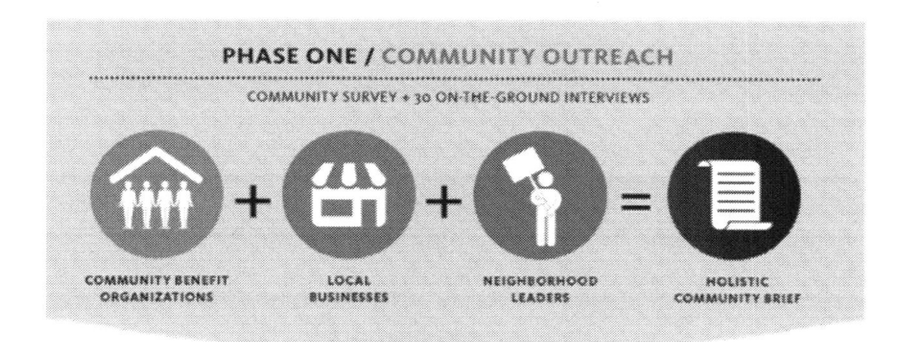
PHASE ONE / COMMUNITY OUTREACH
COMMUNITY SURVEY + 30 ON-THE-GROUND INTERVIEWS
COMMUNITY BENEFIT ORGANIZATIONS
LOCAL BUSINESSES
NEIGHBORHOOD LEADERS
HOLISTIC COMMUNITY BRIEF

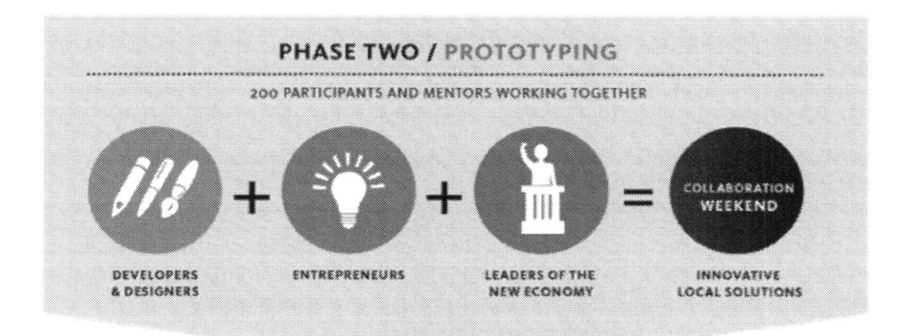
PHASE TWO / PROTOTYPING
200 PARTICIPANTS AND MENTORS WORKING TOGETHER
COLLABORATION WEEKEND
DEVELOPERS & DESIGNERS
ENTREPRENEURS
LEADERS OF THE NEW ECONOMY
INNOVATIVE LOCAL SOLUTIONS

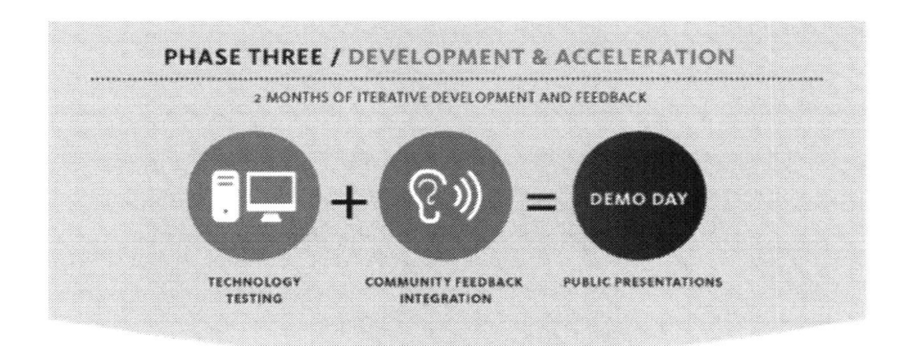
PHASE THREE / DEVELOPMENT & ACCELERATION
2 MONTHS OF ITERATIVE DEVELOPMENT AND FEEDBACK
DEMO DAY
TECHNOLOGY TESTING
COMMUNITY FEEDBACK INTEGRATION
PUBLIC PRESENTATIONS

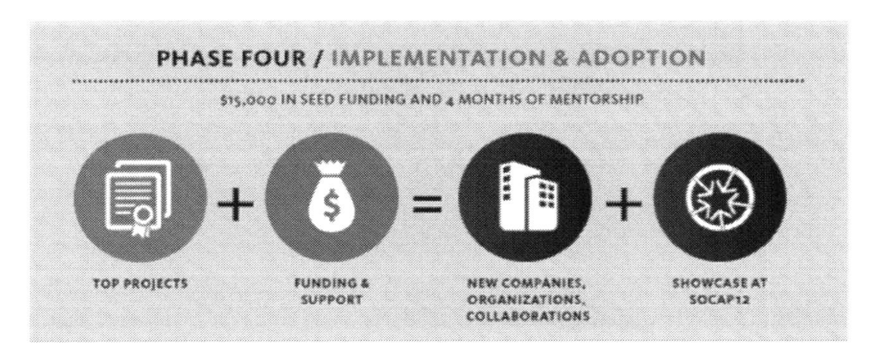
PHASE FOUR / IMPLEMENTATION & ADOPTION
$15,000 IN SEED FUNDING AND 4 MONTHS OF MENTORSHIP
TOP PROJECTS
FUNDING & SUPPORT
NEW COMPANIES, ORGANIZATIONS, COLLABORATIONS
SHOWCASE AT SOCAP12

Figure 5.

Creative Currency Program Model

1. Community Outreach (Community Brief): With an incredible diversity of demographics, interest groups and constituencies, Mid-Market is perhaps one of the most complex neighborhoods in the country. The city has spent weeks on the ground conducting in-person interviews with dozens of San Francisco's leading community benefit organizations, local businesses and neighborhood leaders. To ensure the projects are as grounded as possible in existing local efforts and challenges, the city analyzed hours of discussions and insights and boiled them down into a holistic Community Brief to inform project teams.

2. Prototyping (Collaboration Weekend): This involved leading developers, designers, entrepreneurs, community representatives, and leaders of the new economy in a weekend hackathon called Collaboration Weekend. Participants prototyped innovation solutions to address the pre-identified challenges in the community.

3. Development and Acceleration (Demo Day): In this phase, projects undergo initial technology testing, community feedback integration and solidification before they are presented to a broad audience of citizens at Creative Currency Demo Day.

4. Implementation and Adoption: In this phase, top projects receive funding and support to develop their project into companies, organizations or collaborations with a chance of being showcased at SOCAP12, the world's largest gathering of social entrepreneurs and impact investors.

The projects that emerged from Creative Currency demonstrated the diverse solutions that can applied to community problems:

Trust Score leverages informal networks and relationships to enable engagement in the formal economy, using trust as a form of currency.

YourSQFT connects renters with short-term spaces and labor in Mid-Market.

Bridge is a platform that facilitates real-time information exchange and action essential for low-income and homeless individuals in Mid-Market.

Refresh SF encourages giving through an easy donate system to promote public health and build awareness of homelessness.

Urban Prototyping Festival

Even as the city has developed open data mechanisms and inspiring startups experimenting with data, it was becoming clear that the next great arena for civic innovation would be the physical canvas of the city itself. Online real estate is essentially limitless: multiple companies or teams can build app or web services with the same distributed information. But the physical component of a city is subject to permits, zoning review, and other rules dating back in the city's history.

The city wondered how it could we expose the physical component of the city to the same innovative forces it had seen with data.

San Francisco has pioneered a great innovation: the parklet, which reclaims curbside parking spaces across the city for public open space. This process of "tactical urbanism" brings creativity to the physical façade of the city, building more livable space for citizens everywhere.

This process began to take shape in San Francisco in 2005, when the design firm Rebar created Park(ing) Day, an experiment reclaiming public parking spaces for small parks and other use. In 2010, the San Francisco Planning Department formalized the process by treating the parklet as a new permit type, allowing the creation of dozens of privately operated, publicly accessible spaces throughout the city. This program is now being replicated in cities around the world, a process being made easier with the San Francisco Planning Department's release of the Parklet Manual in 2013.

Building on this movement and the energy behind it, another project began in 2012 called Urban Prototyping (UP) to collect, exhibit and share similar prototypes for improving public space. San Francisco designed UP to gather submissions of designs for new public projects, exhibit them, gain feedback through large-scale outdoor festivals, and then take the projects forward as approved pilots through formal partnerships established in different cities. Led by Gray Area, the first festival brought together a wide coalition of partners, including the San Francisco Mayor's Office of Civic Innovation; Intersection for the Arts, the city's oldest arts nonprofit; Rebar; the design firm IDEO; and Forest City's 5M Project, a mixed-use development in the heart of the city where the festival took place.

For one day in October, UP transformed four blocks of the city into a playground for urban experiments. More than 5,000 visitors from a variety of backgrounds came out to experience and test more than 20 new projects, including sensor-enabled planter bags, environmental monitoring tools and modular urban games that people could play in the street. A program of expert panels and keynote speakers completed the projects focusing on the future of the discipline and its context within San Francisco. The festival was a success and demonstrated that a critical mass exists to take this physical manifestation of shared digital culture to the next level.

Cities around the world curious about how they could bring both the individual projects and the festival as a whole to their own city further validated the overwhelming interest in the program. Singapore and London both launched Urban Prototyping festivals, and Geneva and Zurich participated in a multi-city transportation data challenge. Several projects continue to see success and live lives of their own.

Less than a year later, one project called Pulse of the City—which translates pedestrian heartbeats into electronic music while simultaneously logging and sharing the data to raise awareness about public health—was installed in five locations in Boston as part of its health and public art programs.

Another project, PPlanter—a sensor-enabled public urinal—conducted a pilot in the Tenderloin neighborhood in San Francisco.

Other projects received tens of thousands of visits on Instructables, the open platform for sharing do-it-yourself (DIY) projects used by UP to open source the designs, materials and production techniques for every project in the festival, which was a prerequisite for participation. This openness ensured that anyone in the world could reproduce any of the projects at the prototype scale, allowing them to test them refine them in their own cities.

Figure 6.

The next year, building on the success of UP, San Francisco, launched a Living Innovation Zones (LIZ) program designed to make underutilized public spaces more accessible for creative project and new technology use. The initiative is a partnership between the Mayor's Office of Civic Innovation, the Department of Public Works and the Planning Department. LIZ provides a combination of subject matter expertise, permitting knowledge and political capital to test new approaches to public space reuse.

With current processes, it can be incredibly difficult to navigate the slew of permits and approvals needed to take advantage of city assets for innovative projects in public space. There is potential to use sidewalks, light poles, street signs and other infrastructure in creative ways that are currently unrealized. LIZ helps streamline the process for using these and other similar assets, empowering creative minds to make use of space that enhance the public realm.

The first LIZ involves a partnership with the Exploratorium, an innovative cultural institutions that focuses on the intersection of science, education and innovation. The Exploratorium is adapting one of its physical floor exhibits, some of which take decades of research to develop and construct, on a a sidewalk on downtown Market Street, the city's main artery. The installation includes two large semi-spherical "whispering dishes" that allow pedestrians to hear each other over the din of city traffic while sitting dozens of feet apart.

"The city is partnering with the Exploratorium, one of the most innovative and loved places in our world-class city, to launch San Francisco's first Living Innovation Zone in the Yerba Buena neighborhood," says Mayor Lee. "And what better place than the Exploratorium to help shape a fantastic new public space in an educational, engaging, provocative and playful way, all at the same time."

This first LIZ was funded by a crowdfunding campaign on Indiegogo, making it the first crowdfunding project the Exploratorium or the city has formally endorsed or been involved with. (All of the proceeds go to the Exploratorium for production of the project). The public also has been and will continue to be heavily engaged throughout the design process, with exhibit designers incorporating all types of public feedback to improve and modify the installation.

These types of urban infrastructure "hacks" have already created new types of public space, community participation and socio-cultural development in San Francisco via the success with parklets. LIZ seeks to build on that success and provide innovators with a real-world setting to test new ideas, evaluate next generation technologies, collect data about the impact on street activation and educate the public about innovative solutions. In doing so, LIZ aims to steer San Francisco's tech and creative communities toward advancing sustainable community development, efficient government and a better quality of life for San Franciscans.

Departmental Intrapreneurism

San Francisco's government departments also are at the forefront of the imaginative use of open data to solve urban problems. The people leading the charge to integrate big data and open data into governing are clearly not just data geeks, but also leaders and reformers. They see problems and work to fix them through innovative data use. In this sense, they are "progressives" of the Information Age, and their accomplishments in the city are worth noting.

A great example comes from the San Francisco Department of Public Health (SFDPH), and Dr. Rajiv Bhatia, its Director of Occupational and Environmental Health. In 1999, he pioneered the use of an international tool called Health Impact Assessments (HIAs) in the United States. HIA involves "systematically study[ing] all significant health concerns of a governmental decision." Since the first HIA of a proposed increase in the San Francisco minimum wage in 1999, he has applied HIAs and health outcome data to a number of important issues facing San Francisco communities including labor rights, pedestrian safety, housing and displacement.

In 2004, at the behest of communities facing rapid development pressures, Bhatia and his office launched a multi-stakeholder process involving more than 20 community organizations called the Eastern Neighborhoods Community HIA. The goal was to develop:

- A healthy city vision for San Francisco;
- Objectives to achieve that vision; and
- Indicators to track progress and data on these indicators.

In 2007, 100 of these diverse measures—complete with data sources and methods for their applications—became the open technical resource now known as the Sustainable Communities Index (SCI). In November 2012, SFDPH opened more than 60 of these data sets to the public on San Francisco's open data portal.

Figure 7.

The development of the SCI and the subsequent open data initiative, due in large part to Bhatia's leadership, is one of the most imaginative uses of open data the city has seen.

First, the SCI, as a departmental initiative, is uncommonly holistic. SCI groups indicators into seven broad categories: environment, transportation, community, the public realm, education, housing and the economy. The data sets range from healthy housing code violations (typical) to locations of green businesses and community block parties (not necessarily expected from the Department of Public Health).

SCI rests on the notion that a healthy city is also a green city, walkable city, enjoyable city and so on, and the tools used to evaluate urban policy should reflect the cross-disciplinary nature of urban challenges. The outcome of this systems thinking is that Bhatia made a practical and compelling case for data sharing among city departments.

Moreover, the application of HIAs and the SCI has changed city policy. HIA methodology has been used to improve health impacts of land use plans and housing development designs. Localized air pollution models, or air pollution hotspot maps, have guided safe building code regulations. And creative manipulation of pedestrian injury data has hugely improved traffic calming practices and enforcement priorities. This map in particular was recently featured in The Atlantic's "Best Open Data Releases of 2012."

Finally, the SCI is noteworthy because it provides a scalable framework for public use of open data. Every indicator in the SCI and its corresponding data set includes a description of its relationship to health, a preliminary interpretation, methods for its use, and limitations. Opening data, in this case, does not only mean putting it "out there" for developers and entrepreneurs in the private sector (a good example). It also means providing a robust technical resource for citizens, community groups and public health practitioners to evaluate city policies and projects that affect their everyday lives.

Applying HIAs to policy outside the traditional domain of public health was, of course, an uphill battle. "It was hard," Bhatia says. "We didn't have a mandate to do any of this work. We didn't have resources or funding to do any of this work. But what we did was, we tried."

In most cases, he explains, "We were struggling to get city government agencies to pay attention to, to act on, a social welfare and health concern backed up by data."

The first time he brought up these concerns, there was a fight, as city agencies often have specific mandates, limited staff and limited resources. Eventually, however, city agencies and even developers realized that there was a solution.

"There are people who get collaboration," Bhatia says. "Nothing good is going to come without collaboration, and every good solution is a multi-objective solution."

Bhatia is part of a growing class of social scientists, data engineers and other who recognize the value of open data and cross-departmental collaboration, who have the skills and creativity to make novel use of data, and who have the drive to bring about positive change. San Francisco recognizes them for what they are: innovators, urban entrepreneurs, and yes, data geeks!

PETER HIRSHBERG *is a well know Silicon Valley entrepreneur and chairman of the civic innovation firm Reimagine Group;* ***JAY NATH,*** *Chief Innovation Officer for San Francisco;* ***TIMOTHY POPANDREOU,*** *Director, Strategic Planning & Policy, City and County of San Francisco;* ***JAKE LEVITAS,*** *Mayor's Innovation Fellow, City & County of San Francisco.*

9

Miami-Dade County's Use of Technology in Enterprise Sustainability Projects

Angel Petisco

Miami-Dade County, Fla., which has a population of more than 2.4 million residents, has developed a GreenPrint sustainability plan for building smart cities. In GreenPrint, a sustainable community has a vibrant economy with clean, pedestrian-friendly, tree-lined healthy neighborhoods and provides responsible land use and smart transportation options to benefit residents and visitors. Miami-Dade County's Information Technology Department (ITD) has collaborated with various county departments to enable enterprise sustainability projects using enterprise technology tools. From simple initiatives that produce benchmarks of employees turning off their computers when not in use, to more complex solutions such as capturing energy consumption by county facilities, technology is the underlying platform to enable the county's Enterprise Sustainability Strategy. Through collaborative efforts promoted by the Miami-Dade Office of Sustainability and implemented by ITD, awareness and impact of green efforts in the county has now become second nature.

For instance, IT software and hardware have been instituted to reduce county paper use, greenhouse gas emissions and electrical consumption county-wide and at the enterprise data center. ITD also has been instrumental in developing software programs that, through implementation, affect the environment on a daily basis.

Green Business

Miami-Dade citizens have become more conscious how their day-to-day lives affect the environment. For some, finding environmentally friendly businesses is important, and this is where the green business initiative began. With an online service, business owners in the community are encouraged to apply for a Green Business Certificate certifying their business as "green," encouraging an environmentally friendly community.

To apply, a business owner responds to questions on an online web form to rate business processes. Businesses such as dental offices, restaurants, garment cleaning and retail offices, can apply by going to the county's website where they respond to a series of questions to determine if they are following green practices that are in line with their type of business. If the business does not pass the initial survey, county staff work with the business owner to address the areas needed to pass the certification, verify that the processes are in place and award certification. Through a n et application developed by ITD, county staff can view the surveys and record the status of each application.

The Green Business initiative includes dashboard reports and statistics that provide an analysis of the work accomplished each quarter and lists the businesses that have achieved Green Business Certification.

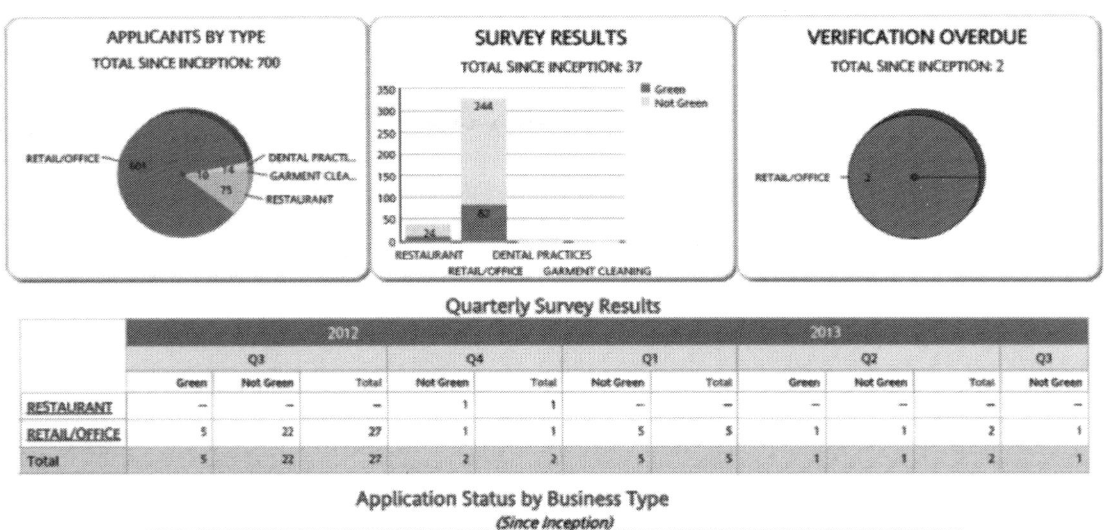

Quarterly Survey Results

	2012					2013					
	Q3			Q4		Q1		Q2			Q3
	Green	Not Green	Total	Not Green	Total	Not Green	Total	Green	Not Green	Total	Not Green
RESTAURANT	—	—	—	1	1	—	—	—	—	—	—
RETAIL/OFFICE	5	22	27	1	1	5	5	1	1	2	1
Total	5	22	27	2	2	5	5	1	1	2	1

Application Status by Business Type

(Since Inception)

	Application Submitted	Application Reviewed	Verification Requested	Verification Completed	Certification Granted	Total
DENTAL PRACTICES	2	3	—	—	—	5
GARMENT CLEANING	1	1	—	—	—	2
RESTAURANT	4	27	—	5	2	38
RETAIL/OFFICE	26	263	2	14	13	318
Total	33	294	2	19	15	363

Figure 1.

GreenPrint

GreenPrint is the county's plan for a sustainable future that addresses goals, strategies and initiatives led by a collaboration of multiple county departments, community groups, and experts from the business community and academia. An annual publication describes progress on the more than 130 initiatives and goal areas over a five-year period. To facilitate collaboration and produce the implementation table for each initiative, the ITD developed the GreenPrint Data Collection and Progress Reporting application. The system allows leaders in each of the goal areas to meet with their teams and capture their work progress in a manner consistent throughout all of the areas. Quantitative measures within the status facilitate the creation of visual graphics and charts to demonstrate progress for the entire plan. Use of the ITD's development tools and business analytics produce a central repository to enter metrics and produce charts and tables of the data.

Figure 2.

Smart Public Safety

The Miami-Dade County Public Safety community has collaborated with ITD to develop computer applications that would streamline tedious job functions, reduce paper consumption and enable the public safety community to work smarter. The applications include:

e-Notify Enables Judicial Court Notifications via the Web—The ITD enterprise data center prints an average of 25,000 subpoenas monthly from the Criminal Justice Information System, Traffic Information System, and Parking Violation System. Previously, the tedious manual delivery process would commence when the printed subpoenas were delivered to the Richard E. Gerstein (REG) Justice Building for the Miami-Dade Police Department Court Liaison Office to manually sort into 19 different districts. The subpoenas were subsequently sent to the Police Department's Court Services Bureau for delivery by 17 couriers to 214 locations throughout the 2,000 square mile county. This daily process required countless hours of administrative processing and navigation through traffic congestion for police officers to receive their notifications for court attendance. Further, the process lacked the ability to notify the judicial agencies in a timely manner when an officer was not found or unavailable to attend court. The obsolete, time consuming and labor-intensive process had been in place since the county was chartered in 1957 and the system was incompatible with the county's growing 21st century needs.

The ITD, under the direction of Miami-Dade county's judicial agencies and its law enforcement agencies, developed the e-Notify System allowing judicial agencies to automatically send court notifications and subpoenas to officers, and immediately receive documented response acknowledgements via the internet. The system is programmed to automatically escalate alerts within the law enforcement agency chain of command to ensure that required witnesses attend scheduled appointments and that court clerks are promptly informed about emergencies. In addition, day-of-court attendance is tracked through the system via a check-in and check-out process at kiosks located in 16 court liaison offices throughout the county. The interfaces to and from mainframe justice applications provide court, case status, officer, officer schedule and subpoena information, and court clerks and administrators within the judicial agencies are able to efficiently reset and confirm new dates to reschedule hearing or pre-file conference appointments.

The e-Notify system provides jurisdictions within the county with a single software platform for electronic submission, distribution, and tracking of court notices and subpoenas to officers from law enforcement agencies within the 11th Judicial Circuit of Florida. The system offers 54 law enforcement and four judicial agencies with the ability to electronically distribute and track interagency subpoenas and notices via the internet. The court notification distribution process that previously took anywhere from three to five days to complete using approximately 40 staff members from the court liaison offices and 17 couriers is now electronically handled for law enforcement agencies using e-Notify. The system now processes approximately 40,000 to 50,000 court notifications monthly, nearly a 200 percent increase in court notifications. In addition to the automation of the printed subpoena distribution process, the e-Notify system also processes more than 50 types of court notifications issued by the state administrative office to law enforcement officers, as well as requests for information and subpoenas issued by private attorneys. This increase in communication between the judicial and law enforcement community guarantees that taxpayer money is used more efficiently.

Since the system was implemented, judicial agencies have benefited from being able to insure witness attendance, while efficiently making use of an officer's time in court. Moreover, law enforcement officers have a system to manage their subpoena appearances and court appointments. The automation of the subpoena process permits law enforcement agencies to redirect resources and increase public safety patrol for the community.

Automated A-Form Solution—The Miami-Dade law enforcement community, represented by county, state and municipal police agencies, serves a large and diverse metropolitan area comprised of 36 municipalities each with their own police department, Miami-Dade County Police Department, Miami-Dade Corrections and Rehabilitation Department, Juvenile Services Department and several state of Florida law enforcement agencies that process more than 220,000 arrests yearly. The approximate incarceration rate for these arrest affidavits translates into 114,000 individuals annually booked into Miami-Dade county's correctional facilities.

Miami-Dade county currently uses a paper arrest form (A-form) to process arrest information. This manual arrest process gives rise to operational deficiencies among all Miami-Dade criminal justice entities. More importantly, it delays the officer's stay at the corrections facility, thereby reducing the ability to protect the community.

The Miami-Dade County Association of Chiefs of Police (MDCACP) is the sponsor of the project funded by the Florida Department of Law Enforcement (FDLE), the American Recovery and Reinvestment Act (ARRA) and a Justice Assistance Grant (JAG) to automate the A-form for county law enforcement agencies. Miami-Dade county acquired an enterprise electronic A-form solution that automates the current manual A-form, making arrest information available at correctional facilities by the time the officer arrives with the arrestee, expediting the booking process. The automated solution incorporates workflows and facilitates data sharing and reporting.

Electronic Crime Scene Processing—The Electronic Crime Scene Processing Request Form designed by the ITD is an online system automating the Miami-Dade County Police Department's Crime Scene Investigations Bureau (CSIB) burglary process. The system uses the county's Electronic Document Management System to create, process and store the completed form. The key features and benefits of the electronic crime scene processing request form are an automated workflow, increased crime scene processing, centralized repository for all CSIB documents, user accountability, and email notification of pending crime scene processing requests. Additionally, it is a green initiative because it eliminates paper and need to physically transport reports.

The Crime Scene Processing project has benefited the Miami-Dade Police Department's CSIB, by eliminating waste, eliminating a defect in the paper-based process, and improving the efficiency and timeliness of crime scene processing. The manual process wasted time, fuel and increased wear and tear on county vehicles. Automating the process has allowed investigators to work smarter and more effectively—saving time and money, and increasing a more rapid response to burglary victims' needs.

Utility Bill Management

To improve the management of Miami-Dade county's 4,500 accounts with Florida Power & Light and to better understand the electric consumption in county facilities, the ITD, Internal Services Department, and Regulatory and Economic Resources Department collaborated to implement a countywide solution for utility bill management. Originally funded from a federal grant to enable electronic data interchange for processing electric bills to measure energy consumption, the system tracks savings and submits Energy Star ratings for buildings. As part of this implementation, energy managers analyze their department accounts, train others on the use of the system, and eliminate paper copies of their bills to meet the savings and accuracy goals. The system allows for more audits and greater accountability for those that approve the energy bills. With its various reports and ease of use, an energy manager can track utility bills over time for facilities and compare statistics between similar buildings and accounts. Interfaces to operational programs include the Enterprise Asset Management System and three enterprise financial systems. Daily alerts ensure that the necessary files are imported and exported, and that the system is running smoothly. Because the system is highly configurable and reliable, the county is looking to leverage the system on utilities, such as water and sewer.

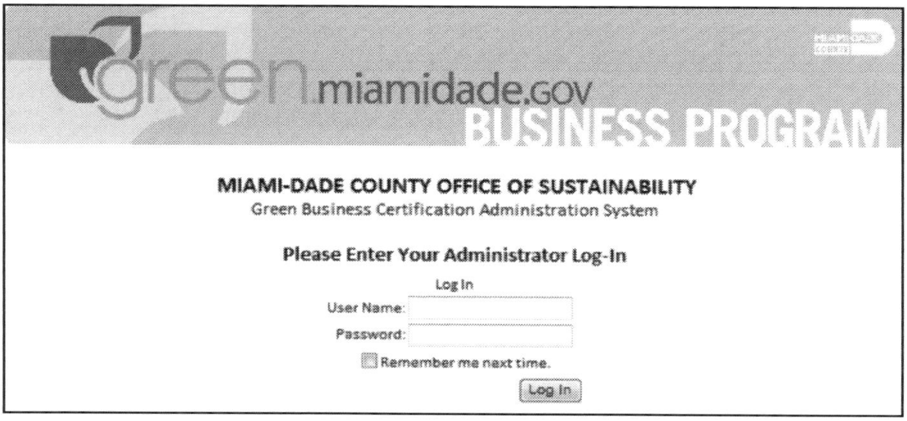

Figure 3.

Enterprise Asset Management

Another federal grant project was the implementation of house meters and submeters to gauge electrical consumption for two of the county's largest buildings, the Stephen P. Clark Center and the Richard E. Gerstein Courthouse. The technology required included software for the current enterprise asset management system, hardware for capturing interval meter readings, and business intelligence dashboards for displays on large monitors in the lobbies of both buildings. Metrics are captured on a daily basis.

Because of the displays, weekly competitions for savings began, and awareness of the importance of saving energy was effectively communicated through behavioral campaigns. Other IT integrations with building management systems and the utility billing system provide data on large equipment such as air conditioning, where an analysis of usage patterns and trends yield opportunities for additional savings.

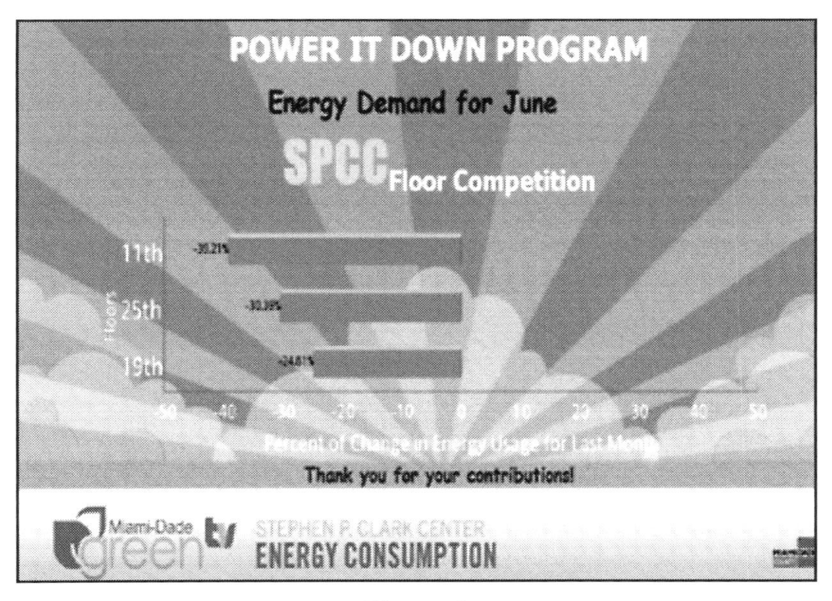

Figure 4.

Power IT Down

The ITD provides technical support for the majority of workstations and servers used by county employees in the facilities and departments throughout Miami-Dade. Following a national movement to turn off computers at night when they are not in use, the ITD explored how to motivate county employees to "Power IT Down." With technology, workstations were polled at night and data was gathered by departments to spark a competition and inspire employees to power down their equipment. By leveraging in-house expertise in business intelligence, ITD designed and created dashboards via drill-through reports that displayed savings by department, month, ranking by percentage and actual savings, and annual totals to the public. The monitoring, compilation and reporting of data are automated, and the system seamlessly produces daily statistics that are subsequently displayed on the ITD website.

When the ITD embarked on another project to install virtual clients and reduce physical personal computers, the Power IT Down system captured and produced charts on the energy savings for virtual clients. Virtual clients are software-based fictive computers that are based on specifications and that emulate the computer architecture and function of a real computer. On average, the county saves approximately $230,000 annually by having its computers power down at night and by using virtual clients.

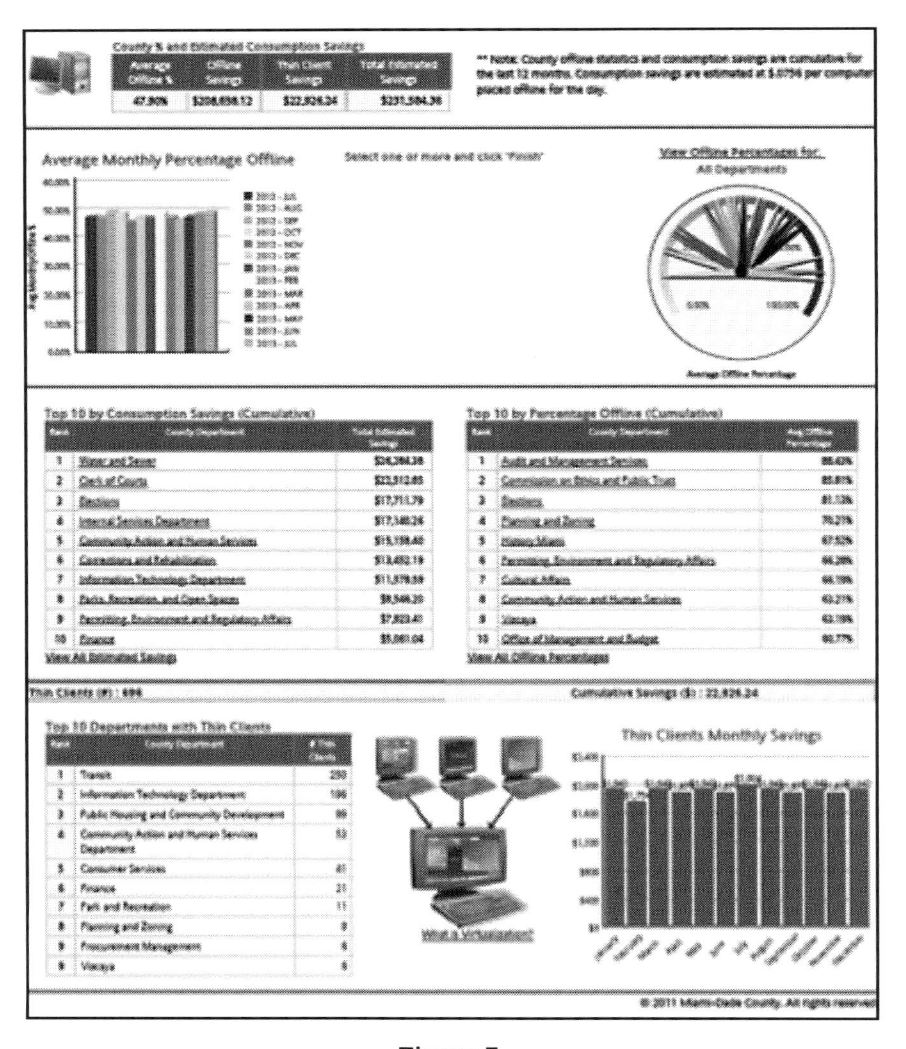

Figure 5.

Smarter Infrastructure

Miami-Dade county requires an availability of information technology services 24/7/365. With an increasing resident population and continuing limited fiscal resources, the county was challenged how to replace aging and out-of-warranty physical servers while maintaining cooling systems running at maximum capacity, and with data centers that could not accommodate required new equipment. To address this challenge, the ITD looked to consolidate its expanding data center and used virtualization to develop a "private cloud," for server virtualization and to deploy virtual desktops for end-users. Miami-Dade county created a private cloud with the goal of reducing the physical footprint of processing hardware at major county data centers by sharing physical resources, providing high availability and business continuity, and providing mobility for entire virtualized applications.

With server virtualization, the county increased the resource use of its physical server hardware from 10 percent to 80 percent, and reduced the physical footprint of processing hardware at the county's major data centers by sharing physical resources. The current infrastructure hosts 500 virtual servers that run on 30 physical servers. The ITD achieved an average consolidation ratio of 20-to 40 virtual servers per physical host. If the county did not use a private cloud, the capital cost for 500 new servers would have been approximately $2.6 million.

The performance of virtual servers and their hosts, the physical servers, are managed and monitored from a central location. The ITD has reduced hardware and operating costs by 20 percent, energy costs by 80 percent, and saved$3,000 annually for every server virtualized. This has decreased downtime and improved reliability for business continuity of county departments.

Below is one example of a comparison illustrating the cost for ordering six physical servers versus six virtual servers. These savings do not include the recurring energy costs related to powering and cooling an additional physical infrastructure.

- Six virtual machines—total cost about $11,520 per year.
- Six physical machines—total cost about $60,000 to $72,000.
- Savings of about $50,000 to $60,000 the first year, with recurring savings of $4,080 a year.

The ITD worked with Microsoft to obtain an operating software license agreement for a cost per socket per host with unlimited virtual servers running on each physical host, equivalent to thousands of dollars in savings. The example below illustrates the utility and carbon footprint reduction of virtualization and blade technology as energy savings.

As virtual servers increase, so do the savings.

By providing a reliable, affordable virtual server infrastructure, county business processes are accomplished more efficiently. Additional virtual servers are offered to replace outdated physical servers. New projects are analyzed to determine if any components can be virtualized. This effort will continue to reduce energy needs for existing services, as well as for new projects. The implementation of server virtualization benefits all county agencies and ultimately its citizens.

Current Power Consumption Per Year Per Server Type		Yearly Power Consumption	Yearly Power Savings
HP460C Blade Server—$300	500 Physical Blades	$150,000	
Virtual Server—$11	500 Virtual Servers	$5,500	**$144,500**

Table 1.

In 2012, ITD began consolidating decentralized departmental computing infrastructure, resulting in the growth of the virtual computing environment. Because of this consolidation, the number of virtual servers exceeds the number of physical servers online.

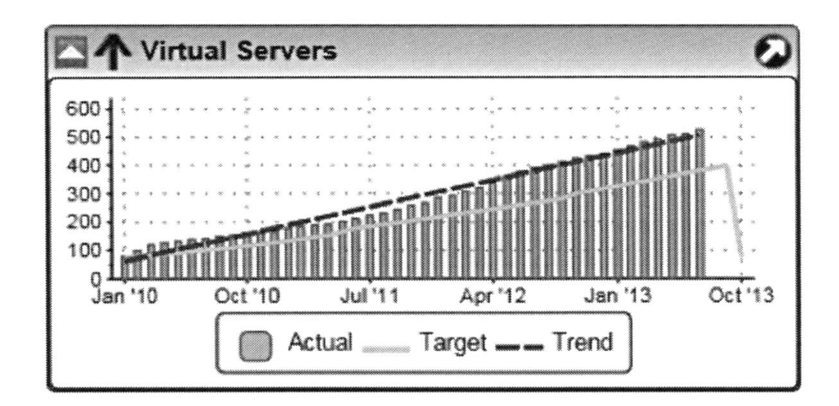

Figure 6.

ITD's current environment of virtual servers saves approximately $12,000 per month in electrical power, based on the highest tier of discounted KwH rate from Florida Power and Light. This tier is for the largest commercial sites in Florida and provides a "no less than x cents per KwH". This cost is calculated on the assumption that the current virtual server environment is all physical blade servers, and are power efficient. As an example, a physical blade server with intelligent power consumption would cost $300 a year; its equivalent virtual server costs $11 a year in power. The ITD is virtualizing 527 servers, a number that is continually growing. The virtual servers consume $5,800 in electrical power a year; if they were physical server blades, the cost would be $158,100, as data centers are one of the biggest consumers of electricity per square foot.

Desktop virtualization also was implemented to provide county employees with a high value, feature-rich desktop virtualization solution designed to optimize user experience, reduce IT workload, improve IT security and lower IT costs. Employees are able to access their virtual desktops from anywhere, anytime and from virtually any internet-enabled device. Users can choose from a range of devices including thin client, desktop, laptop, tablet, netbook, even a PDA or smartphone. When users log in at their workstation, a personalized virtual desktop complete with operating system, configured applications, files and settings, is automatically assembled in the data center and served to the user. The efficiencies have enabled Miami-Dade county to put taxpayers' money to use in the most effective ways, saving the county thousands of dollars.

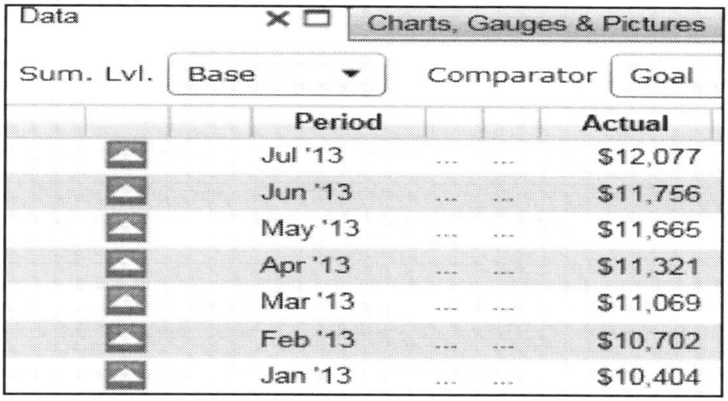

Data | Charts, Gauges & Pictures

Sum. Lvl. Base | Comparator Goal

Period			Actual
Jul '13	...	...	$12,077
Jun '13	...	...	$11,756
May '13	...	...	$11,665
Apr '13	...	...	$11,321
Mar '13	...	...	$11,069
Feb '13	...	...	$10,702
Jan '13	...	...	$10,404

Figure 7.

The desktop virtualization initiative's goals of reducing the carbon footprint, increasing data security and compliance, improving cost efficiencies, providing telecommuting opportunities and ensuring business continuity and disaster recovery has been accomplished. The county can conduct business uninterrupted from any location and virtually any device, thereby improving customer service to Miami-Dade taxpayers while reducing the cost of managing and maintaining the desktop environment.

Desktop virtualization has significantly reduced electrical consumption from 110 watts to 240 watts on average on a personal computer to less than 7 watts per thin client device. Further, the number of calls to the IT Service Center with virtual desktop-related complaints or concerns is nearly zero. Patch and Windows update is at full 100 percent compliance. User productivity has increased because of virtual desktops, and desktop management costs have decreased.

Miami-Dade county directors and staff have been weaving sustainability initiatives into their operations for years and continually seek to learn and improve upon how they do business. County directors are skilled professionals in their fields; their input and ability to grasp and integrate GreenPrint into their operations has been invaluable. Using their skills, they have teamed with the county's ITD to implement a smart design for the future of Miami-Dade county.

ANGEL PETISCO *serves as the Chief Information Officer (CIO) of the Information Technology Department of Miami-Dade County, a diversified data processing and communications organization serving one of the largest metropolitan county government in the nation. Mr. Petisco began his technology career in 1976 with Southeast banking and concluded his tenure as an operations manager overseeing the data center operations. In July of 1979, he joined the Miami-Dade County family in a similar capacity.*

Mr. Petisco continues to work relentlessly to improve overall services, reduce operational and capital costs while increasing service delivery. Mr. Petisco holds a Bachelor of Science in Business Administration from Thomas Edison State College in New Jersey.

10

Montgomery County, Maryland, USA: A Case Study in Smart Counties

Harash (Sonny) Segal

The flight to urbanization in the United States is consistent with similar trends in the rest of the world. According to the United Nations, by 2050 almost 70 percent of the world's population will live in cities. U.S. counties collectively make up a vital part of the overall U.S. public service delivery system and domestic economic engine providing services directly to more than 92 percent of the U.S. population. Montgomery County, Maryland, a nationally leading East Coast urban-suburban U.S. county government of 1 million people in the National Capital Region, has implemented world-class smart county programs that ranked it in first place in the 2013 Digital Counties Survey undertaken by the Center for Digital Government and the National Association of Counties.

Counties' Critical Role: The Need for Smart Counties

The county form of government in the United States is a legacy from the British and may be considered equivalent to a borough or parish. Today, there are 3,069 counties in the United States that account for nearly the entire land area and population outside the nation's cities. County governments are responsible for providing services essential to the creation of healthy, safe, vibrant and economically resilient communities. More than 19,300 elected board members and elected executives in the nation's counties invest USD 482.1 billion annually to serve 296 million county residents across the country. Counties provide a vast array of services through the work of 3.3 million employees (see Figure 1, next page).

County governments are deeply involved in building, maintaining and operating the transportation and infrastructure assets of the United States. By providing efficient transportation and transit options such as buses, trains, light rail and subway systems, counties connect residents, businesses and communities, and strengthen local economies. Beyond transportation, counties build infrastructure, maintain roads and bridges, provide healthcare, administer justice, ensure community safety, run elections, manage solid waste, keep records, treat water and wastewater, remove storm debris, and build roads, schools and jails.

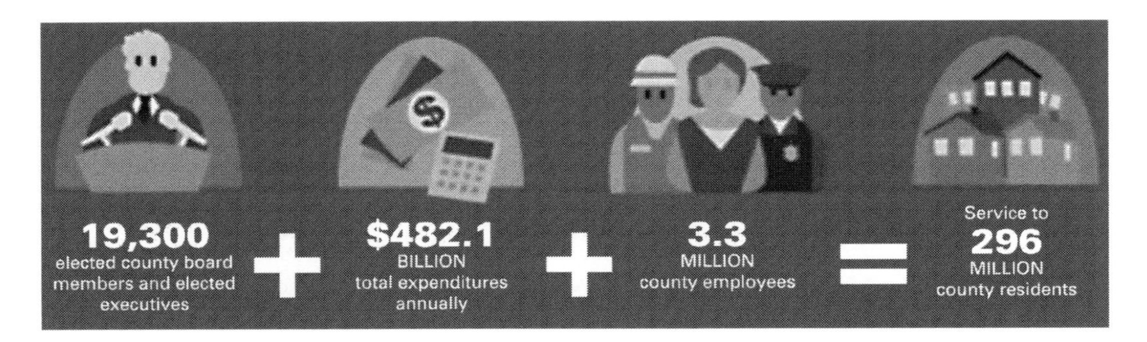

Figure 1. *U.S. Counties Facts.*

Counties own a large share of the nation's infrastructure. For example, counties own 45 percent of the nation's roadways. They also invest substantially in infrastructure. Counties spend USD 106.3 billion annually to build, maintain and operate roads, bridges, transit, water systems, hospitals and other public facilities. Counties spend USD 18.6 billion annually on sewage and solid waste management services. Counties are continually exploring smart ways to curb waste, cut costs, conserve resources for future generations and contribute to a cleaner environment.

Despite the range of services counties provide, county governments receive only approximately 5 percent of their overall revenue from the federal government, according to the U.S. Census Bureau. Collectively, counties receive approximately 35 percent of their total revenue from their home states. Finally, almost 60 percent of county budget revenue is generated from their own sources. Property taxes account for the largest source at 40 percent, and education accounts for the largest expenditure.

What is a Smart County?

With increasingly limited resources, many counties are using process- and technology-assisted innovation to better serve their communities and work with federal, state, and other local governments, nonprofits, and businesses to ensure the prosperity of their residents. Forty counties have merged with their cities to form a city-county form of government. Almost three times as many counties have tried to achieve a city-county form of government, but failed. Nevertheless, more city-county governments will likely emerge as metropolitan cities expand. At present, the city-county form of government is not innovative enough for U.S. cities or counties to deal with the challenges they are facing. Thus, counties must adopt smart city practices if they are to succeed and sustain.

What attributes constitute smart county practices?

The acronym SMART literally stands for "specific, measurable, achievable, relevant and time-based" goals, and most often is used to define a smart jurisdiction framework to include smart grids, smart buildings, clean technology and smart governance. While no rigid definition of a smart city or smart county exists, and each jurisdiction defines it differently, contemporary measures of a smart city or smart county should include an assessment of its investments in human and social capital, as well as traditional (e.g., transportation) and modern (e.g., information communication technology) infrastructures that fuel sustainable economic development and a high quality of life, wise management of natural resources, and participative public action and engagement.

The majority of today's counties run on independent, multiple departments associated with operating systems designed to optimize a specific service in an expert system manner. In a sense, the goal of a smart county is to provide conduits for how these different departments and operational systems can work and learn together—through integration, collaboration and interoperability for synergistic outcomes. For a county to be judged as smart, it must demonstrate sustainable, results-driven smart cities' best practices in all 10 typical county common business areas:

- Transportation
- Infrastructure
- Energy
- Water
- Waste
- Public Safety
- Education
- Healthcare
- Green/Smart Buildings
- Citizen Services

Based on an analysis of U.S. and international smart cities models, it is evident that counties must possess nearly 40 essential traits within 10 business areas in order to be successful in today's environment and considered "smart." These 40 traits may be mapped to six smart county domains (smart economy, smart governance, smart citizens, smart living, smart environment and smart mobility) to form the framework for a smart county model (see Figure 2).

SMART ECONOMY	SMART GOVERNANCE	SMART CITIZENS (HUMAN CAPITAL)
• Ability to transform • Business spaces • Financial promotion (economic image) • Internationalization (global connectedness) • Labor flexibility (attracting talent) • Penetration of Information & Communication Technology • Promoting entrepreneurship innovation • Resilience	• Citizen consultation (e-Democracy) • On-line public services • Political strategies & perspectives • Promoting process & technology • Public & social services • Strategic plans to promote e-Government & ICT • Transparent & open government	• Citizen participation & engagement in public affairs •Cosmopolitanism/ open-mindedness • Human Capital Development (Education & e-Learning) • Level of qualification • Life-long training • Research & Development • Social & ethnic plurality • Social Creativity
SMART LIVING	**SMART ENVIRONMENT**	**SMART MOBILITY**
• Accessibility and e-inclusion • Cultural facilities • Education facilities • Health Conditions • Housing quality • Individual safety • Social cohession (sector interconnectedness) • Touristic attractiveness	• Environmental protection • Green buildings & urban planning • Green energy (end users aware devices) • Monitoring (sensor based) & control • Sustainable resource management	• Availability of ICT infrastructure (wireless/mobile services) • International accessibility • Local accessibility infrastructure • Sustainable, innovative & safe transport systems

Figure 2. *A Smart County Model Framework.*

As traditional counties evolve into smart counties, they need to address social, economic, engineering and environmental challenges. Among the more interesting aspects of smart county initiatives is the closely integrated way that seemingly disparate elements work together. Many smart counties and smart cities are finding that what ties these elements together is the identification and use of authenticated public data. As a practical case, an existing model U.S. county is assessed against these measures next.

A Model Smart County

Montgomery County meets the tests of a smart county. Approximately 490 square miles in area, the county is situated on the northwest border of Washington, D.C. (The dark border in Figure 3 illustrates the county's location in the National Capital Region, as well as its median household income, shown on the scale below the heat map). Spanning an area the size of Rhode Island, the county is home to a growing population of more than 1 million people—greater than that of six U.S. states. The median household and per capita effective buying income levels are more than 170 percent of the national average. Unemployment is well below national levels, averaging a low 5.1 percent in 2012.

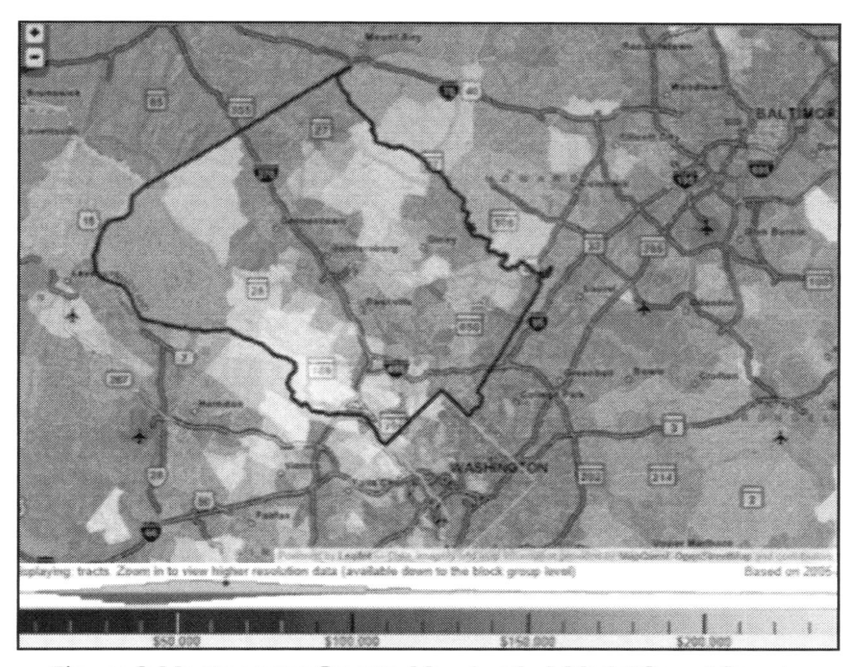

Figure 3. *Montgomery County, Maryland—A Model Smart County.*

The county is recognized internationally as a knowledge-based business and research hub, and a biotechnology center in the U.S. Mid-Atlantic region with a unique agricultural reserve. Indeed, as an urban-suburban-rural jurisdiction, the county boasts dramatically contrasted and physically diverse landscapes, despite bordering on the nation's capital. Montgomery County also admirably seems to balance the challenges of all three types of economies—urban, suburban and rural—through smart county practices. (see Figure 4, next page).

Montgomery County is in the center of the region's federal and advanced technology marketplace. In fact, the county is home to more than 200 biotech companies, representing two-thirds of all those located in Maryland and the third largest cluster of this sector in the nation.

Additionally, the county has a rich history and offers a valued texture of diverse cultures, as well as world-class shopping and dining. The county has a reputation for providing first-rate, award-winning public services.

Montgomery County's most populous communities are Bethesda, Chevy Chase, Gaithersburg, Germantown, Potomac, Rockville and Silver Spring. Together, they form a bustling region and mosaic of existing and new developments and communities.

- Population ~ 1 Million
- Median age ~ 37 years (Digital Natives and Digital Immigrants)
- Land Area ~ 490 sq. miles
- Agriculture Reserve ~ 93k acres
- Median annual household income ~ $93k
- Persons 65 years and older ~ 13%
- Foreign born residents ~ 32%
- Language other than English spoken at home ~ 38%
- Bachelor's degree or higher ~ 58%
- Budget ~ $4.5B
- Median value of owner-occupied housing ~ $470k
- 2013 Digital Counties Rank – First Place

Figure 4. *Montgomery County Demographics.*

The mix of rural and urban settings has increasingly made Montgomery County the community of choice for thousands of families looking for good jobs, excellent schools and safe neighborhoods with relatively low crime rates. Montgomery County residents are among the most educated, diverse and civic-minded in the nation.

The county is served by three international airports and two regional airports, and is literally less than two hours by air from 60 percent of the United States and Canadian populations. With a hugely successful business incubator network, a nationally renowned agricultural preserve, an award-winning small business mentorship program, and world-class conference and performing arts facilities, Montgomery County is an ideal site for both large and small businesses.

Smart Economy

In the smart county model, a county with a smart economy must have the ability to transform; demonstrate an abundance of business spaces; possess effectiveness of financial promotion resulting in a positive economic image; cope successfully with internationalization and maintain a worldwide connectedness appropriate for the new global economy; have labor flexibility in all demographic sectors and in a range of professions;

demonstrate the ability to attract and retain talent; have an evident penetration of information and communication technology (ICT) in the economy; and openly promote entrepreneurship and innovation to sustain a resilient economy (see Figure 5).

SMART ECONOMY
• Ability to transform
• Business spaces
• Financial promotion (economic image)
• Internationalization (global connectedness)
• Labor flexibility (attracting talent)
• Penetration of Information & Communication Technology
• Promoting entrepreneurship innovation
• Resilience

Figure 5. *Smart Economy.*

Montgomery County is one of only eight counties in the United States with a population of more than 1 million and a Triple A (AAA) bond rating from all three major credit rating agencies: Moody's, Standards & Poor's, and Fitch's. The following examples show how the county has successfully achieved a smart economy.

The key industries in Montgomery County are diverse and wide-ranging: life sciences, information technology, health care, communication and satellite, green and clean energy, cyber security, hospitality services, professional (financial, legal and consulting) services, and real estate/construction. Research institutes, including Johns Hopkins University, Howard Hughes Medical Institute, the National Institutes of Health and the University of Maryland, have campuses in the county. Additionally, the county is home to premier higher education institutions and multiple university systems including Johns Hopkins University, University of Maryland and the county-operated community college system, Montgomery College.

As a result of its tax credits, financial incentives, workforce assistance, expedited permitting and ample business spaces for growth, Montgomery County is home to multiple Fortune 500 companies and top industry leaders such as Lockheed Martin, Marriott International, Coventry Healthcare, Catalyst Health Solutions, Host Hotels and Resorts, MedImmune/Astra Zeneca, Discovery Communications LLC (see Figure 6, next page), Human Genome Sciences/GlaxoSmithKline (GSK), Hughes Telecommunications, and GEICO. Additionally noteworthy is the fact that the county has retained the corporate headquarters of many companies:

Discovery, Sodexo, GEICO, Choice and United Therapeutics to name a few. More than 130 foreign companies from around the globe have offices in the county, including BAE Systems (UK), QIAGEN Sciences (Germany), GMV, USA (Spain), Canon U.S. Life Sciences (Japan), Sodexo (France), Daewoong Pharmaceutical Co. (South Korea), Tasly (China), and JOINN Laboratories (China). Eleven local companies made the 2012 Inc. *500 list*, a compilation of the fastest growing privately held companies in the United States. Two companies, E-SAC and Special Operations Solutions, are part of the county's Business Innovation Network. The diverse companies provide a stable and sustainable economic base.

Figure 6. *Corporate Resident—Discovery Communications, LLC.*

Montgomery County is second only to Silicon Valley, Calif., in terms of its concentration of IT and biotech firms in the United States. Conservatively, there are roughly 555 high-tech startups per year in Montgomery County. To achieve this, the county has employed a variety of strategies to help corporations grow here. The county has excellent ICT penetration in its business sectors, as many of its resident ICT companies are firms of international stature and scale.

Montgomery County was a founder and key funder of BioHealth Innovation Inc. (BHI), which is a regional collaboration to commercialize technologies from its research labs. This has resulted in becoming home to more than 350 biotech companies. The county initiated an annual Technology Transfer Conference and worked closely with the Federal Laboratory Consortium to increase its focus on technology transfer. The county's Business Innovation Network houses nearly 160 companies with 850 employees.

To add to this, the county is a ground-zero for bio-health research and development, with world-renowned institutions including public entities (U.S. National Institutes of Health, U.S. Food and Drug Administration) and private entities (Johns Hopkins University, J. Craig Venter Institute, Howard Hughes Medical Institute and Henry M. Jackson Foundation).

The county launched a well-planned Business Innovation Network that offers office and lab space and business support services to its five county-operated business innovation centers (incubators) in all its major municipalities: Rockville, Silver Spring, Wheaton and Germantown. To leverage its 93,000 acres of Agricultural Reserve, the county implemented the Young Farmer Incubator so that future farmers would stay in the county and maintain the agricultural export sector.

The county is home to the National Cyber Security Center of Excellence in conjunction with the existing extensive federal government presence.

The county is considered to have the highest number of entrepreneurs in the nation. In addition, it is home to 19 major research and development organizations.

The county has transformed itself to a more urban economy through a smart growth initiative labeled "Transform Montgomery." This initiative was supported by bond funding, which the county will pay off in 15 years rather than the traditional 30 years that most cities and counties take to repay. The program promotes new urbanism and new sustainable community design, coupled with mixed land use. The program also provides a range of housing opportunities in an otherwise expensive housing market where the median value of owner-occupied housing is USD $470,000.

The state and county have committed more than USD $50 million in financial incentives over the next 15 years to help companies locate and expand in Montgomery County. It also provided direct technical assistance to 300 businesses that led to 10,000 new jobs; 27,000 retained jobs; USD $1.7 billion in new capital investments; and 1.7 million square feet in new commercial space added to the property tax rolls.

Since 2008, the county's Department of Economic Development (DED) has issued nearly USD $500,000 in loans from the Small Business Revolving Loan Fund. Small business is big business in Montgomery County, where 96 percent of the county's businesses have 50 or fewer employees. To help them grow, the county expanded its Local Small Business Reserve

Program, which sets goals for contract awards to local businesses. In fiscal year 2012, more than USD $80 million was awarded to Montgomery County small businesses. The county established a Small Business Navigator program to assist small businesses in their interactions with county government. This resulted in innovations such as shortening of processes, removing roadblocks, or otherwise improving outcomes.

Montgomery County also established the first Local Biotech Tax Credit program. In 2013, the program distributed USD $500,000 to more than 60 investors with total investments of nearly USD $6 million. The county also has established a USD $500,000 Green Investment Incentive Program that started this fiscal year to help spur investment in startup green companies.

The Montgomery County Innovation Network conducts more than100 seminars and training sessions per year for its client companies, as well as CEO roundtables and networking events to address a spectrum of business topics, such as obtaining government funds; good documentation practices; contract negotiations; employment law basics; and strategies for saving employer dollars in the retirement employee benefits market.

The county maintains formal sister city relationships with cities in China, India and Germany. It organizes regular trade and cultural missions through the respective Business Councils. The county, through the state's Maryland Center China in Shanghai, has been assisting local companies in China since 1996 to gain business. This combination of experience and long-term relationship building offers county businesses unique opportunities to explore, enter or expand in the world's most dynamic and fast-growing markets and destinations.

Smart Governance

In the smart county model, the factors that constitute smart governance include citizen consultation to promote an e-Democracy; availability of online public services; smart political strategies and perspectives; promotion of process and technology innovation; availability of ample public and social services; strategic plans to promote e-Government and the wide use of ICT; and the promotion and practice of a transparent and open government model (see Figure 7).

A crowning achievement may be the fact that the Center for Digital Government recently placed the county first in the 2013 National Digital Counties Survey and noted that Montgomery County is the only county government to rank in the top 10 counties in the first decade of the award competition. The following examples show how the county has successfully achieved smart governance.

SMART GOVERNANCE

- Citizen consultation (e-Democracy)
- On-line public services
- Political strategies & perspectives
- Promoting process & technology
- Public & social services
- Strategic plans to promote e-Government & ICT
- Transparent & open government

Figure 7. *Smart Governance.*

An examination of the county's organizational structure and its bond ratings lays the foundation for appreciating why Montgomery County is a smart county. The county has three branches of government. An elected county executive heads the Executive Branch, which comprises 30 functional departments providing approximately 350 government services. The elected nine-member County Council forms the Legislative Branch, whose responsibilities are specified by the County Charter and state law. The Council essentially enacts local public laws for the "peace, good government, health and welfare of the county." The Judicial Branch comprises the courts whose members are appointed by the governor of Maryland or are elected. Montgomery County has created an environment of great professionalism when it comes to objective and constructive decision-making in the interest of the county.

All three branches of government are stable. The mission statement of the current County Executive, the Honorable Isiah Leggett, holds the key to the county's governance culture. It states that the county will "pursue the common good by working for and with Montgomery County's diverse community members to provide a responsive and accountable county government; affordable housing in an inclusive community; an effective and efficient transportation network; children prepared to live and learn; healthy and sustainable communities; safe streets and secure neighborhoods; a strong and vibrant economy; and vital living for all residents." Further, the County Executive states that "as dedicated public servants, the employees of the Montgomery County government strive to embody in our work these essential values: collaboration, inclusiveness, knowledge, competence, innovation, respect for the individual, fiscal prudence, integrity and transparency." The county measures staff performance by these standards.

The current County Executive has been credited with making some drastic fiscal decisions in the past four years by accurately anticipating the Great Recession. He, in conjunction with the County Council, was able to eliminate 1,100 positions from the county's 9,000 strong workforce and hold employees' salaries constant for three years. In 2013, the County Executives of America (CEA) elected the current Montgomery County Executive president based on his long-term visionary performance and collaborative leadership style.

Montgomery County has received the highest award for its fiscal prudence and exhaustive financial reporting from the Government Finance Officers Association (GFOA) for more years than any other county in the nation. The GFOA elected Montgomery County's Chief Administrative Officer Timothy Firestine as president.

The county has a mandatory balanced budget and, as part of the annual operating budget, the county develops a six-year fiscal plan that is actively evaluated. The county enacted laws to maintain a fund reserve as a "rainy day fund." This fund is held for emergencies. The law requires that a 5 percent equivalent of the preceding fiscal year's General Fund revenues be held in reserve for the following year, and a 10 percent equivalent of the Unrestricted General Fund Balance of Adjusted Governmental Revenues (AGR) be held as reserve in the Revenue Stabilization Fund. This is unique and practica, and was put to the test in 2010 when the county experienced an unprecedented USD $265 million decline in income tax revenues, and weathered extraordinary expenditure requirements associated with the H1N1 flu virus and successive and historic winter blizzards. The costs of these events totaled in excess of USD $60 million, only a portion of which was budgeted and planned for. The county's Reserve Fund helps weather such situations and allows the county to maintain its excellent credit and borrowing power in an enviable manner.

One of the keys to the county's success is the way the Executive and Legislative branches actively and objectively interact (in public forums) in the following six committees covering all smart county areas listed. The Education (ED) Committee deals with the public schools' and the county's college system; the Government Operations and Fiscal Policy (GOFP) Committee deals with economic and fiscal policy, spending affordability, county government administrative departments, cable and telecommunications issues, technology issues, personnel and compensation issues, procurement policy, oversight of interagency teams on training, public information and PEG (public, education, and government) cable television channels; the Health and Human Services (HHS) Committee deals with the health and human services agencies, libraries, the arts, culture and humanities; the Planning, Housing, and Economic Development (PHED) Committee deals with master plans and amendments to the zoning laws, issues related to parks and recreation, the Maryland-National Capital Park and Planning Commission, the Montgomery County Planning Board, historic and agricultural preservation, economic development and housing; the Public Safety (PS) Committee deals with criminal justice, including the Police department, the state Attorney's Office, the County Sheriff's Office, the Courts, the Detention Center, the Criminal Justice Coordinating Commission, Fire and Rescue, and Animal Control; the Transportation, Infrastructure, Energy and Environment (T&E) Committee deals with water, sewer and solid waste issues (e.g., incinerators and landfills), environmental protection and forest conservation, and issues relating to state and county roads, including snow removal and street lighting.

The county has been an early adopter of technology and a promoter of transparent and efficient government (see Figure 8). The County Executive is committed to the county being an inclusive, innovative and transparent government that is accountable, responsive and maintains a strong and vibrant economy. The county has been a leader in open government since the launch of its e-Government website initiative in 1992. Since then, the county has sustained a strong commitment to digitizing its information and services. The county has proven its ability to successfully invest in, exploit and sustain emerging technologies on a large scale. This has been shown across many of its business areas including administration and general services, human capital management, public health, public safety, corrections, transportation and public works, and other lines of county business. As a trailblazer and innovative user of technology, the county has earned numerous national awards and recognitions.

The county is publishing county datasets in accordance with its published Open Data Implementation Plan that declares how and when the county should engage the public and hold civic events (such as hackathons and unconferences) for in-person public consultation.

The county is using the power of the web to transform citizens' lives. The county operates more than 400 miles of broadband cable known as the FiberNet. This connects more than 350 buildings across the county, including offices, schools, service locations and low-cost housing projects, to high-speed Internet services and hundreds of Wi-Fi hotspots.

The county passed legislation in 2012 to facilitate its efforts to build a 21st-century open government program to better serve its residents, employees and other partners. Consequently, the county launched its "openMontgomery" initiative consistent with its vision for the future Digital Montgomery County.

The county's Digital Government Strategy document is a "living document" containing a discussion on the roadmap of major programs, activities and milestones the county will follow toward achieving its goals. The openMontgomery strategy includes best practices the county has adopted from leading smart cities in the United States and abroad.

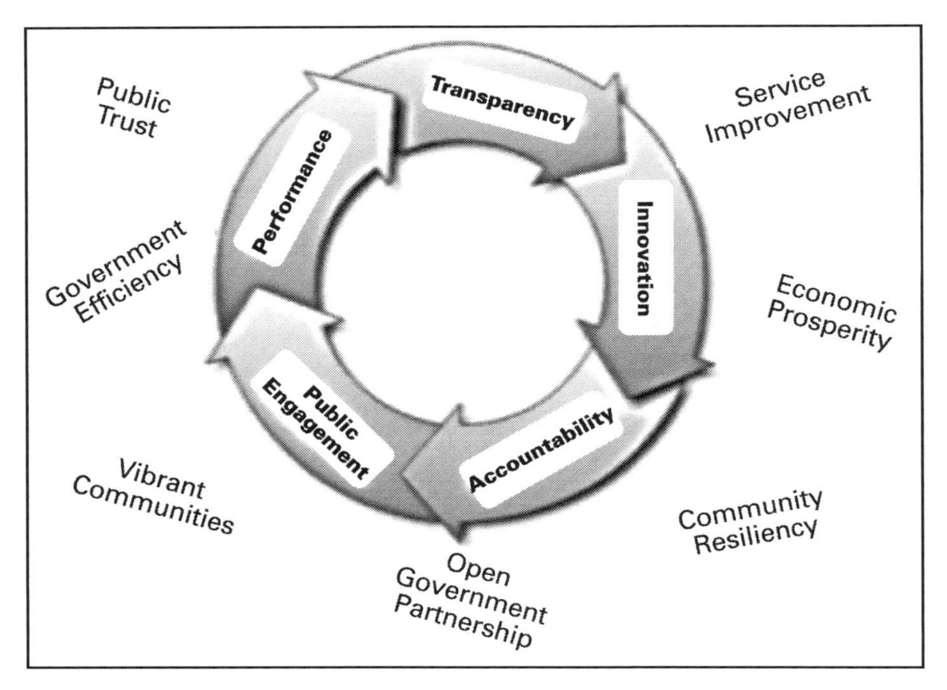

Figure 8. *Montgomery County's Open Government Focus Areas.*

The county's openMontgomery initiative (see Figure 9) embodies four pillar programs: accessMontgomery, dataMontgomery, mobileMontgomery, and engageMontgomery. Underlying the commitment to these programs is the county's ongoing effort to invest in facilitating technologies, business process redesign, innovation and staff development.

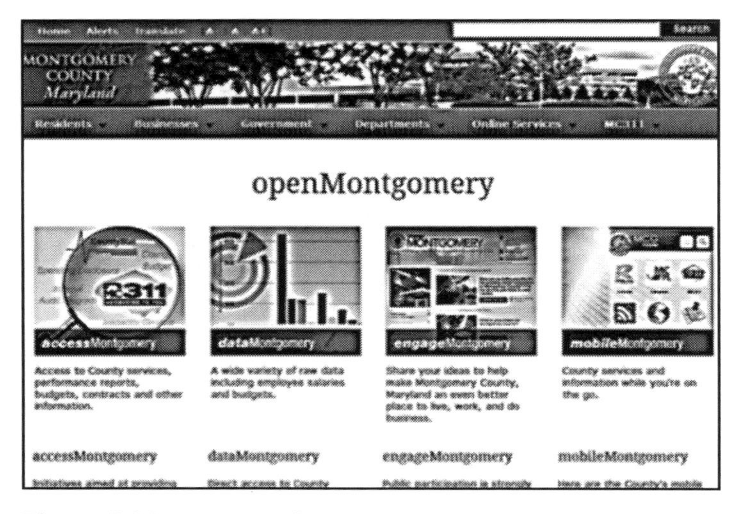

Figure 9. *Montgomery County's openMontgomery Program.*

Some of the major technology modernization initiatives of the county include Enterprise Resource Planning (ERP), state-of-the-art Constituent Relationship Management (CRM), Public Safety System Modernization (PSSM), data analytics and performance measurement (CountyStat), service oriented architecture (SOA), single-sign-on (SSO) and HTML5. These are described further in the county's Enterprise Technology Strategic Plan (ETSP) published on its website. These investments have prepared the county to securely exploit emerging disruptive mobile, social, cloud and information (analytics) technologies going forward.

In addition to its engageMontgomery program, the county directly and extensively communicates with residents through media and social media outlets: YouTube, Facebook, Twitter, the county's cable channel, and expanded distribution lists for electronic publications such as "The Paperless Airplane."

The County Executive has a Performance Management Program Office known as CountyStat. The County Council also has a performance oversight unit known as the Office of Legislative Oversight. In addition, the county has an independent Office of the Inspector General that reviews programs continuously for possible fraud, waste and abuse. The county hires numerous independent auditors to review county programs in great detail and make recommendations to the County Executive. The county posts its audit reports publicly and holds public hearings to discuss the findings and how the government proposes to address recommendations.

The CountyStat program was awarded the 2013 Certificate of Excellence by the International City/County Management Association's Center for Performance Measurement. The CountyStat program works on a results-based accountability system. CountyStat creates a culture of accountability by using real-time data to focus county departments' and employees' efforts, monitor and measure their performance and ensure that they provide an effective and efficient response to residents. This data-driven system provides strategic governance and increased government transparency (see Figure 10, next page). It requires decisions, actions, and policies that are driven by the extensive use of data, qualitative and quantitative analytics, and outcome-focused performance management based on "headline performance measures" that reflect each department's core mission and strategies for how to improve and optimize performance.

This effort creates greater accountability; provides better transparency into county challenges and successes; and ultimately helps ensure the implementation of a culture of "managing for results" in Montgomery County.

The county is constantly learning from smart cities. In recently establishing and funding an Innovation Office and appointing a chief innovation officer, the county was the first county to do so. The county's Innovation Program is fashioned after Boston's Office of New Urban Mechanics for process and service improvement, and has already identified 80 initiatives that will sustain its smart county status.

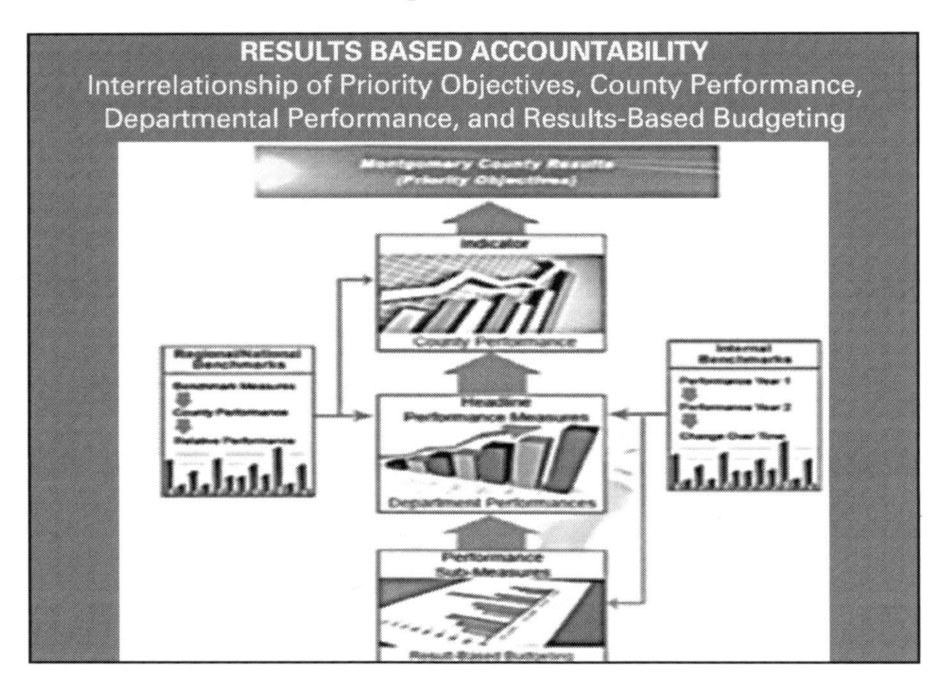

Figure 10. *Montgomery County's CountyStat Program.*

The county offers its web services in 72 languages. A variety of multilingual services for both young and old are made available for residents with limited English under the county's leading English-as-a-Second-Language Program.

The county allocates approximately 50 percent of its USD $4.5 billion budget to kindergarten through high school (K–12) education. All 25 high schools in the county are among the top 8 percent of high schools in the nation in academic performance.

The county has a low incidence of crime. It operates 911 and 311 systems for a highly effective public safety response by police, fire and medical rescue services.

As a part of its mobileMontgomery initiative (discussed above under openMontgomery), county residents are able to download mobile applications from the county's web portal or use the county's many thousands of mobile-ready web pages to find service information, make service requests and order and pay for county services (e.g., paying property taxes or monthly parking permits online with a credit card).

The county uses technology extensively in the communities. For example, it has implemented "pay-by-phone" technologies that allow customers to pay for metered parking using smart phones at approximately 11,000 parking meters, accounting for more than 80,000 transactions monthly.

Real-time bus information is made available at the bus stops on the county's Ride-On bus system, via "Ride-On RealTime" on the county website, smart phones, smart pads and the MC311 mobile application.

To improve public safety services to its citizens, the county has co-located its police, fire, transportation and homeland security functions into an expansive new public safety headquarters building with modern infrastructure and security. Improvements in automation provide all 1,600 officers in five law enforcement agencies the ability to check fingerprints and offender arrest histories, and to make incident reports via 2,000 mobile devices using the mobile AFIS and Law Enforcement Record Management Systems.

Smart Citizens

In the smart county model, the factors that constitute smart citizens include citizen participation and engagement in public affairs; cosmopolitanism and open-mindedness; commitment to human capital development including education and continued e-Learning; level of qualification of the public; life-long training; research and development; social and ethnic plurality; and social creativity (see Figure 11).

SMART CITIZENS (HUMAN CAPITAL)

- Citizen participation & engagement in public affairs
- Cosmopolitanism/open-mindedness
- Human Capital Development (Education & e-Learning)
- Level of qualification
- Life-long training
- Research & Development
- Social & ethnic plurality
- Social Creativity

Figure 11. *Smart Citizens.*

In the past decade of the 20th century, the county's minority population grew from 27 percent in 1990, to 40 percent of the total population in 2000. Almost half of Maryland's Hispanic and Latino population reside in Montgomery County. Almost 38 percent of county residents are foreign born. The following examples show how the county has successfully achieved a smart citizenry.

The county's social and ethnic plurality is evidenced in its ethnically diverse demographics. Approximately 50 percent of the population is white; 17 percent is Hispanic; 17 percent is African American and 14 percent is Asian-Pacific Islander.

The county constituency is cosmopolitan and open-minded. Despite the fact that it is home to world-class communities representing many countries, there are virtually no recorded cases of racial violence or conflict.

The county has one of the highest percentages of registered voters in the nation.

All segments of the county's demographics are well represented on almost 200 formal boards, commissions, task forces, committees and advisory groups, established by the county. Board and Commission members appointed by the County Executive and approved by the County Council have direct access to the County Executive and provide advice on all aspects of county government.

The county boasts one of the highest concentrations of doctorate degree (Ph.D.) holders in the United States. More than half (56 percent) of the adult population has at least one Bachelor's degree (twice the U.S. average) and 30 percent have graduate or professional degrees (almost three times the national average).

The Montgomery County Public Schools (MCPS) system has the following challenging 2011 statistics:

- Number of schools in system: 200
- Enrollment: 144,064 (Largest in Maryland, 16th largest in United States)
- Diversity: Students from 164 countries speaking 184 languages
- Number of Employees: 22,230 (Teachers: 11,675)
- 85.4 percent of teachers have a Master's degree or equivalent
- Special schools and alternative programs: 865

Positive statistics regarding education include:

- Eight out of 25 MCPS high schools made the 2013 Best High School rankings in *U.S. News & World Report*. MCPS had the top six high schools in the state of Maryland. U.S. News also ranked six MCPS high schools among the nation's best for science, technology, engineering and mathematics (STEM) education.
- Seventeen high schools made the annual list of America's Best High Schools, published by Newsweek. Two MCPS high schools made the top 100 nationally.

- MCPS has one of the highest graduation rates among the nation's largest school districts, according to an *Education Week* report.
- The county has a large number of private schools strategically located all over the county.
- The county government partners with its schools and college systems to coordinate and share training strategies and resources to ensure the county's efforts produce a smart citizenry across its diverse demographics.
- The county has one of the largest and most active library systems in the United States, which is continually upgraded as technology changes and the e-culture evolves. Today, the county has digital media and equipment available for check out. The county libraries have Digital Media Labs, supporting the work of students, job seekers, small businesses, teens, seniors and others who need access to modern software tools for business and for creating content. This sustains lifelong learning and collaborative content creation in the county.
- The county's top 10 State University systems are housed at the county's Universities at Shady Grove Campus. The county's Community College system has five campuses with a total enrollment of 65,000 students. The curriculum also caters to residents with an affinity for lifelong learning and continuing education.

When it comes to the workforce, Montgomery County is home to more than 100,000 advanced technology workers and boasts 19 federal research and regulatory agencies. The county's Linking Employers and Applicants Project (LEAP) partners with the county's Commission for Women to present job-skills training workshops. There are extensive training programs for county employees and mandatory core technology competencies for all staff. And the county maintains a high level of creativity and is recognized as having more entrepreneurs than any other county in the nation.

Montgomery County also fosters an emphasis on lifelong learning and qualification building skills through community partnerships, participation in author events, senior and job expos, heritage festivals and business seminars. To maintain a high degree of engagement in public life, creativity and social cohesion, the county organizes volunteers to provide book discussions, programs on business, financial accounting, resume writing and job search assistance. Teen volunteers staff programs on electronic devices such as iPads and Kindle for other age groups. Service to seniors is provided in the libraries, recreation centers and the service centers.

As a demonstration of public involvement, it is worthy to note that the county has a combined career and volunteer firefighting force. In 2012, more than 350 county residents received training and became members of the Community Emergency Response Team to perform rescue services. Overall, there is a high degree of participation and engagement by the citizens in public life. The 200 active boards and commissions mentioned earlier cover every aspect of county services and facilitate smart governance. They engage and work with aware citizens in order to create independent and interdependent groups for public consensus building.

Smart Living

In the smart county model, the factors that constitute smart living include accessibility and e-inclusion; top-notch cultural and educational facilities; excellent health conditions and housing quality; individual safety; social cohesion (sector interconnectedness) and touristic attractiveness (see Figure 12).

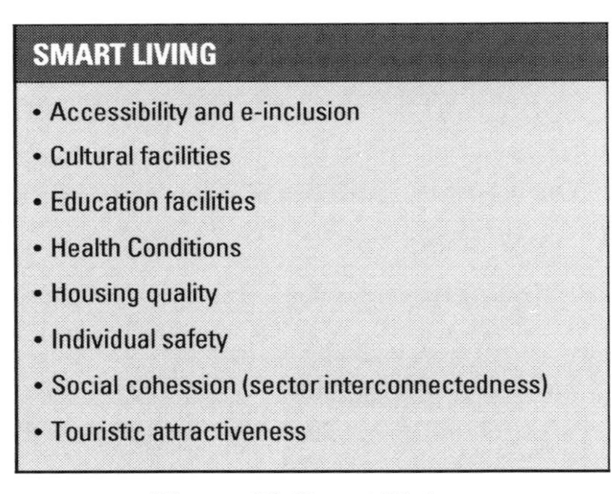

Figure 12. *Smart Living.*

Montgomery County has a robust, creative community that includes more htan 350 cultural organizations and 1,200 artists and scholars. The following are some examples of how the county is promoting smart living.

It is home to a variety of top-quality cultural venues from which to choose—plays, concerts, exhibits, lectures—as well as arts education programs that encourage individual artistic development. The county has 60 galleries; 22 theaters; 50 historic venues; upscale shopping, including 33 department stores; over 900 restaurants serving a variety of cuisines; and 743 boutiques and specialty stores.

The county has a world-class Performing Arts community, which includes the Music Center at Strathmore, a 2,000-seat concert hall whose key resident partner is the Baltimore Symphony Orchestra, which performs 35 concerts a year at this facility; the American Film Institute (AFI) and The Fillmore Silver Spring, both in Silver Spring, Montgomery County's arts district; the Bethesda Blues and Jazz Supper Club, featuring world-renowned music and authentic Creole cuisine, all in a renovated Art Deco cinema palace; Adventure Theatre at Glen Echo Park; Imagination Stage in Bethesda; Black Rock Center for the Arts in Germantown; Montgomery College Performing Arts Center; Olney Theatre Center; and Round House Theatre.

The county's visual arts center in Rockville includes VisArts and Pyramid Atlantic. In addition, there is easy access to a variety of venues in the Washington, D.C., and Baltimore regions, including Merriweather Post Pavilion, Rams Head Live, 9:30 Club, Verizon Center, John F. Kennedy Center for the Performing Arts, Wolf Trap National Park, and many more.

The county's many walkable neighborhoods create a strong sense of place (see Figure 13). One of many examples is the revitalized Silver Spring Business District and neighboring communities.

Figure 13. *Montgomery County, Maryland's Walkable Neighborhoods.*

The county has hundreds of ethnic-based community organizations including chambers of commerce, professional associations, hometown associations, language schools, senior groups and arts organizations. Dozens of foreign language newspapers and other publications for the global communities in the national capital regions are readily available. The Gilchrist Center for Cultural Diversity caters to the needs of immigrants at every step of their life with three locations.

The Maryland-National Capital Park and Planning Commission (MNCPPC) maintains more than 345 parks (more than 30,000 acres) offering a range of recreational opportunities, including Brookside Gardens, an award-winning 50-acre public display garden. The region also has a variety of trails, including the Capital Crescent Trail, which is one of the most heavily used rail trails (now shared use) trails in the United States.

The Maryland SoccerPlex welcomes more than 600,000 visitors a year to its 24 irrigated soccer fields and 5,200-seat capacity Championship Stadium. There is easy transportation access to all four national professional teams (Redskins, Nationals, Capitals, Wizards) that support the region, as well as University of Maryland Terrapins sports teams.

The county has made 105 layers of GIS information available in searchable form. One search criteria is bike trails. The bicycle sharing program features 350 bikes and 50 bike-docking stations located throughout the county. Two communities, Rockville and Bethesda, have been named Bicycle Friendly Communities by the League of American Bicyclists.

The county has a world-class conference center. The Bethesda North Marriott Conference Center is a 100,000 square foot, state-of-the-art facility coupled with a recently expanded, full-service 450-room Marriott Hotel. This facility contains 40,000 square feet of dedicated meeting space, including a 23,408 square foot ballroom and 13,000 square feet of high quality meeting rooms with a 130-seat amphitheater. The facility also houses 20,000 square feet of public open space, which can be used for exhibits, receptions and other pre-function purposes. It has the largest meeting facility in Montgomery County and one of the largest ballrooms in the Washington, D.C. metropolitan area (see Figure 14).

Figure 14. *Montgomery County Conference Center.*

To promote a smart mind in a smart body, the county maintains a large number of centers for learning. The county has created the Circulation Steering Committee and the Senior & Disability Steering Committees to advise and assist in the implementation of services and programs. By contrast and design, and through strong preservation laws, it is also home to 93,000 acres of Agricultural Land Reserve, which provide the backdrop for a thriving agricultural economy.

County public safety operations have a combination of landline, cell and voice over internet protocol (VoIP) 911 trunks, alarm lines, non-emergency lines, and administrative lines. The county's public safety operations receive more than 850,000 calls per year with emergency calls totaling more than 550,000. Cell phones account for 70 percent of calls, and that amount continues to rise.

The county's state-of-the-art non-emergency hotline and service center closed more than 1.5 million service requests in its first two years of operation within specified service level agreements. The county uses data analytics on the data captured about its service requests to continually improve service quality and response.

The county has some of the toughest enforcement of anti-discrimination laws in the country. It has the lowest incidence of hate crimes given the highly diverse population of the county. To keep its streets, schools and neighborhoods safe, the county operates 911 and 311 systems. The 911 system handles emergencies only that require immediate assistance from the police, fire and rescue or ambulance. Non-emergency services are handled by the 311 system, which is also available online and via mobile phone. Trained representatives speak several foreign languages including Spanish, Vietnamese, French, Mandarin and Cantonese. The county also subscribes to a language interpretation service with more than 100 languages available.

To go along with its walkable neighborhood program, the county has increased the number of county police officers by 120, including an increase in the number of school resource officers, based on analysis of crime statistics using workload analysis and deployment studies.

The county also restored 29 firefighter-rescuer positions to improve staffing levels and abate overtime. The county has been awarded a Staffing for Adequate Fire and Emergency Response (SAFER) Grant by the U.S. Department of Homeland Security. This grant will allow for the hiring of additional firefighter-rescuers.

Smart Environment

In the smart county model, the factors that constitute a smart environment include environmental protection laws; green buildings and urban planning; green energy; monitoring and control devices; and sustainable resource management (see Figure 15).

SMART ENVIRONMENT

- Environmental protection
- Green buildings & urban planning
- Green energy (end users aware devices)
- Monitoring (sensor based) & control
- Sustainable resource management

Figure 15. *Smart Environment.*

The following examples show how the county is successfully preserving a smart environment. One-third of the county is open space, including 93,000 acres of preserved farmland (See Figure 16: Montgomery County's Agricultural Reserve) and 27,395 acres of parkland. Three large regional parks complement a network of many local neighborhood parks and green spaces, two state parks and one national park, and 131 acres of lakes. Seven public golf courses and numerous swimming and tennis courts are also available throughout the county. Year-round amateur and professional sports available in the area include football, baseball, tennis, hockey, soccer, and lacrosse, as well as thoroughbred racing. The nearby Chesapeake Bay and Atlantic Ocean beach areas offer a wide range of water recreational activities.

Additionally, the county has a Forest Conservation Law and regulates the loss of tree canopy. The county has passed tree canopy preservation legislation to preserve lush green landscapes and to keep the pollution level low. The amendments are designed to protect and provide for mitigation when forest and tree canopy is lost as a result of development. The proposed approach was developed in consultation with a broad range of stakeholders.

Figure 16. *Montgomery County's Agricultural Reserve.*

The county's waste recycling programs are aggressive and highly successful. They recycle almost 50 percent of the county's waste—one of the highest recycling rates in the nation—with more than 30,000 tons of comingled waste and an additional 55,000 tons of paper products recycled each year. The county also deploys co-generative furnace technology at its solid waste disposal facility. It has also converted its buses and solid waste disposal equipment to use biodiesel fuels. The county requires the use of compressed natural gas (CNG) vehicles by its refuse contractors and other operators.

Being an affluent county, Montgomery maintains an aggressive e-waste recycling program and recycles over 100 tons of consumer electronics each month. Other collection programs include household hazardous waste, yard waste, scrap metal and used oil. The county also has a program for collecting and recycling ash and additional ferrous and non-ferrous metals. This is aimed at recycling construction and demolition debris and other materials.

In a move to encourage consumers to use recyclable shopping bags and to keep its environment clean, the county has implemented a "bag tax" that collects approximately USD $1 million annually from nearly 1,000 registered businesses.

As a part of its Keep Montgomery County Beautiful program, the county sponsors an Adopt A Road (AAR) program that involves residents and businesses in the county to keep more than 700 miles of road litter free.

The county also has implemented an extensive stormwater management program.

All new and significantly modified non-residential buildings over 10,000 square feet, whether funded with public or private money, must be LEED (Leadership in Energy and Environmental Design) Silver certified.

The county is using Energy Efficiency and Conservation Block Grant funds for seven programs to accelerate the adoption of energy efficiency and renewable energy in county, commercial and residential buildings.

The county has installed diesel emissions control equipment on county vehicles through grant awards from the Mid-Atlantic Regional Air Management Administration and the Maryland Department of the Environment.

Meanwhile, Montgomery County leverages state-of-the-art electronic communications employing various web technologies that make it easier and faster for citizens to connect with the county, request services and access information. Such communications channels include:

- Blog: "Talkin' Trash" (with Real Simple Syndication feed);
- Twitter announcements and updates (@GoGreenMC and @ TalkinTrashMC);

- Flickr account for photo viewing and sharing;
- DVD content available as YouTube videos;
- Email subscription service for news alerts;
- Electronic newsletters;
- Text Alerts for mobile devices; and
- Widgets available for homeowners' associations, third-party websites and blogs so that they can feed recycling/trash news directly to their members.

As an example, the county operates numerous online programs that encourage conservation techniques. One such program has to do with connecting users and disposers of cooking oil, which is hard to dispose and keep out of the nearby Chesapeake Bay, a national treasure constituting the largest estuary in the United States and one of the largest and most biologically productive estuaries in the world.

The county has formulated a Watershed Implementation Strategy that includes stormwater permitting, the Potomac River Trash Free Treaty and total maximum daily load (TMDL) limits.

The RainScapes Rewards program, which cost-shares the installation of techniques to capture and treat stormwater on private property in dense, urban settings, is a national model.

To conserve energy, Montgomery County has a program to promote the use of programmable thermostats on home and business heating ventilation and air conditioning systems. The county installed hundreds of such devices for citizens upon request. The county has an active solar energy program and has installed solar panels on county facilities in a joint program with the Maryland Energy Administration, a Maryland-based green energy firm. The county has a program supporting the purchase of renewable energy by the Non-Profit Energy Alliance. The Alliance is an informal collaborative of nonprofit organizations that joined forces to purchase energy at lower cost than utility standard offer service.

The county implemented its Green Business Certification Program, which supports and recognizes county businesses/organizations that take environmentally responsible actions. The program, managed in partnership with the Montgomery County Chamber of Commerce and Montgomery College, has certified 55 businesses with more in the pipeline.

The countywide energy efficiency programs funded Energy Efficiency & Conservation Block Grants to use for 1) improvements to county buildings, 2) grants to private sector entities undertaking energy efficiency improvements, 3) workforce development, 4) energy improvements for housing low income residents, and 5) energy education and outreach.

The countywide energy efficiency programs funded Energy Efficiency & Conservation Block Grants to use for 1) improvements to county buildings, 2) grants to private sector entities undertaking energy efficiency improvements, 3) workforce development, 4) energy improvements for housing low income residents, and 5) energy education and outreach.

Use of computer-based tracking systems allows accurate tracking of and timely response to environmental site assessments and information on code enforcement cases. Several departments jointly model environmental challenges to anticipate illegal activities and create "hotspot" maps.

Smart Mobility

In the smart county model, the factors that constitute smart mobility include availability of ICT infrastructure (wireless/mobile services); international accessibility; local accessibility infrastructure; and sustainable, innovative and safe transport systems (see Figure 17).

SMART MOBILITY

- Availability of ICT infrastructure (wireless/mobile services)
- International accessibility
- Local accessibility infrastructure
- Sustainable, innovative & safe transport systems

Figure 17. *Smart Mobility.*

The following examples show how the county has successfully achieved smart mobility.

The county has been a forerunner in investing in broadband technologies. It operates a 450-mile, high-capacity fiber broadband network known as FiberNet. This connects more than 350 county buildings, including offices, schools, service locations and low-cost housing projects to high-speed internet services and hundreds of Wi-Fi hot spots. The county is one of the most prolific users of e-learning in the country through the use of its networks and communications infrastructure.

This network is used by the county to utilize advanced traffic management systems to synchronize traffic signals, monitor traffic crossings and streets through video surveillance, promote voice data services, and provide back haul networks for public safety radio communication systems.

The county is planning to increase its reach by connecting to and interoperating with the State of Maryland's Inter-County Broadband Network, ICBN, and the National Capital Region's network, NCRNet. The county is making huge gains in providing broadband connectivity to its components. Interconnects to ICBN and NCRnet further promote the county's digitalization efforts.

The rapid commoditization and consumerization of information technology among employees, citizens and business partners is encouraging the county to evolve its open data initiatives and its need to promote the acquisition of open-data-powered applications, whether they are insourced, outsourced or crowd-sourced. The county is focused on improving efficiency and bringing value to its communities. To foster this, the county's goal is to invest in open government programs that contribute to the creation of an ecosystem of interoperable open services within the government, across its external agencies [Ref. 13] (including K–12 and higher education), the private sector and the county's active network of nonprofit entities.

The county is rapidly growing its mobile services portfolio and open-data-powered application offerings. The county is also seeking solutions from its vendors, and subscribing to secure commercial solutions including common cloud platforms to offer even more services to citizens and partners anywhere.

Montgomery County wants to seize opportunities to improve electronic service delivery and sustaining these programs during tight budget periods by obtaining value from internal transparency and decreasing the level of effort required to provide information to residents. As experienced in some European countries, this opening of data could release value for social and commercial entities not only in the county and region, but also on a national and international scale. The county is involving other jurisdictions, research and educational institutions, nonprofits and for-profit sectors to partner in improving services and efficiencies.

The county's openMontgomery program encourages these entities to consume its data (in conjunction with data from other sources, e.g., State of Maryland, Chamber of Commerce, Census, comparable governments) to help make data-driven decisions about the county's services in conjunction with their own services.

Meanwhile, the county deploys low power sensor networks to monitor pollution levels and embedded sensors in roadways and street lights to manage real-time transit and traffic and reduce travel time and fuel inefficiencies.

Montgomery County serves as a regional transportation hub with access to a full range of modes of transportation.

The county has more than 4,000 lane miles of roadways (See Figure 18: Montgomery County's Smart Roads) within its 490 square mile area. The major interstate highways include the Interstate-270 (I-270), commonly known as the "270 Technology Corridor"; I-495, the Washington Beltway;

I-370; US Route 29; and MD 200 known as the Intercounty Connector, a newly opened road which connects the county directly to I-95, Baltimore and points east.

Figure 18. *Montgomery County's Smart Roads.*

The county's highways have high occupancy vehicle (HOV) lanes and it is participating in the regional smart lanes program mainly on its segment of the Capital Beltway.

The county also is served by railways, including the Metrorail rapid transit system that offers 12 county stations, a part of the 103-mile regional network connecting Maryland, Virginia, and Washington, D.C. The MARC (Maryland Area Regional Commuter) train has three stops in the county.

The two major bus systems include Metro Bus and the county's Ride-On bus system. The latter features more than 100 different routes across the county.

Air transportation is provided by three major airports: Baltimore/ Washington International Thurgood Marshall, Ronald Reagan Washington International, and Dulles International. All are less than an hour's distance and together provide domestic and international access on almost all major carriers.

The Port of Baltimore with a 50-foot-deep channel is less than an hour from the county and is a leading automobile and break-bulk port, with seven public terminals including luxury cruise line terminals.

On Becoming a Smarter County

To become an even smarter county, Montgomery County plans to:

1. Continue implementing and maturing the many successful programs it has currently implemented in all six of the smart counties business areas.
2. Evaluate successful strategies for replication or adaption from one business area to another.
3. Span the public and private sectors for examples of emerging innovations, whether people-, process-, and/or technology-assisted, that make for a smarter county, and evaluate them for adoption.
4. Leverage the *Counties Open Government Innovation Partnership* that Montgomery County has proposed to the nation's counties.

Examples of the county's plans to become even smarter in all six smart county domains are listed below along with potential benefits.

- Continue leveraging current economic successes and image to fully consummate trade agreements with sister cities in China, Germany and India to participate in a larger share of the growing global economy.
- Leverage investments in transformation from a suburban to a more urban economy through the revitalization of cities as a part of the newMontgomery Program and the Night-time Economy Program.
- Maintain the AAA (credit) bond ratings to be able to borrow more capital at lower interest rates than other cities and counties pay with lower credit ratings
- Show leadership in continuing to oppose and lobby against the implementation of federal tax laws or law reform that discourage capital borrowing and investment by counties (one such tax law reform is under consideration at the time of this writing).
- Continue investing in education, skills training, and ICT for the benefits of continuing to grow a smart citizenry and future smart workforce that are the very key to current economic differentiators, as well to sustaining a resilient economy.
- Leverage Cloud-based solutions and technologies for interagency sharing.
- Continue growing e-Democracy by being even more transparent and accountable; engaging the public through further implementation of the openMontgomery program, which includes opening more government data under the dataMontgomery program; increasing public consultation through the engageMontgomery

program; mobilizing an increased number of services via the mobile services program mobileMontgomery; continually upgrading information channels, including the expanded use of the award-winning websites and social media channels under the accessMontgomery program.

- Continue to pursue an "open services" model as the next maturity level in the county's dataMontgomery program.
- Maintain smart political policies and perspectives at the state and federal government levels. Leverage the existing governance structure (in all three branches of government) along with performance management and oversight offices to ensure the best return on investments.
- Continue being more transparent and accountable by implementing the vision, principles, and roadmap published in 2012 as a part of the county's Digital Government Strategy document.
- Create an advocacy for the county's open government programs by leveraging the proposal the county sponsored last year at the NACo to form a U.S.-wide *Counties' Open Government Innovation Partnership,* which will partner with the White House's International Open Government Partnership and the City Mayors' Open Government Innovation Partnership. The Partnership proposes to:
    - Provide a forum for the identification and sharing of practices and experiences in improving government transparency, service efficiency and effectiveness, community engagement and collaboration, public-private service coordination, and economic development.
    - Build an ecosystem of open county governments and open government practices that all NACo member counties can share, exchange, and advance to innovate and improve government services and the quality of life in their communities.
- Continue to fully leverage investments in ICT; as an example by extending the use of ERP and Identity and Access Management System (IAMS) to other departments and functions and automating business-to-government (supply chain) processes.
- Continue to develop, implement and maintain technology and cyber security strategic plans to avoid breaches of citizens' data and information, interruption to services, and legal liability.
- Continue to leverage investment in the county's Innovation Program to promote people-, process-, and technology (ICT)- driven innovation.

- Capitalize on the opportunity provided by the President's Healthcare Reform Act grants to overhaul the way the county delivers public and social services.
- Invest in technologies that support integrated case management, electronic health records, and electronic records management.
- Continue to stay actively engaged with the 200+ public advisory boards, committees and commissions.
- Continue to leverage CountyStat and OLO programs to measure the effectiveness of government programs and to recommend corrective actions for executive level consideration and implementation.
- Pilot the next generation City 24/7 revenue generating kiosk in downtown Silver Spring and Bethesda.
- Continue attracting highly qualified individuals into the county through the Management Leadership Service at competitive compensation levels.
- Create IT expert and functional expert job series to establish career paths for highly skilled, hard-to-attract professionals within county government.
- Leverage public-private partnerships to benefit the constituents' services and lessen fiscal burden on government and the taxpayers.
- Increase citizen participation and engagement in budget formulation and development policies.
- Increase commitment to human capital development including education and continued e-Learning.
- Continue to attract research and development organizations to foster and promote innovation in high technology fields for future strength and job creation.
- Leverage the Transportation Reserve Fund to manage impact of growth and decrease congestion.
- Maintain social and ethnic plurality in order to preserve harmonious and progressive communities working together for best overall outcomes and vibrancy.
- Ensure all sectors thrive through the living arts in order to foster social creativity and imagination.
- Continue expansion of accessibility programs and e-inclusion programs in the public schools, public libraries, citizens services centers, elder and senior living centers.

- Continue examination of changes required in current law that could accelerate the expansion of the use of broadband networks in all demographic sectors through public-private partnerships and revenue sharing models.
- Continue investment in educational facilities to promote smarter future generation for the global economy.
- Continue publishing data regarding health conditions and inspections to promote compliance with county laws and objectives to promote sound public health for all.
- Continue affordable housing programs even as property values and rentals increase with a strengthening economy; continue the Moderately Priced Dwelling Unit Program and the Section 8 housing programs.
- Continue to fund the Technology Modernization Program by funding the Public Safety Systems Modernization to include upgrades to the public safety radio systems infrastructure, the computer-aided dispatch system and the fire station alerting system; continue to integrate the county's customer relationship management with back-end work order fulfillment systems; and upgrade the county's voice and data communications infrastructures for improved constituent services.
- Continue to pursue a nighttime economy to promote safe "hang-outs" and places for people to congregate to foster continued social cohesion.
- Continue to lead regional inter-jurisdictional efforts to promote public safety and disaster resilience across local borders.
- Continue to pursue increased interconnectedness, cooperation and sharing of knowledge and solutions (e.g., shared IT services and platforms connected by the county's fiber network or the cloud) between the county's external agencies (e.g., the Washington Suburban Sanitary Commission, the Maryland-National Capital Park and Planning Commission); this will promote improvement of a longer chain of services.
- Continue the tree canopy preservation legislation and other programs that promote touristic attractiveness to grow the local economy and preserve the environment.
- Continue to plan for use of emerging technologies (e.g., internet TV-based kiosks) for use in areas where the customers have limited mobility (e.g., seniors' centers).

- Expand the county's night time economy by adding more walkable neighborhoods, creating a strong sense of place using the revitalized Silver Spring Business District as a model.
- Continue funding from federal grants (Community Development Block Grant (CDBG), the HOME Investment Partnership Grant (HOME), and the Emergency Solutions Grant (ESG) to provide funding for affordable housing, rehabilitation, commercial revitalization, focused neighborhood assistance, public services, and preventing homelessness.
- Continue to expand services to low density population areas.
- Add two Linkages to Learning sites to provide prevention and early intervention services, including physical and mental health, social services, and educational support to students and their families.
- Make employment opportunities available for retired residents and young people to intern in government and the private sector.
- Improve the capacity to serve Montgomery County's immigrant population by strengthening the network of public and private partners.
- Strengthen the county's safety net, by adding nearly USD $2.8 million to the county's refundable earned income tax credit (EITC) to provide expanded support for low income working families in Montgomery County. The county's EITC will serve almost 39,000 residents in the county in 2014 and increase the match of the state's EITC from 75 percent to 85 percent.
- Establish a senior transportation initiative through a partnership between county agencies and the nonprofit community, to enhance access to county facilities and programs serving older adults. Leverage senior centers as the base for expanded senior transportation initiatives.
- Substantially increase the county's investment in e-books to meet significantly increased customer demand, while continuing to meet the diverse needs and high demand for print and media library materials. Expand the range of the e-books collection to include more items in more topic areas.
- Fund and support the successful implementation of the Electronic Health Record System to interface with the state of Maryland's Health Information Exchange.
- Launch the "Be Active Montgomery!" campaign. The campaign aims to improve the overall health and wellness of county residents by encouraging active participation in county recreation and park facilities

and programs. The initiative will serve as a public and private partnership between county agencies and private organizations.

- Develop and implement a food recovery system to increase food donations that will be distributed to people in need.
- Continue working toward the implementation of universal 911 call-takers to improve emergency response.
- Create tsenior,disability and circulation steering committees to address special needs programming on the county's public, education and government (PEG) TV channels.
- Continue to implement and scale environmental protection laws to promote green buildings and urban planning.
- Invest in mobility monitoring, coordination and optimization systems along with public communication systems.
- Work with the power industry to promote the use of green energy; incent the public to participate in energy conservation programs through the use of smart sensors and devices.
- Promote sustainable resource management.
- Expand investment in high availability, high capacity ICT infrastructures (wireless/mobile services) to the public.
- Continue growing international accessibility through electronic and physical means.
- Continue to grow the local accessibility infrastructure for a bus rapid transit (BRT) vehicle system and a light rail line to further connect various cities and locals both within and outside the county to shorten commute times, reduce dependence on cars and reduce pollution.
- Develop sustainable, innovative and safe transport systems.
- Continue efforts to develop toll roads and to maximize the use of smart interoperating infrastructures to enhance quality of life.

Potential Challenges

In previous discussion, we examined Montgomery County's specific smart county traits. The potential challenges in developing smart county traits are not specific to Montgomery County. They relate to many of the U.S. counties, and may even be applicable to their suburban and urban equivalents around the globe.

In inculcating and sustaining smart county traits, most counties will encounter and must overcome some potential barriers in the following areas to move closer to smart county status. They are:

- Statutory limits in the county code and legislation that unintentionally serve to limit transformation options.
- Long-term contractual obligations and debt service that impede or preclude timely actions.
- An increase in the numbers of local natural disasters due to climate change requiring heavy investment in public safety response (including 911 and 311 systems), recovery and community involvement.
- Growing ethnic diversity in the U.S. communities and in the public schools (See Figure 19) levy a demand for language and culturally targeted services, including education and health services.

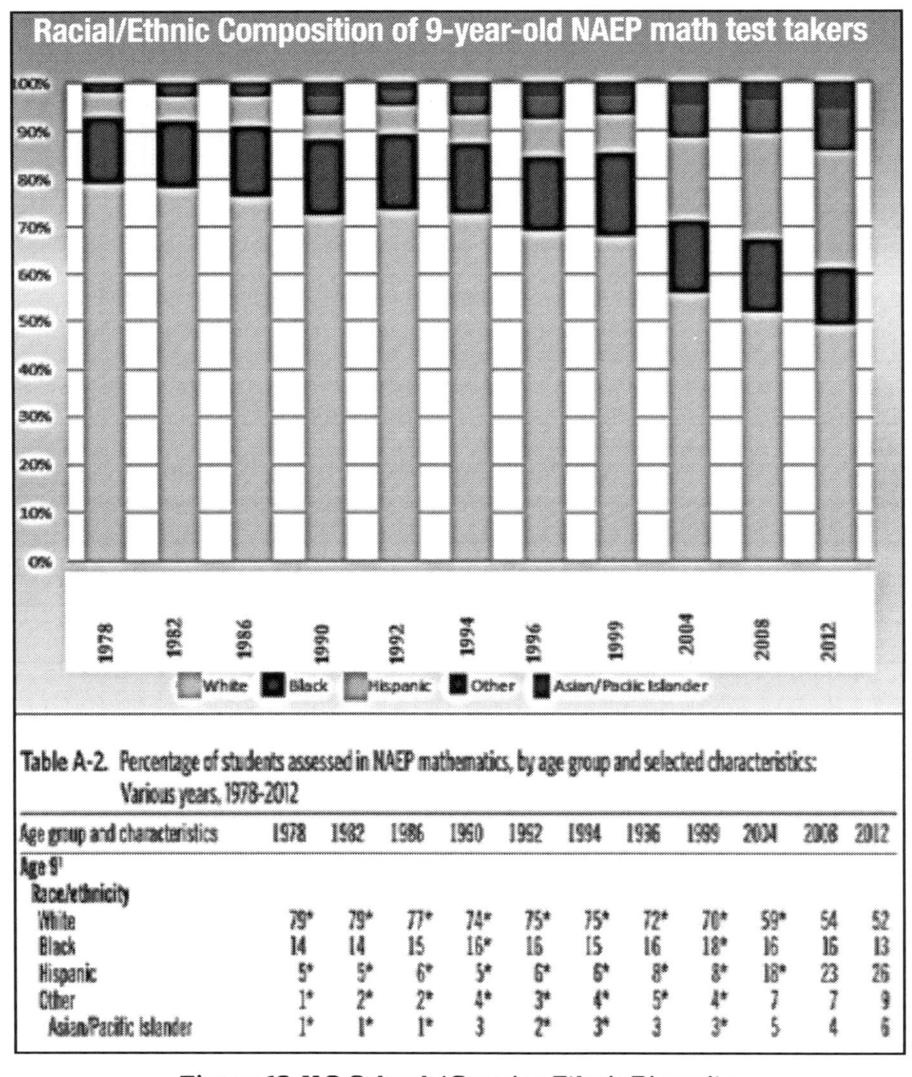

Table A-2. Percentage of students assessed in NAEP mathematics, by age group and selected characteristics: Various years, 1978-2012

Age group and characteristics	1978	1982	1986	1990	1992	1994	1996	1999	2004	2008	2012
Age 9[1]											
Race/ethnicity											
White	79*	79*	77*	74*	75*	75*	72*	70*	59*	54	52
Black	14	14	15	16*	16	15	16	18*	16	16	13
Hispanic	5*	5*	6*	5*	6*	6*	8*	8*	18*	23	26
Other	1*	2*	2*	4*	3*	4*	5*	4*	7	7	9
Asian/Pacific Islander	1*	1*	1*	3	2*	3*	3	3*	5	4	6

Figure 19. *U.S. Schools' Growing Ethnic Diversity.*

- An increasingly educated constituency (see Figure 20) coupled with the consumerization of technology (e.g., smart phones and the internet of things) with growing expectations for more and increasingly sophisticated services from local government.

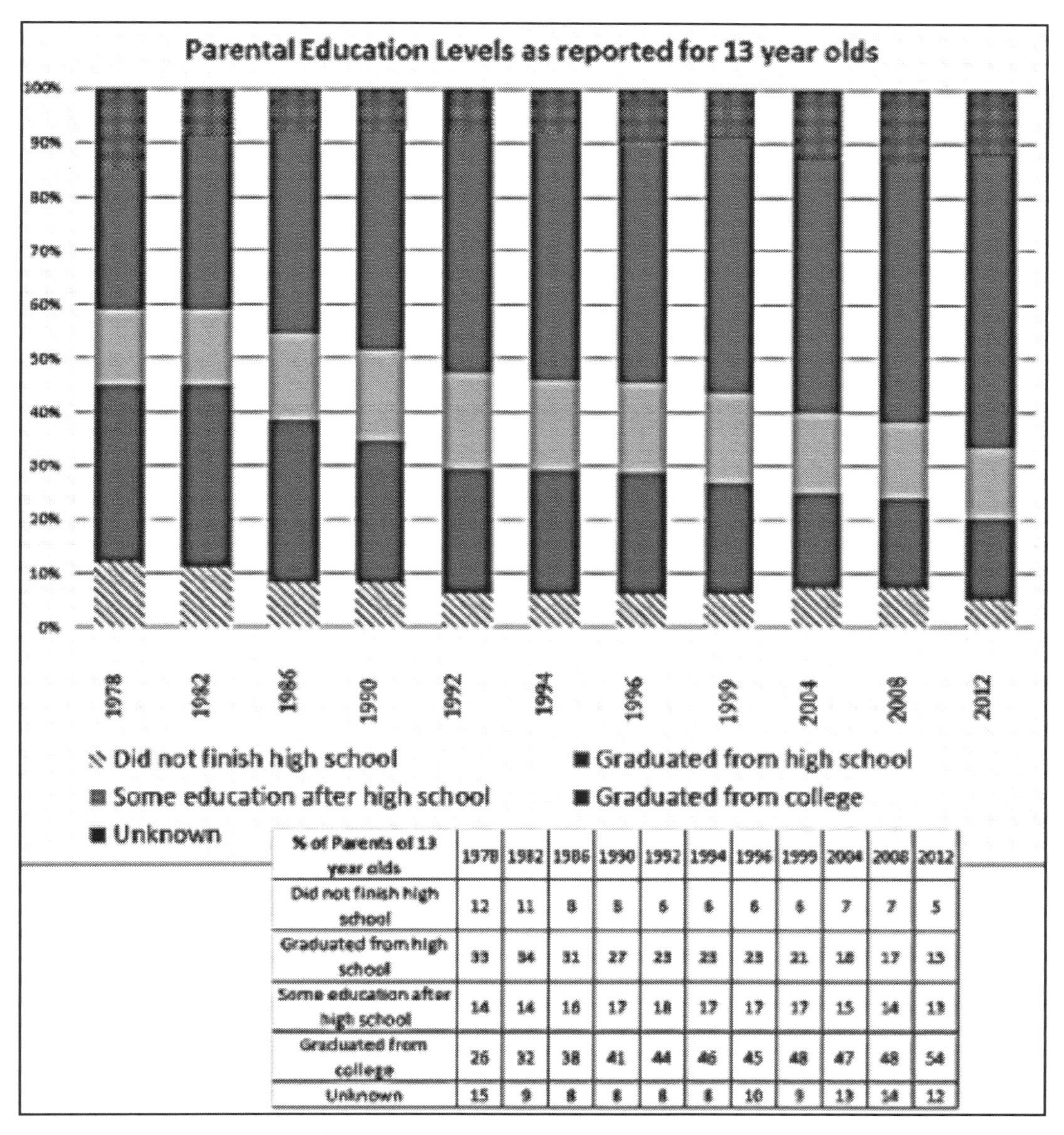

% of Parents of 13 year olds	1978	1982	1986	1990	1992	1994	1996	1999	2004	2008	2012
Did not finish high school	12	11	8	8	6	6	6	6	7	7	5
Graduated from high school	33	34	31	27	23	23	23	21	18	17	13
Some education after high school	14	14	16	17	18	17	17	17	15	14	13
Graduated from college	26	32	38	41	44	46	45	48	47	48	54
Unknown	15	9	8	8	8	8	10	9	13	14	12

Figure 20. *U.S. Adult Education Trends.*

- A growing digital divide among the Millennial and Baby Boomer generations (almost 60 years apart in age) requiring e-Government services to be designed for a wide range of demographics. Millennials are digital natives and live in a digital world, while Baby Boomers are digital immigrants who foray into the digital world to pay bills and such.

- An aging U.S. population requiring targeted services to ensure quality and mobility.
- Growth of the sector of economically disadvantaged or disengaged populations requiring sustainment services.
- Power and ICT services availability in expansive, low-density rural areas typical of counties.
- The escalating cost of services exacerbated by a deteriorating economic outlook and revenue.
- Growing competitive pressure to attract and retain top talent and businesses, while providing quality public service and balancing tight budgets.
- Lack of willingness among sectors to partner, e.g., public-private sectors, to alleviate the stress on government budgets and services by cross-pollinating best and smart services practices and by fostering 'open services" in more lines of government business (e.g., by sharing open data for projects in the public commons).
- A lack of standards across jurisdictions so data and information can be more readily shared and consumed to make smart decisions and enunciate policy.
- A lack of central control over all agencies of government (e.g., education, utilities, land development, public housing) keeps the Executive and Legislative Branches from realizing the full benefit; the challenge is that some agencies (e.g., education) have state and federal funding they are responsible for using under strict guidelines from the funders.
- State levied controls. Whereas state laws allow counties considerable flexibility in their governance structure and policies, many states, reeling from their own fiscal woes, impose levies on the counties such as asking the counties to pay school teachers' pensions or share local telecommunications revenues (e.g., cable franchise fees) with the state. Often, the states use the revenue to distribute iaid more evenly among their counties or to maintain state provided services.
- Federal controls. State and local governments financed more than USD $1.65 trillion of infrastructure investment in the past decade (2003–2012) through the tax-exempt bond market. Ninety (90) percent of infrastructure muni bonds financing went to schools, hospitals, water, sewer facilities, public power utilities, roads and mass

> transit in the past 10 years. Eliminating the deduction or including it as part of any cap on deductions would increase the borrowing costs that public entities will have to pay for infrastructure improvements. In short, by repealing the tax exempt status of municipal bonds by the federal government for infrastructure purposes issued over the past 10 years is more than USD $495 billion. The effect will be increased costs to the public for infrastructure and, therefore, less funding for teachers, fire and police officers, hospital workers, librarians and construction and maintenance workers. Any change to the tax-exempt status of municipal bonds will result in less overall infrastructure spending, fewer jobs and dampened economic activity.

Finally, local government policies could serve to perpetuate a cycle of change and need that emanates from the very policies that they implement to become smart counties. For example, the more certain counties invest in public health and education and economic development programs, the more people they attract. This perpetuates growth in all sectors. This growth requires a commensurate government response, which brings even more growth and need for services. Ultimately, this makes it imperative for the counties to embark on sustainable smart government programs.

Summary

As demographics shift to the world's urban areas, smart cities and smart counties are differentiating themselves by inculcating almost 40 traits discussed in this case study of Maryland's Montgomery County, an East Coast smart county in the United States. These traits permeate all six domains (i.e., smart economy, smart governance, smart citizens, smart living, smart environment and smart mobility) that encompass local government services. By growing such smart traits, cities and counties can ensure that the evolving needs of the constituents, communities and environment are met in transportation, infrastructure, energy, water, waste, public safety, education, health care, buildings and citizen services. Finally, smart counties and smart cities cannot achieve this status solely by acting individually or regionally. They must learn from and work with each other to create best practices and bodies of knowledge using public data analytics. To this extent we discussed Montgomery County's proposal for a Counties Open Government Partnership that could connect with corresponding open government partnerships at the city, state and national levels to enable governments to work together to create a sustainable environment.

HARASH SEGAL *is Montgomery County, Maryland's Chief Information Officer. He serves as the chief technology manager for the county and is responsible for an operating budget of USD $35 million plus a capital budget of USD $300 million. His responsibilities include information and communications technology management, including technology and cyber security strategy planning, broadband communications, technology acquisition and operations, technology innovation, and coordination of the growth of the county's ICT sector. Segal is a member of the county Executive's cabinet; a member of Governor Martin O'Malley's Maryland State-wide Interoperability Executive Commission; a member of the Metropolitan Washington Council of Governments CIOs Committee; a member of the National Association of Counties CIOs Committee; and a member of the Public Technology Institute CIOs Forum.*

Thanks goes to ***TRACY A. PARKER*** *for her contributions in researching, reading and editing this article. She has published and edited for several national organizations, including the Chemical Heritage Foundation (CHF), Philadelphia Museum of Art, San Francisco Museum of Modern Art, and the Art Institute of Chicago.*

ENDNOTES

http://www.montgomery countymd.gov

http://www.montgomery countymd.gov/open/

http://www.montgomery countymd.gov/open/Resources/Files/openMontgomery-Digital-Government-Strategy.pdf

http://www.montgomery countymd.gov/open/partnership.html

http://www.city-data.com/ county/Montgomery_ county-MD.html

http://www.mcinnovationnetwork.com/why-montgomery- county/

http://www.naco.org/Counties/countiesdo/Pages/Why-Counties-Matter2_1.aspx

http://www.mhfi.com/about/Global-Institute/white-papers/Creating-the-Sustainable-City

http://www6.montgomery countymd.gov/content/DED/downloads/Incubator%20 Report%20Final1.pdf

http://visual.ly/anatomy-smart-city

http://www.nlc.org/build-skills-and-networks/education-and-training/event-calendar/predictive-data-analytics-how-cities-can-get-ahead-of-the-curve-and-improve-performance

http://datasmart.ash.harvard.edu/news/article/citizen-centered-governance-278

http://www.schneider-electric.com/documents/support/white-papers/smart-cities/998-1185469_smart-city-cornerstone-urban-efficiency.pdf

http://www.cities-localgovernments.org/committees/cdc/Upload/formations/smartcitiesstudy_en.pdf

http://quickfacts.census.gov/qfd/states/00000.html

https://data.montgomery countymd.gov/

http://gfbrandenburg.wordpress.com/2013/07/02/more-on-long-term-us-education-trends/

http://www.thedigitgroupinc.com/RICS_SMARTCities2012.pdf

http://www.accenture.com/SiteCollectionDocuments/PDF/Accenture-Dispelling-the-Myths-Preventing-Government-Transformation-US.pdf

http://mobithinking.com/mobile-marketing-tools/latest-mobile-stats

http://www.smart-cities.eu/

http://proximityone.com/counties0010.htm

http://www.gartner.com/technology/home.jsp

http://public.dhe.ibm.com/common/ssi/ecm/en/pub03003usen/PUB03003USEN.PDF

Caragliu, A; Del Bo, C. & Nijkamp, P (2009). "Smart cities in Europe". Serie Research Memoranda 0048 (VU University Amsterdam, Faculty of Economics, Business Administration and Econometrics)

11

Moscow: Moving to Smart City Through Smart Technologies

Evgeny Styrin

Moscow has unique context for smart city development. Moscow City is the capital of Russian Federation. Moscow is often named as "heart of Russia" and can be considered as the main and most important Russian city. Moscow accumulates governmental, financial, cultural development in one and the same time. Not only Federal Government but also Governments of Moscow and Moscow region (Moscovskaya Oblast) reside here. Moscow has status of a region that is why mayor of Moscow can be called by law the Governor of Moscow. Moscow Government consists of departments. The key role in smart city project besides mayor belongs to the Information Technologies Department, Departments of Transport, Education and Utilities[1]. The population of Moscow is 12 mln. people with average density 10588 people per square kilometer. Disproportional development of Russian regions makes Moscow economically attractive not only to Russians but for majority of people from former Soviet Republics. That is why the key challenge to the city is to make life of each Muscovite comfortable and secure in spite of the objective problems with transport, ecology, multyethnicity, quality of public services, effective usage of housing utilities[2].

Historical background, cultural heritage were reflected strongly in Moscow urban planning process. Here are some of the examples: specific road planning combining radial and circle highways structuring traffic in the city, dense location of financial, governmental and cultural areas in the city center, very unstructured or pointed building in 90-es and 00-es, stable growth of cars in the city (297 cars per 1000 inhabitants in 2013). In the same time Moscow remains one of the worlds' most concentrated scientific center with hundreds of institutions and universities and almost 2000 schools.

The key idea and a challenge for Moscow Government is to control and manage effectively city infrastructure by saving costs and bringing new quality. Department of Information Technologies plays a key role in this goal implementation because the most efficient driver for this goal is information technologies. Moscow follows main world tendencies in technological enactment in education, road trafficking, healthcare system, public services provision, citizens' security and privacy, interactive education system, housing and utilities.

In the same time Moscow remains one of the most powerful Russian regions with financial budgets which enable Moscow Government to solve really challengeable problems.

Managerial Approach.

The key tool to manage smart city based on technological means of improvement is Moscow Program "Information City 2012-2016". It has several key directions:

- Intellectual city management system,
- ICT development for citizens quality of life improvement,
- Media and communications development,
- Formation of special informational environment or ecosystem.

The overall budget of the Program is approximately 10 billion USD from which 6 bln. USD go from Moscow budget, 0,7 bln USD from federal budget and the rest goes from investors.

Each direction of the Program has measurable indicators. For example for citizens' quality of life effective indicators are:

- the number of PCs for 100 pupils in schools,
- the number of PCs for medical professionals,
- e-services quality (for example, electronic enrollment to the doctor).

For intellectual city management system it is actual to measure:

- the number of CCTVs for observation in mass public spaces and mass housing sector,
- the state of utilities in housing sector (intellectual houses with the amendment that these are no less than 16 floor apartment blocks with hundreds of flats where it is necessary for Moscow authorities to know electric, water, heat consumption),

- typical ICT solutions to manage housing area, health enterprises, schools and etc.

Finally effective ICT environment is measured with:

- high speed Internet penetration for each household,
- digital TV development and usage,
- 4G coverage.

In the area of media and communications development the Moscow Government has to keep at a high value such indicators as:

- number of printed and electronic media,
- electronic and printed books issuance and availability.

Following, we will examine in more detailed form key directions of Program implementation and key ICT-tools which support each direction.

Official City Portal—Gorod.Mos.Ru.

This project was resumed and relaunched from 2011 and is based on new philosophy of Mayor Sobyanin's administration which is basically in citizen's inclusion in city governance. Citizens never before had direct connection with governmental services and authorities on different levels. In other words, there were no system control over citizens' complaints and claims. Now through the portal Mayors administration controls the process of citizens' claim and bids implementation by Moscow local or area (sectoral) authorities responsible for the result.

The process works as following: citizen forms a request which goes through portal moderator team. If the request is complete it is being redirected to the local authority from the area to which the bid or claim is related. In a certain officially established period of time the local authorities must react to the problem, fix it and report to the Mayor administration and to the citizen.

One of the most interesting things on the portal is initial role of Mayor's administration in problem formulation. Citizens can't just send any request. On the contrary they obliged to choose from a list of typical bids and claims concerning four areas: housing utilities, hospitals and clinics, roads and road utility objects (traffic lights, lighting stands, road marks etc), territories near houses. For each of these four areas there is a number of typical questions which citizens might have problems with.

For example, for house nearby territories the questions might concern the quality of children's playgrounds, quality of yard cleaning, broken objects in the yard, left cars and etc. The evolution of the questions formulated in each area can happen only if citizens massively request administration about something which has not been included in the list of questions before.

In case new problem is massive then it becomes typical and enters the list. Also there are seasonal requests which come and go periodically. For example, seasonal weather can cause problems with management of the snow consequences in winter and heat in summer.

One of the obvious problems is sufficient difficulty for the citizen to send a request which will be approved by moderator team. The citizen has not only to describe the problem he/she is sometimes obliged to make and attach photos of the problem noticed. The citizen should comply with moderator rules by using only appropriate vocabulary, providing trustful information etc. otherwise their request will be declined.

The authorities want to have insurance from false problem or claim and also want to have clear reason to initiate investigation. The positive effect for the Mayor administration and the citizens is the ability to create the rating of local area authorities in Moscow based on the number of existing problems in the area and the speed of solving these problems. Citizens can also evaluate many objects in the city: transport routes, public hospitals, public toilets, places of trade, parks and pharmacies. With all this Moscow Government can analyse and report on most painful problems for the citizens, can see evaluation of Moscow infrastructure objects, use this analytics for Moscow general development plan improvement. The portal is connected with ten information systems which contain information about roads and trafficking, household utilities, hospitals and pharmacies, trade enterprises, yards, public services provision centers. To the current moment 130 thousand requests (bids, claims) have been resolved and 165 thousand citizens have been registered on the portal. Because citizens leave the exact address of the place where the problem was encountered Moscow Government attaches the problem to the map and it is possible to rate local sectors of the city from the problem resolution perspective as well as to observe the problem map of the city.

Using Medical Services in the City

According to sociological surveys one of the most popular services among Russian citizens is enrollment to the doctor. In Moscow by means of Joined Medical Information system electronic enrollment to the doctor was implemented. The system integrates different application channels (personal visits, phones and internet). The queues in the clinics disappeared, the doctors can appoint and plan new visit and also electronically readdress patients to specific narrow professionals. Up till now 547 medical centers participate with more than 3000 doctors going online every day and more than 5 mln. patients served, 18 000 working stations installed. Also 49 000 doctors are already registered in the system and 15 000 from them passed through ICT-skills improvement to interact with the system. Cost efficiency analysis will be performed to prove the effectiveness of service provision in electronic form. Probably the bad side of this direction concerns general problem with shortage of family doctors in Moscow in general. Though joined medical information system can perform perfectly special health policy in Moscow must be redesigned to involve necessary professional in the area.

Modern School in the City. Fast middle class formation among Muscovites increases the demand in qualitative education. The school plays the leading role in personality formation by bringing cultural, behavioral societal requirements to future generation. Moscow Departments of IT and Education collaborate to not only invest in technology equipment by providing schools with smart boards, tablet PCs, servers and high speed Internet but also to provide high quality services in school and around the school. For example, necessary technological solutions and public services concerning school search and enrollment have been implemented in the electronic form. Electronic enrollment services are used to provide extra education services, summer camps, inform parents about pupils marks, timetables and food in school canteens.

In 2015 Moscow Government plans to launch joined e-textbooks library project which will serve to Moscow teachers as a single bank of different textbooks which can be used in education. The system will work as a textbook constructor which helps teachers generate new textbooks based on electronic material published by their colleagues. The system will build a rating of most popular textbooks and based on this rating most popular teachers will get extra rewards. In 2017 a ICT certification system will be launched. It will assure the acceptable level of technological equipment in each Moscow school.

The complex approach to school education will be reflected in "healthy" school. Each school will lead a health record of the pupils by fixing vaccination map and clinical examinations.

Another dimension is distance learning and inclusive education for the child either at home or in school. Each school will provide up to 2017 distance learning system for the pupils. Parents will get control and information on pupils success in school, presence at the lectures by getting alarm messages by e-mail or SMS. In 2015 in addition to school activity information parents will be able to know when their child entered the school and how much money he/she spent on the food. This security aspect in school will be implemented by means of pupils e-card.

To the end of 2015 Moscow Government will provide single typical IT-system for financial and human resource management. All schools will use unified approach to managerial activity and Moscow Authorities will get macrocontrol over financial spending in school education and also will manage high quality data register containing full information about teachers in Moscow.

Moscow Open Data Portal (www.data.mos.ru)

Open data became a new trend in national and regional development in the world[3]. Open data serves not only for better transparency and accountability but also enables economic development[4]. Moscow open data project from the very start got intensive development. It is the best way for Moscow Government to decrease the number of informational requests from the citizens, ease their time in searching information by providing open data based services. The most popular areas for open data search are: sports facilities in the city, election results, transport and traffic. Around 200 datasets have been already published, 11 mobile applications and 88 informational services are available for the users. The data is structured according to citizens' categories (pensioners, young moms, children, students and etc). Users often request data about low quality fuel stations, traffic rule breaking statistics, road CCTV locations. The project team plans proactive datasets disclosure. One of the key problems here is sufficient taxpayers money investments in datasets preparation and publication process with very weak feedback and usage from the citizens. It is possible to say that only 10% of all datasets are of a sufficient interest whilst funds should be spent to support growing number of datasets. Very serious advantage which potentially makes Moscow one of the leading cities in open data is automatic linking between open datasets layers and Moscow geographical map in the form of objects which relate to datasets. This immediately enables citizens with powerful visualization tool and helps them quickly find necessary information. Future plans of this project is to open seasonal datasets (for example, summer or winter leisure places), open 76 datasets to the end of 2013 especially about advertisement constructions in the city, utility rates, bookstores, privatized property.

Managing Payments From the Citizens

One of the biggest challenges in Russian practice of governance is effective arrangement of payment systems which would enable fast and reliable way of accepting payments as fines, taxes, etc. More than 1.5 bln. USD each year is accepted by Moscow authorities from the Muscovites as payments in Moscow budget. The main problems here were: big amount of legacy systems not communicating well with each other as well as sufficient number of public organizations involved as information systems owners. Often payment from the citizen could be rejected, could not be managed or acceptance could take more than critically assumed time. The idea is to enable citizens with different payment channels: mobile applications, internet banking, ATMs. The challenge is the necessity to create formal regulations among private agents, Moscow Authorities and Federal Authorities who are also involved according to laws and procedures. The payments must be fast, reliable, traceable and transparent. Up to year 2015 2500 public organizations (schools, libraries, hospitals, public services provision centers, official state departments) will be connected to a joined payment gateway. Up to 2018 the number of these organizations will reach 8000. Moscow Government launches single payment gateway enabling citizens' payments through credit cards or electronic purses. Key Russian private agents (including banks) which own their payment systems will be also connected to this gateway. Usually these agents own wide payment infrastructure (payment machines and terminals all over the city) and will provide it to citizens as means of payment to Moscow Government. One of the typical challenges is to sign agreement about interests division on each transaction payment going through diverse payment agents' network to authorities. Banks will get the right to establish their interest rates with the only precondition that they will inform the user before the transaction takes place. Technological solution behind the payment gateway is called Information System of Payments Registration and Crediting (ISPRC). Moscow Government developed clear rules on the ISPRC interface to which other payment agents can be connected. Payment agents will have to care all the expenditures to adjust their systems to ISPRC interface. The ISPRC contains security and authentification component, web-services execution component.

Payment gateway launch will let citizens pay online or through their mobile phones for sport and leisure facilities, extra medical and educational services, fines and penalties.

Developing Housing Utilities System

The problem of housing utilities was named as one of the most touching for Russian citizens. Moscow is not an exclusion due to the high level of deterioration of housing infrastructure (water pipes, electric cables, bad state of houses facades and internal facilities). For the last twenty years starting from 1990-es housing was not managed properly in the sense that responsibility division among authorities, utility management companies, utility suppliers and citizens were blurred. The key idea in this area would be to use technological solutions in a way that would lead to efficient financial control over the funds from Moscow budget spent to improve the situation. Another expected outcome would be detalization of the bills for utilities so that citizens could see clearly what they are paying for. This outcome brings to another useful side effect: citizens can be educated and more responsible for the resources they consume. Citizens also move to the ideology of resources saving which is very valuable for city's sustainable development. For the authorities it is very important to create high quality register for utility management companies and make them be more transparent and accountable in the way they use citizens' money in the same time authorities need to demonstrate transparency in utilities billing formation process. Utilities inspection authorities want to have immediate information picture about each apartment as well as about the whole apartment building utility consumption and resources usage efficiency. They will be able to react very fast in case of accidents. Because of the long time absence of formal regulations among key stakeholders in the utility consumption area it is very hard to bring back formal agreements which can be implemented in the supporting information system.

Current supporting technological solution is called "Joined Information and Calculation Center" (JICC). This information system is very distributed in terms of branches across the city and its operator is responsible for billing, managing and inspecting utilities. The system interacts with migration control system. JICC is also used to record population.

Each month the system accounts information about 4 mln. bills including 2.3 mln. bills for citizens with benefits and bills for 45 000 legal entities. The system gathers information from 79 000 devices for the apartment blocks and from 3.9 mln. devices for individual apartments. The system serves for 33 000 houses (80% of all living facilities in Moscow) or in other words for 3.8 mln. of individual apartments. Each month system issues 705 000 references concerning information about apartment characteristics including utilities. The system accepts 10 mln. requests per year, at least 1 mln. requests were managed in last half a year in communication with other agencies information systems 4200 working places are installed all over Moscow and more than 30 different level official authorities use information from the system.

The system is very vulnerable to human factor because for many information requests the personnel has to prepare responses in manual regime. Another side effect is constantly growing number of personnel and absence of service quality control.

Moscow Government uses legal, organizational and technological approaches to improvement in housing utilities area. First of all legal framework is modified to enable legal significance to all the requests exchange going among the system's stakeholders. In other words JICC will become official transport environment for documents exchange among system's stakeholders.

System will be connected to payment gateway so that citizens can pay online and manage their personal accounts electronically. Citizens will get tools to compare details of their utilities consumption from month to month. The ywill also get opportunity to visualize details of the bill. Another outcome would be saving of 7.5 mln USD for not issuing bills in paper form. Benefits usage by the citizens will be put under strong control and bring to the financial savings.

Full automation of information collection process will lead to possibility to release information about utility management companies in open data format. This will open new possibilities for statistics and analytics in the area and in its turn to competition among utility management companies.

One of the key decisions that Moscow Government has to take is to choose centralized or decentralized mechanism of billing process. First puts the city in the role of financial controller and supporter. Second is in its turn very flexible and adjustable to citizens needs but doesn't help to keep integrated picture in the area. Probably final decision about approach to billing will be made after consultations with system stakeholders.

Finally integration of the billing information details will enable citizens' access to new informational e-services from mobile devices and strengthen feedback and communication process with them from utility services providers.

The success of this project can be measured with sociology by reporting about satisfaction dynamics from the citizens about utility services quality.

Conclusion

Due to the very specific and unique context of development Moscow can serve as attractive, safe and comfort environment for citizens only by implementing intellectual or smart solutions or in other words moving to smart city conception implementation[5]. Growing population, transport and ecology problems can be resolved only under strong control and reuse of existing resources and investments in human capital. This will become possible only by means of ICT. This is clearly understood by Moscow Government and sufficient funds are spent for "Information City" Program. Growing welfare situation for Muscovites stimulates demand for better solutions and transparent control of resources expenditure by Government. Another clear trend in Moscow is sufficient efforts spent for legacy systems umbrella integration and interagency collaboration improvement by means of ICT. The speed of change in public services quality will depend on the pace of new citizen oriented services appearance. The Internet penetration growth will continue and push Moscow Government to further development of electronic feedback environments for citizens. Finally payment integration mechanisms in services provision will stimulate electronic payments and better budget transparency.

Moscow will be moving fast to a smart city implementation but with the necessity to overcome unpredictable challenges of multystakeholder large scale centralized city management information systems improvement.

EVGENY STYRIN PH.D., *Senior research analyst, Institute for Public and Municipal Administration, Higher School of Economics, Moscow, Russia.*

REFERENCES

1. Moscow Government Information Technologies Department—www.dit.mos.ru
2. Makhrova, A. G., T. G. Nefedova, and A. I. Treivish. "Moscow agglomeration and "New Moscow": The capital city-region case of Russia's urbanization." Regional Research of Russia 3.2 (2013): 131-141.
3. Gurin, J. Open Data Now: The Secret to Hot Startups, Smart Investing, Savvy Marketing, and Fast Innovation. McGraw Hill Professional, 2014.
4. Vickery, G. Review of Recent Studies on PSI-Reuse and Related Market developments, Information Economics Paris. 2012.
5. Nam. T, Pardo T. "Smart city as urban innovation: Focusing on management, policy, and context." Proceedings of the 5th International Conference on Theory and Practice of Electronic Governance. ACM, 2011.

12

Smart City Case Study: Tallinn, Estonia

Maria Lille

The public sector provides a variety of services that are essential or serve public interest or social benefit. Regardless of whether the city service is a public good or a convenience, providing services at the minimum cost, maximum convenience and according to modern world possibilities, is essential. To achieve those criteria Tallinn, Estonia, has integrated smart city concepts into city strategies and development plans, with the aim to engage the public, implement sustainable practices and enhance the quality of life and environment in the city.

One of Tallinn's priorities has been to develop efficient information communication technology (ICT) applications and e-services that integrate existing databases and provide additional convenience to citizens and other users of city services. According to survey (Citizen Satisfaction with Tallinn Public Services 2012), 81 percent of Tallinn citizens use the internet daily, and 25 percent are expecting that city focus more on e-service development. Nearly half of Tallinn citizens (48 percent) prefer to interact with the city using electronic channels.

To serve citizens more efficiently with the emphasis on the stakeholder engagement, Tallinn has implemented innovative services: the Citizen Service Portal, Citizen Self-Service Payment Portal (including Mobile Text Messages Platform) and Statistical Atlas.

Citizen Service Portal

Citizen Service Portal is an innovative tool that enables the public to reach city services at one point. With the city providing more than 500 services, the portal encourages citizens to apply for services digitally, point out service delivery gaps on feedback forms and pay for services using e-banking links.

In the portal, every service has its description, links to service-providers or databases, contact information, updated price information, regulations, feedback forms and applications (see Figure 1).

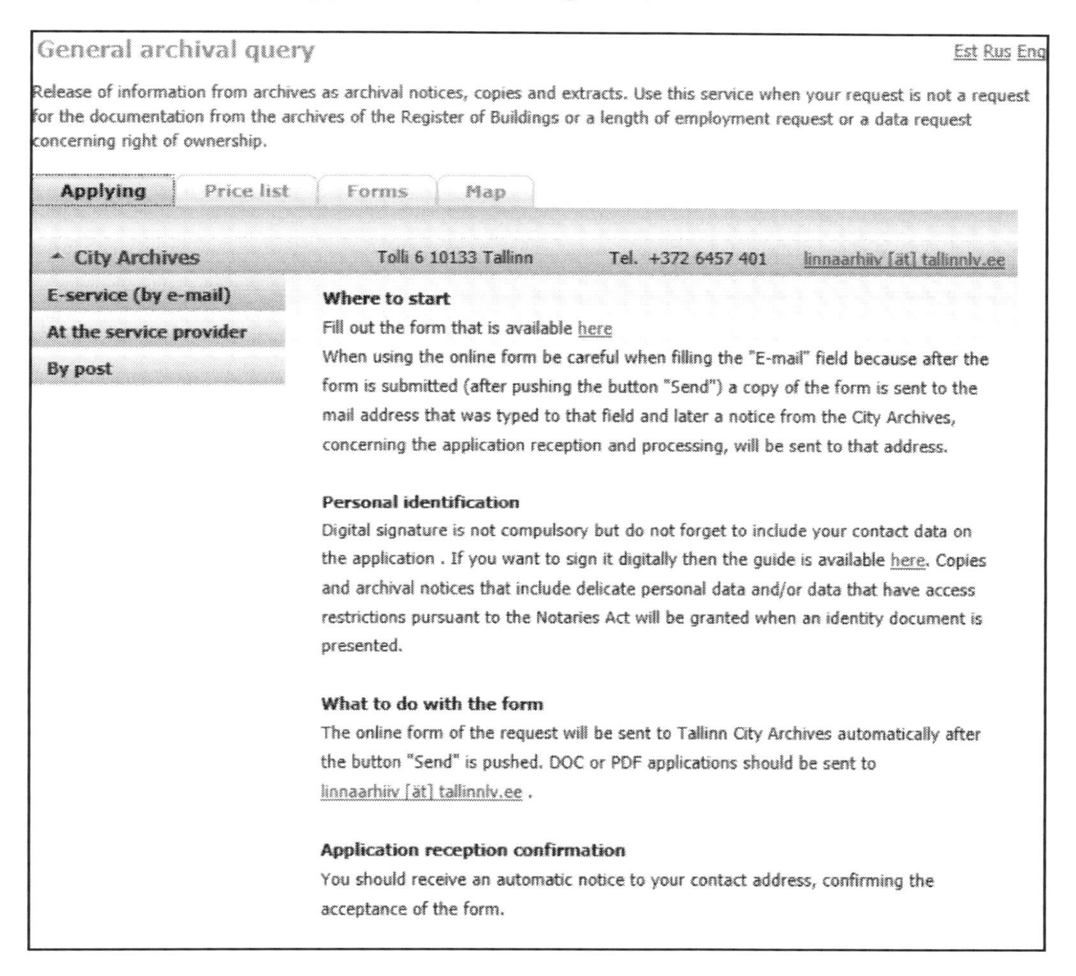

General archival query

Est Rus Eng

Release of information from archives as archival notices, copies and extracts. Use this service when your request is not a request for the documentation from the archives of the Register of Buildings or a length of employment request or a data request concerning right of ownership.

Applying | Price list | Forms | Map

City Archives — Tolli 6 10133 Tallinn — Tel. +372 6457 401 — linnaarhiiv [ät] tallinnlv.ee

E-service (by e-mail)
At the service provider
By post

Where to start

Fill out the form that is available here
When using the online form be careful when filling the "E-mail" field because after the form is submitted (after pushing the button "Send") a copy of the form is sent to the mail address that was typed to that field and later a notice from the City Archives, concerning the application reception and processing, will be sent to that address.

Personal identification

Digital signature is not compulsory but do not forget to include your contact data on the application . If you want to sign it digitally then the guide is available here. Copies and archival notices that include delicate personal data and/or data that have access restrictions pursuant to the Notaries Act will be granted when an identity document is presented.

What to do with the form

The online form of the request will be sent to Tallinn City Archives automatically after the button "Send" is pushed. DOC or PDF applications should be sent to linnaarhiiv [ät] tallinnlv.ee .

Application reception confirmation

You should receive an automatic notice to your contact address, confirming the acceptance of the form.

Figure 1. *Service Description.*

The portal is integrated with Tallinn's Financial Information System and updated with every price information change. In addition to financial information system integration, the portal interlinks a mobile texting platform and payments self-service database.

The city has appointed 34 administrators to insert service information, as well as to reply to or organize responses to citizen inquires. The Department of Social Welfare and Health Care, followed by City Vital Statistics, which is responsible for services of family matters such as marriage and birth registration (See Chart 1, next page), have received the most citizen feedback. The majority of feedback deals with service inquiries and questions. Complaints are received second-most frequent.

The city typically responds to feedback within five working days, but no later than within 30 working days as stipulated by the Estonian Response to Memoranda and Requests for Explanations Act (RT I 2004,81,542). The exemptions are requests that require more time. However, if a response will take longer than a week, the city sends the citizen a notification letter with an updated response date. Responses are registered and sent via the Service Portal Database. If the response is delayed, the city's chief administrator is notified by email about the unanswered request.

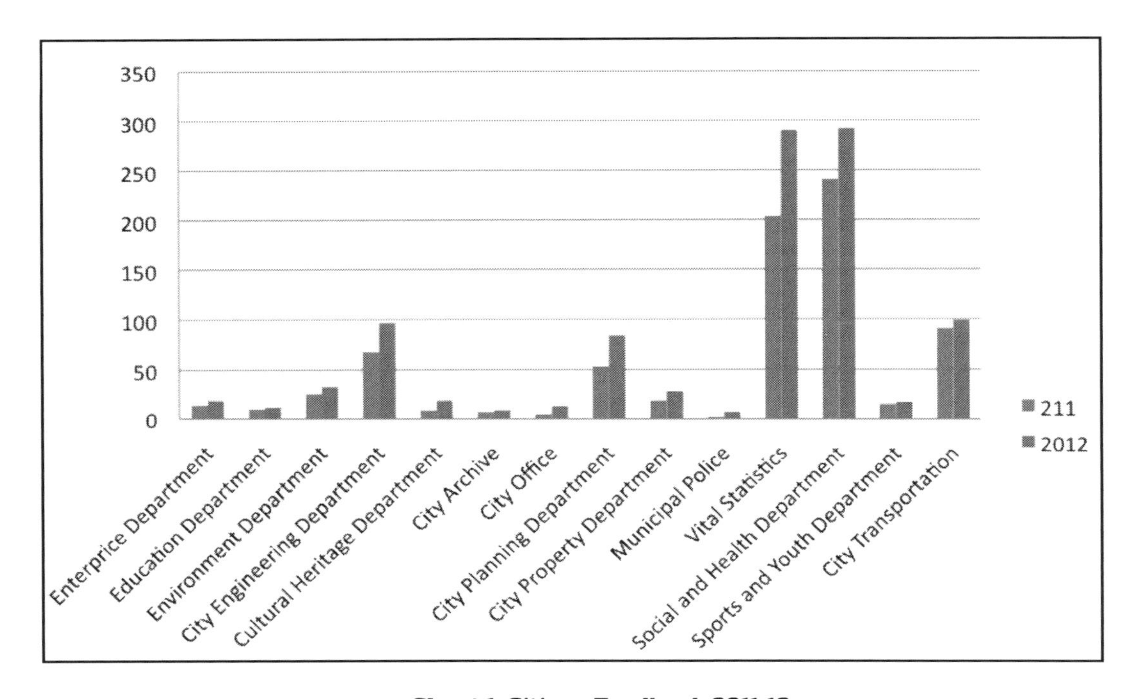

Chart 1. *Citizen Feedback 2011-12.*

In 2012. Tallinn citizens submitted 1,019 feedback forms with questions, requests, complaints, proposals, etc.—39 percent more than in 2011 (City Government 3rd of April 2013 Session Protocol, No 31). This verifies the service portal is popular among citizens. In 2012, citizens visited the portal more than 600 000 times, a 15 percent increase since 2011. Primarily, citizens were interested in was finding contact information of service-providers and learning how to apply for the services digitally. Citizens were next interested about finding information about service prices.

The most popular services that citizens visited were in two categories:

1. Social benefits (pension support, birth allowance, living support); and
2. Family matters (changing residential address, marriage registration, divorce).

Portal use with Russian language selection was four to two times lower than by Estonian language selection. English speakers searched for different hobby activities, such as martial arts clubs, swimming pools and, like other groups, marriage registration and residential address change information.

In summary, the service portal provides valuable information about citizens' needs and interest, which services need to be improved, and where are the gaps or delivery problems. Some valuable proposals have been included into service development.

Payments Self-Service Portal

The second large service application Tallinn implemented is a payments self-service portal. Users of the Se-Service Portal are able to see and pay for the following:

1. Rental bills in municipal housing;
2. Invoices from municipal kindergartens;
3. Invoices from municipal hobby schools and schools of interest;
4. Property sale payments;
5. Fines;
6. Municipal taxes; and
7. Other invoices issued by the city of Tallinn.

Tallinn structured the application with a simple design that provides information about bills and the due date, as well as provides an overview about payment history (see Figure 2).

Tasumata arved | Arvete ajalugu | Teenusportaali maksete ajalugu | Isikuandmed ja teavitused | Juhendid

Otsekorraldusteenuse kasutamisel kuvatakse Teie arveid juba tasutuna arvel märgitud maksetähtajaga!

Arve kp. Kõik Kuupäeva valik

Nõude saldo Kõik Nõude nr Nõude esitaja Otsi

Kuupäev	Tähtaeg	Nõude nr	Nõude esitaja	Summa	Tasuda	Maksa
13.05.2013	27.05.2013	5501803462	Kunstikool	25.00 EUR	0,00 EUR	
25.04.2013	09.05.2013	5501772572	Kunstikool	25.00 EUR	0,00 EUR	
25.03.2013	08.04.2013	5501748372	Kunstikool	25.00 EUR	0,00 EUR	
25.02.2013	11.03.2013	5501717145	Kunstikool	25.00 EUR	0,00 EUR	
25.01.2013	08.02.2013	5501687883	Kunstikool	25.00 EUR	0.00 EUR	
19.12.2012	02.01.2013	5501658749	Kunstikool	25.00 EUR	0,00 EUR	
26.11.2012	10.12.2012	5501631126	Kunstikool	25.00 EUR	0,00 EUR	
26.10.2012	09.11.2012	5501603609	Kunstikool	25.00 EUR	0.00 EUR	
25.09.2012	09.10.2012	5501573430	Kunstikool	25.00 EUR	0.00 EUR	
04.09.2012	15.09.2012	5400034559	Rahvaülikool	32.00 EUR	0.00 EUR	
19.07.2012	02.08.2012	83005257	Tallinna Linnakantselei Finantsteenistus	31.00 EUR	0.00 EUR	

Figure 2. *Payments History at Self-Service Portal.*

The payments application is integrated with the State Business Register, so and after identification, the system makes an inquiry with the register to determine whether the user has legal business with the city. If the answer is yes, then the user can decide whether to pay personal or business invoices. After the user makes a selection, the system provides relevant data.

Beside the State Business Register, the self-service portal is linked to the city financial information system and a mobile text messages application. All the invoice data comes from the financial system. If payments are overdue, the system automatically sends the citizen a mobile text message reminding him or her about the unpaid invoice..

The city has found this tool to be effective in improving payment behavior. Eighty percent of the self-service portal users who were late with their payments made their payments are receiving an SMS notification about the unpaid invoice.

Mobile Text Messages

Another part of the self-service portal is a mobile texting service. Portal users can request to receive notifications from city officials for the following services:

1. Building construction permit;
2. Notifications from kindergartens (personal and group notifications);
3. Notifications from schools (personal and group notifications);
4. Initiation of the city Detailed Plan in the user's living area;
5. Municipal job offers; and
6. Other notifications related to user applications.

After selecting and clicking on the texting services, users add their phone numbers and, in case of the Detailed Plan notification, their residential address.

With the exemption of the Detailed Plan notification service, users give their permission or send a request to service provider before they can receive notification. For example, teachers at schools gather permissions from all parents and add them into the class group created in the mobile texting database. After a parent accepts the portal's terms and selects the service, the mobile number is activated. The number messages sent varies among schools. On average, 800 SMS per year are sent by one school. The messages can be personal or of a group nature. For example, if the child does not feel well, or a reminder about a class field trip.

City Detailed Plan notification does not require prior requests. Every time a new Detailed Plan initiation is enforced, the automatic notification is sent to all users who have indicated their residential address within a 500 meter radius of the plan area (see Figure 3).

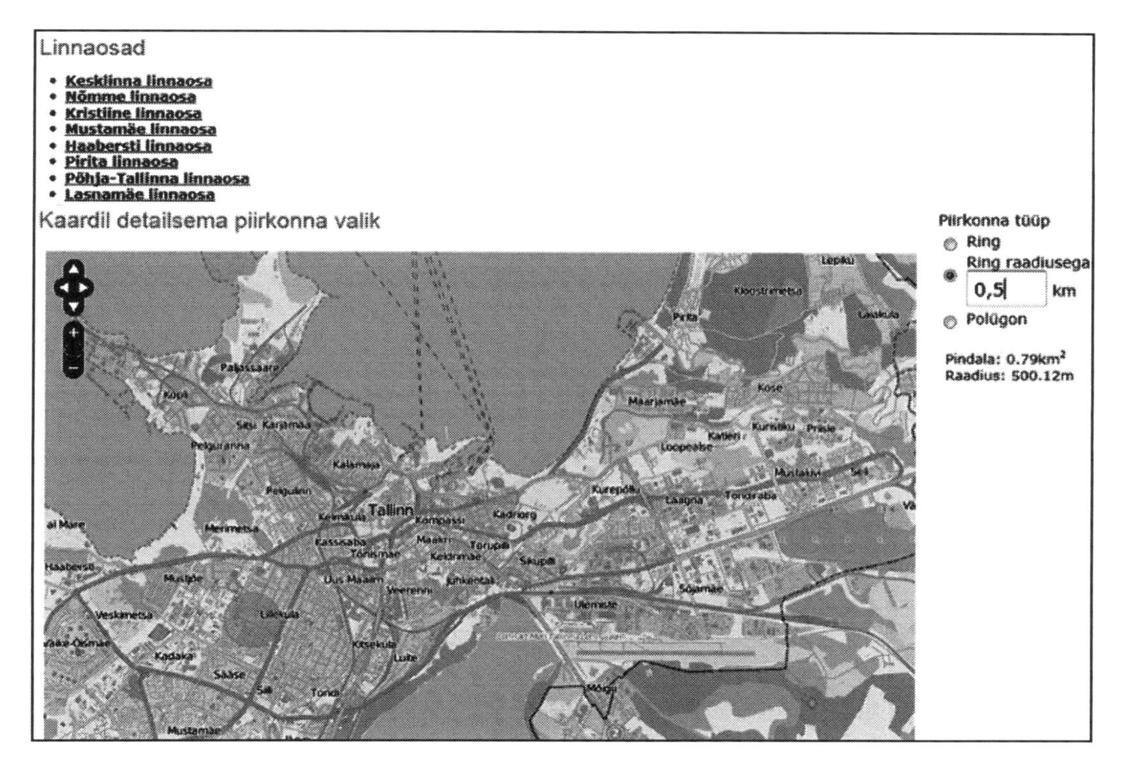

Figure 3. *Labeling the Area of an Initiated City Detailed Plan.*

This Detailed Plan notification service is a good example of citizen engagement. People need to know whether the city has planned new construction or other changes. Often, the information does not reach target groups by conventional means because it is complex to find plans for the specific area. With the notification service, the city can engage users in the beginning planning stage.

Overall, the objective of the mobile texting platform is to provide certain services or additional data faster and through more convenient channels. The second objective is to improve users' satisfaction with the city. By combining different options with services, some external side effects could be enforced. In the case of Mobile Texting platform, the target was improving payment behavior and at the same time developing better services.

Statistical Atlas

In 2012,Swedish Innovation Agency VINNOVA approved implementation of a citizen-focused statistical atlas project in frame of the program "Citizen-Centric eGovernment Services." A collaboration with Iceland

University, Umea University and Regio Ltd., developed a new user-friendly statistical tool for displaying data (see Figure 4). The atlas aims to provide data that is easy to find, use and understand. To achieve this, the group focused on presenting data from the perspective of different users, ranging from general users to experts.

One of the central elements of statistics is making the data as comparable as possible to reveal differences, correlations and trends. Statistics allows users to compare numbers on differences between various groups, changes over time or both. Statistics can give absolute and relative numbers. Numbers also can be presented as percentages, rates or ratios. The decision whether to give absolute numbers or percentages; how to compute percentages, how to design tables, colors, shades; and which titles to make is based on the user's perspective. Experience users can customize a statistical output that is most useful to them, such as by nominal or relative numbers. Users also can create templates for different output layouts. For basic users, predefined output templates are provided, and users can bookmark a particular output (CitizMap PA pp3-5).

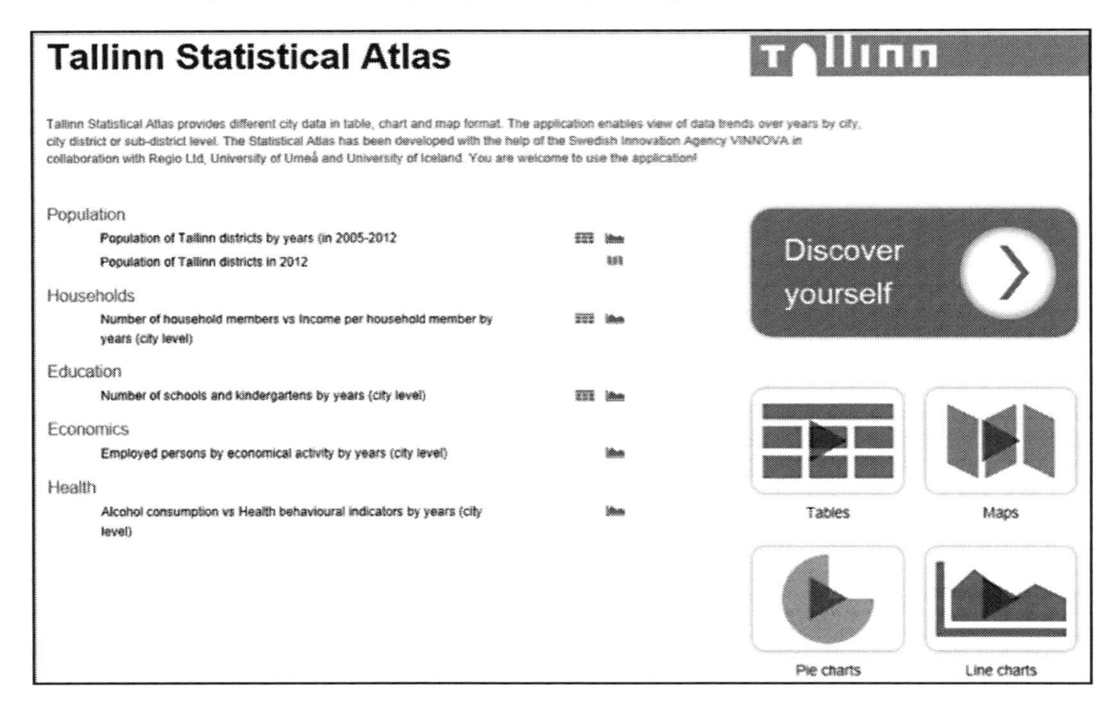

Figure 4. *Tallinn Statistical Atlas.*

In an user-focused approach, data plays an important role. There are innovative ways to present available data. Beyond traditional demographic and socio-economic statistics, it is possible to integrate different data to address the interests of general users. There are primarily two data types:

1. **General statistical data and geographic information.** This type of data contains traditional quantitative and qualitative data of populations, households, the economy, labor market, environment, etc. Geographic information can contain terrain and land-use information, as well as traffic and transport information.

2. **Data about services.** There are two types of data related to services. First, service providers, such as number of schools, hospitals, kindergartens, swimming pools, etc. Second, there is data about service use, such as number of pupils in a school, trainings, kindergartens, etc. (see Figure 5).

Users can combine all this data with the territorial aspects. For example, the number of children in certain school at a given district. Additionally, data about free places in those schools can be integrated as well. Thus, statistics has practical value to citizens who are looking for suitable schools in their community. The data also can be combined with municipal training activities at the schools, and as such, provide extra value when looking at school locations, number of vacant places and training possibilities.

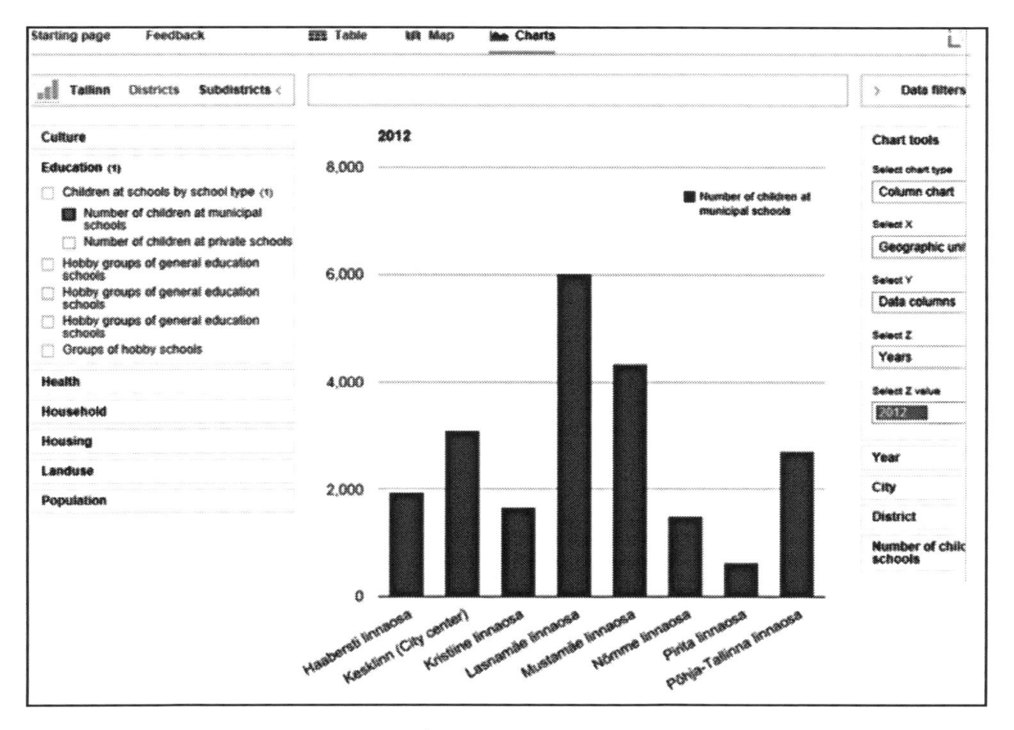

Figure 5. *Data Display.*

Data can be displayed on a map, as tables, pie charts, bar charts, line charts, column charts and area charts, allowing for user-friendly functionality. In addition to external uses, data can be avaluable tool for municipality officials so that they can analyze existing services and plan new services.

Tallinn's citizen-centric developments are contributing to smart city stakeholder engagement objectives. Constant evaluation and analysis of existing possibilities and efficient integration of recourses provides flexibility in how citizens interact with the city. Moreover, citizens are able to provide valuable information about how to enhance their living environment and how to create sustainable practices. Because of its efforts, the Intelligent Community Forum selected Tallinn as among the top seven communities in the world in 2012, and the city aims to continuously improve the delivery of its services.

MARIA LILLE *is chief specialist in the Department of Public Services and Research at Tallinn City Development Service.*

REFERENCES

City Government Session (03.04.2013) Protocol 31 "Informatsioon Tallinna linna avalike teenuste andmekogu ja teenuste arendamise kohta"—Information on Development of City Services and Tallinn Service Database

CitizMap PA between Iceland University, Umea University, Tallinn City Office, and Regio Ltd, 2012

Citizen Satisfaction with Tallinn Public Services 2012—Elanike rahulolu Tallinna linna avalike teenustega 2012, Uuringu raport, OÜ Eesti Uuringukeskus

Response to Memoranda and Requests for Explanations Act (RT I 2004,81,542)

13

Education and Economic Development: A New Approach Critical for Jobs and Growth

Mary Keeling and Mary Olson

The world's economy is evolving. Cities will thrive or decline on their ability to muster a workforce that has the skills suited to this emerging environment. Increasingly, citizens need to have broad awareness and experience paired with deep expertise in a specific domain; often referred to as having "T"-shaped skills. The breadth of their experience allows them to be flexible and adaptable as situations change and they must put new learning into context. These T-shaped skills are essential for entrepreneurs, as well as employees.

Many factors are at play in this transformation, and education is one of the most important "core" systems that supports economic vitality (see Figure 1, next page). These systems are drivers of innovation, job creation and growth, as they influence the quality of life in cities, counties and regions and help to attract and retain knowledge workers and innovative businesses in those locations.[1] They also affect economic activity through the quality and efficiency of the services and employment they provide. Moreover, they are an important indirect contributor to growth, as many other related industries and activities consume these services as inputs to their own activities.

With that in mind, there are specific steps communities can take now to ensure they have an educational ecosystem that is adaptable, responsive and conducive to job creation and growth.

---

[1] Dirks, S., Gurdgiev, C., and Keeling, M. "Smarter cities for smarter growth: How cities can optimize their systems for the talent-based economy." IBM. May 2010. ftp://public.dhe.ibm.com/common/ssi/ecm/en/gbe03348usen/GBE03348USEN.PDF.

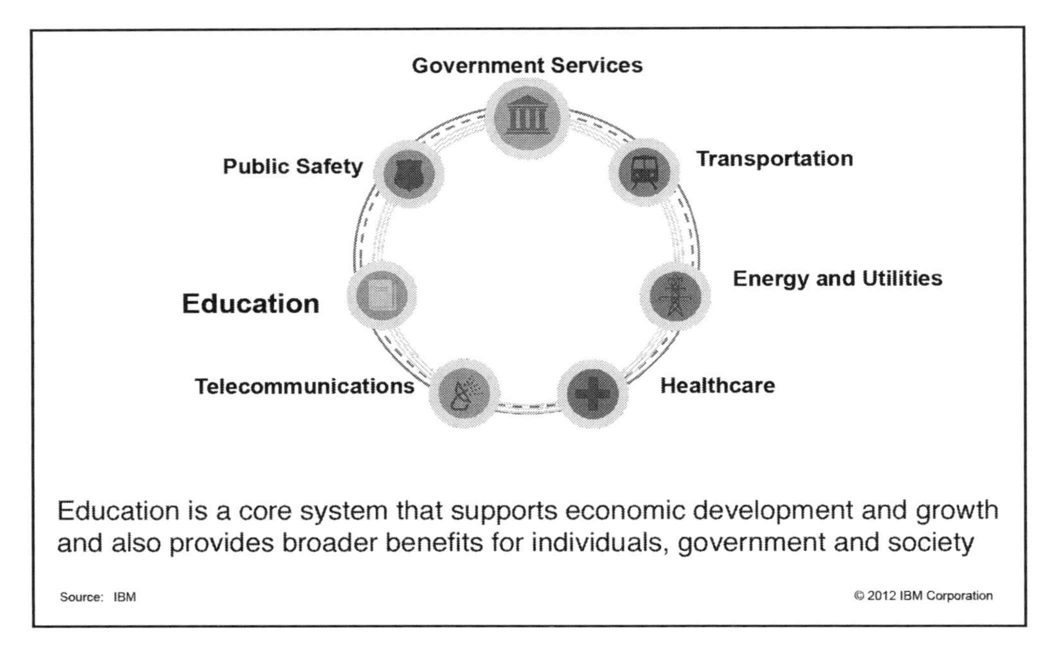

Figure 1.

Why Education Matters Now More Than Before

There is widespread evidence on the role of education as a critical enabler of growth. Both the quality and quantity of education in the economy increases human capital, which increases labor productivity.[2] Evidence shows that an additional year of schooling and improvement in student test scores boost growth.[3,4] Yet there are a number of drivers and forces that make education more important now for cities, counties and regions.

Education facilitates the diffusion of knowledge needed to process new information and implement new technologies.[5] As the speed and pervasiveness of technological change accelerates, this places education front

---

[2] Hanushek, E. and Wößmann, L. "The Role of Education Quality in Economic Growth." World Bank. 2007. https://openknowledge.worldbank.org/bitstream/handle/10986/7154/wps4122.pdf?sequence=1.

[3] An additional year of schooling raises the growth rate on impact by 0.44% per year. See Barro, R.J. "Education and Economic Growth." OECD. 2000. http://www.oecd.org/innovation/research/1825455.pdf.

[4] A one standard deviation increase in student achievement test scores increases growth by 1%. See "The High Cost of Low Education Performance." OECD. 2010. http://www.oecd.org/pisa/pisaproducts/pisa2006/44417824.pdf.

[5] Hanushek, E. and Wößmann, L. "The Role of Education Quality in Economic Growth." World Bank. 2007. https://openknowledge.worldbank.org/bitstream/handle/10986/7154/wps4122.pdf?sequence=1.

and center as an even more powerful lever for fostering growth. Education also helps to increase the innovative capacity of the economy, which promotes growth,[6] as knowledge intensive services become more important in economic activity. This again places increased weight on the importance of education as a means to generate much needed growth (see Figure 2).[7]

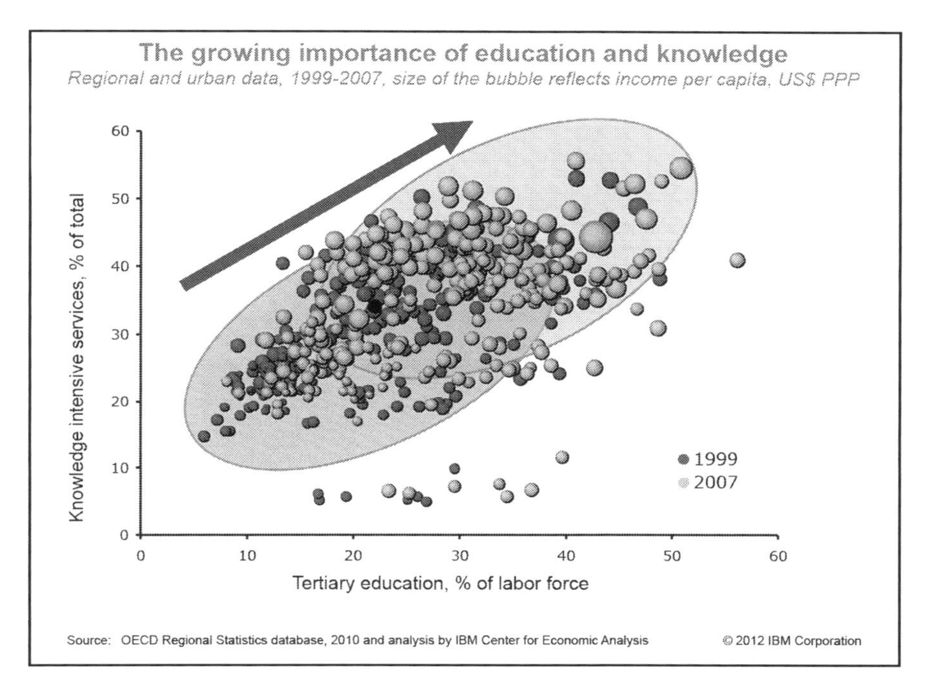

Figure 2.

If that wasn't a sufficient reason to put focus on education, policymakers at city, county and regional level can generate several other positive spillover benefits as a result of the benefits education brings to individuals, government and society. This emphasizes the need for cities, counties and regions to make education a priority.

For individuals, education improves employment prospects. Employment rates are higher and unemployment rates are lower as education level increases. In the European Union (EU), for example, the employment rate of those with tertiary education was almost 84 percent—much higher than the 54 percent employment rate for those with primary or lower secondary

---

[6] Ibid.

[7] OECD Regional Statistics database, 2010. http://stats.oecd.org/OECDregionalstatistics/. Dirks, S., Gurdgiev, C., and Keeling, M. "Smarter cities for smarter growth: How cities can optimize their systems for the talent-based economy." IBM. May 2010. ftp://public.dhe.ibm.com/common/ssi/ecm/en/gbe03348usen/GBE03348USEN.PDF.

education. It also is higher than the 73 percent employment rate those with an upper secondary and post-secondary non-tertiary level of education.[8]

Education also improves earnings potential. Each additional year of schooling raises earnings by about 10 percent in the United States, and lifetime earnings for graduate degree holders is at least double that of those with only a secondary school education.[9,10] By the same token, the economic penalty for not finishing high school is steep—almost $9,000 per year.[11] Having some postsecondary education, even without earning a degree, adds nearly one quarter of a million dollars to lifetime earnings. With median earnings of $2.3 million over a lifetime, Bachelor's degree holders earn 74 percent more than those with just a high school diploma.[12] Similar evidence is available for other countries. For example, in the United Kingdom, employees with a minimum of a degree earned 85 percent more than those educated to around the lower secondary level.[13]

Governments benefit from investing in education as returns from investing in education outweigh the costs, with larger benefits relative to costs at higher levels of education.[14] The public return[15] from investing in secondary education is more than 8 percent in the Organization for Economic Cooperation and Development countries (OECD) over the course of the learning period.[16] The public return from investing in tertiary education

---

[8] Eurostat Statistics Database. http://epp.eurostat.ec.europa.eu/portal/page/portal/eurostat/home/.

[9] "Education Counts: Towards the Millennium Development Goals." United Nations Educational, Scientific and Cultural Organization. 2011. http://unesdoc.unesco.org/images/0019/001902/190214e.pdf.

[10] Carnevale, A., Rose, S. and Cheah, B. "The College Payoff: Education, Occupations and Lifetime Earnings." Georgetown University Center on Education and the Workforce. 2009. http://www9.georgetown.edu/grad/gppi/hpi/cew/pdfs/collegepayoff-complete.pdf.

[11] Ibid.

[12] Bachelor's degree holders earn 31 percent more than workers with an Associate's degree and 74 percent more than those with just a high school diploma. See Carnevale, A., Rose, S. and Cheah, B. "The College Payoff: Education, Occupations and Lifetime Earnings." Georgetown University Center on Education and the Workforce. 2009. http://www9.georgetown.edu/grad/gppi/hpi/cew/pdfs/collegepayoff-complete.pdf.

[13] "Labour Force Survey: October-December 2010," Office for National Statistics. 2010. http://www.statistics.gov.uk/hub/labour-market/people-in-work/earnings/index.html

[14] "Education at a Glance 2011." OECD. 2011. http://www.oecd.org/education/skills-beyond-school/48631582.pdf.

[15] The gain to the public sector on an investment in education over a specified period, expressed as a percentage increase over the initial investment cost. See "Education at a Glance 2011." OECD. 2011. http://www.oecd.org/education/skills-beyond-school/48631582.pdf.

[16] "Education at a Glance 2011." OECD. 2011. http://www.oecd.org/education/skills-beyond-school/48631582.pdf.

is even higher at 11 percent.[17] Benefits for governments include additional tax revenues generated. Each four-year-equivalent degree creates direct fiscal consequences over an average lifetime. State income taxes increase by about $52,500, local property taxes increase by $38,000, and state and local sales taxes increase by more than $27,000 due to the higher spending power of more educated individuals.[18] Total tax revenue increase by about $471,000 over an average lifetime.[19]

Governments also benefit because they end up paying less money to educated individuals. Medicare benefits decrease by $9,500, Social Security benefits decrease by $9,000, unemployment compensation decreases by more than $1,500 and spending on public health care decreases by almost $5,000 over an average lifetime.[20]

Educated individuals are also less likely to be involved in crime.[21] This not only means that the crime rate can be lower, which affects the locational attractiveness of an area to other individuals and companies and means governments spend less on criminal justice and incarceration. U.S. evidence shows that a 1 percent increase in the high school graduation rate can lower crime rates and create $1.4 billion per year in reduced costs from crime incurred by victims and society.[22]

The good news for society is that there are also broader benefits from having more educated citizens. People with higher levels of education tend to be healthier and report higher life satisfaction levels.[23] Evidence from the United Kingdom shows that those in lower skilled jobs were over twice as likely to die over a three-year period as those in the highest

---

[17] Evidence based on OECD evidence for males; figure is 9.5% for females. See "Education at a Glance 2011." OECD. 2011. http://www.oecd.org/education/skills-beyond-school/48631582.pdf.

[18] Trostel, P. "The Fiscal Impact of College Attainment." New England Public Policy Center. 2007. http://www.bos.frb.org/economic/neppc/wp/2007/neppcwp0702.pdf.

[19] Total tax revenues include state income tax, local property tax, state and local sales taxes, federal income tax and federal payroll tax. See Trostel, P. "The Fiscal Impact of College Attainment." New England Public Policy Center. 2007. http://www.bos.frb.org/economic/neppc/wp/2007/neppcwp0702.pdf.

[20] Ibid.

[21] Machin, S., Marie, O. and Vujic, S. "The Crime Reducing Effect of Education." IZA. June 2010. http://ftp.iza.org/dp5000.pdf.

[22] Lochner, L. and Moretti, E. "The Effect of Education on Crime: Evidence from Prison Inmates, Arrests, and Self-Reports." 2003. http://elsa.berkeley.edu/~moretti/lm46.pdf.

[23] "Education at a Glance 2011." OECD. 2011. http://www.oecd.org/education/skills-beyond-school/48631582.pdf.

skilled jobs.[24] Evidence from the United States shows that more education reduces the risk of diabetes by almost 20 percent.[25] An additional four more years of schooling reduces lost days of work to sickness by 2.3 days each year (relative to 5.2 on average).[26] Education improves social capital and has broader societal benefits. For example, 87.2 percent of citizens with tertiary education vote compared to 79.4 percent with upper secondary education and 74 percent for those with below secondary education.

To reap the benefits to the economy and society that education can produce, education systems will have to focus on overcoming several critical challenges.

Education Systems Face Several Challenges

In the face of all the potential good that can come from education, there are several challenges that education systems globally are facing. These challenges are constraining the ability of the system to support economic growth and development, and to deliver the potential benefits to cities, counties, regions, individuals, government and society. The longer they go unaddressed, or the longer it takes decision makers in cities, counties and regions to take action, the greater it will constrain growth.

With the slowdown in growth in the aftermath of the global recession in 2007, many national and local governments have been forced to cut back on spending, with the axe falling on areas such as education that traditionally might have been ring-fenced from cuts. This reduced funding for education leads to increased demand on social programs and perpetuates a vicious cycle forcing tradeoffs between discretionary spending and entitlements. Although there has been some recovery in spending since 2008, greater competition for less or limited funds means that public spending is subject to much greater levels of scrutiny than previously. Given budget issues, there is an urgent need to improve performance measurements and in the education system to provide clear return on investment (ROI) and outcome measures while improving the productivity of the system to manage costs.

While systems face issues with static or shrinking budgets, demand for education services is rising. This is due to a combination of demographic trends, the growing demand for higher skilled workers, a decline in job

---

[24] Johnson, B. and Al-Hamad, A. "Health Statistics Quarterly—Trends in socio-economic inequalities in female mortality, 2001-08. Intercensal estimates for England and Wales." Office for National Statistics. 2011. http://www.ons.gov.uk/ons/rel/hsq/.health-statistics-quarterly/no—52—-winter-2011/art-1—-hsq-52.html .

[25] Cutler, D.M. and Lleras-Muney, A. "Education and Health." National Poverty Center. March 2007. http://www.npc.umich.edu/publications/policy_briefs/brief9/.

[26] Ibid.

opportunities for lower skilled jobs, and the fact that many jobs will require lifelong training and continuous skills updating.[27]

Between 1990 and 2007, the number of university students increased by 22 percent in North America, 74 percent in Europe, 144 percent in Latin America and 203 percent in Asia.[28] Demand for knowledge workers with specialized skills is growing by 11 percent per year.[29] Applications to British universities increased by 22.3 percent between 2007 and 2012 to just more than 650,000.[30] These trends pose huge challenges for education service providers as they try to provide more services to more people with fewer resources.

Despite the declining opportunities for lower skilled workers and increasing demand for skilled occupations, a significant number of students do not complete or are late completing secondary and tertiary education. Some 32 percent of students do not graduate from upper secondary school on time.[31] Eighteen percent of young people are under-educated and will not complete upper secondary education. There is a large degree of variation in these rates across countries ranging from rates as high as 75 percent in Turkey to 3 percent in Germany. Similarly in tertiary education, while on average 31 percent of students who enter tertiary education leave without a degree the rate is as high as 54 percent in the United States and as low as 11 percent in Japan.[32]

Simultaneously, the quality of basic skills of students that manage to complete their education possess is declining in many countries.[33] This makes it more difficult for cities, counties, regions and countries to generate growth as they churn out graduates from the education system that do not have basic math or literacy skills that are a necessary prerequisite to

---

[27] Dirks, S., Gurdgiev, C., and Keeling, M. "Smarter cities for smarter growth How cities can optimize their systems for the talent-based economy". IBM Institute for Business Value. 2010. http://public.dhe.ibm.com/common/ssi/ecm/en/gbe03348usen/GBE03348USEN.PDF. "Skills supply and demand in Europe: medium-term forecast up to 2020." CEDEFOP. 2010. http://www.cedefop.europa.eu/EN/publications/15540.aspx.

[28] "Education at a Glance 2011." OECD. 2011. http://www.oecd.org/education/school/educationataglance2011oecdindicators.htm.

[29] "Education for a Smarter Planet". IBM. 2012. http://www.ibm.com/smarterplanet/us/en/education_technology/ideas./

[30] UCAS. 2012. http://www.ucas.ac.uk/about_us/stat_services/stats_online/data_tables/datasummary.

[31] "Education at a Glance 2011." OECD. 2011. http://www.oecd.org/education/school/educationataglance2011oecdindicators.htm.

[32] Ibid.

[33] "PISA 2009 key findings". OECD. 2010. http://www.oecd.org/pisa/pisa2009keyfindings.htm. "Reading for change: Performance and engagement across countries. Results from PISA 2000." OECD. 2002. http://www.oecd.org/education/school/programmeforinternationalstudentassessmentpisa/33690904.pdf.

the economy shifting up the value chain. This not only imposes greater costs on the public purse, but it also reduces the employment and earnings prospects of these individuals.

To illustrate the significance of the impact of improving basic skills, it has been estimated that boosting PISA scores by 25 points in the next 20 years could increase OECD gross domestic product (GDP) by US$115 trillion.[34] In addition, demographic trends in many developed economies where workforces are shrinking and dependency ratios are rising means that the quality of a shrinking workforce is more important. The wages of those fewer people will determine tax revenues that governments have available to support social and other services for a growing aging population. Lower wages will mean less revenue, while higher wages from more skilled workers will translate into more revenue.

In tandem with ensuring that basic skills improve, the education system faces a challenge to ensure that students develop the right types of skills that are required in the job market by employers. This relates to two things. First, ensuring that students develop a new, broader skill set is increasingly important. Employers are now increasingly looking for T-shaped individuals who have depth of skill in a specific area but also broader skills across other areas.[35] The combination of skills enables a capacity to learn and an adaptability that makes ideal employees.

The number of jobs that require some type of information and communication technology (ICT) skills is increasing. Estimates from the EU show that by 2015, 10 percent of jobs will not require some type of ICT skill.[36] This is not a matter of putting an ICT module on the curriculum for children, but thinking long and hard about how to deliver knowledge to these students and how to take advantage of ICT to change the mode of delivery across the curriculum of subjects.

Second, the system needs to ensure that specific occupational skills—professional, managerial and technical—in traditional trades and expanding fields are available. Look at the level of structural unemployment in the labor market to see the extent of mismatch between the skills of those who are unemployed possess while there are significant vacancies going unfilled in the job market. The United States had 14 million people unemployed in September 2011 but had 3.4 million job vacancies. The EU had 23.3

---

[34] Ibid.

[35] Harvey, M. "Look for Opportunities to "Go Deep"." Stanford Technology Venture Programme. January 2011. http://stvp.stanford.edu/blog/?p=2539 Perkins, N. "Will 2012 be 'T-shaped'?" Econsultancy. December 2011. http://econsultancy.com/uk/blog/8539-will-2012-be-t-shaped-2.

[36] Kolding, M., Mette, A. and Robinson, C. "Post Crisis: e-Skills Are Needed to Drive Europe's Innovation Society." IDC. 2009. http://ec.europa.eu/enterprise/sectors/ict/files/idc_wp_november_2009_en.pdf.

million unemployed in the third quarter of 2011, yet also had 1.3 million vacancies. Fifty-two percent of U.S. employers said they were having difficulty filling mission-critical positions within their companies, up from 14 percent in 2010.[37]

These challenges in the education system are reducing benefits for individuals, government, society and constraining the ability of cities and counties to generate much needed growth. Thus, a new approach to education is urgently needed to address these concerns.

What Needs to Change

When looking at the daunting challenges that the education system is facing, the good news is that there are more means at our disposal to effectively address these problems. Yet many education systems have not taken full advantage of these new tools and solutions. Education remains one of the few services in which the delivery has virtually not changed in several decades.[38]

So what are the core competencies and functionality that education services need to develop to more effectively address these problems?

First, they need to collect the right data and take full advantage of data they already have on students and constituents. Second, they need to bring this data together from across the system and integrate it. The power of integrating the data lies in putting the puzzle pieces together to form a complete picture of what drives student success. Third, they need to take advantage of advances in modern information technology to make sense of vast amounts of data and turn it into insightful information to make better decisions and shift from reacting to predicting. For example, predicting future workforce needs can help resolve the skills alignment challenge. This data-driven approach enables the creation and execution of personalized learning pathways that allow students to gain the right skills in ways that are most effective for them.

Today, education organizations are increasingly using analytics to find ways to deliver better education more efficiently. They are connecting data systems and tracking student marks, mobility, attendance and behavior. They are measuring instructor and curriculum performance against funding sources and spending goals. They are able to spot troubling trends early, take action and align daily activity with common goals. A broader view of information across silos provides the new intelligence

---

[37] "2011 Talent Shortage Survey Results." ManpowerGroup. 2011. http://us.manpower.com/us/en/multimedia/2011-Talent-Shortage-Survey.pdf.

[38] Summers, L. "What You (Really) Need to Know." New York Times, January 2012. http://www.nytimes.com/2012/01/22/education/edlife/the-21st-century-education.html?pagewanted=all&_r=0.

needed to make education truly effective.[39] By connecting academic, operational and financial data, and coupling it with the right reporting and analysis capabilities, education organizations can: track student performance across institution, cohort, course and more; monitor attendance, mobility and intervention patterns and take remedial action; and analyze instructor development and curriculum effectiveness at any level. The result is increased completion rates.

Data-driven analysis of student behavior provides education administrators with an understanding of the factors contributing to retention. The predictive analytical model—based on hundreds of variables that previously had to be compiled by hand—makes connections across datasets, including those that were not readily apparent. Now it is possible to spot, in real-time, anomalies in students' behavior indicating whether they are at risk of dropping out.

Administrators can then quickly build intervention strategies and ensure that the right interventions are applied. This optimizes the deployment of financial aid, counseling and curriculum development resources to keep at risk students in the program and on target to graduation. The predictive analytical model boosts student retention and academic excellence by better predicting the likelihood of students staying on course or dropping out. Thus, it helps to facilitate timelier and better quality monitoring of progression and outcomes in the short term. It also provides insight about trends in enrolment, student demographics and outcomes that can help long term strategic planning.

Higher education institutions are also leveraging data to resolve the growing funding gap. They use deep analytics to manage fundraising, advancement and alumni relations to create a more sustainable base. This data-driven approach can help deal with budgetary pressures by improving services and making efficient use of existing resources. A precise, detailed picture of the entire education continuum can help stakeholders make better decisions about how to allocate resources.

In other areas, technology can be applied to lower the cost of teacher, faculty and staff computing resources, for example, through desktop cloud services. Upgrading aging infrastructure can reduce waste and manage resources more efficiently.

Technology also can help address rising demand by facilitating modes of delivery other than face-to-face, such as eLearning, creating tangible benefits for students. For example, it can help to increase the effectiveness

---

[39] "IBM Business Analytics software for education." IBM. http://www.ibm.com/smarterplanet/us/en/education_technology/nextsteps/solution/S292500W43329H30.html

of learning.[40] It also helps to lower costs by using standard/pre-existing software, drawing on the open standards, increased material re-use and sharing, and greater course standardization.[41] There is evidence that blended learning supports faster progress.[42] Of course, using technology to deliver subjects right across the curriculum can enhance students' digital literacy by giving users the opportunity to practice computer and internet skills, as well as more advanced ICT-related skills.[43]

In addition, technology can help to align the supply of skills with where demand is and ensure closer response of the education system to the needs of employers and the labor market. This approach helps to develop existing and new skills that are becoming increasingly important in the labor market. It fosters collaboration with fellow students at home institutions and other schools/universities around the world. Students will enter the job market with a better understanding of how collaborative technologies and communities are used in the real world.

Call to Action

Provinces, cities and institutions can take some practical steps to ensure that their education system is fit for its purpose and plays its rightful role in supporting growth. Leveraging data and analytics as a cornerstone of process transformation is essential to making wise decisions on resource allocation. Across the educational eco-system, we should act now to:

- Create a unique persistent view of students over time;
- Incorporate data-driven decision making into the instructional culture;
- Develop a consistent and pervasive framework for student assessment; and

---

[40] Learners learn more using computer-based instruction than they do with conventional ways of teaching, as measured by higher post-treatment test scores. See Tobias, S. and Fletcher, J. "Training and Retraining: A Handbook for Business, Industry, Government, and the Military." American Psychological Association. 2000.

[41] "E-learning in Tertiary Education." OECD. December 2005. http://www.oecd.org/internet/35961132.pdf.

[42] Watson, J. "Blended Learning: The Convergence of Online and Face-to-Face Education." North American Council for Online Learning. 2008. http://www.inacol.org/research/promisingpractices/NACOL_PP-BlendedLearning-lr.pdf.

[43] "Digital Transformation: A Framework for ICT Literacy." Educational Testing Service. 2002. http://www.ets.org/Media/Tests/Information_and_Communication_Technology_Literacy/ictreport.pdf.

- Leverage analytics to identify opportunities for interventions with a feedback mechanism to evaluate and improve effectiveness of the interventions.

The digital learner of the 21st century needs a digital curriculum. Following are essential elements to consider when building a digital curriculum:

- Develop a migration strategy to digital, adaptable and interactive content;
- Create common learning objective standards by grade level that are rooted in the needs of employers and society;
- Foster science, technology, engineering and mathematics (STEM) and T-shaped skills as these are becoming increasingly pervasive for most occupations;
- Enable alignment to economic development goals for the system and individuals;
- Enforce IT standards for curricular content to ensure interoperability and investment security and avoid being tied to a single content provider; and
- Enact common IT standards for student tracking and reporting that will facilitate ongoing evaluation and improvement the digital curriculum.

Digital instructional tools for learning hold great promise to cost effectively tailor and personalize education. In deploying these tools:

- Focus on blended learning to merge the best of online and classroom-based learning into a seamless model for students;
- Build upon open technology standards to foster ongoing innovation from vendors and educators;
- Focus on teacher enablement and success, followed by student engagement and success; and
- Build toward a model of personalized lesson plans and learning pathways that are informed by the requirements and opportunities in the marketplace.

Pervasive ICT access is fundamental to successful deployment of digital learning. Communities must have a robust IT infrastructure and device deployment model to:

- Support high speed network connectivity in the classroom, on transit, in public spaces, as well as home access;
- Facilitated shared services across many institutions to drive common processes and lower costs; and
- Build an infrastructure that's "device neutral" to support changes in the consumer market and student preferences.

Funding the required infrastructure and enhancements to curriculum is always a challenge. Organizations that can drive efficiencies in administration and operations are able to shift funds to support learning. Significant cost savings can come from:

- Shared services across institutions to gain efficiencies;
- Integrated decision support systems to improve financial performance;
- Automated facilities and operations to lower costs; and
- Analytics systems to identify and reduce risk and unexpected costs.

While education is crucial to jobs and growth, it is an evolving effort. The system should be aligned to support economic development goals as they change over time.

- Incorporate 21st century skills into the curriculum. Seek input from employers on emerging trends and the skills that are most needed for the foreseeable future.
- Engage industry in support of the educational system through mentorships, apprenticeships and career alignment projects..
- Create pathways and support tools for individuals to navigate the education continuum to career objectives.
- Leverage analytics to provide insight into system-wide performance, aligned to objectives.
- Build in a feedback mechanism to ensure the system adapts and thrives as society transitions to new industries and business models.

Making wise investments now to build smarter education and learning systems will help to drive economic development and employment growth for many decades to come.

DR. MARY KEELING *is manager, economic analysis for the Global Smarter Cities program in IBM. She is responsible for the economic analysis underpinning IBM's smarter cities solutions including the financial and business justification for the solutions.*

MARY OLSON *has worked in the technology industry for 30 years, starting her career working for a University then State Government. After earning her Masters degree, she joined IBM in field sales for numerous industries. She is currently responsible for helping government and education clients use technology to solve some of their toughest challenges.*

14

Building Smarter Cities

Jennifer Bremer

The term "smart city" is more than just a tag line for large consulting and information technology (IT) companies. Smart cities are those cities that find new ways to enable economic growth and sustainability by really listening to their constituents and providing innovative ways to provide necessary services in this new digital age. While every city needs the basics of water and sewer services, public safety, public education, etc., smart cities take extra measures and provide easy and affordable (even free) access to the Internet. They make digital education a priority, and they attract high-paying jobs—not through a tax incentive for a home office or factory to relocate, but rather by providing a higher quality of life for employees and their families.

Economic development is now more about where one wants to live, not where one wants to work. With the 24-hour access to information and the enhanced collaboration tools available today (such as Cisco TelePresence® and WebEx®), many employees are choosing to live in one place and telecommute to another location, sometimes many states away.

The new world of economic development is about developing talent and *keeping* collective intelligence in your municipality, not trying to bring it in from another city or state. After all, if you can tempt a business to move from a different locale to your area, other areas can lure that same business away from you. On the other hand, creating a cultural and community bond that establishes an emotional connection with the employee and his/her family is more difficult to break. The tax base becomes stable, and the types of jobs that allow for technology-based "commuting" are usually high-paying, skilled jobs that provide higher wages and subsequently higher tax revenues (property, sales and income taxes). This stable base allows for other businesses and services to be established, such as retail or even entrepreneurial startups. Educational needs will change and grow, allowing for new research and development advances. And the cycle continues, becoming self-sustaining over time.

To achieve this new vision of being a smart city, municipalities are tasked with balancing a large set of priorities and challenges including economic health, employment, increased longevity of the population, safety and security requirements, environmental concerns, aging infrastructures and planning for future IT models. Additionally, new groups of people are coming into the workforce, and their expectations are vastly different from the previous workforce. The new workforce believes technology is no longer a nice to have; it is truly a necessity.

Public and private industry have a tremendous opportunity to work together to address the needs of citizens and partners in the new digital world, especially as they relate to education, health care, transportation, telecommunications, safety and security, building systems, utilities, and sports and entertainment. The key to succeeding in this balancing act will reside not only in the collaboration of partners, but also in establishing clear IT priorities around information and connections.

Cities are looking to serve citizens by developing or transforming urban settings to offer advanced, connected communities that attract businesses, boast innovative design, and lay the groundwork to achieve long-lasting economic, social and environmental success. Increasing amounts of data from both humans and machines present opportunities for citizen engagement, enhanced quality of life, and previously unimaginable opportunities within the smart city.

Factors driving smart cities include:

- **Need for Talent.** To remain competitive, cities need to attract and retain talented and skilled workers. Smart cities will provide an advantage when compared to potential competitor cities due to their strong innovation ecosystems and long-term growth plans. This results in even further job creation and growth

- **Need for Infrastructure.** Traffic congestion, utilities and finite resources are pushing cities to think more strategically about how to use their limited budgets. Technology offers capabilities to more efficiently manage and use existing infrastructure, as well as to plan for future growth. The term infrastructure now must include a digital backbone for the municipality, not just a physical backbone (road system).

- **Access to Resources and Data.** The population has become accustomed to immediate and unlimited access to information and services. The demands that once were reserved for private industry are now being asked of governments. This has forced city leaders to rethink service delivery models for citizens.

Along with the inherent and evolving needs of citizens, emerging technology is pushing American cities to rethink current procedures and systems to better serve citizen needs and to create smarter, more efficient cities. The more data generated and shared, the greater the opportunity to understand the unique behaviors and needs of a given population. Moreover, thanks to a number of driving factors, the potential to unlock greater cost savings, efficiency and intelligence can become a reality. To ensure a successful long-term strategy and implementation, the following components must be present:

- **Strategy.** Clearly defined business goals serves as the foundation of any smart city project, while strong leadership defines the vision for the smart city, facilitates collaboration, and implements proven solutions that best fit the vision.

- **Culture.** Communicating with and understanding the people for whom the city is built will prove essential to the success of a smart city project. This includes the community's willingness to experiment with innovative ideas and technology.

- **Process.** Developing structure around how change will be implemented, with regard to organization, budgeting and performance measures, provides a clear sense of direction and set expectations. Establishing structure and process around partner relationships creates smoother interactions.

- **Technology.** Technology is the driving force behind smart cities. Architects should design structures to meet the needs of each specific community, and overall IT strategies should account for the adoption of broadband infrastructure and data capture devices.

- **Data.** The use and access to data will define the potential of the smart city. The greater utilization of data also will allow for continued improvements to citizen services, while the availability of data will create a more informed and collaborative population.

- **Security.** The possibilities offered by technology and data utilization are infinite and awe-inspiring, but they can also be fraught with danger. Any citizen-centric digital plan must include a robust, multipronged approach to network security and the assurance of data integrity.

The IT Factor

Planning the grand development of a smart city is exciting, but to make those dreams a reality, clear IT strategies and models will be required. The task is a daunting one, as chief information officers (CIOs) and IT leaders work to create integrated, architecture-based strategies that enable the sharing of ideas, plans and budgets among the public and private partners. Successful smart cities have a vision that leverages the network as the platform to transform communities into tightly integrated and widely connected communities capable of achieving economic, social and environmental sustainability through networked information.

Looking Ahead: A City Connected Through the Internet of Everything

The Internet of Everything (IoE), or the connections among people, data, things and processes, creates enormous amounts of data. The sheer volume and complexity of connections that can be achieved through the IOE will serve as a key factor in the planning of future smart cities.

New technology ideas like big data and analytics, secure mobility, social media and cloud will provide the foundation for meeting smart city goals. When analyzed and used intelligently, the data produced through IoE has the ability to provide remote security monitoring; monitor energy consumption; trace essential supplies like food and medicine; and monitor devices, vehicles and people from afar.

A more robust future IoE environment could help uncover even more information through sensors, making it possible to make real-time decisions that provide faster response times during emergencies and create direct connections for citizens to the public services they need and desire.

Cities around the globe are facing a crossroads as they plan for the future and attempt to incorporate future technologies and deal with existing infrastructure. Communities are just beginning to unveil the potential for smarter cities. Nevertheless, municipalities around the country are making strides to create better communities that operate efficiently, effectively and productively.

Lake Nona, FL: America's First Smart City

As the first fully developed U.S. smart city project, Lake Nona, just outside Orlando, Fla., is poised to become an integrated city for working, living, learning and playing. Cisco will work with Lake Nona over the next 15 years to collaborate on developing a global model and standard for sustainable urban development. Leveraging Cisco® Smart+Connected Communities™ solutions, Lake Nona will integrate the latest networking technologies and digital infrastructure to design a smart city experience for more than 25,000 residents.

The Lake Nona Community relies on IT implementations and the network to achieve urban development goals of becoming an integrated community that is home to excellent education, recreational facilities, a medical city, diverse workspaces, retail centers, entertainment choices and residential options. The community is designed with advanced technology at the center of its ecosystem to enable community dwellers and visitors to work, live, learn and play in new and more sustainable ways.

Lake Nona community features will include:

- **Unified Lake Nona Medical City:** Increased integration, coordination and collaboration between medical care and life sciences stakeholders within the Lake Nona Medical City will enable a unified lifelong medical care delivery system. This type of platform will help to reduce technological barriers and increase information sharing to improve quality of care and reduce costs, with a focus toward increasing the overall quality of human life experience across the full cycle of wellness.
- **Virtual Safe Community:** Through integration, coordination and collaboration between local law enforcement, emergency management and justice ecosystem partners and organizations, Lake Nona will have the ability to more effectively and efficiently identify and detect risks, issues or other activities that require action by law enforcement, safety and security, emergency management, or justice resources through machine-to-machine or machine-to-man field sensors, cameras, video, tracking devices and other technology-enabled capabilities.
- **Unified Life-Long Learning and Education:** Using the network to integrate voice, video, data, advanced collaboration tools and high-speed broadband access across the education system will empower students, faculty, staff and administrators to become more informed and connected. The integrations will provide access to information anywhere, on any device, and will help to enable inclusion of outside experts and content to create rich learning environments.
- **Smart Work Centers:** Lake Nona will offer public spaces for the community, providing residents with places to work, meet and use shared services. This will create greater opportunity for flexible work schedules. Highly secure wireless Internet access, TelePresence, collaboration tools and business services, including reception, catering and daycare, will be available. The proximity of these work centers within the environment also will help to reduce commute times, greenhouse gas emissions and traffic congestion.
- **Transportation, Sports and Entertainment, Retail:** Intelligent transportation platforms will help to reduce traffic congestion and pollution while easing the commuting experience. Residents will enjoy more intelligent entertainment experiences, as well. Providing connections to retail infrastructure will enable better collaboration among retail employees and suppliers, resulting in greater revenue and reduced operating costs, while enhancing the shopping

experience. Sports and entertainment options will be personalized through greater connections between fans and their favorite teams, and with each other.

City of Midland, TX: Upgrades Traffic Management System with Wireless

As the nation's demand for energy expanded, the city of Midland, Texas, situated in the heart of oil and gas country, experienced exponential growth. The previous traffic management system was outdated and unequipped to handle the city's 10 percent annual population growth, and 17 percent growth in traffic.

The legacy traffic management system in place was managed using a combination of fixed time intervals for peak inbound and outbound traffic for major highways, while city traffic used a grid, changing signals at fixed intervals set for each inbound and outbound traffic. Costs to replace parts, and operate and maintain the systems were high because of the aging technology and need for manual intervention.

After assessing options and selecting an advanced traffic management system (ATMS), the city Transportation Department turned to wireless networks to revamp its system. In 2008, the traffic department began implementing a web-based ATMS Central Software Suite, running on a robust and secure wireless network. The revamped citywide system began operating at the beginning of March 2009, using 180 wireless access points. As a result of the ATMS deployment, Midland saved US$1.2 million through efficiencies in traffic management and gained wireless coverage, including an estimated 27 percent reduction in total delays per vehicle, 18 percent reduction in total stops per vehicle, and 10 percent reduction in fuel consumption.

Key capabilities of the ATMS include:

- IP network-enabled arterial management applications that detect traffic flow and take rapid preemptive action to mitigate congestion.
- IP-connected controllers send immediate notification of signal malfunction, enabling remote management to resolve signaling problems, optimize traffic flow by changing signal offsets and splits, and adjust traffic signals for major events affecting traffic.
- Web-enabled devices at intersections and connected in extended wireless LAN allow for secure monitoring and management. This monitoring allows traffic policies to be programmed to respond to predefined conditions such as congestion.

Investing in a single, scalable, converged IP network as a platform has allowed the city of Midland to focus on downtown revitalization and economic development initiatives by alleviating traffic challenges, saving money and providing wireless coverage to 95 percent of the city as a result of the broader project. As mobile devices become more prevalent and anytime access becomes the norm, extending the free 802.11 Wi-Fi access to outdoor spaces could increase the attraction of the downtown area as a destination for businesses and professionals.

The city of Midland plans to incorporate approximately 70 wireless IP video cameras to stream live video from the field back to Traffic Control Center (TMC), enabling greater monitoring of high accident intersections. Cameras will be used to alert emergency dispatch of accidents more quickly, provide citywide coverage for transportation-related services, and alert the department of hazardous material spills or fires.

USAA FBI Chicago: Sustainable Buildings

Sustainable or "green" buildings hold a significant economic and environmental opportunity and growth, as 39 percent of carbon dioxide emissions, 40 percent of energy consumption, 13 percent of water consumption and 15 percent of gross domestic product are produced through U.S. buildings each year. Aside from meeting 85 percent of future U.S. demand for energy, creating more efficient buildings presents a potential for 2.5 million new jobs.

Understanding the need for more efficient buildings, the USAA Real Estate Company (USAA RealCo) sought to team with building tenants to improve efficiency and reduce the environmental impact. USAA RealCo, in cooperation with the Federal Bureau of Investigation (FBI) and the General Services Administration (GSA), sought to maximize occupant comfort and improve financial performance by seeking Leadership in Energy and Environmental Design (LEED) Platinum certification (the highest level of certification) for the FBI Chicago Regional Office. The certification is based on five categories, including indoor environmental quality, sustainable sites, water efficiency, energy and atmosphere.

Beyond the LEED certifications, USAA RealCo sought to earn the Energy Star label, and worked to develop and implement a plan that optimized the FBI building's energy performance.

USAA RealCo looked to Cisco Network Building Mediator (Mediator) to collect energy consumption data from the building's newly installed sub-meters, and communicate that data to the building's enterprise energy management platform using the IP-based network as the platform. USAA RealCo also turned to EFT Energy Inc. for its web-based energy management platform software for data analysis and reporting.

USAA RealCo submetered the major energy systems, programmed the building's equipment to run at its highest efficiency, and introduced an enterprise energy management capability to track and analyze energy consumption. These measurements allowed the building operations team to understand which equipment uses the most electricity, at what times, and under what conditions.

The network-based framework creates a common, standards-based, open platform for applications and cloud services, enabling disparate building/IT systems to communicate. Since deployment, the FBI building's engineering team is able to collect energy consumption data in real-time, and communicate that data to the building's EFT Energy Manager as an enterprise energy management solution for analysis and reporting. Equipment operation schedules can be adjusted to better reflect building occupancy. Programming for after-hours and weekends increases efficiency. Overall, the goals of lower energy costs and better work environment were achieved. In December 2008, the building was awarded the U.S. Green Building Council's first LEED Existing Buildings Operations Maintenance (EBOM) Platinum certification in the world.

In the LEED Energy and Atmosphere category, the building achieved 25 points out of 30 points, and succeeded in increasing its Energy Star rating from a highly efficient score of 78 to an exceptional score of 95 (out of 100), thereby indicating that the project is operating in the top 5 percent of the market in terms of energy efficiency. By developing and implementing a building commissioning plan that included real-time data monitoring and analysis, USAA RealCo not only achieved its immediate business objective, but also established the infrastructure that will permit an ongoing commissioning process to ensure that the facility continues maximizing its energy efficiency.

USAA RealCo demonstrated that by using technology such as the Cisco Network Building Mediator and EFT Energy Manager, energy consumption can be better managed to increase efficiency and lower energy use on near-real-time intervals.

City of Raleigh, NC

As a city, Raleigh, N.C., lacked a unified vision for technology and how it could drive improvements for the city and its citizens. Disparate legacy technologies were in use throughout the city government, and technology was seen as a footnote rather than a key to the much needed revitalization of downtown Raleigh. Technological infrastructure was used for internal purposes, and the city missed out on opportunities to leverage technology to drive the mission and vision of Raleigh.

Leadership looked to revitalize the city and began the initiative with the convention center, a city institution that many had given up on. Revenue for the convention center was down, and it was increasingly difficult to attract large trade shows and conferences to the city with a venue that had outdated technology. This lack of visitors, in turn, adversely affected local retail shops, restaurants, hotels and other businesses. The mall was facing decline because it was positioned in an area of downtown that was no longer frequented by businesspeople or students as it had been in the past. This trend had severe consequences for the financial well-being of the area.

Raleigh residents, especially those in low-income neighborhoods, were falling behind the technology curve, as computer literacy is increasingly important for workers and students.

Planning a major overhaul of existing technological infrastructure, the city of Raleigh and Cisco partnered to revamp the city's entire network infrastructure, using a mesh access architecture, power over Ethernet and Cisco Unified Computing System™ (UCS®), and then deploying voice over IP, video and wireless connectivity.

This infrastructure extended to the conference center, which now has a fiber optic data network and high-speed Internet access with both wired and wireless connectivity. In addition, the city's comprehensive technology initiative, "Raleigh Connected," provides free Wi-Fi throughout downtown, including Fayetteville Street, which attracts businesspeople and students. It also extends wireless access to nearly 2,000 households in low-income areas.

The city received federal stimulus funds and corporate support to make technology available and affordable for those who need it, and started a "Digital Connectors" program that offers computer training in Cisco networking and other technologies to people ages 14 to 21 who are from low-income households.

Since the overhaul began in 2006, the city's technology infrastructure has been modernized. Businesses, workers and students have returned to downtown Raleigh. In fact, the city has made such great strides with technology that *Forbes* named Raleigh "America's Most Wired City" in 2010.

The convention center, formerly a symbol of decline, is now a state-of-the-art example of the city's progress, and it can compete with any other in the world. The 19th International World Wide Web Conference (WWW2010) and the Internet Summit of 2011 were both held at the Raleigh Convention Center.

Meanwhile, the city continues to improve, working to implement an optical ring, consisting of 125 miles of fiber that is part of its traffic light network, connecting the city to the local universities and other government entities to support the community in even more ways. In addition, because fiber is already in place, the city will realize tremendous cost savings by leveraging existing infrastructure and getting rid of many leased lines.

Every city's needs are different, and every city will define "smart" in its own way. It is important to remember that this new digital world requires a new approach to economic development. That approach must include technology, but not simply for technology's sake. It must be used to create a community with a high quality of life for its citizens. That high quality of life will be the engine that drives truly sustainable economic growth for the future.

__JENNIFER BREMER__ is director of public sector marketing for Cisco Systems Inc. She holds a Bachelor's degree in English from North Carolina State University, as well as a Masters in Technical Communications from East Carolina University. She has focused her career on the effective use of technology in government and education, and has written on topics such as the use of video in public safety, the use of technology for underserved populations, and new ideas for economic development in a digital world.

15

Slicing Data Center Costs in Half

Adam and Cal Braunstein

Data centers managers and IT executives that take aggressive actions to address growing data center inefficiencies and waste can reap benefits that can approach 50 percent of a data center's operating budget. In fact, recent Robert Frances Group (RFG) studies show a typical data center operation can double capacity while reducing costs by up to 50 percent and cutting energy expenditures by up to 80 percent. By implementing strategic plans for highly efficient data center operations, companies and governments can realize significant savings and improve their competitive stance against traditional shops and those using cloud offerings. IT executives should build a five-year plan to transform their data centers into optimized IT-as-a-service operations.

Business Imperatives

- Transforming the data center is a three-phase process. Phase one employs basic production best practices and eliminates customs that have resulted in excessive operational expenditures. These inconsistencies take the forms of both process and technology, and achieving singularity will require willingness to conform to best practices and common platforms. Ultimately, it is not difficult, but it requires having an open mind and willingness to give up old habits. IT executives should perform a gap analysis between best practices for applications, infrastructure, networking, processes, servers and storage and their existing environments, and address those items that need improvement.
- The tougher phase is the implementation of transformational processes that enable a quantum leap in operational effectiveness and quality of service (QoS). This stage requires IT executives to rethink their processes so that they can scale-up their operations and create highly efficient network, server and storage pools. While there are

technology aspects to this phase, it is more about cultural change, highly efficient processes, reorientation of people skills and standardization. This stage of improvement will result in staff reductions and new work efforts and environments. Thus, IT executives should communicate the new data center vision, restructure data center practices and procedures using those that are willing to change, and transition out those that are steadfast to the old ways.

- The final step is the move to agility, automation, optimization and IT as a service. The big gains made during this phase result from locking in the advances learned in phase two through automation, optimization and the use of hybrid, private and public clouds. The objective is to fuse business with IT and make IT operate as a service. IT executives should determine what to keep in-house or move to external clouds, and create software defined data centers with the required interfaces, management controls, processes and tools to achieve the goals.

A study by Jonathan Koomey, WHO IS HE?, shows IT executives are making gains on energy efficiency and power usage (See Figure 1). RFG studies have found that most enterprises are not operating anywhere near maximum effectiveness levels. Consequently, a typical data center operation could slice costs by up to 50 percent and reduce energy expenditures by up to 80 percent. If one includes data center consolidation and use of cloud computing, the operational expenditure savings can greatly exceed 50 percent.

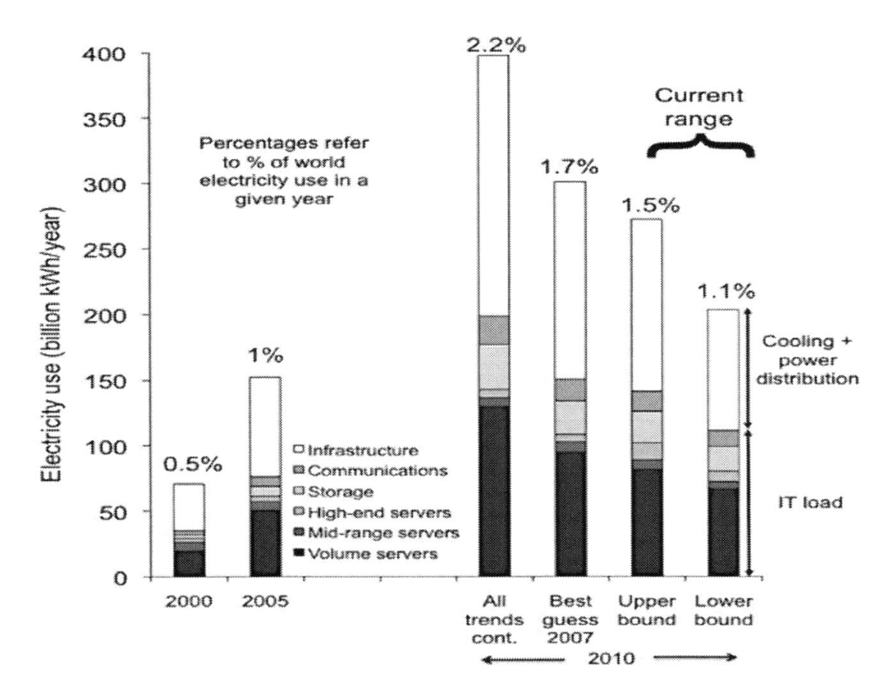

Figure 1. *Worldwide Data Center Electricity Use, 2011 Koomey report.*

Going Green

A decade ago, the concept of "going green" was a priority for few enterprises outside industries directly tied to environmental issues or legislation. Now, many companies and governments increasingly understand how the alignment of sustainable initiatives and cost optimization are not mutually exclusive. Moreover, the elimination of wasteful practices extends beyond adopting cleaner, more efficient technologies to include best practices in strategic planning, processes, technologies and quantitative measurement. While overnight results may be few for already-efficient enterprises, ongoing positive monetary improvements can be realized using a three-phase framework incorporating tight controls, objectives and carefully timed improvements.

The transformation needed to eliminate waste and adopt an IT as a service-delivery model is a three-phase effort that can extend between five and 10 years before completion (See Figure 2). While the total time may be daunting, enterprises can make gains annually and within each phase. All phases should have clearly delineated goals and include quantifiable measurements to track progress and keep stakeholders abreast of goal attainment.

The three phases are as follows:

- IT production improvements;
- Business transformation; and
- IT as a service.

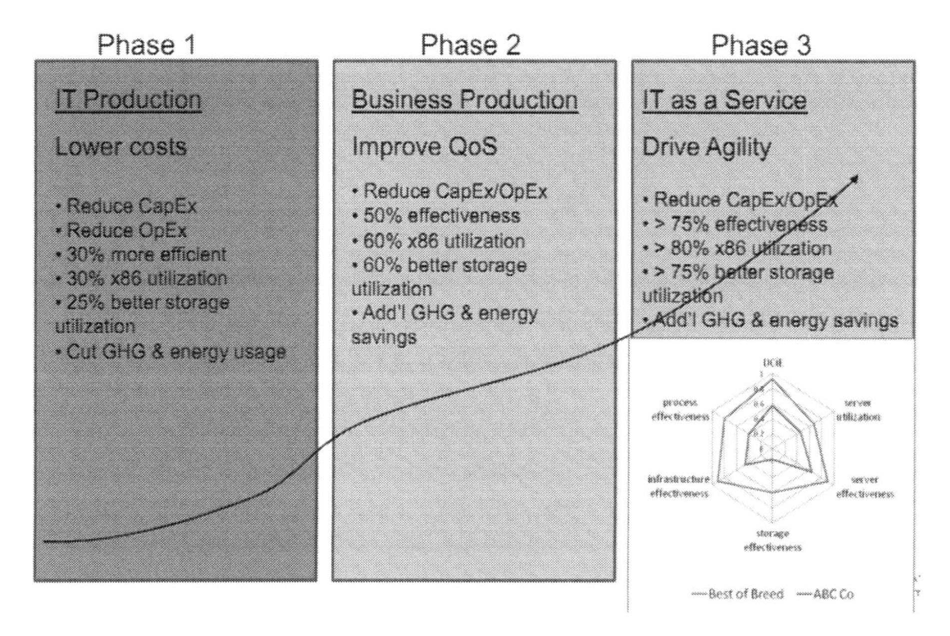

Figure 2. *IT Transformational Approach.*

The first step is to lower operational costs as much as feasibly possible. RFG estimates that this process will improve server use by 25 percent to 30 percent, and increase storage use by up to 25 percent. This step also will lower infrastructure costs so that the data center can obtain a power usage effectiveness (PUE) rating of less than 2.0. These are not breakthrough results, but get an organization poised to begin transforming the business of IT.

Designing for Green

Infrastructure elements including data center builds, maintenance and cooling are significant operational cost centers for corporations that can reduce expenses by adopting new, but already proven, designs. Modular data center designs available from numerous vendors offer enterprises abilities to build new facilities up to 75 percent faster and less expensive than traditional methods, although enterprises need to embrace new realities while jumping into the fray. Many of these designs are "containerized pods," which enterprises can combine rapidly to bring new processing and storage capabilities online. Pods are either linked together or laid end-to-end. Containers incorporate channeling for cooling, lighting, networking and power.

Techniques that rely less on costly and inefficient computer room air conditioners (CRACs) offer 50 percent or more savings over traditional systems, depending on how aggressive enterprises are with heat management and data center location. For instance, Google Inc. is using seawater to cool warm air in its new Finnish data center, while Facebook Inc.'s Oregon data center uses an outside air exchange (DX) approach coupled with a misting chamber to add humidity. The smaller, enclosed pod space requires less cooling, and the company eliminated raised floors in favor of centralized backplanes that combine networking and power. Ducting is unnecessary, and cool air blows directly onto servers, many of which have open, caseless designs to allow heat to escape.

Caseless designs are one part of the more effective layouts used in pods and other new data center architectures. Other envelope-pushing architectures include forgoing large UPSes in favor of on-board battery backups, the use of single rail voltage to reduce energy losses, temperature sensors coupled with slower fans to save power, and the elimination of unneeded ports in motherboards. The design also supplements hot and cold aisles with modular aisle enclosures and top-of-rack heat exhausts. Many of these elements are on the bleeding edge and should serve more as reference for long-term planning than short-term quick fixes.

RFG has written extensively on approaches to cutting infrastructure costs. The research brief, dated May 2013, "Data Center Effectiveness Metrics" discusses this in detail.

IT Production Improvements

Other keys to IT production improvements are rationalization, standardization and virtualization. As these elements have a number of components, IT executives should identify quick hits, near-, intermediate- and long-term project gains. For example, standardizing archiving, development and test beds, processes, and tools across all business units globally can take years.

One approach that has proven successful is to implement changes within an influential group and to demonstrate the gains achieved through standardization. One major financial institution found that it could save more than $100 million per year in storage costs by archiving "golden records" only. Golden records are the primary sources of data; all other copies are secondary and not kept long-term.

An all-encompassing rationalization effort should address applications, data, servers, storage and workloads. Most large enterprises have multiple applications performing the same functions. This inefficient approach requires redundancy in hardware and personnel, necessitating multiple copies of software licenses and maintenance, as well as development and support teams to keep these applications current. Each of the duplicate applications has its own sets of databases that enterprises back up, archive, synchronize and aggregate into data warehouses and reports. In many cases, the reports need manual reconciliation before final use. Companies that have aggressively focused on correcting this flaw have reduced the number of business applications by 75 percent or more.

Companies can develop a similar story for the number of physical servers required for development, test and production. There are four ways companies can reduce the quantity of servers. The obvious approach to server consolidation is through virtualization. Most organizations should be able to achieve a minimum of a 4:1 virtual to physical server ratio of x86-architected servers without a transformational effort. This ratio rarely results in server utilization of more than 25 percent to 30 percent.

The second way to eliminate server quantity is through shorter server lifecycles. RFG studies have found that a 36- to 40-month lifecycle is more economical than a 60-month lifecycle. By turning over technology more rapidly, enterprises tend to reduce the number of servers required while increasing computational power.

Standardizing development and test environments further reduces processors in data centers. Lastly, studies find companies and governments tend to have at least 10 percent of their servers in operation but not in use. For varying reasons, these boxes remain idle but run and occupy space. In a similar vein, power management can reduce the number of servers running at various periods of the day to consolidate workloads and power down idle servers.

Another way to do server rationalization is by workload. There are four types of critical workloads: business applications; transaction processing and database; analytics and high performance computing (HPC); and web, collaboration and infrastructure. Each of the four workload types has different computational, network and storage characteristics, and their underlying platforms should be purpose-built to optimize availability, cost, energy-efficiency, performance, quality of service, scalability and security. Major hardware providers have addressed this challenge with appliances and converged architecture or expert systems solutions, which are optimized for targeted workloads and administrator productivity. In the similar vein, RFG studies find that organizations that move and consolidate their x86 databases onto a mainframe (the original multi-workload processor) can reduce their operational costs by at least 50 percent for those ecosystems.

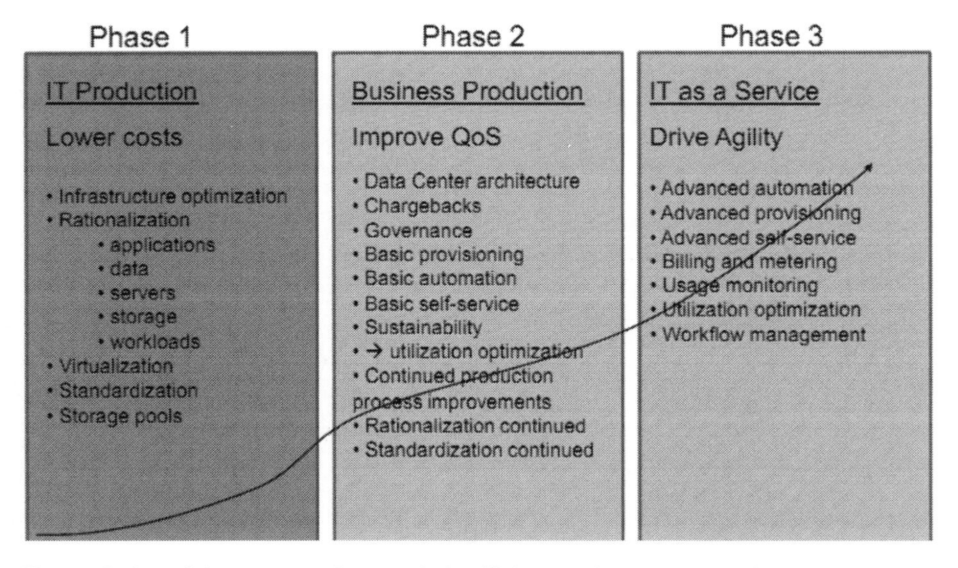

The majority of data centers is grossly inefficient and costs enterprises at least twice as much to operate than necessary. Companies that do not tackle this problem may find themselves priced out of the market due to their expensive, inflexible infrastructure cost structures, while governments will be stuck supporting these costly legacy infrastructures for a digital eternity. IT executives should develop and gain executive buy-in for a five-year data center transformational plan that addresses business agility and capacity requirements, technological roadmaps, and state-of-the-art capabilities. The plan should close the gap between current levels of performance and the future state of an IT as a Service operation.

Figure 3. *Components of IT Transformation Approach.*

Moreover, RFG finds IT does not manage its storage environments very well and that more than 60 percent of existing storage space is either not used or not well used. According to studies, about 10 percent of overall usable disk capacity was once appropriately allocated but becomes orphaned when the server that uses it goes away and the space is not returned. Another 15 percent of capacity tends to be allocated but unused, while 5 percent is inappropriately used. Lastly, up to 40 percent of disk capacity is inert (i.e., the space was allocated and used but not accessed or referenced for six months or more).

With the right tools, IT executives can locate and recover the wasted space, thereby doubling disk capacity without additional storage purchases. Additional gains can be made by using compression, deduplication, flash storage, tiering, thin provisioning, and golden records. Thus, IT executives can jump from 20 percent to 30 percent effective disk utilization to greater than 60 percent utilization and lower costs by optimizing data placement on storage tiers, archiving and three- to four-year refresh cycles.

Business Transformation

The business transformation stage involves more than just gains made from better use of technology. In this phase, work efforts and processes are re-engineered to take advantage of the latest best practices. Instead of resources dedicated to application servers or underutilized, siloed scale-out processor environments, IT executives re-architect the data center so that it optimizes and pools people and technology resources, and thereby minimizes waste. IT executives will find that the new software defined data centers, networks or storage pools improves and shortens the transformation process while lowering overall costs.

Then there is the inclusion of cloud computing into the mix. There are multiple approaches to use cloud technologies. The question should not be if one should employ clouds but where and how should cloud technology be incorporated as part of the business transformation. The supplemental use of clouds can reduce costs by up to 40 percent if done correctly, which includes having already consolidated, standardized and virtualized the components one is contemplating shifting to cloud services. Off-premise clouds are not always less expensive, so executives should be cautious and perform a cost/benefit study before leaping.

The transformation will require staff to adjust to a major cultural shift and re-learn their jobs, objectives, business processes and tasks. The data center operational staff will now be responsible for software-defined resource pools, user/vendor relationship management or physical infrastructure, and will no longer be fully knowledgeable on an application and its entire environment. When there are complex application or system failures or problems, operational staff will need second-level support from individuals with detailed understanding of the applications or systems.

The consolidation to virtual environments means that fewer people will be required to handle daily operations. IT executives will need to determine which personnel is able to effectively adapt to new roles and transition out those that are no longer needed.

Also as part of this stage of development, new governance policies and procedures may come into play. Frequently, chargeback initiatives based on business factors (rather than IT metrics) are implemented in this phase. RFG also sees other QoS initiatives, such as basic automation, provisioning and self-service functions initiated.

The result of the business transformational phase is the achievement of utilization levels in the 60 percent range. Additionally, with advances in rationalization and standardization, IT executives are positioned to start addressing the entire IT operation as a business service.

IT As a Service

The IT as a service concept means the encapsulation of all IT services into a service catalog combined with the agility to rapidly provision, fulfill and charge for any service request. To attain this capability, IT executives will have enhanced their operations with advanced levels of automation, provisioning and self-service functionality. Accurate and flexible billing and metering tools must be in place along with workflow management.

These enhancements will enable users to provision and execute their own services, as well as allow operations to run with reduced staff and highly utilized systems. Additionally, once IT has data on its true operational expenditure and performance baselines, IT executives can determine whether applications should be executed onsite or offsite on a cloud. RFG expects that for large enterprises in most industry sectors, up to 25 percent of all applications will run on an off-premise cloud. IT executives should evaluate whether cloud computing can satisfy some horizontal functional needs (such as development or test) or temporary capacity relief (such as supplemental server capacity).

Data Center Resource Optimization

Transforming data center architecture and operations is more than just optimizing operations. It is about converting IT operations into a least-cost automated business support environment. Because most data centers are relatively inefficient, it should be possible to reduce operational costs by half while improving capacity and performance. Data center resource optimization is a journey requiring a long-term view coupled with improvements that reduce cost and resource requirements in a predictable and regularly demonstrable manner. Organizations that take aggressive action to address growing energy use and waste can reap benefits that can exceed one-third of a data center's operating budget. By implementing strategic plans for highly efficient data center operations, companies and governments can deeply cut costs and reduce power-consumption while providing more capacity. For-profit organizations also can improve their competitive stance against traditional shops and those using cloud offerings.

Enterprises should address issues from a holistic standpoint that encompasses the data center, its architecture, and the lifecycle of the computer and infrastructure equipment installed. Most IT executives do not have a detailed view of their data center effectiveness and are unable to pinpoint areas for improvement. A hard look at operations will reveal areas for improvement, and IT executives should prioritize based on integration complexity, corporate value, cost and phase appropriateness. IT executives should have the ultimate say in designing and implementing these data center improvements. However, understanding and buy-in from stakeholders is essential as improvements will affect asset management, hardware and software selection criteria, operations, and IT support methodologies.

Establishing baseline metrics and gap analysis measuring operations against best-of-breed should be conducted in preparation for building the strategic plan and in educating stakeholders in the efficiency and cost-optimization opportunities. Business and financial executive management can be instrumental in establishing priorities, transformational funding, and in establishing measurement techniques and goals.

ADAM BRAUNSTEIN *is Principal Research Analyst and Director of End User Computing Strategies and Owner, Robert Frances Group,* ***CAL BRAUNSTEIN,*** *is CEO/Executive Director of Research, Robert Frances Group.*

16

How to become a Smart City: An EPIC Roadmap for Smart Cities

Michel Dirkx

In recent years, the concept of a smart city has been widely used by cities and commercial organizations to communicate and promote different types of initiatives or solutions in a city context, especially in the policy arena where the concept of smart city has been fashionable. As a result, there are various definitions for what a smart city is, or which characteristics define being smart. The European Union (EU) Platform for Intelligent Cities (EPIC) vision believes that a truly smart city is one that is able to:

1. Benefit from the innovative developments of citizens, small and medium enterprises (SMEs) and other actors from across Europe rather than just within their own cities;
2. Leverage a service infrastructure that is capable of delivering "one-stop government" through the integration of services, interoperability of systems and use of actionable intelligence in service delivery;
3. Contribute to a multinational service-oriented ecosystem by providing and sharing open business processes as services with other cities.

EPIC aims to create the first scalable and flexible pan-European platform for innovative user-centric public service delivery by combining innovation ecosystem processes, as well as fully researched and tested eGovernment service applications within a cloud computing environment. The resulting overall vision for EPIC can be defined as:

> *"To be the first choice service innovation and delivery platform (with roadmap) for medium sized (50.000–500.000 habitants) cities across Europe, where any city can cost-effectively share, access and adapt a range of services to work smarter to meet the needs of most, if not all, their citizens, visitors and a wide range of business/social relations"*

A Roadmap for Smart Cities

To achieve this vision, a business-focused roadmap is developed that promises to support European cities and SMEs in transitioning toward a smart city. This roadmap provides a comprehensive guide for a pan-European exploitation of the EPIC and covers the important aspects and required steps for a successful adoption, including possible strategies, program management, business cases, business models and key building blocks.

The phases in this smart city roadmap focus on the development of a smart city vision and strategy, the definition of project plans, and the implementation and operation of smart city services using the EPIC. As shown in following figure, the roadmap describes the planned series of actions, tasks and steps in becoming a smart city by adopting the EPIC and taking advantage of the EPIC service catalog. The practical and concrete tools, templates and descriptions are provided in this roadmap for city administrations and SMEs to start their journey toward smarter cities.

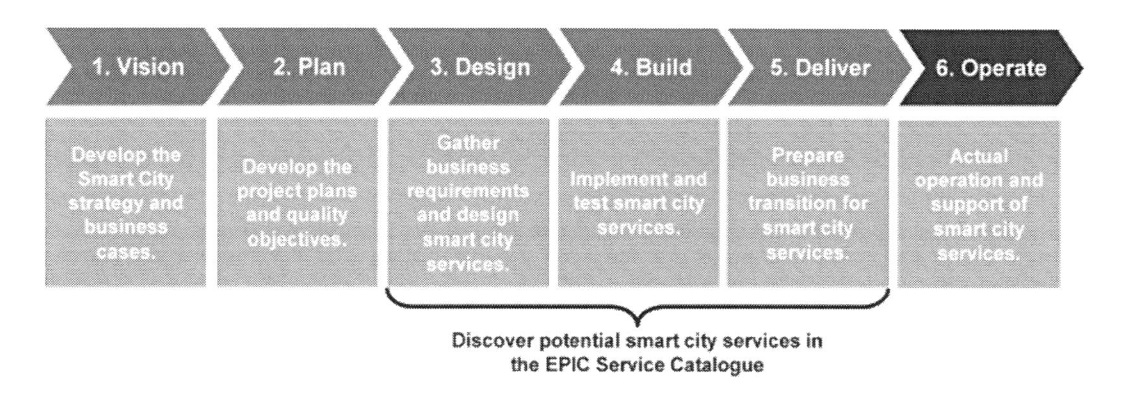

Figure 1.

Defining the Smart City Vision and Strategy

The vision phase helps cities in elaborating and defining their smart city vision and strategy, based on a smart city framework that structures the strategic smart city domains and characteristics. This framework helps to assess a city's maturity according to strategic axes to identify and define potential strategic smart city initiatives.

The concrete implementation of the identified strategic smart city initiatives will require city administrations and SMEs to develop a comprehensive business case, highlighting the benefits, potential risks and financial impact of the smart city initiatives to the relevant stakeholders.

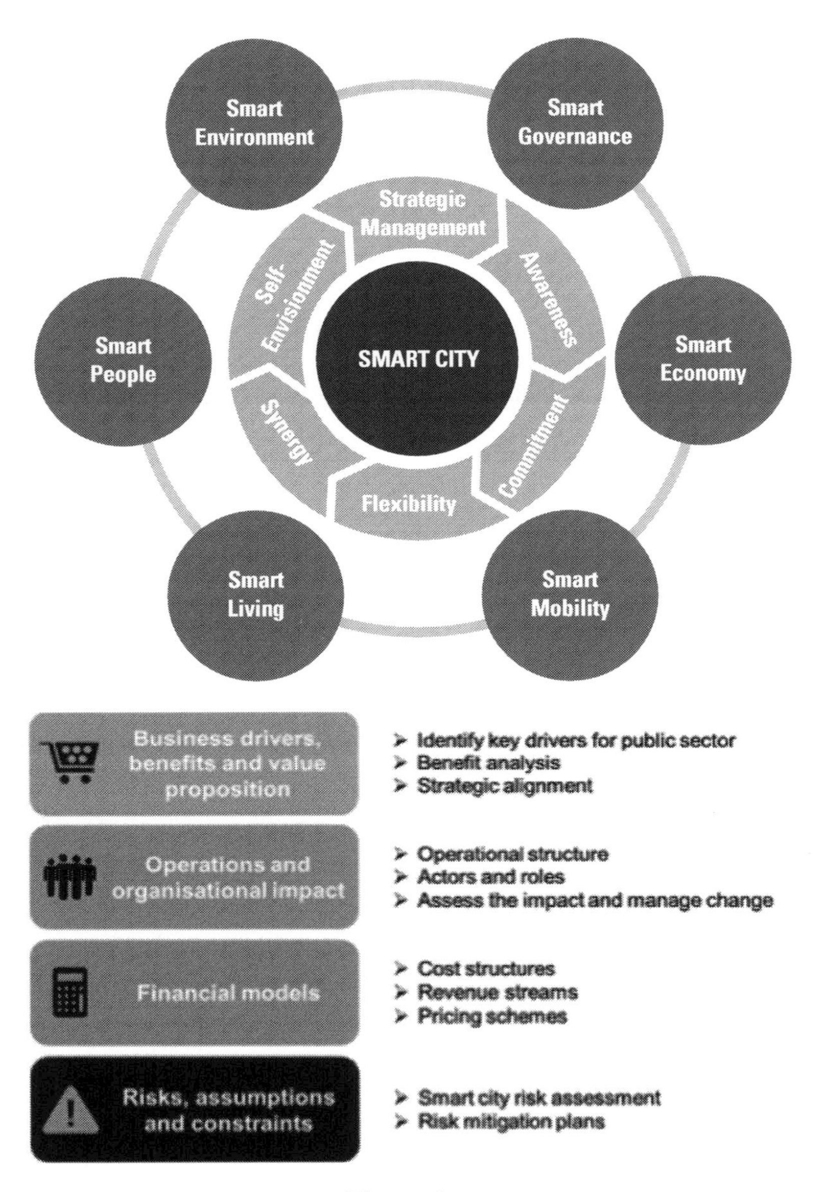

Figure 2.

Readiness for a European Platform for Intelligent Cities (EPIC)

After taking a decision on the business case, the possible implementation of the smart city services will drive the need for concrete and innovative solutions, such as the EPIC. The best way to decide on the actual take-up of the EPIC is to perform an assessment of the city's readiness for providing smart city services using the EPIC. This assessment is done across four areas, including strategic/legal, financial, operational and technical.

An EPIC Operating Model and Service Catalog

The EPIC provides the necessary infrastructure and platform (as a cloud computing-enabled platform) for efficient implementation and delivery of smart city services that could be integrated within the city's ecosystem and with external suppliers, integrators, or even citizens and businesses. In the operational model for the EPIC, the use of open standards and technologies are promoted to ensure broad exploitation opportunities for developed smart city services.

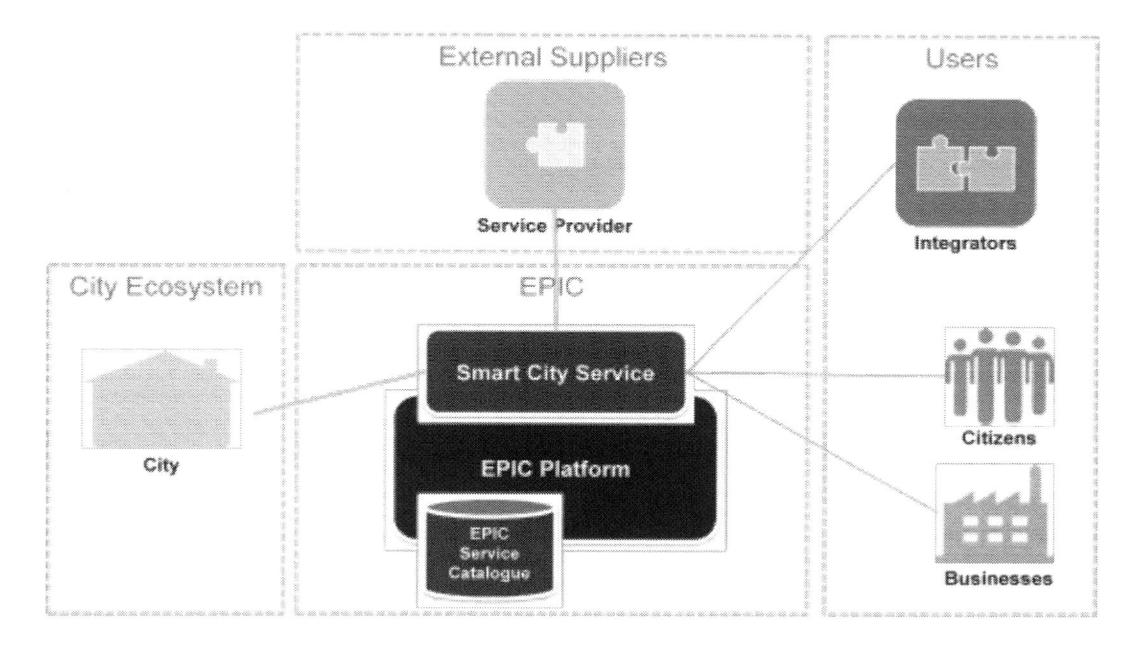

Figure 3.

A service catalog for the EPIC provides the cornerstone for delivering and managing the smart city services available or developed for the EPIC. It will provide the starting point for any city administration or SME to investigate the possibilities of the platform and to leverage or learn from existing smart city services. Or, it will help potential service providers in developing and delivering a smart city service on the EPIC, taking into account the service life cycle management and the EPIC certification procedures.

This service catalog contains information about two types of services: the customer-facing services (or smart city applications) that are visible to the business, and the supporting services (or smart city service) required by other service-providers to deliver customer-facing services. As such, the EPIC service catalog allows the service-provider or external integrators to carefully define and select the available services for their purposes.

The creation of service provision agreements between the EPIC service catalog and the different providers and consumers of the smart city service ensures the correct operating, controlling, maintaining and financing of the smart city services.

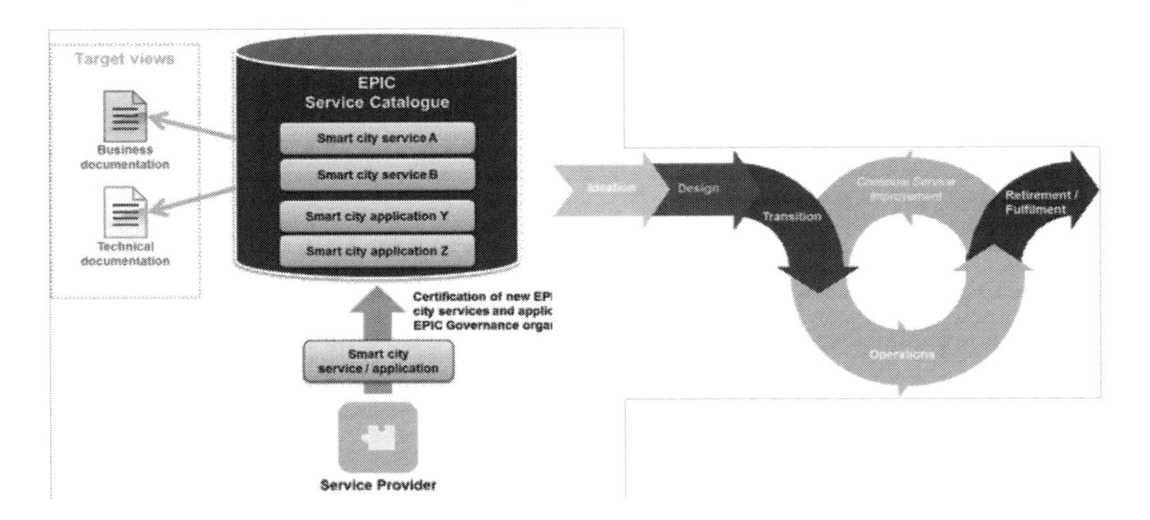

Figure 4.

Financial Conditions for Delivering Smart City Services on the EPIC

As an important element in every business model, the financial implications and especially the cost structures, including both fixed and variable costs, should be investigated and understood. It is easy to understand that the users (or integrators) of smart city services would pay a certain amount (or could be free) for the use of the service on the platform. It is also easy to understand that there are some fixed costs in operating the smart city service on the EPIC platform and the service catalog. The more difficult cost and revenue streams are to be identified for the service-provider and the city ecosystem that are responsible for setting up and making available the smart city services.

For each stakeholder in this EPIC operational model, the specific pricing mechanisms could be defined for making available and operating the smart city services. These pricing mechanisms could include both fixed pricing schemes (e.g. pay per use or menu prices) and differential pricing schemes (e.g. service features or customer characteristics).

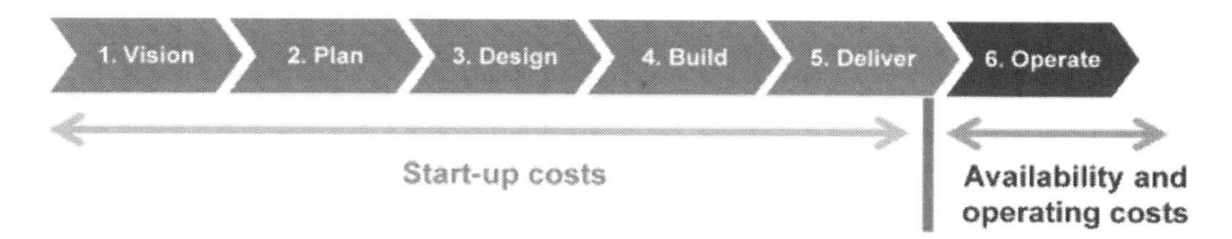

Figure 5.

The EPIC pilots have indicated that pay per use and service features are the preferred options for making the smart city services available within the ecosystem of small- to medium-sized cities. For city administrations and involved SMEs, the initial startup costs for developing the smart city services and making them available in the EPIC service catalog should not be underestimated. However, the potential returns from leveraging existing smart city services from the EPIC service catalog in multiple cities around Europe would compensate for the startup costs. This is in essence the leveraging power of cloud computing and, in particular, the EPIC.

Testing the Roadmap in Tirgu Mures, Romania

The roadmap for smart cities was developed and tested in collaboration with the city of Tirgu Mures in Romania, to make it more concrete and practical based on their experiences and feedback. As main stakeholder, the Tirgu Mures City Hall was interested in developing new technological standards for eGovernment solutions and better and faster ways of communicating with citizens and businesses.

Because of the testing, the following considerations and conclusions for the use of the EPIC roadmap were made:

- Explicit need for the alignment of the roadmap phases with the strategic management, project planning and the technical developments of the smart city services;
- Due to specific expertise and skills needed in the different phases of the roadmap, the collaboration and involvement of various stakeholders is needed at both the city management and IT level;
- A smart city vision and strategy should be the main driver for implementing the concrete smart city solutions and services, as was the case with the Digital Mures strategy[1],

[1] See more information on the Digital Mures strategy with following link: http://www.digitalmures.com/

- The most value of the EPIC and the roadmap would be gained from the increased number of smart city services that are made available in the EPIC service catalog.

For the use of the EPIC roadmap, it was important to take time explaining and convincing the city administrations and involved stakeholders of the benefits of implementing the smart city strategy and the specific business cases for the smart city services.

This article provides a summary of the roadmap for smart cities that was developed for the European Platform for Intelligent Cities (EPIC). The more detailed explanations of the phases, activities and steps can be found in the complete roadmap documentation, which also includes detailed descriptions of the tools and templates that could be used to support and facilitate the use of the roadmap in a smart city.

More information on the EPIC can be found at www.epic-cities.eu. For more information, email hugo.kerschot@is-practice.eu.

MICHEL DIRKX *is senior consultant for Deloitte Belgium.*

17

Smarter Water Management for Smarter Cities

Carey Hidaka

As water demand increases and resources dry up, smarter water management can address the impending challenges to keep water resources flowing. Fresh water, a fundamental requirement for life on the planet, is becoming a scarce resource as the world's population grows and competition increases for fixed resources of available water. It is estimated that by 2050, approximately 70 percent of the world's population will live in cities, stressing an already fragile infrastructure that provides basic city services like transportation, water, power, wastewater collection and treatment. In the United States, the American Society of Civil Engineers in 2009 developed a Report Card for America's Infrastructure and assigned an overall grade point average of D, with drinking water and wastewater both achieving grades of D-.

Against this backdrop, the world's cities will require new and innovative approaches to address these significant challenges. Business-as-usual and traditional approaches will not suffice on their own.

Water supply and distribution systems and wastewater collection and treatment systems generate and rely on tremendous amounts of data. This includes data from:

- Supervisory, control and data acquisition (SCADA) systems that collect sensor data (flow, pressure, water quality), operate and control;
- Computerized maintenance management systems (CMMS) and enterprise asset management systems (EAM);
- Geographic information systems (GIS); and
- Web-based data, such as data from the U.S. Geological Survey.

This data typically resides in separate systems and data repositories within and outside an organization. Thus, finding needed data for analysis, study and planning may be difficult and time consuming

A common complaint in water/wastewater management is, "We have tons of data; we just don't have any information!" However, Smarter water management leverages new and existing data sources and applies analysis/visualization/optimization tools to provide information and insights to make better and timelier decisions. Better decision-making, whether in treating/conveying drinking water or in repairing/replacing infrastructure prior to catastrophic failure, ultimately improves water/wastewater operations and efficiencies. Smarter water management facilitates planning processes, as well as maintenance and repair operations to better manage and forecast future water/wastewater needs and requirements. In combination with the discovery of new sources of fresh water, smarter water management can help address the impending water challenges facing the planet.

Preparing for the Future

Fresh water is becoming a scarce resource, and many areas of the world are already approaching a water crisis. The world's population during the 20th century grew nearly three times, to nearly 6.8 billion people by early 2013; the corresponding use of water has increased six times[1]. Experts predict the world's population to grow to more than 9 billion by 2050, which could adversely affect water resources. Many regions of the earth are experiencing drought, even those not typically associated with water scarcity.

For instance, the Midwestern United States in 2012 suffered its most intense drought since 1988, on par with droughts of the 1950s[2]. At the end of 2012, two of the Great Lakes, Michigan and Huron, were at their lowest levels in 94 years [3]. Water levels in the Mississippi River were so low at the end of 2012 that the U.S. Army Corps of Engineers dredged critical sections to keep the river open to barge traffic [4]. Because transporters used land-based methods as an alternative to river transport, prices increased, as did energy use and the carbon footprint.

Meanwhile, water infrastructure is deteriorating and collapsing with alarming frequency. Water main breaks/bursts and sewer cave-ins are commonly reporting in the media. Municipalities have neglected buried infrastructure, which is out-of-public-sight (and mind), as the economy deteriorated and funding sources face financial pressures. Some areas of the United States have distribution and collection systems that are over a century old[5]. In some cases, they still rely on original materials, such as wood, to transport water. More than 770 U.S. cities discharge untreated wastewater into the environment and suffer sewer backups into residential basements during heavy rain, resulting in Clean Water Act violations and concerns for public health.

Additionally, the United Nations Environment Programme (UNEP) said in 2010 that more people around the world die from contaminated water than from wars and other violence[6]. Statistics indicate 1.8 million children under age five die from water-borne diseases, equivalent to about one infant every 20 seconds. The Vice-Minister of Water Resources for China said in 2012 that 20 percent of the country's rivers were so polluted that water quality is too toxic for human contact; up to 40 percent of China's rivers were seriously polluted[7]. In the United States,

These problems are daunting and require significant investment to reverse further deterioration. Yet given today's challenging worldwide economic realities, water and wastewater utilities must do more with less. Communities need to determine whether there are better ways to address the growing and threatening problem of fresh water sustainability. Smarter water management is a critical means for tackling these challenges.

Water/Wastewater Infrastructure is Falling Apart

There are several global water concerns regarding the availability of fresh water, the challenges associated with water contamination and water quality, and the condition or lack of infrastructure for supplying clean water and treating wastewater. The problem is not whether the industry has the expertise to treat and deliver potable water and safely collect, treat and release wastewater to the environment. Instead, the worldwide problem is:

- Getting clean, safe drinking water to those who really need it, notably in developing areas of the world where there may be no infrastructure at all;
- The affordability, cost and logistics of maintaining or replacing existing infrastructure that is approaching or beyond its design life;
- The affordability and logistics of creating new infrastructure to support rapidly growing urban populations; and
- The cost and logistics of collecting, treating and discharging wastewater so that it does not contaminate drinking water supplies and cause downstream public health problems.

Problems may not seem imminent in the United States and the developed world yet, but they are a serious fact for other parts of the planet. In China, 320 million people have no access to clean drinking water, and 190 million are drinking water severely contaminated with hazardous chemicals[8]. In the most populous areas of India, the public has no access to drinking water 24 hours per day, 7 days per week.[9] And although not as dramatic, changing weather patterns in the United States have created drought-like conditions in many areas, while other areas have experienced storms that have damage infrastructure and contaminated water supplies

In March 2013, the American Society of Civil Engineers (ASCE) estimated the investment need by 2020 at $3.6 trillion to address the water infrastructure problem[10]. In like fashion, the American Water Works Association (AWWA) stated in a February 2012 report, "Buried no Longer: Confronting America's Water Infrastructure Challenge," that the cost of replacing drinking water pipes at the end of their useful lives will total more than $1 trillion across the United States between 2011 and 2035, and exceed $1.7 trillion by 2050[11]. The problem is so daunting that the President's 2011 State of the Union Address highlighted state of America's infrastructure.[12]

Lots of Data, No Information

With available funding significantly constrained and an overwhelming infrastructure overhaul required, there is a need to prioritize and apply limited available resources in a rational way. The water/wastewater industry collects and uses large amounts of data, from a variety of sources, such as:

- SCADA systems that control water and wastewater treatment and lift and pumping station operations, and collect data on water level, flow, pressure, rainfall, etc.;
- Wastewater collection systems (interceptor and trunk sewers), sometimes combined with SCADA system data, including water levels and flows;
- GIS that provide geospatial context about the area being served and the underlying infrastructure;
- EAM and CMMS that collect information about assets such as pumps, valves, sensors, piping, blowers, clarifier motors and assemblies, etc. Information about work-order creation, processing, maintenance and failure history is included in this category.
- Web-based data from external sources such as the USGS (including river gauge flow and water level data), the U.S. Army Corps of Engineers (including reservoir/lake level data), and the National Weather Service;
- Laboratory information management systems (LIMS), including water quality data;
- Enterprise resource planning (ERP) systems, including financial systems, customer information systems (CIS) and water billing systems; and
- Research data from universities and other academic institutions.

Data tends to reside in silos with little or no interaction across organizational boundaries. Or, data may be analyzed for specific purposes like operational or environmental compliance reporting, generating key performance indicators (KPIs), capital budgeting or monitoring real time system operation (see Figure 1). Consequently, the data itself can be highly variable, comprised of structured data in databases or spreadsheets, or unstructured data on hand-drawn maps, logbooks or non-digital records (e.g., strip charts).

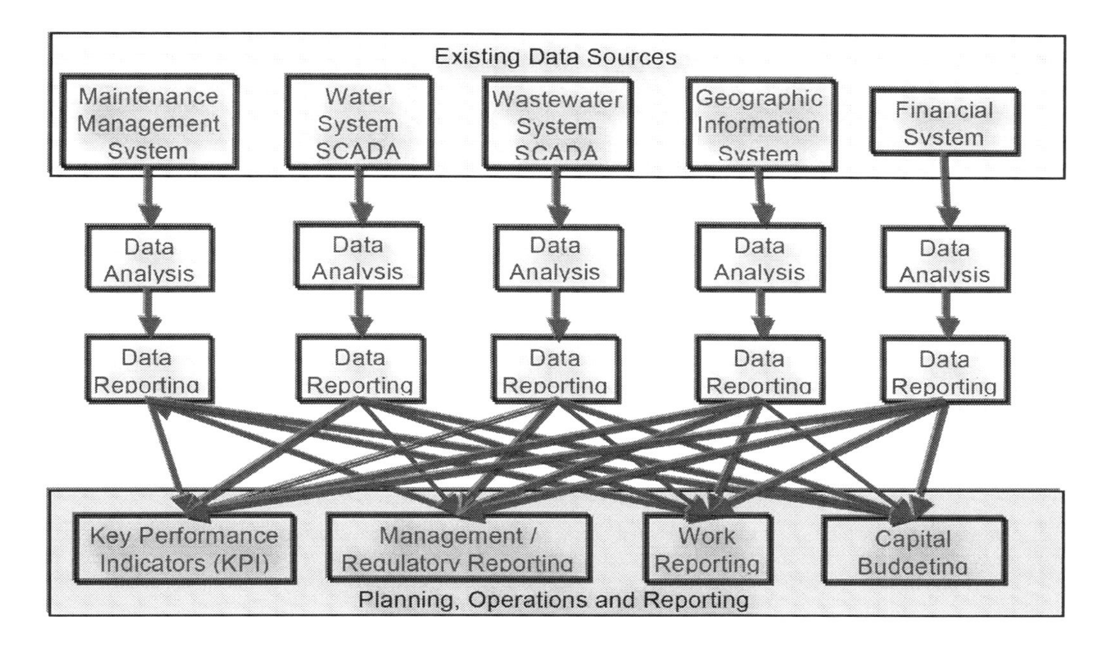

Figure 1. *Organizational Data Silos in Water/Wastewater.*

There is so much data, residing in disconnected repositories and collected over long periods, that organizations do not know where to begin digesting and making sense of the data chaos. In other words, many organizations are drowning in a sea of data without a logical way to organize or analyze it in a meaningful way.

What is Smarter Water Management?

While volumes of data are collected as drinking water is sourced, treated and distributed, and as wastewater is collected, treated and discharged, not much of that data is used to prevent the next crisis. Nevertheless, such data could detect system anomalies that could presage the next infrastructure failure, or provide operational insights to address the looming challenges of scarce water supplies and shrinking budgets. That is because organizations are "data rich and information poor;" there is little aggregation and integration of the data across system and organizational boundaries. Often organizations may manually enter data multiple times to meet reporting deadlines. As a result, they may make decisions based on incomplete, inadequate or inaccessible information.

However, smarter water management would allow data, complemented by analytics tools that transform data into information, to support the planning, anomaly detection, failure prediction, and insight generation to work smarter and stretch budgets further.

Smarter water management does the following:

- Uses existing and new sources of data to meet water/wastewater operational objectives, comply with environmental regulations, and efficiently operate and maintain water supply and wastewater collection/treatment systems;
- Uses data and historical information supported by analytical tools to detect performance anomalies, trends and patterns, and provide insights for cost effectively meeting demands for clean water and complying with environmental regulations;
- Uses predictive analytics with past performance and maintenance information to anticipate asset malfunctions and failures, recommend preventative maintenance, and subsequently get the most out of installed infrastructure by eliminating catastrophic failures and improving system performance;
- Provides valuable input to traditional engineering analysis and design to address future objectives, resulting in smaller capital infrastructure investments; and
- Models real world operations into "supply chain" environments that allow data sharing to provide an enterprise view and recommendations.

Smarter water management supports and complements traditional day-to-day, routine operations by revealing alternative views that identify previously undiscovered insights and dynamics. Take, for example, a city that separately monitors the operations of its water treatment plant(s), distribution system, wastewater treatment plant(s) and collection system. A smarter water management solution would provide an overarching view of the entire system, revealing dynamics and interactions between the component parts. This would provide the opportunity to optimize the operations for each system and the total water system in aggregate.

Essentially, smarter water management overcomes the challenges of a traditional siloed data environment by introducing the following major functions that characterize smarter operation:

- ***Data Aggregation,*** collecting existing data residing in different systems and in different, disparate formats to provide an aggregate, consistent view of water and wastewater operations ("one version of the truth").

- ***Data analytics,*** visualization and optimization tools, and expertise that operate on the collected data to detect anomalies and provide insights for fact-based decision making and contribute to more efficient and proactive operation and maintenance of water and wastewater systems. Predictive analytics, visualization and optimization tools would combine and operate on previously isolated but related data with a goal of transforming it into useful information for innovative decision-making.

- ***Display of visual key performance indicators*** that provide a "health index" of water and wastewater operations. The KPIs provide "at-a-glance" measures of system performance to potentially head-off problems and service disruptions before they occur.

- ***Automatic, regular and routine reporting of KPIs and key management reports*** to track system performance on an ongoing basis, providing documentation to support regulatory compliance. Aggregate real time status of water and wastewater operations would note whether standards are being met and, if not, which systems are affected and what actions must be taken to address potential violations. This would support proactive problem resolution and decision-making system operation more efficient, and reducing costs by eliminating catastrophic system failures and break-fix expenses.

Building on Figure 1, Figure 2 (see next page) illustrates how segregated data can be combined and analyzed to support more efficient operations and reporting. With smarter water management, data act as the source of insights that stimulate innovation.

The resulting smarter water system would enable decision-making to:

- Support supply and demand allocations of water as a scarce resource;

- Complement and support engineering, operations and maintenance recommendations to provide operational efficiencies;

- Reduce costs by supporting preventative/predictive maintenance and prevention of catastrophic failures; and

- Address the challenges of an aging workforce by capturing data and using information systems to document experience using standard operating procedures and workflows.

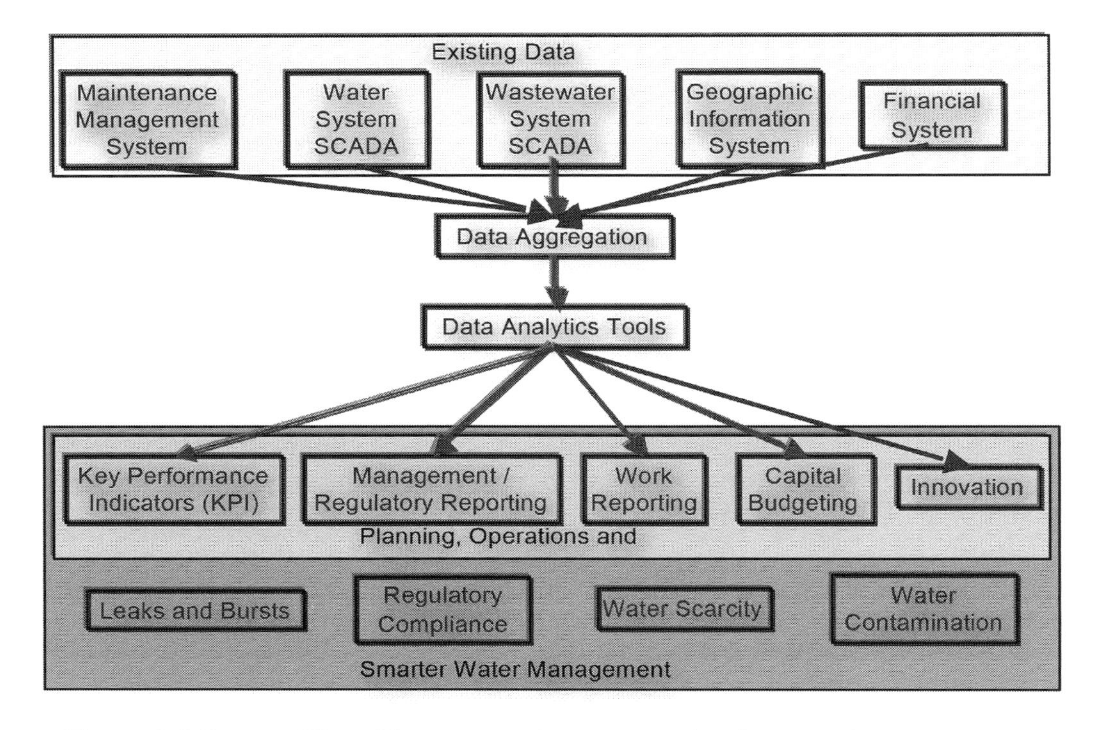

Figure 2. *A Smarter Water Management Implementation Creates a Smarter System.*

Smarter Water Management in Use

Case Study for Coastal/Marine Environment—SmartBay Galway, Ireland

Ireland's Galway Bay encompasses 220 million acres of underwater area and represents the close linkage between the economy and the environment. The Bay is a center for seafood, shipping and innovative water monitoring technology, including wave-generated electricity. It has also been the historical focus of marine and coastal ecosystem research, as environmental pollution and climate variation affect the bay.

To a large degree, organizations that produce data associated with the centers of economic, technology and research activity keep that information for reasons of ownership, security or convenience. Access to this data by others may or may not occur. However, the SmartBay project implemented a collaboration platform that uses an information technology based, smarter water management solution to bridge organizational and operational data silos and facilitate information sharing.[13]

Initially, the Marine Institute of Ireland, which leads national efforts for sustainable marine and coastal research and development, started the SmartBay Galway project with an initial focus on scientific research.

Throughout the Bay, it deployed "smart buoys" equipped with wireless communications and sensors to collect data on sea state, weather conditions, water quality and other environmental data, much in real time. This data was the basis for innovation to create new commercial opportunities and economic development.

SmartBay's collaboration platform solution combines multiple sources of data to provide integrated data monitoring, analysis, visualization, and data access for a diverse group of stakeholder users. These include marine and coastal research, commercial fishing, aquaculture (fish and shellfish farming), the Galway Bay Harbour Master for flood condition warning, sustainable energy research and development (wave energy), advanced sensor development, and public health (beach health conditions). Using collected data, the collaboration platform provides customized web applications to users via the Internet. The combination of scientific and day-to-day operational management perspectives on the single platform is both unique and representative of collaboration needed in the industry today.

For instance, SmartBay has improved data access by making weather, shipping and environmental data collected from Bay and other locations available to multidisciplinary users in marine and coastal research, sustainable energy research and development, public health and tourism. The data is also helping local anglers manage aquaculture farms and the harbormaster proactively monitor and predict flood conditions. As the need for data grows, SmartBay can add new sensors and data sources to the platform because the platform infrastructure uses open standards and is agile and flexible.

Case Studies for Water Supply, Distribution and Consumption—Sonoma County Water Agency, Miami-Dade Parks, Recreation and Open Spaces, and Desert Mountain, Arizona

As another example, three communities used smarter water management to address challenges in water supply distribution and consumption, eventually optimizing operations and making tools available to encourage water conversation and limit nonrevenue water (NRW).

NRW is drinking water that communities source and treat for delivery that is "lost" before it reaches customers. Losses occur through theft, leaks and bursts that occur in the water distribution system. This results in lost revenue and increased costs to treat and deliver water to replace the losses. National studies show that on average 14 percent of treated water is lost to leaks. Other water systems in the world have losses of more than 60 percent[14]. The World Bank estimates that water leaks have annual worldwide costs of $14 billion[15].

With smarter water management, Sonoma County, Calif., Water

Agency improved water operations using pressure management; Miami-Dade County, Fla., Parks, Recreation and Open Spaces conserved more water through improved consumption monitoring; Desert Mountain, Ariz., detects when water is needed for irrigation using water conservation sensors; and the city of South Bend, Ind., Public Works Department (PWD) is improving synergies to maximize its wastewater collection system.

Sonoma County Water Agency (SCWA) is a water wholesaler in California responsible for managing the flows of the Russian River and meeting the recreational and environmental needs of a service population of 600,000. SCWA supplies drinking water sourced from the Russian River to several regional retail water providers that, in turn, distribute water to consumers. SCWA's service area includes the world-famous wine industry, as well as endangered fish populations. However, drought has heighted the need for water conservation in the area. In the past, wholesale water purchaser Valley of the Moon Water District (VOMWD) continuously and manually adjusted water pressure valves in the distribution system by trial and error to maintain optimum operating pressure across the system. This was time consuming and inefficient.

So, VOMWD worked with SCWA to apply analytics and optimization technologies to conserve water by operating parts of VOMWD's distribution system at lower pressures. The system optimizes pressure settings,-reducing valves in the distribution network based on data from existing sensors, including pressure gauges and flow loggers throughout the water system. In other words, the system collects input data from existing SCADA systems, applies analytics and optimization tools targeted at pressure management, and provides recommendations for water pressure adjustments in VOMWD's distribution system based on usage, weather and environmental conditions. With detailed information, staff can optimize valve settings based on what is happening across the entire system, eliminating guesswork.

The benefits of improved pressure management include reduced water loss, energy savings and reduced wear on the distribution system infrastructure. Operating a distribution system at lower pressures can decrease pumping and stress on the system. Better pressure management also can improve the quality of the water in the system by optimizing storage tank turnover to maintain required levels of chlorine residual.

Miami-Dade County, Fla., has a sprawling parks system—the third largest in the United States—which includes 263 parks spanning 12,845 acres of land, including a zoo, beaches, marinas, pools, golf courses, educational nature centers and preserves. In 2009-2010, the parks system incurred more than $4 million in annual water and sewer costs, consumed more than 360 million gallons of water and managed more than 300 water accounts to manage.

In the past, the Miami-Dade County parks system's aging water infrastructure required manual inspection to detect leaks or other problems. However, rising water costs and the labor-intensive process of acquiring, integrating and analyzing historical water consumption data taxed parks department resources. Consequently, the county decided to focus on smarter water management and analytics to create information that improves efficiencies.

Using Smarter Water Management, Miami-Dade County employees monitor water consumption, detect leaks and share information with colleagues among the county's parks and facilities. When fully implemented, the solution will include a web portal to view water consumption data, enable better monitoring and management of overall water usage, and detect leaks or potential leaks more rapidly. Smart irrigation technology also automatically optimizes irrigation on park properties where water use is highest, such as for landscaping and golf courses, to maximize savings. Ultimately, the parks department estimates the smarter water management solution will yield a 20 percent reduction in water use annually with savings of about $860,000 per year.

Arizona's Desert Mountain community in the Sonoran Desert in Scottsdale includes 4,500 residents and six championship golf courses (550 acres of turf). The community is a leader in water conservation and is the largest reclaimed water user in the area (1 billion gallons per year) using 11 on-site pumping stations to move water for irrigation. Buried sensors measuring soil moisture, temperature and salinity levels at turf root level collect data several times per hour daily to monitor soil conditions. The community uses this data to determine when to irrigate the turf and when to flush salts and alkali from the soil.

Prior to implementing a smarter water management solution, data collected and the four systems used to monitor water and energy usage were separate, disparate and siloed. This forced the operations staff to manually collect updates and data on turf and soil conditions, which sometimes took 30 days to gather and verify data needed for irrigation decisions. However, the smarter water management solution pulled data into a single location, and combined it with dashboard, KPI and analytics tools. The solution captures, analyzes and displays data, including water flow, electrical usage and lake levels, in a single, unified view of usage across the property. This provides an integrated view of golf course conditions and direct feedback on water and power requirements. Desert Mountain has been able to gather needed data in real time (up to six times per hour, 24 hours per day) and make decisions within 15 minutes.

Ultimately, smarter water management eliminates guesswork, reducing salt/alkali flushing in the soil from 20 times per year to six, saving 3 million to4 million gallons of water and decreasing turf fertilization 10 percent to 15 percent. The community plans to expand its solution to the rest of tits six golf courses in the next three years. Desert Mountain projects this will result in a 10 percent energy savings in pumping and distribution costs, a 10 percent reduction in water usage, and an overall efficiency increase of 50 percent.

The city of South Bend PWD is responsible for providing drinking water and conveying, collecting, and treating the wastewater for a population of 122,000 in the city and surrounding unincorporated areas. Like many cities in the Northeast and Midwest USA South Bend has a collection system partially comprised of combined sewers that convey sanitary waste and stormwater. During periods of significant precipitation and runoff, combined sewer overflows (CSOs) can result in discharging untreated wastewater to the environment and backing up into residential basements.

To mitigate this problem, the city implemented a network of sensors in its collection system to monitor water levels at critical locations. It has also initiated limited real-time control of throttling devices to take advantage of available inline storage in the collection system, to reduce the potential for CSOs and residential basement backups. The sensor implementation helps the PWD monitor and maintain the collection system to optimize the system's ability to convey wastewater to its wastewater treatment plant. It also helps to make better use of available storage in the collection system.

The PWD independently operates its water supply and wastewater collection/treatment systems using separate SCADA systems. Historically, the PWD has not had an aggregate view of both systems to monitor overall water and wastewater operations. However, the PWD recognized the two systems have interdependencies that, if monitored in combination, could provide insights into the condition and operation of the respective systems. For example, if the city schedules a water supply filter backwash during a rainfall event, backwash volumes contribute to collection system flow, exacerbating an already challenging problem during rainfall events.

Consequently, PWD wanted to compare its potable water production with wastewater treatment flows to evaluate nonrevenue water in its distribution system and for assessing the impact of infiltration and inflow (I & I) on the collection system. Yet the data for these evaluations were housed in different databases or locations and required significant effort to obtain. As a result, the PWD recently implemented a smarter water management solution that builds on the work already begun to monitor and evaluate its wastewater collection system. The solution:

- Provides information-based decision making by collecting data from current water supply and wastewater treatment systems and combine it with collection system sensor information;

- Helps reduce the number of CSOs by using new sources of data for more effective water, collection and wastewater treatment system operation; and
- Provides enhanced communication between city departments to establish information-based action plans before problems arise.

The solution provides an executive dashboard-style operations center and geospatial view of the collection system, including critical overflow points. PWD management and operations uses these tools to rapidly assess the condition and performance of city water and wastewater systems, notably during rainfall, to monitor and track CSOs. The solution combines selected SCADA system data from the water supply and wastewater collection and treatment systems, USGS data on water levels in the nearby St. Joseph River, and existing city GIS system data.

To date, the smarter water management solution has helped reduce wet weather overflows by 23 percent and has virtually eliminated dry weather overflows from 27 to one in the first year of operation. The solution also has allowed South Bend to improve storage and collection system performance while avoiding costly infrastructure investments, as well as helped the city avoid fines relating to Clean Water Act violations.

What's Next?

Addressing infrastructure and operational challenges in water and wastewater utilities and more broadly water scarcity and contamination is a major opportunity. Replacing and repairing crumbling assets to prevent water main breaks, sewer cave-ins, and operational challenges such as CSOs will clearly require traditional engineering solutions and massive physical upgrades. They may—and probably will—take decades to complete. In the meantime, the more data water and wastewater authorities have about their infrastructures, and the more that data is transformed into useful information to prioritize actions and improve decision making, the better prepared utilities will be to make improvements and reduce resource consumption process.

The five smarter water management case studies demonstrate that collecting, sharing, visualizing, and analyzing data can foster collaboration and offer new perspectives that may lead to improved decision-making, research and commercial application. In contrast, decisions made in isolation and with incomplete information can lead to shortsighted and error prone conclusions that may negatively affect our environment, lead to inefficiencies, and increase costs.

Moreover, improvements in water and wastewater systems can serve as a model for revamping other city services. The same data analytics system used to manage water and wastewater utilities can manage electric utilities, solid waste collection, transportation, emergency services, law enforcement, social services and more. Imagine cities with smarter systems transforming data into information across and between all their departments to operate more efficiently and effectively, while planning.

Other important water and wastewater dynamics using data management that should be evaluated include:

- The energy-water nexus—the intimate and inextricable relationship between energy consumption/generation and water delivery and wastewater treatment. The preference for coal-fired power plants over nuclear in China and India (as a result of the Fukushima disaster in Japan), requires three times more water as natural gas generating stations, creating increased competition for water in energy production over agriculture and drinking water[16].
- Potential groundwater contamination from new technologies (e.g., hydraulic fracturing, or "fracking," are a significant new source of oil and natural gas), that may pose serious, future environmental concerns.
- The water-food-energy nexus—the complex interplay between fresh water scarcity and food and energy security, is looming on the horizon as a significant environmental challenge[17]. The agriculture sector internationally is the single largest consumer of fresh water, accounting for about 70 percent of the total volume of fresh water withdrawals from lakes, rivers, and aquifers[18].
- A "system of systems" view of water that links information about consumers, fresh water generators and water/wastewater research. This collection of fragmented and previously disconnected data sources when analyzed in combination may provide new insights and stimulate innovation by providing perspectives not considered before.
- Micro-weather forecasting—provides the ability to model the earth's atmosphere to predict weather at fine resolution (down to one or two square kilometers) with high levels of precision, This would allow cities to anticipate and prepare for flooding, improve collection system operation to prevent environmental contamination, and support smarter agricultural practices.

Given these trends in the context of fresh water scarcity, the world's next wars will be fought over water, not oil[19]. Water management is required for the survival of life on the earth. Smarter water management is a critical component for planning and managing fresh water resources to address the resilience of the planet.

CAREY HIDAKA *is a Client Solutions Professional in IBM Software Group with experience in Smarter Water Management business development. He has 31 years of information technology experience and practiced as a consulting environmental engineer and registered Professional Engineer (PE, State of Illinois), focusing on water resource planning and water and wastewater treatment plant designs and implementations for public and industrial sector clients.*

He has a Master of Business Administration degree with finance specialization from the University of Chicago, a Master of Science degree in Environmental Engineering from the University of Illinois at Urbana-Champaign, and a Bachelor of Science degree, with honors, in Civil Engineering from the University of Colorado at Boulder.

ENDNOTES

1. World Water Council, Water Crisis. [Online]. Available: http://www.worldwatercouncil.org/index.php?Id=25.
2. Huffington Post Green, 11/29/12.
3. Associated Press, February 6, 2013.
4. Chicago Tribune, 12/26/12.
5. NY Times, April 19, 2009.
6. ABC News, March 27, 2010.
7. The Straits Times, February 2, 2013.
8. Water Pollution in China, Greenpeace East Asia, http://www.greenpeace.org/eastasia/campaigns/toxics/problems/water-pollution/.
9. India's Water Nightmare, Environment South Asia, Shreyasi Singh, http://thediplomat.com/2010/09/22/india%E2%80%99s-water-nightmare/.
10. 2013 ASCE Report Card for America's Infrastructure, http://www.infrastructurereportcard.org/a/#p/home.
11. Buried No Longer, AWWA, http://www.allianceforwaterefficiency.org/uploadedFiles/Resource_Center/Landing_Pages/AWWA-BuriedNo-Longer-2012.pdf.
12. State of the Union Address, http://www.asce.org/About-ASCE/Annual-Report/2011-Annual-Report/Annual-Report-2011—Infrastructure/#State_of_the_Union.

13. Collaboration Platforms in Water Management, Water Practice and Technology, 2011.
14. EPA. Water: Sustainable Infrastructure, http://water.epa.gov/infrastructure/sustain/wec_wp.cfm.
15. The Challenge of Reducing Non-Revenue Water in Developing Countries, The World Bank, Paper No. 8, December 2006, http://siteresources.worldbank.org/INTWSS/Resources/WSS8fin4.pdf.
16. Asia Risks Water Scarcity Amid Coal-Fired Power Embrace, Natalie Obiko Pearson, September 10, 2012, Bloomberg, http://www.bloomberg.com/news/2012-09-09/asian-water-scarcity-risked-as-coal-fired-power-embraced.html.
17. What is the Water-Food-Energy Nexus?, Blog, http://www.water-energy-food.org/en/news/view__1130/what-is-the-water-food-energy-nexus.html.
18. Worldometers, Real Time World Statistics, http://www.worldometers.info/water/.
19. Water: The Epic Struggle for Wealth, Power and Civilization, Steven Solomon, 2010, HarperCollins.

18

Beyond Smarter City Infrastructure—The New Urban Experience

Norm Jacknis

Much of the focus of the smarter cities movement has been on managing the physical infrastructure of the city—its buildings, transportation, water supply, energy and the like. These are important, because no urban resident would be happy if the foundations of city life were unreliable or breaking down. However, using technology merely to manage an industrial, almost mechanistic, model of the modern city limits the potential of both the city and technology.

A truly smarter city of the future takes full advantage of technology to enhance the experience of being a city resident or traveler. Indeed, developing information and communications networks, along with new ways of providing interfaces to these technologies, make possible new urban experiences and delights.

This in happening in a new context for cities: Their traditional role as engines of economic production has been and will continue to be undermined by trends in the economy and technology. Cities, of course, will have an important role in the future, but it is not in perpetuating an older industrial model. Instead of centers of production, cities can be centers of consumption or, more broadly, centers of living. Almost any city that jumps to these new opportunities will thrive as a desirable location to live.

Part of that urban quality of life will be civic engagement—are the residents not just in a city but players in its management? Here, too, new technologies enable people to participate in the running and designing of the city in ways not possible before.

Changing Economic Role of Cities

To understand why aspects of city life go beyond infrastructure, it is important to elaborate how the role and demands on cities are changing and what foundations smarter cities need to create for their future.

Examine economic growth going back to Adam Smith. Two things lead to economic growth in a stable society: One is specialization and the other is creating new knowledge and innovations. This is why cities during the industrial era in the United States, Europe and Japan became the engines of economic growth. They put people together. When millions of people were together, they could accelerate the process of innovation and specialization. It was what engineers call a positive feedback cycle or economists call a virtuous circle.

In sub-national government circles around the world, there has been much talk about clustering businesses. However, this is not a new phenomenon or a new idea. There is a wonderful picture from 1922 showing the (later-to-become) major film studios in Hollywood already clustering together. This clustering occurred before there was sound or color in movies—and before the movie industry was a major cultural force.

The cluster effect is a good example of how the lessons of previous economic history have taken hold in the minds of public leaders. But how well is the cluster effect working in today's 21st century economy?

Princeton University Economics Professor Paul Krugman is perhaps best known as a left-of-center commentator for the *New York Times*. But he is also a well-respected economist who won the Nobel Prize for his work on the "new economic geography." This was part of the intellectual foundation for much of the cluster strategies government officials have been pursuing.

At the awards ceremony in Stockholm a couple of years ago, Krugman expressed his gratitude for the prize. He then went on to say that the clustering effects he observed when he wrote about his research 20 years ago were now diminishing.

> *"[Clustering] may describe forces that are waning rather than gathering strength ... The data accord with common perception: many of the traditional localizations of industry have declined (think of the Akron rubber industry), and those that have arisen, such as Silicon Valley, don't seem comparable in scale."*

Meanwhile, Dr. G.M. Kunkle's University of North Carolina dissertation research tracked the growth and survival of a cohort of more than 300,000 companies operating in Pennsylvania from 1997 to 2007. According to his findings:

> *"Industry cluster theory has ... an inability to explain economic dispersion and the presence of high-growing firms that thrive in non-clustered industries and locations ... Firm characteristics are 10 times more powerful than industry and cluster characteristics, and 50 times more powerful than location characteristics in explaining and predicting establishment-level growth and survival"*

The diminished effect of clustering goes beyond the United States. A 2011 study in Norway concluded:

> *"Business clusters could be less relevant as drivers of innovation than has been commonly assumed. The Stavanger Centre for Innovation Research analyzed 1,600 companies with more than 10 employees located in the five largest Norwegian city-regions. Rather than national clusters, international cooperation or 'global pipelines' were identified as the main drivers of innovation."*

The song "New York, New York", which the singer Frank Sinatra made a hit a few decades ago, has this famous line: "If I can make it in New York, I'll make it anywhere." The implication was that an ambitious person should move to New York. Many did and many continue to do so.

But changes in the economy have turned this theme on its head. Consider one of the world's most famous and long-standing clusters—Wall Street. Of course, many New Yorkers know that a large part of the financial industry in the city is actually in midtown, not on Wall Street or streets nearby.

A couple years ago, there was a story in the *New York Times* that the New York Stock Exchange had lost about half of its market share in the trading of American securities. One of its biggest competitors, which garnered more than 10 percent share of the market in just a few years, is the BATS Exchange. It is located in Lenexa, Kansas, about 14 miles outside Kansas City. It is fair to say that most Americans would not have considered Lenexa a center of high finance when they were growing up. But with the internet today, it is possible to set up an exchange anywhere.

There was a story about a year ago from the *Associated Press* about the New York Stock Exchange that reads, in part, "What you do when a cathedral of capitalism becomes antiquated? You turn it into New York's best party space." While the point was supposed have its humorous side, it also highlights what is happening to cities, even the most successful global cities like New York.

Cities that were built as centers of industrial production are now much more centers of consumption and of living—party spaces, indeed. This change calls for a different perspective on re-creating cities, big and small.

Even the idea of the importance of size in the success of cities has changed. It used to be that the richest cities were the biggest cities, like New York, Chicago, a Detroit and Philadelphia. Z.P. Neal of Michigan State University compared the leading cities in 1900 with those in 2000 and found:

> *"Well-connected cities, regardless of their size, are more likely to develop robust regional economies ... A city that can draw on the resources of the whole world through extensive network connections to other cities, whether it is a metropolis or a hamlet, is likely to thrive."*

At the height of the industrial era, an observer could see thousands and thousands of men—and it was almost all men—coming into huge factory plants. These industrial plants concentrated jobs. Then a dramatic shift in employment began occurring more than 50 years ago. In 1900, 71 percent of the American labor force was making things or food. By 2000, that had reversed and 79 percent were providing services of some kind, often intangible services and knowledge creation delivered via the internet. Europe has followed a similar pattern.

When it became clear that more people would be working in the service sector of the economy, city leaders expected office towers to concentrate employment just as factories had. They would concentrate white-collar employment. And they did for a while, although it was often outside downtown in the suburban parts of the metropolitan region where office blocks grew the fastest.

That concentration of employment is also changing. Global real estate company Jones Lang LaSalle completed an analysis in 2011 of commercial office space. The analysis noted that the traditional rule of rule of thumb is that a company needs 200 square feet per employee. Within two years, that rule of thumb will be down to 50 square feet.

Why? Many employees no longer have to be in the office. For example, Jones Lang LaSalle reports that half of IBM's employees do not work in a space that says IBM on the door. This is true of other technology companies as well, where even their executives are not working in the office.

Moreover, this phenomenon is not found only in high-tech companies. It is true for the advertising industry or for any kind of business where people do not have to physically be in the same place.

This transition in the role of the city is paralleled by a transition in thinking about economic organization. In 1937, the Nobel Prize-winning economist Ronald Coase introduced his theory of the firm. He wanted to explain why, if the market was so efficient, people banded together in large corporations. His conclusion was that the transaction costs of going to the marketplace for all the services needed in a business were too costly. It was simpler to ask someone in another part of your company for the needed service or part.

Then a few years ago, Professor Clay Shirky of New York University wrote, "Here Comes Everybody: The Power of Organizing Without Organizations." He pointed out that the internet can provide that same kind of organizational glue. Perhaps the most successful example of this is Wikipedia, whose encyclopedic content is a result of collaboration made possible by the internet.

While we continue to think of manufacturing as part of the industrial age, almost a museum of yesteryear, even manufacturing has been affected and decentralized by the communications revolution and the global cooperation that it makes possible. This will increase with the use of robotics. Moreover, the developing technology of 3D printing may also help to decentralize the once monolithic, centralized nature of manufacturing.

Technology's Impact on Cities

All this change is occurring in a world where most of the internet-based interactions with other people are limited to text, a few pictures and sometimes voices. Instinctively, people know that face-to-face communications counts for more than text alone. For this reason, many cultures have some version of sayings like "seeing is believing."

The relatively minor role of the text of a conversation compared to all of its visual cues has been long established by research going back more than 40 years ago by scholars such as Albert Mehrabian and Michael Argyle. When the equivalent of face-to-face communications start to be delivered over the internet as an everyday event, there will really be dramatic change.

There are various ways that people try to achieve the effects of being physically near each other. Roughly two-thirds of corporations use video conferencing. There are numerous consumer examples as well, including Apple's FaceTime on its mobile devices, Google's Hangout, Facebook's video and Skype.

It is not just 20-somethings who use video. Services like Skype have become popular with many grandparents who want to spend more time with their grandchildren, often many miles away.

This is, however, in its early stages. The internet today is much like where the telephone system was in the 1920s. Many of the features of the phone system that we take for granted today were available, in a sense, back then. There was long distance, although it was expensive and not simple to use. There was even ship-to-shore communication that was a precursor to the mobile phone most of us carry today. But again, it was not widely available.

This is the case with the visual and collaboration tools available on the internet today. The quality is uneven, the software still gets in the way and there are other technical issues that prevent widespread use. That is rapidly changing.

As usual, a technology's possibilities will precede its actual use. Here, too, the analogy to the phone system is useful. The generation that grew into adulthood a hundred years ago was eventually aware of the possibility of making long distance calls, but shied away from doing so because the habit never developed during their youth when the costs were high and service difficult. As video and collaboration technologies become easier to use and more ubiquitous, their widespread use may also have to wait for a generation starting its adulthood to take these capabilities for granted.

The New Urban Quality of Life

Not today, but certainly by 2030 at the latest, urban residents will live in a world of ubiquitous, high-quality visual interaction anywhere they might be. When that happens, economic activity for most people will no longer be tied to a particular place, office building, store or factory. While the "laws of economics" as described by Adam Smith will not change, physical proximity will no longer be required for human collaboration. Many people will be able to earn a living anywhere or even in multiple places, depending on their whim at the moment. Thus, being in a big urban region will no longer be the strong requirement for wealth creation that it has been.

Going forward, the smart city will not only need to be well run, but it also will need to stand out as a place someone, with choices where to live, would want to live. This is often referred to as quality of life, although different qualities attract different people, so there is plenty of opportunity for a city or a neighborhood in a city to create a relatively unique appeal.

For that reason, more urban leaders will have to start thinking like business marketing strategists for a consumer experience, identifying what their city's special appeal might be to various "segments of the market" (also known as potential residents). The city itself must perform to keep its residents and their economic potential in competition with every other city.

Blending the Virtual and the Physical

While urban leaders have had an understanding of the phrase "quality of life," in this century it will not be just about the existing physical aspects of their cities.

To stand out, city leaders can use more imaginatively many of the technologies that enable smart management of infrastructure and some technologies that go beyond what is needed for infrastructure. In an age of ubiquitous communications and computing resources, cities will be able to blend physical and virtual spaces to create new destinations and new experiences.

In his article, "Augmented Reality Will Make Boring Cities Beautiful" (http://www.smartplanet.com/blog/cities/video-how-8216augmented-reality-will-make-boring-cities-beautiful/691), Christopher Mims notes that:

> *"Once augmented reality is widespread, the difference between a great and a mediocre city won't just be its built environment. To some extent, it will also be the degree to which that environment is a suitable tapestry for the creatives who will paint it with their augmented reality brush. Digital artists who learn to re-appropriate the city with the most innovative augmented reality add-ons won't just bring themselves fame and fortune—they'll also be attracting others to the places they love."*[1]

There are many examples of blending of the virtual and physical.

In the most basic way, iPavement, from a Spanish company, provides continuous connectivity by building it into the sidewalk so pedestrians can gain access to heavy bandwidth applications (http://news.cnet.com/8301-17938_105-57420548-1/ipavement-adds-apps-to-the-ground-beneath-your-feet/).

- In Aarhus, Denmark, the public library opened a public space for residents to use their mobile devices and create a collective work of digital art that could be "posted" on the walls.
- In Times Square in New York, retail outlet Forever 21 put a fashion model on a display screen. She took pictures of the real crowd below and then showed it on the screen. The event was so successful, that police supposedly asked the company to shift the angle of the screen because drivers were stopping to look.
- Just as work goes to people, instead of people going to work, so too have retailers started to bring the store to where people are instead of trying to entice them into stores. As an example, PeaPod converted the walls of the Chicago Transit Authority into virtual supermarket display cases where people can use their smart phones to buy food that will later be delivered to their homes.

---

[1] http://www.smartplanet.com/blog/cities/video-how-8216augmented-reality-will-make-boring-cities-beautiful/691

- In Australia, partly as a public health measure to encourage walking instead of escalator use, the city painted some stairs to look like piano keys and then linked that to computer generated sounds. As people walked on the stairs, they played music, creating a "wow" experience that was not expected by residents.

Due to improvements in connectivity, software and optics, there various forms of projection mapping have begun. Mostly, these have used the city's buildings as a canvass for otherwise unrelated artistic efforts. One good example is the video artwork in 2012 that was projected on 30,000 continuous square feet of the Manhattan Bridge in Brooklyn, N.Y. In 2013, the well-known artist Leo Villareal started a two-year display of 25,000 LED lights on the cables of the 1.8 mile, 500 foot tall San Francisco-Oakland Bay Bridge.

But projection mapping offers the possibility of creating truly new kinds of spaces and transpositions of existing urban places.

- A beginning in that direction was an effort by the Vienna Tourist Bureau to project a taste of Vienna, Austria, on the façade of an old building in London. Of course, it is also possible to create videoconferencing gateways between cities so that a person might sit near a video wall at a restaurant in London and have a conversation with a person similarly situated at a restaurant in Amsterdam, as if the two tables were side-by-side.

- Mercedes Benz has demonstrated "transparent walls" on which is projected what is happening on a side street. This allows a driver to see something coming before it would normally be visible. The safety benefits are obvious. For a video, see http://www.youtube.com/watch?feature=player_embedded&v=LqCMv3Nz4ZQ#!

- Another automobile company, BMW, displayed an alternative streetscape based on a one-to-one conversion of cars on the street into their futuristic versions.

- Transposition in time and space opens all kinds of possibilities. So a city might project on the wall of its train station what is going on in a concert hall many miles away, or what the sunrise looked like six months ago.

Citizen Experience and Cooperative Management in the Future Smart City

The quality of life that a person experiences in a city also includes the experience of being a citizen. The smart city of the future thus will engage its citizens smartly in part because people who are deeply engaged in a community will want to stay.

There is a substantial and growing proportion of the population that wants to have a role in shaping the environment or a role in creating and delivering public services. The rest want to know that they have the opportunity, even when they do not avail themselves of it.

By way of illustration, consider two examples. The first is Betaville, as described by Carl Skelton, co-founder of the Gotham Innovation Greenhouse and its originator when he directed the Brooklyn Experimental Media Center of New York University/Polytechnic Institute.

> *"Betaville is an open web-based environment for real cities, in which ideas for new works of public art, architecture, urban design and development can be shared, discussed, tweaked and brought to maturity in context, and with the kind of broad participation people take for granted in open source software development ... If a user-generated TV network is possible (YouTube), why not a user-generated city? How could this not be fundamental to the concept and practice of citizenship?"*

(More detail can be found in his video presentation from the Municipal Arts Society's 2012 New York City Summit, entitled "From Science Fiction to Future-Making in Real Communities."—http://youtu.be/cOvzSJucQto)

In the past, decisions about the future of cities have been dominated by urban planning professionals, architects and real estate developers, as well as mayors at times. This supposed professionalism, with insufficient public participation, clearly has not guaranteed the best results over time. That was part of the last century's fundamental dispute between the voice of wise, top-down planning (represented by Robert Moses in the United States) and the voice of a more bottom-up, organic approach to urban development (represented by Jane Jacobs).

An even earlier historic case in point was the planning and design for what is now Central Park in New York. After an initially disappointing professional design for the park, the New York City park board ran an open contest in 1860 for a design. From among 30 proposals, they decided that Vaux and Olmstead's proposal was the best—even though Olmstead was not yet considered an experienced professional.

In this century, Betaville can be the platform for a range of contests to envision critical parts of a city. It would enable more people to participate and provide a wider range of ideas for urban amenities of the future that will be as successful as Central Park turned out to be.

Another example is Oakland County, Mich., which now constitutes the most populous jurisdiction within the Detroit metropolitan area. The Great Recession in Michigan presented the county with a combination of a 20 percent decline in property tax revenues combined with increased demand for services. Public officials realized that Oakland County had an active group of residents, empowered by widespread deployment of internet connectivity and technology.

The city chose to facilitate the delivery of some public services by enabling residents to help each other, rather than paying full-time employees for the first line of interaction with someone needing help. Of course, the government's paid employees could join in the conversation to help when more or specialized expertise is required. Because of its more conversational nature than traditional computer applications, Oakland rolled this out using social media.

Both of these examples and other ways that technology enables better collaboration by citizens opens up new ways for cities to use the smartness of their residents. Beyond an industrial, if automated, "smart city," there can be a new "soft city" in which blended virtual/technological and physical space enables a fully engaging urban experience—a city where people will be pleased to live. This is what will ensure success for future cities.

DR. NORMAN J. JACKNIS *joined the Intelligent Community Forum in November 2013, as Senior Fellow. He is also the Co-Founder and Chairman of the Gotham Innovation Greenhouse, as well as a leader of several organizations focused on libraries. Before ICF, starting in 2008, he was Director, Cisco's IBSG Public Sector Group, working especially with the US Conference of Mayors. Prior to Cisco, he was the CIO of Westchester County, New York for ten years. He received his Doctorate, Master's and Bachelor's degrees from Princeton University.*

19

The FUPOL Project: An Integrated Approach to e-Governance, e-Participation and Policy Modeling

Giorgio Prister

Nowadays, private companies consider social networks, blogs, e-participation websites and social media web 2.0 facilities the new frontier of marketing and business opportunities. Although public organizations have different objectives, e-marketing tools also are at the core of many of their initiatives—especially cities that represent a specific and vast community with shared interests and goals.

For years all media including the increasing dominant role of Social Media have been effective arenas for politicians to launch their political messages and to collect feedback and requests from their citizens. Increasingly, the results of the policy decisions and of the elections depend on the wise, effective and extensive usage of social media.

Smarter Cities have launched initiatives that deal with the overall prosperity of their community, such as in the areas of green power and grids, traffic and transportation, health care, public safety, education, green buildings and others,. Often these initiatives are decided with the involvement of the constituents. However, the amplitude of the players in the city is a major challenge in getting opinions, in evaluating the wide inputs that the community can provide and in enabling effective two-way participation of the citizens.

Because of those challenges, cities struggle to properly manage policy decisions by leveraging the social media wealth. Positive and negative examples show how difficult this is. Years ago, the city of Stuttgart, Germany, faced major opposition from its citizens. Public demonstrations resulted due to a negative reaction against the decision to build a new underground railway station without input from the local community.

Something similar happened in Barcelona, Spain, as well, regarding the major refurbishing of the very important road, the Avenida Diagonal. Citizens were consulted too late in the process and were not involved in the definition of the plan. Consequently, they reacted negatively and rejected the plan in a public poll, while city administration wasted time and resources defining the plan. As another example, the Gezi Park riots in Istanbul represent the initial trigger of population issues against the government. However, these issues started because there was a lack of citizen participation and approval in the decision to create a new commercial area that replaced green space.

On the other hand, positive examples show the value of citizen participation. Many cities worldwide engage citizens in decisions, such as the allocation of the yearly budget or when setting city priorities. These decisions are usually made using traditional forms of communication, such as through public assemblies or by publishing budget information on the city website and opening it to online discussions and suggestions. This has an interesting effect on policy decisions and shows the willingness of the citizens to have their say in the decisions that affect their life and the life of the whole community. Nevertheless, this form of dialogue is just a beginning. The methods are clearly still a rudimental and limited way to address the complexity of policy decisions and e-participation in the era of social media.

Many cities have defined policies and guidelines on how to manage social media in their relationships with citizens.

Engaging Citizens in Policymaking

Engaging citizens in the policymaking process results in better decisions and is a core element of good governance. The idea behind citizen engagement in policymaking is to get more ideas and information to meet current challenges under conditions of increasing complexity, policy interdependence and time pressure. Citizen engagement strengthens trust in politicians and governments, and contributes to an increase of the quality of democracy. This should help to reverse the steady erosion of voter turnout in elections and falling membership in political parties.

The internal jobs and responsibilities of city administrations are evolving because of the above challenges. The city public relations and communication departments are more involved with internet—not just to publish information but also to establish a permanent two-way discussion with citizens on social media. It is becoming clear that information communication technology (ICT) should play a major and evolving role in supporting PR and communications activity. Discussions should not only involve social media, but they also should help to manage the huge amount of data and information that should be collected, leveraged and analyzed to extract intelligence and support city decisions. Some cities have already appointed new management positions such as "data manager" and "city social media manager," whose jobs are closely linked with the chief information officer (CIO) and the information technology (IT) manager.

Some key guidelines and policies should regulate the engagement of citizens in policymaking, such as:

- **Rights**—Citizens' rights to access information, provide feedback, be consulted and actively participate in policymaking must be firmly grounded in law or policy. Government obligations to respond to citizens when exercising their rights must also be clearly stated.
- **Commitment** to participation in policymaking is needed at all levels (politicians and government administration).
- **Clarity**—Objectives and limits of the participation during policymaking should be well-defined from the beginning. In particular, the roles and responsibilities of citizens (in providing input) and government (in making decisions for which they are accountable for) must be clear to all.
- **Time**—The time period of participation has to be specified.
- **Resources**—Adequate financial, human and technical resources are required. Government officials must have adequate human resources (skills, training), There also should be an appropriate organizational structure.
- **Objectivity**—The information provided by government during policymaking should be complete and objective.
- **Coordination**—Initiatives should be coordinated across all government levels to avoid duplication and to ensure policy coherence.
- **Accountability**—Governments have an obligation to use citizen input. Measures to ensure that the policymaking process is open, transparent and amenable to external scrutiny and review are crucial.
- **Evaluation**—Governments need tools to evaluate their performance so that they can adapt to new requirements.
- **Active Citizenship**—Governments benefit when citizens actively deliver inputs for decision-making.

Participation differs between active participation and passive participation. Active participation is the involvement, by either an individual or a group of individuals, in their own governance or other activities, with the purpose of exerting influence. Active participation is executed by traditional surveys, roundtable discussions, social media and e-participation. Passive participation involves finding out citizen opinions about specific topics by crawling media, social media, blogs, etc.

	E-Participation	Traditional Participation
Active Participation	• blogs • e-participation website • social media	• traditions surveys • round tables • plebiscite • referendum
Passive Participation	• social media analysis • crawling of media • blogs	• traditional surveys • media • newspaper • analysis

Figure 1. *Examples of Active a ssive Participation.*

E-Participation

Public participation is generally defined as "the practice of consulting and involving members of the public in the agenda-setting, decision-making and policy-forming activities of organizations or institutions responsible for the policy development." E-participation is defined as the use of ICT to support the provision of information to citizens concerning government activities and public policies, the consultation with citizens and their active participation. The development and increasing penetration of information and communication technologies—particularly the internet—in many countries has enabled the extensive application of the above principles through electronic media.

All cities face five key challenges when building an urban model fostering e-participation:

1. Societal pressures and expectations of participating groups;
2. Heterogeneity in the practices of the groups;
3. Complexity and "messiness" of the issue to be modeled: urban sustainable development and planning in this context;
4. Imprecision and open-endedness of final users and concrete practice applications; and
5. Change and innovation processes implied for both science and planning.

Thus, it is important to consider the interconnection of these challenges to foster e-participation (see Figure 2).

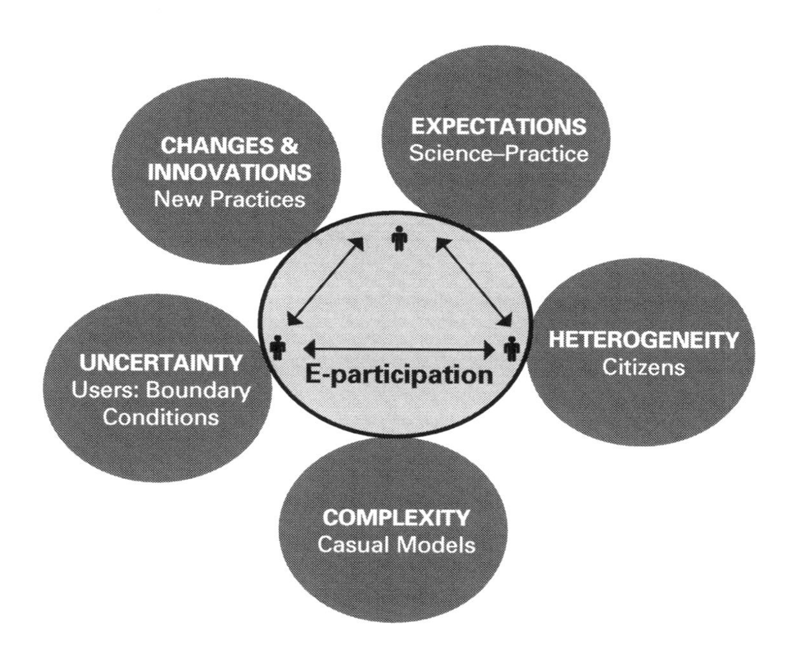

Figure 2. *Interconnection of Challenges When Fostering E-Participation.*

The participation process involves heterogeneous practices in knowledge production.

The FUPOL Project

The objective of FUPOL is to introduce a new governance model to support the openness of policy design and implementation lifecycle supported by innovative IT solutions. The results are expected to enhance the capabilities of constituents and policymakers to reduce uncertainties and make better decisions. The solution covers uncertainties related to the potential impact of policy measures and to the related reaction of citizens.

The transparency of the policy design process is enabled by multichannel social computing, policy topic sensing and extraction, multilingual semantic analysis, dynamic agent based simulation, cloud computing, idea management system (IMS) and geographic information system (GIS) presentation technologies. Those elements integrated with classic e-participation form a system to facilitate e-governance.

Typical policy modelling problems are characterized by complexity and dynamics. Because of the complexity, it is often difficult to solve such problems mathematically. One of the prospective approaches in simulation is the agent-based simulation approach.

The FUPOL project aims to apply this model, among others, to policymaking. The new governance model builds on new technologies as well as on existing expertise and open government data to create better policies and decisions based on the citizens' expectations. The approach being developed seeks the active involvement of all stakeholders, including policymakers, civil servants, citizens and companies in the policymaking process. The FUPOL consortium is executing a comprehensive plan to advance the research and development in simulation, urban policy process modelling, text analysis, visualization and integration of those technologies.

The project, which has a budget of $12.5 USD (9,1 M€) is an integrated European Commission program under objective 5.6 in the seventh call FP7 EU research program. The project duration is four years (October 2011—September 2015). The FUPOL consortium[1] consists of partners from Europe and China, including research partners, IT-industry, local governments and political cluster organizations. The solution developed is being tested in five pilot cities: Zagreb, Croatia; Barnsley, United Kingdom; Pegeia, Cyprus; Skopje, Macedonia; and Yantai, China.

Following are the key specific deliverables and outcomes of FUPOL:

- A new governance model to engage all stakeholders in the policy design lifecycle;
- A cloud computing based ICT solution for scale take-up and acceptance;
- Multilingual training and accompanying material;
- A comprehensive urban policy knowledge database;
- Piloting and evaluation of FUPOL in European cities and China; and
- Large-scale dissemination of results through clusters of cities in Europe and worldwide.

FUPOL should not be considered as a policymaking solution for developed cities only. Developing countries also can take advantage of FUPOL because although they have still poor communication infrastructures, the mobile telecommunication services are widely used by citizens of all classes, including poor people in slums.

The United Nations Human Settlements Agency is teaming with the FUPOL project and with the Kenyan authorities to take advantage of the country's technology boom so that people in all walks of life can use their mobile telephones and other devices to join in programs aimed at combating poverty, especially in urban slums.[2]

---

[1] www.fupol.eu

[2] http://www.unhabitat.org/content.asp?cid=11847&catid=592&typeid=6&subMenuId=0 and http://www.fupol.eu/it/node/222

FUPOL's Benefits

FUPOL provides major benefits for politicians, civil servants, citizens and enterprises.

FUPOL supports cities by:

Increasing engagement of citizens and creating better understanding of citizens' needs and businesses' activities. The wider use of ICT tools results in higher potential of innovation concerning interaction of citizens with the government. A key technology that enables increased engagement of citizens is social computing. It helps citizens, enterprises and third-party organizations to express views instantly and to have more influence in the policy formulation process. To enable citizen engagement, FUPOL is designed to provide a social computing user interface that overcomes present technological barriers by integrating multiple channels into a single social computing environment (social computing cockpit).

Improving prediction of impacts of policy measures and enable better decisions. FUPOL's objective is to significantly improve the effectiveness and efficiency of the implementation of the government policies and to better identify the benefits and consequences for citizens and businesses. FUPOL assists the long-term strategic planning of policy operators in urban regions and enables improved prediction of impacts of policy measures to better address and shape future developments so that the demands of citizens and economy are met.

Improving transparency. FUPOL is designed to improve transparency of information related to the impact of decisions on the economy and on the society and to improve capacity to react to main societal challenges. Transparency of information is targeted by advanced visualization mechanisms. The deliberative approach with simulations increases the transparency of decisions, and therefore increases the trust of stakeholders and the public in governance.

The Policy Lifecycle

A major step represented by FUPOL from a political and participative point of view is related to the possibility to follow step by step the policy lifecycle to avoid the negative citizen engagement in the evaluation, discussion and decision process, and to avoid negative feedback because of a lack of understanding citizens' points of views or a lack of citizen involvement.

The FUPOL project aims to build a single process model, which is supported by integrated technology components. The building blocks of the policy lifecycle are as follows (The overall proposed workflow is summarized in Figure 3.).

Automatic "Hot Topic" Sensing—In the first step, the political blogosphere is searched and weighted to find out current "hot" political topics. The information is harvested with a web crawler.

Topic extraction—Topics are extracted from the raw text data and clustered based on semantic similarity. A core multi-language political ontology for automatically proposing good aggregations is built. It defines the background knowledge used for pre-processing and the selection of relevant views. Text classification is established by human analysis experts.

Analysis and Visualization—The characteristics of the hot topics analysed, clusters weighted and results are visualized in a user-friendly and understandable way. Analysis and visualization include a visual tool to compare previous results to show political hot topic shifting across time and to alert policymakers to emerging topics.

Open deliberation—At this stage, the policymaker decides to pursue a given topic further. If not, the topic-sensing process can be repeated at a later time to determine whether new topics have developed or whether there has been a major shift in citizens priorities.

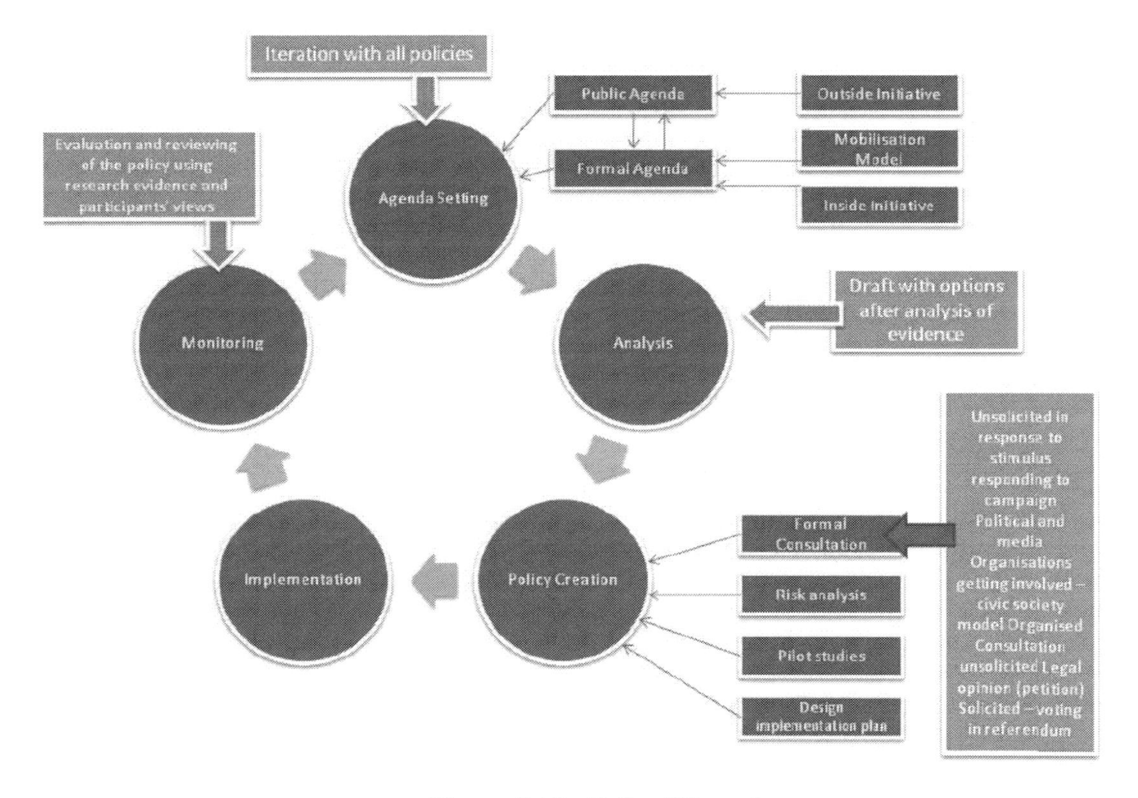

Figure 3. *The Policy Lifecycle.*

Idea Management System (IMS)—A policy issue is opened for public deliberation on the web, social networks, etc. The IMS, accessible by any citizen, is deployed. During an initial period, e-citizens have the opportunity to answer open questions related to a given topic. The idea management system is an enhanced discussion forum to enable open deliberations, as well as a crowd-sourcing tool for the public through an open call. This may include an outline of different policy scenarios, or it could be open. The creativity of citizens and stakeholders is used to generate new ideas and insights into the topic. The responses and corresponding analyses are stored in a response database for further analysis.

Opinion Analysis—The large number of potential contribution needs to be aggregated and summarized. This data aggregation step is crucial for e-governance because it expresses the citizens' voices. The text response is analyzed with semantic analysis tools and used with the multiple-choice response by subject matter experts to build policy alternatives and scenarios. It will be determined whether a document or a section thereof is subjective or objective, and whether the opinion expressed is positive or negative using a mixed-initiative framework that combines human annotations and automatic annotation based on machine learning/natural language processing techniques. The strength of the expressed opinion also will automatically be determined.

Opinion Summarization—Opinion summarization aims at giving the overall sentiment of a large number of opinion resources at various granularities. The presentation and visualization is to a large extent unexplored and new research field. Results of the opinion extraction as well as the underlying raw data will be classified and linked with the topic, so users can drill down to see the single stakeholder opinion. Likewise, the data will be linked with related results of a classical survey.

Policy Simulation—Based on the opinion summarization of stakeholders, policy scenarios are simulated. An agent-based policy model to accommodate the scenarios is built out of a predesigned standard model for the specific policy area. The scenarios and their potential impact over a timeline are simulated using available data. Eventually, data from other public administrations is obtained through data import facilities based on the World Wide Web Consortium (W3C) recommendations on "Publishing Open Government Data".

Visualization of the Results—Visualization comprises expert matter users (civil servants, political operators) and other political stakeholders (citizens, enterprises, etc.). They get insight into the topics by simulating alternatives, and they may change their original opinion. Instead of the design and development of isolated and singular visualization solutions, the FUPOL visualization consists of a frame where different components can be "plugged-in" as modules. Context-specific visualization environments can be configured. This allows users to visualize the impact of policy decisions and to answer "what-if" questions.

Ideas obtained from social networks will be related to the geographic information system (GIS) as far as possible. A starting point is the "MEIPI" approach. This is a collaborative space where users can upload information and content around a map.

Publication—The results of the simulation are published and advertised to get feedback from stakeholders or to prepare for finalization of the development lifecycle.

Reiteration or Finalisation of the policy design—A decision whether to get stakeholder response again or finalize the policy design lifecycle is made. The option of returning to the Opinion Analysis step to get stakeholder response has been introduced to show the results of the simulation to stakeholders and to eventually get different feedback from them because they may change their opinion once they see the impact of their original opinion.

The City Pilots

Each city pilot foresees a scenario and a set of basic actions and steps that have been defined and are being implemented:

- Measurable objectives;
- Actors to be involved;
- Real context of application;
- Scenario to be executed;
- Required input data;
- Simulation processes;
- Output products;
- Time planning; and
- Key performance indicators (KPI).

The following is an overview of each city site scenario. The pilots are being implemented or are scheduled to be implemented soon. Therefore, the final results will be available later.

Barnsley Council, United Kingdom

The policy domain selected is the Provision of Land for Employment Creation. The objective is to search foropinions and ideas on the availability of sufficient land for employment purposes and the elements the that need to be taken into account to move to specific recommendations regarding where such land should be allocated.

The Barnsley Council wants to increase the quality of the land available for economic development initiatives because land already allocated is no longer suitable. The Council wishes to do this without causing alarm or controversy to citizens.

The policy lifecycle being developed in the pilot includes:

- Investigating the current feeling of the people about the areas already allocated in the city;
- Collecting suggestions and ideas regarding possible improvements; and
- Collecting feedback on issues that are thought to be the most important when the policy is refined. It is an iterative process.

Municipal Council of Pegeia, Cyprus

The policy domain selected is Sustainable Tourism. It includes two scenarios: one to gather tourists' positive/negative experiences and opinions to develop the best recommendations for improving the area of Coral Bay; and the second to provide the best solution to promote Yeronissos as an archaeological attraction.

Pafos District, where the municipality of Pegeia is located, has been selected as the European Capital of Culture for 2017. The Municipal Council of Pegeia identified tourist seasonality as the major issue requiring immediate action, and sustainable tourism initiatives as a possible solution.

PromotingYeronissos island as an archaeological attraction requires specific actions to avoid harming the landscape and affecting excavations. The surface area of the island is quite small, so bringing tourists to the island could affect the ecosystem. Consequently, the FUPOL platform will collect feedback from stakeholders and identify the best ways to promote tourism while taking into consideration archaeologists', citizen's and visitors' concerns.

Municipality of Zagreb, Croatia

The policy domain selected is Land Use & Improvement of Social Infrastructure. It includes two tests: one for setting the policy in the area of social infrastructure, and the other to solicit opinions regarding the center for autism.

The City of Zagreb ensures the necessary infrastructure for the education for preschool (kindergartens) and school (schools) children, for their everyday involvement in sports activities and for access to the city's cultural facilities. Involvement in sports activities and access to cultural facilities should be enabled for all other Zagreb's citizens and visitors, too. Consequently, when drafting of the city's development strategy, key issues in the area of social infrastructure have been identified. To define the new policy to improve the social infrastructure, a dialogue with the public is being held. Public presentations, discussions and collection of written remarks and suggestions are organized. The topics will be open for discussion on the city of Zagreb's websites and social network pages. Moreover, media will be informed, and blogs will be launched on their websites. The city will use the FUPOL platform to allow the involved actors to investigate the most used social networks to collect people's opinions. Such opinions also can be geo-referenced through a specific opinion map.

Once such content is available, the municipality will be able use the specific platform functionalities to extract the most debated issues and to use graphical representations to submit the results to the decision-makers. The planned dialogue with the public is iterative and it follows the entire process, including agenda setting, policy creation, implementation and monitoring.

The second scenario refers to land use domain and aims to build the Centre for Autism. FUPOL used for better communicate with all interested parties and to ease the project implementation. The city has identified an area in which it wants to build the Center for Autism, including a new elementary school with all the necessary utility infrastructures. For this area, a detailed plan is being defined, including how the area should be used and decorated according to the planned purpose, public and social needs, and respecting the values and specificities of the surrounding area.

The transformation of this area includes the construction with spatial-functional determinations to offer a high quality of living to future inhabitants. Because the local population is very interested in using the surrounding land for its own needs, it is necessary to examine the construction of the Center for the Autism regarding its high significance.

Yantai Municipal Government, China

The Yantai pilot plans to focus on two domains— the Economic Domain regarding economic development analysis and policymaking, and the Urban Administration domain regarding parking area planning.

Every year, the Yantai municipal government develops new economic policies, which are related to all industry domains of the city. The objective is to review the status of economic development and make strategic decisions regarding upgrading the existing industry to meet the needs of the local social and economic development. The government plans to orient it's policy toward clean energy, low carbon and efficiency. The decision-makers of the city want to base their decision on existing data, such as electricity consumption, pollution emissions, etc., to make a better policy toward future year's economic development. Before starting the new year economic plan, Yantai's decision-maker wants to investigate citizen and stakeholder opinions and suggestions about the current economic situation and to collect opinions about policymaking standards. FUPOL will support a participatory approach from Yantia citizens that increasingly demonstrates their willingness and capacity to participate in public affairs discussion and the city development policymaking process.

Yantai will use the Urban Administration domain in parking area planning. Presently in Yantai every 100 city and township households has 37 cars. With the increase use of private cars, parking is becoming increasingly problematic and more parking areas must be planned. The results of the pilot will be used by planning officers. They will present relevant decisions and their plan to the public on a map, based on preliminary ideas. On the map, all planned parking areas in urban area will have one allocation. Then, there will be a consultation process that will help to refine the list of suggestions for chosen parking areas and consider the new factors that should be considered when making decisions. FUPOL tools will enrich existing processes and will be followed to give the pilot a very solid foundation. The result should be a new improved and refined map.

The Municipality of Skopje, Macedonia

There is an urgent need in Skopje to undertake measures and activities in order to provide a healthy environment for its citizens. One such measure is fostering inter-modality in the daily transportation of people and goods, more specifically, the use of bicycles.

FUPOL is supporting policy decisions for modernization of current transport being made by using several simulation tools as well as mechanism for collecting citizens' opinions. Sophisticated tools for survey analysis and social networks are being used as input in the developed model; it will also provide more precise data on planning sufficient infrastructure, like parking lots, bike paths, resolving the conflicts and overcoming the constraints.

The FUPOL IT Solution Features

Data Integration—The FUPOL Core Platform provides access to a comprehensive set of data. This includes:

- Statistical data from various sources (Eurostat, regional/local data, etc.);
- Semantic data, mainly from social media;

- Geographical data;
- Knowledge data; and
- Operational data (user accounts, user activity data, clients, journals, etc.).

The FUPOL Core Platform acts as a multipurpose data store and provides the ability to store and forward data between the modules.

The central repository integrates data from multiple source systems and ensures data consistency across all steps of the policy lifecycle. It provides a single common data model for all data of interest regardless of the data's source. Data generated in one policy lifecycle process are used for the next step.

Policy Indicator Dashboard—The policy indicator dashboard visualizes various indicators and flags if they are below/above thresholds or if certain conditions are fulfilled. The dashboard is intended as a tool for decision-makers and advisors to set context and perspective when evaluating the current state of policy domains in the city. The policy indicator dashboard is an efficient tool to monitor policies on the management level.

Social Network Aggregation and Single Window Display—Read posts from various sources, all in one place.

Social network aggregation is the process of collecting content from multiple services such as Facebook, Twitter, Blogspot or the FUPOL opinion map, and pulling them together into a single location. This also includes the same channel with different accounts (e.g. Facebook pages). Sources are from the city itself, but also other relevant sources such as citizen initiatives, for example. The postings are displayed as a "single window." Postings from various sources are displayed on the same screen. A multichannel "single window display" enables users to better grasp the public opinion.

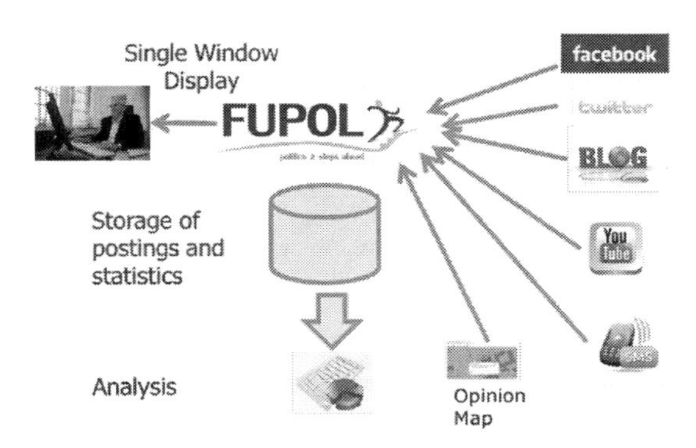

Figure 4.

Hot Topic Sensing and Topic Summarization—Get relevant topics and summaries automatically.

Hot topic sensing (HTS) is a web and social network analytics tool that analyzes data from social networks, newspapers, forums, blogs, etc., and identifies relevant topics.

The purpose of the HTS is to help identifying community needs. Postings from various social media are analyzed and "hot" topics are extracted.

Figure 5.

Topic Summarization—Also a summary of postings is created to reflect the opinions of the postings in brief. A quick identification of issues that are not yet on the public-policy agenda allows for better recognition of citizen needs.

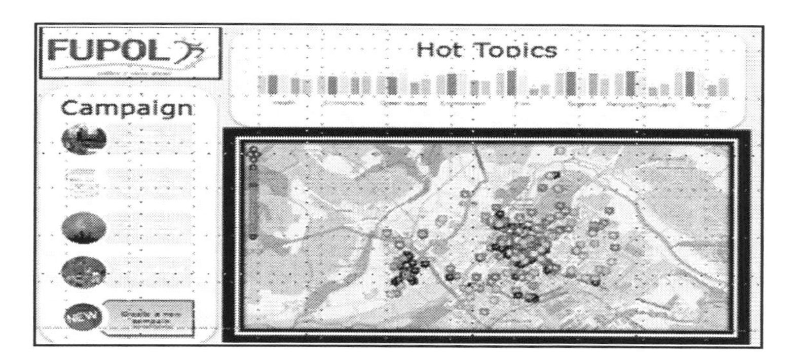

Figure 6.

Community Feedback Platform—The Community Feedback Platform is inspired by crowdsourcing platforms and is designed to enhance cognitive processes. The purpose of the system is to facilitate the idea analysis and selection processes.

- Create a campaign focused in a desired topic.
- Start ideation process: communities write ideas and comments, and vote on them.

- Select promising ideas and rank them from different point of views.
- Implement the best promising ideas.

The Community Feedback Platform enhances the capabilities of social network aggregation and single window display with additional features such as:

- Commenting/voting as a facilitator; and
- Analytics toolkit (i.e. computing: trends, topics, sentiments).

This leads to greater productivity and efficiency when staff analyze citizen feedback and needs. Staff also will be in a better position to recognize citizen needs through the advanced analytical tools.

Visualization of Statistical Data—In the described process of policy modelling, problem identification plays a key role in the whole policy design process. The need to get valid information about certain topics and policy indicators is essential to agenda-setting and for a new possible policy. Visualizing valid and proven data provides a more useful instrument to gather information by comparing, associating, correlating and identifying data, data-attributes or indicators.

In FUPOL, various visualizations are used to visualize:

a. Time-series of single or multi-variable data;

b. Geo-located variables and influences on geographical maps;

c. The combination of various visualization types, e.g. for comparing and identifying relevant and influencing indicators.

Visualization enables the stakeholders to evaluate data quicker leading to resource rationalization, greater productivity and efficiency.

FUPOL Knowledge Database and Visualization—In various steps of the FUPOL process model, the acquisition of information and the generation of knowledge play an essential role. The web provides increasing and rising knowledge repositories that enables, for instance, experts to validate hypothesis or explore options. The FUPOL Knowledge Database and Visualization uses web sources, that are interlinked with formal knowledge descriptions in combination with the knowledge provided within FUPOL.

It enables a user to search for knowledge in different external (web) data and internal (FUPOL) sources. It also combines visualizations in a visual cockpit metaphor for various policy tasks. A user is able to view web knowledge to validate, for example, an identified policy problem and to gather related implicit information.

FUPOL's visual knowledge database provides the ability to visually search, provethe given information and compare it to the web knowledge. It provides an efficient tool to increase the amount of linked open data.

Outgoing Multichannel Social Media Single Window Messaging—This is the capability supported by FUPOL to post messages to various channels (social media targets) without the need to manually post to each site separately.

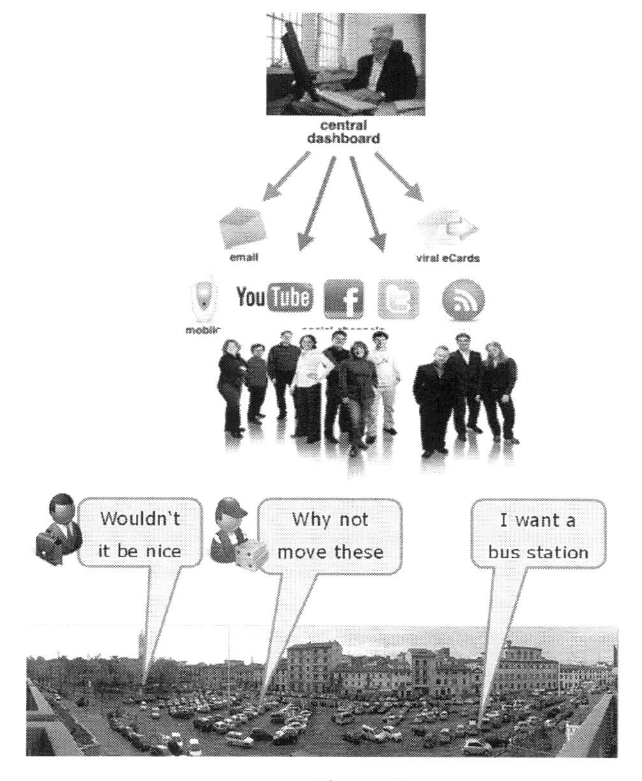

Figure 7.

FUPOL uses existing social media as a channel to the citizens. No new accounts are required (i.e. there is a low barrier to entry).

FUPOL supports:

- Twitter;
- Facebook;
- Blogspot;
- Sina Weibo;
- RSS/Atom; and
- Drupal.

Opinion Maps—Many political debates in a city have a reference to some specific spots. People have opinions on upcoming construction projects, on the place for a new bus station, or they just want to notify someone that there's a broken traffic light.

FUPOL provides a tool for geo-referenced interaction: The opinion maps. Opinion maps are interactive electronic maps that can be integrated into almost any internal or external website. So, for example, the municipality can use the city's existing blog to start a political debate related to some construction project. The opinion map can be integrated seamlessly into the city's blog, and eCitizens are able to express their opinions by interacting with that map.

Simulation and Impact Visualization—The simulation enables a virtual evaluation of policies. Therefore, the statistical history of indicators is used to generate forecasts based on mathematical models, in dependency of identified influencing indicators that can be addressed with a policy. A simulation tool is advantageous because the impact of a policy can be tested in a de-facto laboratory environment and can be evaluated to decide whether a certain change is desirable or not. The opportunity to evaluate a policy before it is implemented is useful in two ways:

- Evaluating an identified solution in the analysis phase to ensure that a planned policy will address and solve the problem.
- Simulating in the monitoring phase, after a policy is implemented, to predict the function of a policy, especially if a complex policy needs a longer reaction time.

In the FUPOL policy process, simulation plays an important role because it allows users to identify predicted impacts on policy indicators or other influencing factors. After the computation of the simulation, the visualization provides a detailed analysis to determine the impact of a planned policy.

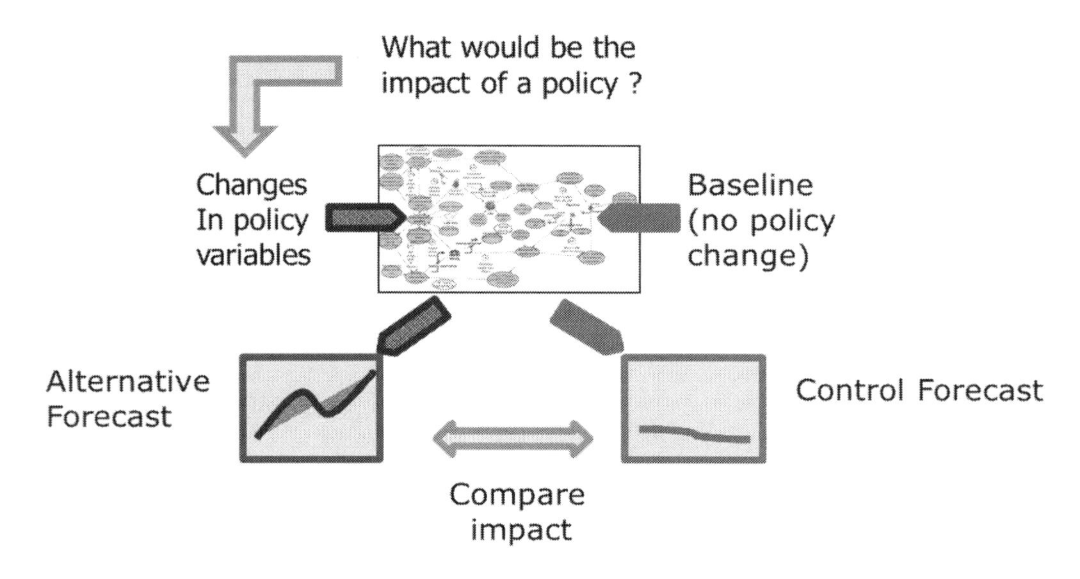

Figure 8.

Therefore it is advantageous for decision-makers to simulate and analyze a planned policy before it is implemented because insufficient policies can be avoided.

FUPOL status and further evolution

In October 2013, the FUPOL project entered its third year and is in the middle of its development, being implemented according to the plan.

Although multiple risks and obstacles exist, they have been identified and analyzed. Simulation techniques, GIS, social networks and automatic text analysis are being combined with classic e-participation to facilitate integrated e-governance. The solution covers uncertainties related to the potential impact of a policy measure, as well as uncertainties related to the reaction of the citizens. In today's volatile environment, this is important.

The core platform and most of FUPOL's key features are partially ready or in an advanced stage of development. Pilots have been launched and initial results are expected soon. To support the deployment of FUPOL, extensive online education, including tutorial videos and training materials, have been developed[3]. Valuable deliverables already have been published, such as the FUPOL guidelines for policy for cities and municipalities, and social media project implementation in cities and municipalities.

Wide dissemination through conferences, meetings and publications have been performed successfully. This has raised great interest, and other cities are candidates to join the project and to test the FUPOL solution.

In parallel contacts with potential partners heve been established in Europe and worldwide to deploy and exploit the FUPOL solution. Special focus is also given to the deployment of FUPOL in developing countries.

GIORGIO PRISTER, *President of Major Cities of Europe, www.majorcities.eu.*

[3] Training material http://www.fupol.eu/node/110?q=node/223

20

Can Smart Cities Exist in Africa?

Samia Melhem

The smart city concept is a fairly new one in mainstream literature. It has emerged powerfully in the past few years and is associated with concepts of information communication technology (ICT) innovations in the context of urban management. The smart city concept has been adopted as one of the main pillars of leading ICT companies such as IBM, Cisco, Siemens, Microsoft, Google and others. It seems to incorporate notions of climate change adaptation and mitigation (green city, eco city), resilience and preparedness for disasters (safe city), architectural design, efficient use of public resources, high speed affordable connectivity (digital city), and an aggregation of skills, technological know-how, and new service industries (knowledge city).

Add to that picture the capabilities of sensors on trash and recycling bins to minimize costs and the environmental footprint for city waste, water sensors in public facilities to ensure water is used more intelligently, space sensors in parking areas to indicate empty spaces (minimizing driving time and emissions), and sensors on streetlights that detect movement and daylight- and adjust the illumination accordingly. Imagine a city with well-designed, strategically located charging stations for electrical vehicles, bike parking racks, pet-friendly zones, children-safe playgrounds, recycling bins, food and clothes donation stations, and several other measures to reduce the citizens' environmental footprint and optimize the use of space under advanced design principle. Who would not want to live in a smart city? But can global advances in smart cities, and their impact on ICT and urban strategies be applied in Africa?

Smart Use and Re-Use of Resources

A smart city recycles almost everything. Some 1.3 billion tons of municipal solid waste (MSW) are generated globally each year, a volume that is increasing rapidly with urbanization and mass consumption. The volume of MSW generated globally is projected to double by 2025. It is expected home and office electronics (old phones, laptops, printers, monitors, appliances, etc.) will significantly increase MSW. This indicates the need for city planners to think seriously about sustainability, innovation and low-carbon waste management solutions, enlisting in the process the good will, knowledge and creativity of citizens.

Cities like Barcelona, Copenhagen[i] or Songo are showing a desire to proactively engage citizens and the private sector to modernize their energy, transit and health care systems to reduce waste and improve efficiency. So are the cities of Nairobi, Dakar, Ouaga and Dar.

A smart city leverages its social capital, utilizes the innovation and energy of its youth, maximizes on its volunteers' knowledge and connections to keep improving and evolving—while respecting the environment. What are the incentives to sustain this virtuous circle? Time will tell, but for now, co-creation, ownership, active citizenry, social responsibility and such shared values seem to be the main drivers.

What About "Other" Cities?

One World Bank client recently said: "There are no smart cities. There are smart administrations, smart services and smart citizens. How can a city be smart by itself?"

Meanwhile another client asked: "Are there any stupid or dumb cities? Please name me one or two."

Jokes aside, the path to becoming a smart city is evolutionary, not revolutionary. It would be much easier to design a smart city if starting from scratch with an empty drawing board and with plenty of resources and skills at hand. But very few policy makers have that luxury.

Smart Cities for Smart Development Champions

At a recent "Smart Rwanda" International conference[ii] which took place in Kigali, Rwanda, with a smart city discussion ensued with the Minister of Youth and ICT and the mayor of Kigali. The discussion was part of the larger picture design of "Smart Rwanda," and an objective of the government of Rwanda's vision 2020. The Smart Rwanda concept is based on the principle of using the transformational powers of ICT in Africa[iii] to embrace smart solutions to tackle pressing development problems, such as poverty and access to basic services. The smart approach will enable Rwanda to leapfrog and accelerate growth and development to the benefit of all citizens.

The conference brought together more than 250 representatives of government, private sector, academia, media, and civil society, plus online participants from around the world, to co-create the Smart Rwanda concept. This was Rwanda's first co-creation event, and with more than 500 online followers each day, it was one of the biggest crowdsourcing exercises conducted by the World Bank in Africa. Experts from 11 countries shared experiences in using ICT to create innovative solutions to development problems such as transportation, education and agriculture.

The Smart Kigali vision, the leaders explained, is a city where government uses open data to improve public transportation efficiency, and to enhance public safety—analyzing data around road accidents, traffic patterns, petty theft and urban flooding levels. The minister and the mayor want to reduce carbon emissions. They aspire for Kigali and the other major cities to become efficient places to live, with lower per capita greenhouse gas emissions, with efficient land use and transportation alternatives, towars a climate change mitigation culture. They aspire for smart youth to live in the city, help it grow, improve it, sustain it and improve it.

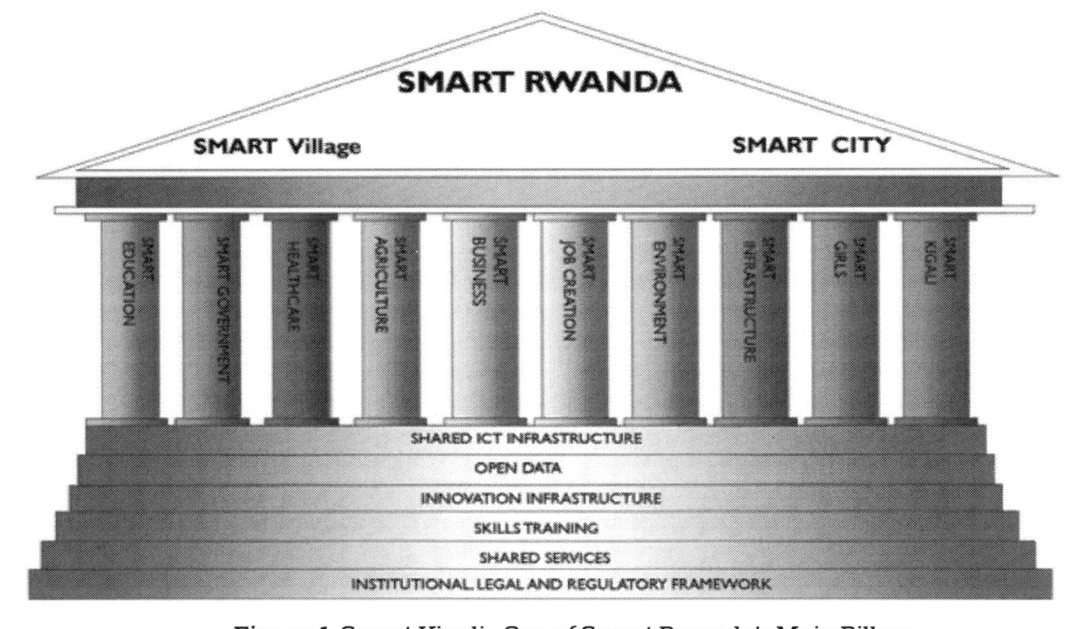

Figure 1. *Smart Kigali—One of Smart Rwanda's Main Pillars.*

Urbanization and Population Growth

During the 20th century, the global population saw its greatest increase in known history, rising from about 1.6 billion in 1900 to more than 6 billion in 2000. By 2000, there were approximately 10 times as many people on earth as there had been in 1700. In 2013, there are about 7.2 billion people, or 50 times the number of people who lived on earth in 1700. Two centuries ago, humans were predominately rural dwellers, with just 3 percent of us living in cities. According to United Nation estimates, the balance tipped sometime in 2008, when more people lived in urban areas than in rural communities—a first in the history of humanity. Thus, climate change mitigation and adaptation is important as we rethink how we can make cities management smarter, and consumers of city life and services more conscious about choices and behaviors with the hope of improving citizen's quality of life. Competitiveness also is a factor, as cities need to create quality jobs and need to attract educated entrepreneurial people.

Why We Need Smart Cities

Urbanization is one of the most dominant trends of the current decade. For the first time in history, more than half the world's population lives in urban areas. More than 90 percent of urbanization is taking place in the developing world. Urbanization, population growth, exodus from rural areas, combined with regionalization and globalization, has changed the patterns of urban development. In addition, transport and ICT revolutions have helped to create large industrial economic zones, boosting local and regional competitiveness around clusters zones.

In the flagship report "eTransform Africa[iv] commissioned by the World Bank, several case studies feature ICT innovations delivering home-grown sevelopment solutions in Africa. These solutions are helping to createg jobs in most Africa cities—through the explosion of mobile apps innovation labs and hubsin Nairobi, Dakar, Cairo and Cape Town. Some African capitals are living labs to innovation around open and big data. The challenge for local government is to catch up and come up with innovative ways to use, analyze and curate its own data toward service-delivery improvements.

Birth of Smart Citizens

The adoption of cellular phones by the world's population at an unprecedented rate also has helped connect all citizens to a common set of global goods and consumer applications, from social networking apps such as Twitter, Facebook and LinkedIn to search engines such as Google. In today's social networking culture, citizen participation in governance is a disruptive and powerful force challenging existing concepts of local public administration's quality of service and that of "classical" city management. The local or municipal agencies in a smart city treat their citizens like a retailer treats customers: professionally, promptly and productively.

A smart city enables its citizens to crowd-source ideas, solutions and feedback into the day-to-day life in that city, from status reports on the state of schools, water mains, water fountains, public restrooms, bus driver attitude, etc. Mobile based applications to geo tagging of public assets and service points have tremendously empowered citizens. Through Open 311[v], an open source application allowing citizens to interact with local city management, or Check my school, an application monitoring school teachers' performance, local government can monitor anything including abandoned vehicles, potholes, urban floods traffic and teacher absenteeism. Monitoring is the first step toward redress and service-delivery improvement. Addressing and fixing of the problems is another story, and has to do with the science of delivering local government.

The European Union (EU), in particular, has devoted constant efforts to devising a strategy for achieving urban growth in a smart sense for its metropolitan city-regions. The OECD and EUROSTAT Oslo Manual stresses the role of innovation in ICT sectors and provides a toolkit to identify consistent indicators, thus shaping a sound framework of analysis for researchers on urban innovation based on a citizen-centric approach. Out of the top 10 cities generally recognized as "smart cities," more than half are European: Barcelona, Helsinki, Amsterdam, Stockholm, Oslo, Copenhagen, Vienna, Lyon, London, etc.

In such cities, data quality is necessary, and so is the ability to act on data-driven warnings, signals and triggers. Intelligent systems are useless if their remediation part is unreliable. This is where smart civil servants, smart back-end systems and smart administration kick in. This is where big data, open data, ICT innovations, public sector reform, and science of service-delivery intersect—resulting in a high outcome, high quality experience for all stakeholders, and increasing trust between local government and its constituents.

Citizens as Feedback Provider

Today's World Bank-supported projects push to enable two-way information flows between citizens and governments. Based on experience in Nairobi, Rabat, Ghana and other cities, two-way information flow has proven to greatly improve project outcomes by enhancing the accountability of service-providers, improving transparency of decision-making and service delivery, building ownership and empowering citizens. Making the development practice inclusive and participatory is a key aspect for any activity's sustainability.

To this end, several of the World Bank's projects work with implementation units in government to streamline collection of citizen feedback by establishing a common platform that supports SMS and Web feedback loops between government, public service-providers and citizens in the local languages used, and in a transparent and consultative manner.

Several such platforms have been implemented, mostly using open source applications that are available for others to re-use. The Open

Development Technology Alliance team at the World Bank group has been compiling and collecting such public goods (www.odta.net). The Ontrack Platform has been used in Nepal[vi], Brazil and Zambia,[vii] and may be used in other countries such as Morocco, where local government is actively seeking citizen feedback around service-delivery foron-time bus and tramway schedules, providing building and construction permits in a timely fashion, water service provision and effective waste management by the municipality, among other projects.

Access infrastructure is critical to a smart city. This was referred to a decade ago as the "I" (Infrastructure) before the "E" (eGovernment), and the statement is still valid today. Most of the World Bank Projects in the ICT sector provide governments with the enabling legal and regulatory framework for broadband infrastructure. In the regional connectivity projects financed by the World Bank in Africa, countries like Kenya witnessed a 40-fold drop in the price of the 1 megabites per secon (Mbps) in Nairobi due to increased competition.

Smart Cities for the Connected Youth

In the next two decades, cities are expected to expand by another 1 billion residents, as people, mostly youth, move in unprecedented numbers from rural areas to pursue hopes and aspirations in cities. More than 90 percent of this urban population growth is expected to occur in the developing world, where many cities are already struggling to provide basic needs (water, electricity, transport, health services and education.) Smart cities will need to provide youth centers, equipped with counselors that can assist in career management, housing, vocational training, continuing education, etc. Special programs to assist the under-privileged and distressed youth, especially young girls and women, are needed. Partnerships with (CSOs) and the private sector to connect youth to private sector opportunities (internship, training, jobs, etc.) are valuable. Youth centers are connected and host useful educational content and entertainment. Youth centers could host innovation labs, or hackathons, for specific projects and social experiments, such as financial inclusion schemes and micro-work training.

The Harvard Kennedy School of Business[viii], for instance, recently funded an innovation lab in June 2013. The objective is to catalyze on the youth's energy and creativeness toward creative solutions to urban problems. These structures help create a "can do" attitude, where youth take it upon themselves to fix problems that the local administration could not handle. A common starting point is mapping the city's resources and points of interest using open source maps (open street map for instance) or proprietary map applications from Google or others.

In Tanzania, which has been, along with Kenya, pioneering mapping activities using youth equipped with mobile phones and mapping apps, the streets of Dar El Salam are now fully mapped. Local government and youth partnering in such projects has helped to create temporary jobs, create skills, and promote inclusion, participation and trust between youth and local authorities.

Making Sense of the Sensors

Technological innovations such as crowdsourcing and big data provide city administrators evidence to improve service delivery to citizens in terms of effectiveness, quality and volume. Use of wireless sensor networks is a specific technological innovation to support smart cities. The distributed network of sensors can measure several parameters and deliver the data in real time using the wireless network of the smart city. It is then up to the appropriate authorities to use the data to tweak the specific service.

For example, citizens can monitor the pollution concentration, traffic, water levels, temperature, and bus stops on each city street. They can get automatic alarms when the temperature rises to certain level, triggering an emergency call to the nearest fire station. It is also possible for authorities to optimize lighting in city zones where crime or petty theft are high; re-route traffic in areas routinely congested at specific times; and fix and clean public facilities where hygiene matters, such as at recreation areas, parks, school zones, latrines, etc.

The World Bank's Contribution to the Smart Cities Research

The World Bank Group has been funding urban development and decentralization for several decades. The group also has been investing in policymaker capacity building, and in South South Exchanges of experiences. In the past few years, the World Bank supported research on smart cities by financing the following global public goods and reports:

a. Planning, Connecting and Financing-Now: What City Leaders Need to Know[ix], provides a framework for urban growth planning and finance, backed by 12 case studies, to help policymakers on good practices, policy options and technical solutions that have proven to work. Launched at the Global Energy Basel Conference, the report provides a policy guide that local officials can use to create jobs, housing and infrastructure needed to turn their cities into hubs of prosperity for current and future residents, in other words, into smart cities. To help policymakers prepare for and manage growth, the report distills lessons learned from 12 countries across all geographic regions and stages of urbanization—including

Korea, India, Colombia and Uganda. The report then translates the global lessons into practical policy advice around smart grids, transport, green growth, etc.

b. The Urban Knowledge Platform (UKP): The UKP was prepared by leading authors and academics in urban development. It is a global public good and provides helpful lessons on urbanization and smart citiy development. The UKM examines specific concepts for policymakers championing smart city concepts:

1. Open city data initiatives such as a "Mayor's Dashboard" enable smarter urban decision-making and global benchmarking in partnership with a number of private sector partners and others from academia and civil society. The Dashboard helps make sense of a range of agency and bottom-up data sources through compelling visualizations to facilitate smarter urban decision-making (modeled in part on MIT's *Singapore Live!* project).
2. A global research collaboration on the spatial development of cities brings together planners and decision-makers from many of the world's megacities for hands-on peer learning in partnership with the World Bank.
3. A data-driven city management lab uses big data and draws on experience from the MIT Senseable City Lab[x] or the Ash Center for Democratic Governance and Innovation at Harvard Kennedy School (Data-Smart City Solutions)[xi]. Both labs are based on the concept that big data and analytics should transform the way local government operates. Bringing together industry, academic and government officials, these labs offer city leaders a national depository of cases and best practice examples where cities and private partners use analytics to solve city problems This enables a city to build a "lab" around an innovative initiative being implemented by a partner city in which other cities then participate, both to observe and to help provide input through the lab's open data infrastructure and resources.
4. Discussions about developing a shared open city data agenda were envisaged for a potential "Science of Cities" workshop. The goal of this workshop was to convene a sizable number of city representatives (from both the developing and developed world) to sign on to a common framework for open data at the city level (modeled in part as a city-level version of the Open Government Partnership (OGP)).
5. Assisting individual cities and groups of cities through demonstration projects emphasize data-driven city management and performance based management. These activities are requested officially by local governments.

c. The Open Development Technology alliance (aka the ICT knowledge platform, a sister platform to the UKP) has researched civic tech applications for smart cities—and their re-use across the planet. The alliance highlights a few successes, looking into lessons learned from ongoing initiatives such as the European Initiative on smart cities , the European network of living labs (ENOLL), successes from Singapore, South Korea and Toronto. A particularly potent concept are learning labs inspired in part by similar initiatives in the open government and civil hacking community (including hackathons). While never formally defined, a learning lab essentially focuses on facilitating hands-on peer learning and collaborative problem solving in an open environment where cities can jointly dissect not just their successes but also their failures. In particular, the term lab implies a willingness to experiment and try new innovations, with a much higher tolerance for failure —but also a commitment to learn from failure (i.e. to "fail forward"). Here, a 'smart city' is one that takes advantage of the opportunities ICTs offer to increase local prosperity and competitiveness. The approach implies integrated urban development based on multi-actor, multi-sector and multi-level perspectives. Urban development is a complex area and most solutions to urban development problems are multi-sectoral and thus necessitate the sustained collaboration of a variety of actors—all motivated by a shared vision of their smart city.

SAMIA MELHEM *is Lead ICT Policy Specialist of the World Bank Group. The views represented in this chapter are that of the author and do not represent the view of the World Bank Group nor its board of directors.*

ENDNOTES

[i] http://topics.nytimes.com/top/news/business/columns/smart_cities/index.html

[ii] Smart Rwanda Days Event

[iii] Report: eTransform Africa: The Transformational Use of Information and Communication Technologies in Africa

[v] http://open311.org/

[vi] Poverty Alleviation Fund, Nepal, http://ontrack-ms.esri.com/nepal/node/8

[vii] Existing OnTrack platforms and following description: Promoting Innovative Approaches to Peri-Urban Sanitation Improvement Project, Zambia, http://ontrack-ms.esri.com/zambia/node/38

[viii] http://www.hks.harvard.edu/news-events/news/press-releases/ash-center-data-smart-city-solutions

[ix] http://intranet.worldbank.org/WBSITE/INTRANET/SECTORS/INTURBANDEVELOPMENT/0,,menuPK:336395~pagePK:151716~piPK:176772~theSitePK:336388,00.html

[x] http://senseable.mit.edu/livesingapore/

[xi] http://www.hks.harvard.edu/news-events/news/press-releases/ash-center-data-smart-city-solutions

[xii] http://setis.ec.europa.eu/implementation/technology-roadmap/european-initiative-on-smart-cities

21

The Role of e-Government and Citizens in a Smart City

Eikazu Niwano

The argument for smart cities has mainly been to improve society's infrastructure. However, smart technology also can improve society's initiative, self-motivation, spontaneity and autonomy by allowing citizens, regional communities, enterprises and public/governmental entities to cooperate, coordinate and collaborate.

To connect stakeholders dynamically, governments should considered what is required for electronic government and governmental entities to be "smart."

In the current environment, where there is tougher competition in a global market, an increase in elderly-people, expansion of an economically stratified society, diversification of a living environment, local government's funding issues, and a lack of mutual aid between families/neighbors by the increase in living alone. Therefore, it is important for governments to offer a system in which it is convenient to support life from four aspects: connection, individual, community and safety (see Figure 1).

- **Connection:** Society where all information* and services* required for a life are digitized, and the user and provider are connected simply.
- **Individual:** Society in which everyone can use information* and service* required for life, and enjoy those ones that are optimal to the individual
- **(Regional) Community:** Society where use/offer gap of the information* and service by the area is narrowed, and those contribute to the life security and promotion/vitality in the region
- **Safety:** Society that ensures and guarantees the relief and safety at the time of information* and service* use, such as providing citizens with air or water in emergencies.

**A public sector system and a private sector system are included.*

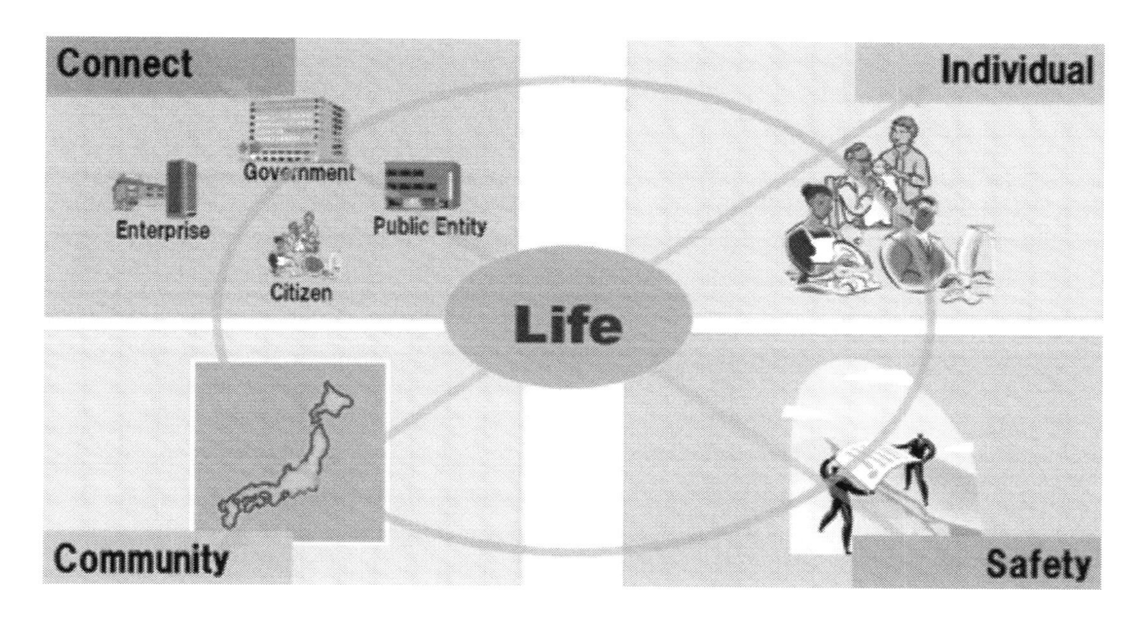

Figure 1. *SICS Vision: 4 Aspects to Support (Regional) Citizens Lives.*

The Approach for Realizing Society

To create a connected life, governments need to improve the digital information circulation environment and integration of data. Technology makes it possible to use necessary information anywhere, and with various appliances and terminals to integrate the scattered and various types of information can be connected and used.

To create an individual life, it is important to create a participatory type society that supports: 1) various citizen lifestyles; 2) participation of city administration/planning and the regional community; and 3) establishing its channel, with the capability of optimizing information according to the attributes of individuals, such as concierge type information dissemination and a usage environment.

For "(regional) community" life, governments will need to have an open-ubiquitous-universal type connection environment. This means according to the isolation of a regional information technology (IT) environment, the connection environment should: 1) support activation and vitalization of economic activity and communication in the region, 2) self-support human and financial resources, 3) transmit information from the regional community and rectify gaps between regions.

For "safe (and relief/ease)" life, governments need to provide a secure service/information integration IT platform. This provides the mechanism by which trust in net society can be checked, based on trust in the actual world. Conversely, trust in net society will elevate trust in the actual world. Based on reliable/trustworthy IT information, communities will realize relieved social security and living, which alleviates an information divide.

The concept of LifeHub (see Figure 2) can help governments satisfy the above requirements. In the LifeHub, government or a public entity is the hub for regional stakeholders.

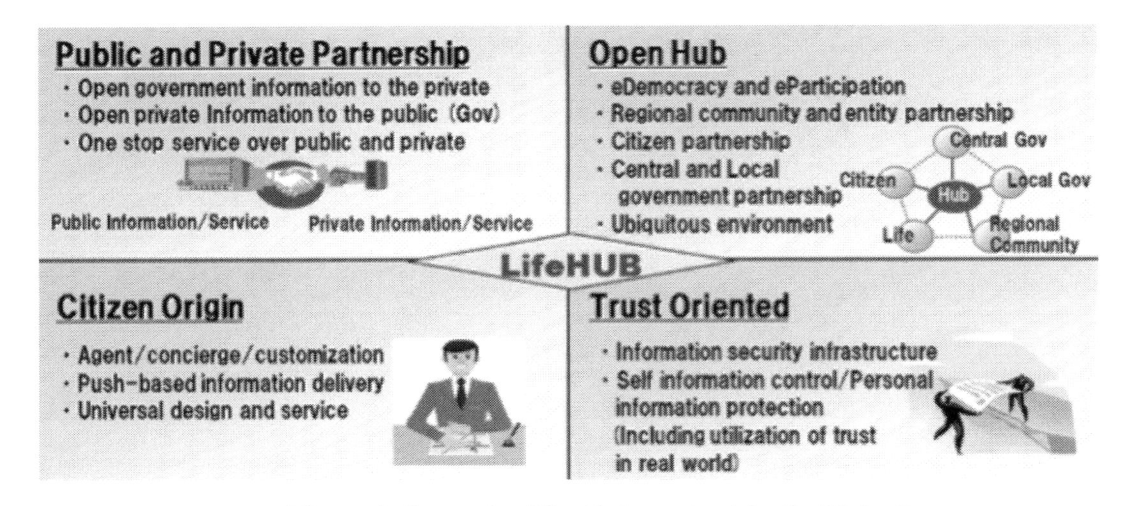

Figure 2. *Concepts—What Is Important for the Vision?*

- **Public and Private Partnership:** Offers new information and services, improvement in convenience and simplicity because of the public-private partnership..
- **Open Hub:** All subjects (administration, self-governing body, company, people, etc.) and all information services are connected. There is mutual participation between subjects with the goal of improving the convenience and simplicity of an information service.
- **Citizen Origin:** According to citizen situations (an attribute, environment, a life stage, etc.), there is optimization of the contents of offer of an information service, and the offer method is attained.
- **Trust-Oriented:** Information and service circulate to provide relief and improve safety. The information platform that can control information, authority, etc., are offered.

CONCEPT		CONTENTS
Public-Private Partnership	Opening to the Private Sector Administration Information and Service	The information and service that administration holds is opened to the private sector, and the private sector provides private information and service, or combines the information.
	Opening to the Governmental Agency private Sector Information and Service	The information and service that the private sector holds is opened to the public sector. This provides a public information and service.
	One-Stop Government and People Information Service	Administration and private information/service are provided at one stop.
Open Hub	eDemocracy and eParticipation	People and administration are connected, and the hub enables them to perform electronic voting, or solicit direct participation from people in the policymaking process.
	Regional Community	Local residents and a self-governing body are connect-ed, and it enables a local resident to participate in local administration.
	Hub for Living	The public service (donor) concerning a life of people and people are connected. The convenience and simplicity of service are improved.
	Cooperation Between Government and a Self-Governing Body	The central government and a local government are connected to provide citizen convenience and simplicity when following a government procedure, or sharing information and service.
	Regional Cooperation, Citizens Cooperation	Self-governing bodies and people are connected, so that information regarding a government procedure or service can be improved. (i.e., sharing medical examination information on a new address, etc.)
	Ubiquitous	Anyone has access to use information and service from any terminal at anytime, anywhere.
Citizen Origin	Concierge type/ Customized Type	According to every citizen's attributes, environment, needs, etc., there is optimal information and service.
	Push-Based Information Delivery	According to a life stage of a citizen, required information and service are actively provided directly from the provider side.
	Agent Type	For elderly, a disabled person, etc. the mechanism by which an individual can act for himself or herself, or for those cannot easily use a public service.
	Universal Design and Service	Public services (operability, correspondence apparatus, etc.) that are easy-to use by all people.
Trust-Oriented	Information Security Platform (confidentiality, complete-ness and availability)	Confidentiality at the time of use that provides information and a service, etc. are secure and guarantees relief and a safe circulation platform.
	Self-Information Control/ Private-Information-Protection Platform	The security environment reflecting trust, authority, etc., of the actual world and the circulation platform that can be controlled by itself.

Personal Information Use for a Service-Provider-Driven Environment

- To realize this concept, using personal information becomes a key issue. Consequently, consider the following model: Omotenashi-Ozendate-based Service Provisioning
- Diversity-Oriented Secure Device Management

Omotenashi-Ozendate is a service-provider-driven environment that consists of three components, such as user driving initiative, service-provider as a driving force, and distributed personal information/big data/life log (see Figure 3).

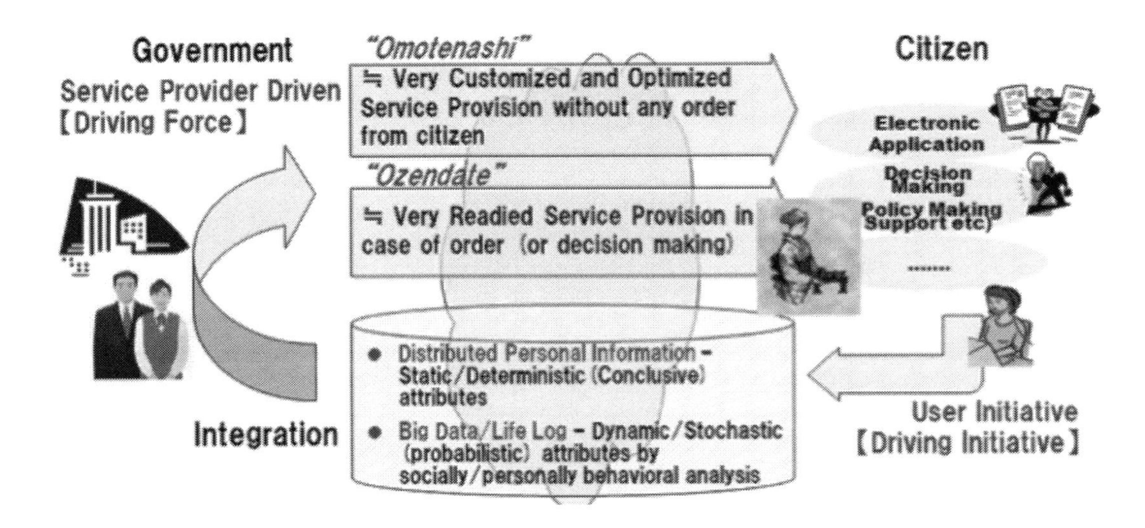

Figure 3. *Omotenashi-Ozendate-Based Service Provisioning.*

In this environment, the service user becomes the driving initiative for all personal information. In other words, a service user can control disclosure/delete self-information. Then, the service-provider can use a service user's distributed personal information, social information such as big data and life log to provide the user with convenient service under the user's initiative. The driving force exists on service-provider's side; it offers the mechanism by which a citizen can choose, make a contract of and use governmental services easily and safely.

Omotenashi is a Japanese word that means to convey consideration, compassion and sympathy without the right side and the wrong side by using thing and object faithfully and sincerely. It is used like hospitality in providing service. Under the service-provider-driven environment, this creates a customized and optimized service provision without input from the citizen.

Ozendate is also a Japanese word meaning to get ready for the meal, and to reach the state in which you can eat immediately. It also means to prepare so that you can start it immediately. In other words, it is akin to setting the stage for, completing the arrangements, setting the table, etc. It means not only getting ready for an event or action, but also laying the groundwork for decision-making. Under a service-provider-driven environment, it means readying service provisions in case there is an order (or decision making) by the user.

An example of the omotenashi service is recommendation service in private sector. An example of ozendate" service is a pre-populated/filled tax return.

The difference in the "Omotenashi-Ozendate" offered in a private sector field and the administration field is the following point.

In the case of a private sector field, some amount of money is paid when the service is used, the trade-off/counter value is quite prudent. On the other hand, when using governmental service, the tax payment has been made, so interest is only to know and use governmental services without dropping.

The function that notifies the service with a pre-filled application document dynamically in the administration field is very useful and highly convenient in the sense that you do not need to note advantages and disadvantages when evaluating service.

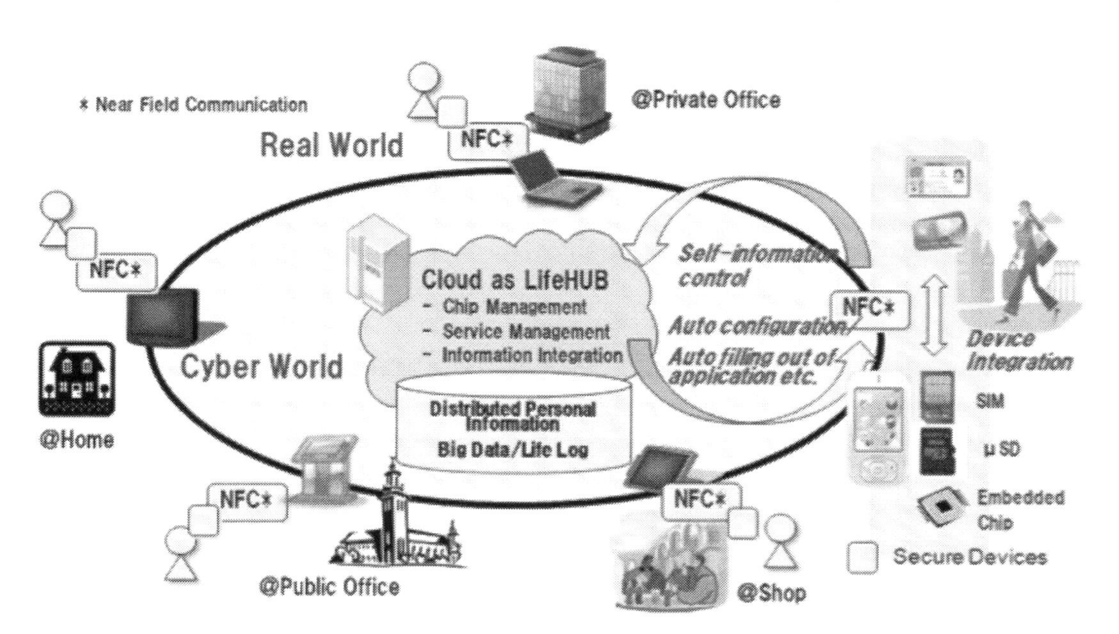

Figure 4. *Diversity-Oriented Secure Device Management.*

Moreover, when doing this calculation about personal information, it should be based on what private information the user permitted others to view, and what the user wants protected and static. Dynamic/stochastic (probabilistic) attributes by socially/personally behavioral analysis by the big data/life log will be applied to context-based services.

Moreover, as a means for providing both civic private information protection and convenience, governments should provide service management and multiple secure device management capability, in addition to information and service integration capabilities. Using the secure device as a civic agent allows the service provider and user to perform service management and use securely and safely anytime, anywhere.

Citizens' Role When Forming a Self-Governing Organization

What is the role of a citizen in sustainability?

The following concepts are inspired from the expression of "municipal/local government" in Japanese. In Japan, municipal/local government usually is called a self-governing body. There are many types of self-governing organizations, such as a vigilante group, committee, neighborhood council and student council. Those entities are loosely connected to each other and sometimes collaborate with each other dynamically in the case of disaster, etc. Many cities have supported these kind of citizen-oriented, self-governing activities in the real world.

To create a sustainable society, it is important that with information communication technologies (ICT):

1. Self-governing organization can be created spontaneously and dynamically, and can act autonomously.
2. Mutual concessions and sharing is made for self-help and mutual aid among those organizations;
3. There is cooperation with other organizations according to a time or a situation. A necessary organization consumes a necessary thing, not excessively but self-effacingly;
4. Hand over the current culture to the next generation.

Sustainable society has the function to manage an arbitrary, self-governing organization dynamically, efficiently and effectively, then connect and federate each other by ICT.

eSelf-Governance/Government

In eGovernment, the concept of eDemocracy and eParticipation has been discussed in this order for a long time. This is raising the degree of how citizens relate to government activities.

- In addition to ICT support for citizen relations to government, ICT support for citizens to construct self-government organizations and perform self-government activities must be provided. This scheme can be called "eSelf-Governance/Government" (see Figure 5), and basic requirements are as follows: Citizens can construct eSelf-governing organization spontaneously and dynamically through electronic means.
- Governmental agencies or a public entity can support the generation, maintenance, revitalization and the cooperation over the eSelf-governing organizations in wide areas through electronic means.

This aims at the model that government and citizen are loosely connected and cooperate autonomously each other.

Figure 5. *A Topic Direction in eGovernment.*

Sectors for Basic Citizen Life

When discussing sustainability, there are two axis. When taking sustainable development into consideration, it is certain that revitalization of a town is an important element, but a fundamental life must be guaranteed in advance. There are four fields of fundamental sectors: environment, disaster prevention, medical treatment and education. eSelf-Government by citizens and regional communities, in conjunction with governmental/public entities as LifeHUB, lead to activation or revitalization of towns, such as "local production for local consumption," welcoming citizens/enterprises and then sightseeing. This also is caused by financial feedback to the governmental entity, and benefits the citizens/regional communities in this virtuous cycle.

Then, eGovernment can support eSelf-Government schemes and service/information integration capabilities of these four fundamental fields by applying ICT as the LifeHUB.

- When creating a continuous smart city, it is important to recognize the role of electronic administration and the civic Government Role. Entity: Connects the eSelf-governing organization dynamically.
- Citizen: Accepts the support of eGovernment, and configures the eSelf-governing organization autonomously.

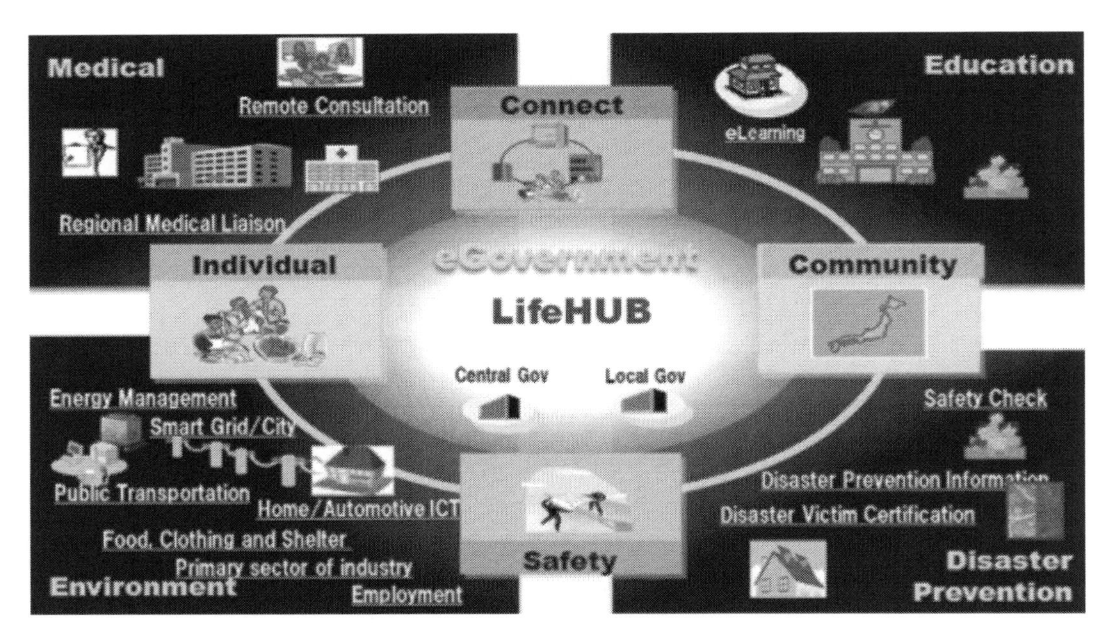

Figure 6. *Important Sectors for Basic Citizen Life.*

ESelf-governnance/government is one of important issues to be considered to create a sustainable society, in addition to sustainable smart city infrastructure and eDemocracy-eParticipation in eGovernment. The scheme with four fundamental sectors —health, education, disaster prevention and environment—will be fundamental to citizens lives. It will imply activation or revitalization of towns, also ultimately can lead to a sustainable society.

EIKAZU NIWANO, *Producer Research and Development Planning Department, NTT Corporation, Japan*

REFERENCES

1. E.Niwano, "Through the Experience of Great East Japan Earthquake/Tsunami 3.11-Social Information Infrastructure and eGovernment for Basic Citizen Life—Proceedings of Global Forum 2011.
2. E.Niwano, "Omotenashi-Ozendate": Towards Realizing Service Provider Driven eGovernment, Proceedings of Global Forum 2012.

22

Citadel on the Move: Open Data Unlocking Cross Border Innovation

Geert Mareels, Susie Ruston, Julia Glidden and Jesse Marsh

Citadel on the Move is an European Union (EU)-funded CIP-IST Smart City project that consists of partners from five European countries including the Flemish eGovernment Authority (CORVE), the Linked Organisation of Local Authorities (LOLA) and the cities of Gent, Issy-les-Moulineaux and Athens in a common effort to empower citizens to use open data to create "smart" mobile applications that can be potentially shared by cities across Europe.[1]

Citadel on the Move believes that a truly "Smart city" is one that is able to:

1. Benefit from innovative developments of citizens, small and medium enterprises (SMES), and other actors from across Europe, rather than just within their own cities
2. Harness the power of 100 percent freely available and easy-to-use open data to unleash the creative potential of citizens to develop smart, interactive and on-demand mobile solutions that can be used on any device, anytime, anywhere.
3. Contribute to a multi-national, service-oriented ecosystem by providing and sharing mobile technology services with other citizens and cities across Europe.

To unleash the true potential of these smart city trends, however, local government cannot rely on technology alone. Instead, public

[1] *Citadel on the Move* is intentionally designed to build upon and advance the Citadel Statement which was launched in December 2010 following extensive consultation with over 60 organisations (including all of Europe's leading local government organizations) from over 200 cities across five continents. The Citadel Statement called upon EU and national decision makers to provide tangible support for local eGovernment in terms of shared services, open data and citizen participation.

administrations must do part of the work themselves by opening up data and engaging citizens in the creation of new public service-oriented applications. Although doing so may sound easy, perennial political, administrative and legal constrains often hamper public sector innovation. Additionally, local governments also face a number of challenges surrounding standards, interoperability and technology.

There is a need for common standards or approaches to make it easier to open data from various sources and transform it into a publicly useable format—in other words to move beyond "open data" toward "open access." Even if local governments have heard about open data, many—particularly at the smaller, local level—do not know where or how to begin in terms of making the information it holds available to citizens.[2] Similarly, even where they do succeed in opening data, many local governments are unsure how to help citizens use it to create value.

Citadel on the Move aims to address these challenges by making it possible for local governments across Europe, regardless of their size or resources, to combine open access data and mobile technologies to create "smart," innovative citizen-generated services that can be used across Europe. The project does so by promoting a "Citadel Approach" to publishing government data and developing mobile app templates to transform this data into new services.

Citadel Principles

Citadel on the Move is based on three principles that the project has identified as strategic guidelines to help drive smart city innovation:

- Citizens as developers;
- Common approaches to standards; and
- Open data for universal participation.

Citizens as Developers

In the open government data realm, Citadel on the Move contends that actions should be taken to answer the fundamental question: "Who is in a position to make use of newly available data?"[3]. The answer implicit in most of the discussions on the subject—and explicit in Tim Berners-Lee's TED

[2] Obstacles within public bodies include a lack of technical knowledge on publication of Open Data, legal and licensing issues, and lack of resources for publishing Open Data.

[3] http://firstmonday.org/htbin/cgiwrap/bin/ojs/index.php/fm/rt/printerFriendly/3316/2764

talk[4]—is that "everyone" has the potential to make use of the data.

Berners-Lee's contention builds on a trend that has been in vogue for some time. As long ago as 2006, *Time* magazine named the computer user as "Person of the Year" in recognition of the increasing role of user-generated content. For all the talk of user-generated content, when it comes to public services, the divide between producer and consumer has remained stubbornly intact.

Citadel on the Move seeks to address this challenge by helping local government to provide citizens with new tools to become developers and create public value. In this regard, Citadel's concept of the "citizen-developer" is not just a technical concept but a new form of empowerment and democratization of internet technologies. Citadel will enable mobile applications to be designed by the same people that will use them, rather than devised in far-away research laboratories. As such, these service applications can "belong" to a city and its citizens in a new and more integral way.

Common Approaches to Standards

As defined by ISO, standards are "requirements, specifications, guidelines or characteristics that can be used consistently to ensure that materials, products, processes and services are fit for their purpose."[5]

Standards help to ensure interoperability, making sure goods and services can flow effectively between companies or across national borders. For example, ICAO 9303 sets out a global standard for passport sizes, ensuring citizens of all countries can easily move across borders[6].

For open government data, however, this one size fits all standard is not necessarily the most effective way to ensure interoperability, as 1) different types of data have different format requirements and 2) many cities and governments have already begun to publish their data in a variety of formats.

Rather than approach open government data standards in terms of a narrowly predefined way of doing something, it is more useful to think of standards in terms of defining a path toward a specific objective—in this case the seamless interoperability between datasets.

With the specific goal of interoperability in mind, the question of open data standards can be reexamined from a bottom-up perspective. The path toward standardization in open government data from this view is "demand-led." In other words, cities will publish their data in a common way

---

[4] http://www.ted.com/talks/tim_berners_lee_the_year_open_data_went_worldwide.html

[5] http://www.iso.org/iso/home/standards.htm

[6] http://www.icao.int/Security/mrtd/Pages/Document9303.aspx

because citizens and users ask for it. Standards result from the convergence of technologies and social demand.

In relation to open data, a number of key areas can be identified where there is a demand for standardization. These areas include technology platforms (including from web servers to hand devices), data structures, metadata, vocabularies and repositories. As technologies in each of these areas emerge, a variety of standards come into existence as developers generate new solutions to more effectively serve their customers. However, as the technologies in these areas mature and the market becomes more efficient in selecting "winners," a limited number of standards prevails.

The strategy of Citadel on the Move in relation to standards is to articulate clear, pragmatic practices that raise the understanding of interoperability among public sector stakeholders. Citadel on the Move does not advocate conformity to any single standard for publishing open data because, should standards then change, this would place undue burden on cities. Instead, Citadel on the Move raises awareness of existing standards, particularly those that support the broadest interoperability, and advises cities to follow clear, pragmatic steps to ensure they publish open data in a way that is "friendly" to interoperability middleware.[7]

In short, Citadel on the Move offers a step-by-step approach to make cities "standards aware" and ensure that they take the most appropriate and cost-effective actions in publishing their open data. Under this scenario, Citadel on the Move understands standards as common approaches to the publication of data sets that enable citizens to use the same methods to access data from different sources secure in the knowledge that the data will interact with each other. This objective is sometimes referred to as a web of data' or, more commonly, the Semantic Web.[8]

Open Data for Universal Participation

Open government data is rapidly becoming a new principle for local government to 1) increase the transparency of administration's actions and 2) improve public services through collaboration between the public and private sector.

Open Data means data that can be freely used, reused and redistributed by anyone, subject only, at most, to the requirement to attribute and

---

[7] Middleware refers to any tool or program that stands an original source and the end user, performing an intermediary function. Specifically in reference to open data, middleware tools exist which can translate between different standards. These technologies allow for 'on-the-fly' interoperability, removing the burden of standardization from cities and governments.

[8] http://www.w3.org/2001/sw/

share alike. The key elements of this open data principle can be summarized as follows[9]:

- **Availability and Access:** The data must be available freely, directly accessible via the internet. The data must also be available in a convenient and modifiable form.
- **Reuse and Redistribution:** The data must be provided under terms that permit reuse and redistribution including the intermixing with other datasets.
- **Universal Participation:** everyone must be able to use, reuse and redistribute. There should be no discrimination against fields of endeavor or against persons or groups. For example, non-commercial restrictions that would prevent commercial use, or restrictions of use for certain purposes (e.g. only in education), are discouraged.

The data sets that are opened by public authorities/bodies in the public domain are often referred to as public sector information (PSI). These sources of data are regularly used and reused by private businesses that have the technical skills required to build applications using the data. However, in terms of universal participation, while citizen developers have the opportunity to access PSI, complications arise when sourcing resources to help them use the data. The current online open data ecosystem is a fragmented variety of tools, interfaces and toolkits, mostly designed for use in silos (i.e. with a specific data set or application.)

Citadel on the Move uniquely overcomes this challenge by creating and bringing together online tools and services for publishing, and using open public data that is not specific to a given dataset or application. This approach is considered a "commons:" a collection of reusable items that belong to the community and can be used by any section of the community (i.e. facilitating universal participation).

The commons is a self-sustaining resource as gaps in data or tool availability become filled by "donations" of new data or applications developed by the community as it innovatively creates new public services—a win-win situation.

Citadel on the Move's open data commons (ODC) approach is intended to benefit local government data providers and citizen application developers by providing a shared, dynamically constructed resource center for linking citizens-developers to available open datasets and facilitating the collection and take-up of application programming interfaces (APIs) and software development kits (SDKs) to build mobile application templates and apps.

---

[9] http://gurstein.wordpress.com/2013/02/03/is-open-government-data-a-product-or-a-service-and-why-does-it-matter/

From addressing standards in how to make public data open to reducing the investment required to create a new application, Citadel on the Move's ODC is designed to improve the ease of interaction between stakeholder groups. Under this model, governance of the ODC resource becomes a collaborative effort between the local administration, citizen developers and businesses, with the public sector partner taking responsibility to ensure that the process is open and fair. All parties discuss and decide upon the most appropriate open data strategies for their city (i.e. which datasets to open and what applications, standards, privacy and security recommendations from Citadel on the Move should be adopted).

With the ODC, the role of the public sector is elevated from data provider to the stewardship of the collective interest.

Citadel Considerations

To advance the overarching goal of developing open data-based mobile applications for public sector innovation, Citadel on the Move has identified key issues that require attention:

- Privacy;
- Citizen Capacity;
- Semantics; and
- Future Proofing.

Privacy

With more than 250 million Europeans online and a virtual tsunami of data-capturing mechanisms coming to market, data protection and privacy is an increasing concern for many citizens. According to a recent survey, more than 70 percent of EU citizens are worried about the misuse of their personal data disclosed online.[10]

In January 2012, the European Commission presented a proposal for reform of the whole legislation on privacy in EU27 aimed at strengthening the rights of individuals and improving the clarity and coherence of national rules for personal data protection.[11] The upcoming EU regulation, for

[10] DG Justice Fact Sheet

[11] This proposal is now being debated at the Council and the European Parliament, before it becomes a Regulation. According to Article 288 of the Treaty on the Functioning of the European Union, while a Directive allows Member States of the EU the chance to adjust the legal text to align with national requirements or to ensure that it fits the national legislation of that State, a Regulation is binding in its entirety and immediately after its approval in each Member State—thus having a much higher and more direct impact depending on their objectives.

all its good intentions, raises potential risks of over-protecting certain personal rights and excessively increasing the cost of publishing and maintaining open datasets by the EU public sector authorities.

Analysis of the prospective effect of this new EU regulation on the value chain of public sector information reuse has led Citadel on the Move to conclude that local government can minimize potential pitfalls by undertaking a preliminary privacy impact assessment (PIA) to understand the bearing that opening a particular dataset will have on all stakeholders from the administration to citizen developers and end-users of services that may be built using the data.[12]

The PIA will highlight any risk of breakdown in the anonymization of the data at any stage of its use. These findings will help government understand whether to publish the data, and if so, whether any tasks of cleaning up and upgrading the published datasets are needed.

To maximize privacy protection in a manner that does not impede the opening of government data, Citadel on the Move proposes to embed the logical "privacy as a service" (PaaS) into technology design. PaaS is designed to allow strong security and privacy protections that are easy to use and apply uniformly across platforms and applications.[13]

PaaS' goal is two-fold:

1. To support data subjects willing to share their datasets online by enabling automatic consent to publication and therefore encouraging take-up, transformation and usage at the lowest cost;
2. To encourage both data owners and collectors for developing purposes (including citizens as "hackers") to think about how they can assess the risk implicit in several possible releases of the privacy protection principle.

The approach is intended to help reduce the impact of privacy concerns on at least two key aspects of the Citadel on the Move collaborative ecosystem:

1. The potential conflict between personal data anonymization and socioeconomic utility of a smart service, which heavily relies on user data collection and upgrading on the fly;

---

[12] Privacy issues that arise from the personal data generated by newly created apps (such as who has been accessing the application when and where) fall outside the scope of the Citadel project. Nevertheless, the developers and the users of mobile apps should always be aware of the potential misuse of their data and breaches of Privacy Regulation.

[13] *Privacy-as-a-Service: Models, Algorithms, and Results on the Facebook Platform*, E. Michael Maximilien et. al. http://w2spconf.com/2009/papers/s4p2.pdf

2. The integration of third parties (and especially normal citizens) in the familiar business cycle of application development, thanks to the support offered by the ODC.

Citizen Capacity

As governments and cities struggle to meet the demand for improvement in the delivery of public services, the concept of co-creation offers a potential solution for delivering sustainable, long-term services in the midst of fiscal constraints. However, to maximize the participation of citizens in a service co-creation ecosystem, it is essential to first overcome the "digital divide" and provide stakeholders with the necessary enablers for service/application development.

Citadel on the Move takes a step toward unlocking the innovative potential of citizens by helping local government to equip them with the open data and tools they need to generate their own public services. A key concept in this vision is the development of web-based mobile application templates that allow citizen developers to produce PSI-based applications, accessible from any smart mobile device.

A template is, in essence, a working application optimized for mobile devices but also accessible by a browser of a desktop machine[14]. In common office software, templates are ready-to-go models for standard uses such as a business letter or a monthly budget, allowing non-experts to add the content and finishing touches. Citadel on the Move uses mobile application templates to assist less technically adept citizens (non-professional developers) by providing software code that exploits real, available open data sources and allows end-users to easily modify or extend them to create custom applications.

Citadel on the Move template applications aim at a number of predefined application scenarios, working across more than one city and making use of web, mobile and geo-location technologies. The templates act as modules that carry out the technical work of, say, accessing a database of events or air quality data and visualizing the information contained therein. Citizen-developers, defined initially as those with some familiarity of HTML5[15], can then piece the modules together to build mobile applications

---

[14] The front end of this application is based on HTML5 and PHP. Javascript and JSON are also used to enhance the user experience and allow the communication with the application's back end and data respectively.

[15] HTML5 is a markup language for structuring and presenting content for the World Wide Web and a core technology of the Internet. Its core aims have been to improve the language with support for the latest multimedia while keeping it easily readable by humans and consistently understood by computers and devices. http://en.wikipedia.org/wiki/HTML5

such as an app to advise those with allergies as to whether or not to attend an open-air concert.

By building templates to facilitate mobile application development and by exploiting geo-location technologies, the Citadel on the Move open innovation ecosystem will facilitate the development of new applications that are available anywhere and anytime, while advancing the "build once, use-by-many" principle.

Semantics

A shared semantic approach enables local government to publish their datasets in a manner that will, for example, enable a transport application built using a timetable dataset in Ghent, Belgium, to also work in Athens, Greece.

Citadel on the Move facilitates the development of public services that can be used by citizens as they travel or work across Europe. Citadel on the Move accomplishes this by promoting the adoption of shared semantic standards that provide a common language for public administrations to use to open their data in a uniform and organized way. Citadel's common semantic approach works at three levels:

I. Format—how data is structured and presented;

II. Metadata—descriptions used to describe and find data; and

III. Links—connections between datasets to enrich navigation.

The two key focal areas of Citadel on the Move's semantic work are transport data and georeference and points of interest data.

Transport data

Citadel on the Move recommends that all local governments publish public transport data as a starting point in their open data journey. Transport is a natural place to begin because it forms the key component of a city's circulatory system, generating a wealth of information about a local area including transport routes timetables, parking spaces and energy consumption.

By publishing open transport data, local government presents an opportunity for citizens to not only leverage this information to better understand their local area, but to also create new service applications that enhance their transportation experiences within the city. Transport data, when mixed with other data sources like noise levels, crime or pollution hotspots, can generate innovative applications that improve quality of life. A group in the United States, for example, recently linked bus transport data with safety records to create an application that allows users to easily choose the safest bus connection between, to and from New York and other cities[16].

To fully realize the added value of opening transport data, transport applications must be mobile and able to work wherever a citizen is while traveling, whether within a particular city, country or across a border. These mobile services need to be context and location aware so they can retrieve relevant data needed for the service to work. This need places a demand upon local government to publish open transport data on the internet in a manner that enables the applications to easily find, access and use the information regardless of its origin. Linked geodata is one method Citadel on the Move is exploring to achieve this aim.

Georeferenced Data and Points of Interest

To geo-reference an item means to define its existence in physical space or, in other words, to establish its location in terms of map projections or coordinate systems. Recent open data initiatives launched by governments and organizations worldwide have released a wealth of useful geo-referenced or location-based data into the public domain. Literature shows that more than 80 percent of all decisions in the public sector are based on georeferenced data.[17]

Points of interest (POI) constitute an important element of geo-referenced open data, particularly in transportation and tourism.[18] As GPS-enabled devices as well as software applications that use digital maps become more available, so too are the applications for POI expanding.[19]

Despite the growth of POI data, when geo-information and open data meet, the time datasets are in raw output formats, especially XLS and CSV, which are largely proprietary and do not allow for easy representation of metadata to provide semantic interoperability. To overcome this challenge, Citadel on the Move recommends that data managers avoid XLS and CSV

[16] http://blog.semantic-web.at/2011/12/11/experiences-from-teaching-linked-data/

[17] Thanks to the rapid explosion of new technology—such as smartphones & tablets—the figure is likely to be closer to 95% today. http://agile.gis.geo.tu-dresden.de/web/Conference_Paper/CDs/AGILE%202011/contents/pdf/shortpapers/sp_158.pdf

[18] http://www.w3.org/2010/POI/documents/Core/core-20111216.html

[19] According to the Editor's draft of the Points of Interest Core of W3C, "in general terms, a 'point of interest' is a location about which information is available. A POI can be as simple as a set of coordinates and an identifier, or more complex such as a three dimensional model of a building with names in various languages, information about open and closed hours, and a civic address." http://en.wikipedia.org/wiki/Point_of_interest

and instead use open and expressive formats such as JSON[20], XML and RDF that allow for the inclusion of metadata.

Linked geodata provides a good starting point for RDF. Linked geodata uses the information collected by the OpenStreetMap project and makes it available as an RDF knowledge base according to the linked data principles.[21] It interlinks this data with other knowledge to add a spatial dimension to the web of data/semantic web.

The World Wide Web Consortium's (W3C) Semantic Web Interest Group (http://www.w3.org/2003/01/geo/) has defined a basic RDF vocabulary that provides the semantic web community with a namespace for representing lat(itude), long(itude) and other information about spatially-located things[22]. Citadel on the Move builds upon the W3C effort by defining a common way of representing POI datasets to foster the interoperability of the project's mobile application templates.

Ultimately, the Citadel templates will be able to consume POI data coming from diverse sources and produced in various formats, thereby ensuring that applications created using the templates can be used in different cities across Europe.[23]

Future Proofing

Citadel on the Move is a solution developed to meet the ongoing needs of local government. To ensure Citadel continues to deliver in a world of fast-paced technological development, the project has embedded a "future-proofing" strategy at the core of its efforts.

Future-proofing can be defined as the process of "making ready to meet potential future requirements, or make use of potential future opportunities"[24]. In the context of open data and smart cities, the greatest opportunity for future development comes from the group of technologies known collectively as the 'internet of things' (IoT).

IoT is commonly defined as a future vision of the internet in which machines, not people, are the main creators and exchangers of data. Kevin Ashton, originator of the term, defines IoT as a shift from traditional

---

[20] XLS: Microsoft Excel file format—CSV: comma-separated values—JSON: JavaScript Object Notation—XML: Extensible Markup Language—RDF: Resource Description Framework

[21] Linkedgeodata.org is directly derived from OpenStreetMap.LinkedGeoData and provides one of the largest LOD knowledge bases.

[22] In effect, this initiative attempts to define a common, flexible and lightweight data model and syntax to express POI data, and consequently of such information.

[23] Existing or new POI datasets must be transformed in this common format using a set of tools (translators, plugs, etc.) provided by Citadel's Open Data Commons.

[24] http://en.wiktionary.org/wiki/future_proof

visions of the internet where humans create data manually to an internet of machines (things) that sense data without the need for human input[25].

In addition to referring to machines that collect and exchange data, IoT also refers to the range of supporting technologies and services that enable the process of sensing, collecting and exchanging data without the need for human input.

For local government, IoT has the potential to provide huge amounts of new open data about a living environment. Within the smart city context, IoT refers most commonly to sensor networks or monitoring mechanisms that provide local data to city administrators or to citizens.

IoT presents a range of challenges to decision makers. The key challenge, from the perspective of city administrators, is that available technologies are often highly specialized, ranging from simple monitoring tools to highly complex systems. Different applications often require different sensor types and management systems.

A second significant challenge for IoT is the role of "closed" corporate solutions. The majority of current IoT sensor networks are sold as packages that include sensors and back-office management software. These IoT packages are, in the majority of cases, proprietary technologies, which vending companies protect through developing different data output formats. Proprietary solutions such as these can trap cities into procuring solutions that are sometimes larger, more complex or more expensive than they require.

The *Citadel on the Move* solution is future-proofed for IoT by ensuring, through ODC, that data generated by IoT sensors can be accessed and used in open, interoperable output formats. To ensure that data is uploaded in interoperable formats, Citadel on the Move encourages IoT users to explore the options for interoperability middleware to standardize their IoT outputs.

Citadel on the Move's focus on middleware and output standards, rather than technology standards, provides benefits for both city administrators, who can choose to link IoT solutions from different providers as "modules" in wider solutions, and IoT system developers[26].

Future Issues

Citadel on the Move believes that open data and mobile web technology hold the key to making European cities smart through the creation and

---

[25] http://www.rfidjournal.com/article/view/4986

[26] This White Paper recommends that the aggregation and messaging middleware used in IoT systems is open—examples of such middleware include RESTful API and XMPP. This allows for the possibility of interoperability between systems where the use of proprietary middleware may not.

delivery of innovative-shared services that can be used across borders and on any platform. Nevertheless, the project has identified a number of issues that need to be addressed to realize this vision.

Local government must strive to protect the privacy of its citizens without allowing data protection and privacy concerns to become an obstacle to openness. Citadel on the Move believes that it can do so by conducting privacy impact assessments before opening data sets and embedding privacy as a service (PaaS) in its technology design principles.

Secondly, local government must realize that it is not enough to simply open data. Local government must do so in a manner that makes data accessible and easy to use. In addition to releasing data in open and expressive formats such as JSON and RDF, Citadel on the Move recommends that local government advances the concept of the "citizen developer" through the creation and use of mobile application templates that make it easier for citizens with basic technical skills to create service applications of their own.

Third, local government must not remain content to unleash innovation in its own backyard. Rather than forcing developers to adapt applications on a city-by-city basis, local government should adopt shared semantic standards for opening data that enable mobile apps to consume POI data from diverse sources and formats, and work anytime, anywhere.

Finally, local government should constantly look forward. To ensure that its open data efforts anticipate future change, particularly with regard to the projected explosion of new IOT-enabled data gathering devices, local government should explore options for interoperability middleware within the context of ODC.

In advancing these recommendations for local government, Citadel on the Move seeks to promote a comprehensive new approach to help European cities work together in a smarter and more open manner. In so doing, Citadel seeks nothing less than to advance the digital materialization of European integration through the creation of "smart" mobile services that can potentially be shared and used anywhere.

GEERT MAREELS, *eGovernment Manager, Vlaamse Overheid;* ***JULIA GLIDDEN,*** *Senior Research Fellow at the Institute of European Studies, Vrije Universiteit Brussel & Managing Director, 21c Consultancy;* ***SUSIE RUSTON,*** *Managing Partner, 21c Consultancy;* ***JESSE MARSH,*** *Consultant, Alfamicro*

23

Cities and the People in Them: The New Hearts and Souls of our Nation

Kim Nelson

Cities and the people in them are becoming the new hearts and souls of our nation. For the first time in history, more than 50 percent of the world's population lives in urban areas. By 2050, nearly 70 percent of the global population—more than 6 billion people—will live in cities.[i] Cities create 80 percent of the world's GDP.[ii] And despite only representing 2 percent of the world's surface area, cities are responsible for upward of 80 percent of the world's energy consumption and 75 percent of carbon emissions.[iii]

As we have become a more urban nation, cities and their leaders have risen in prominence. A higher profile brings broader awareness of the daunting issues these leaders face in the march toward urbanization, but does not make the challenges easier to address. The need to modernize aging infrastructure in older cities, while scaling the demand for natural resources, and sustaining the health and safety of citizens is all unfolding in the midst of an extended global economic downturn. Additionally, far-reaching austerity programs have often reduced citizen services to the barest minimum and often limited economic growth.

Historically cities, like all forms of governments, have worked through economic downturns by attempting to do "more with less." The recent recession, however, has forced cities to not only reduce, but eliminate, many long-standing programs. Aging infrastructure, new hazards to public health and safety, and the inherent uncertainty of natural disasters, climate change, and global and national economic forces are stark realities. City leaders even in less urbanized areas must meet these growing demands with tight budgets and greater citizen expectations while working across complex, siloed agencies. The current economic environment coupled with the needs of future generations require city leaders to change the focus of their conversations.

The Age of Cities

We have entered an "Age of Cities" that reflects a profound shift in human populations. The world is undergoing an urban renaissance as more people move to cities to build better lives. Cities are gathering places for higher education and advanced innovation in healthcare, science and energy—the engines of new ideas and businesses that drive breakthroughs and economic growth.

Many high-profile city innovation projects focus on making infrastructure "smart" by embedding sensors and upgrading networking capabilities. While this is a critical foundational step, limiting the conversation to infrastructure misses an enormous opportunity to unlock the human potential within a city. Next-generation cities also empower people in government, businesses and the community through innovation to build a more sustainable city across economic, environmental and social spheres. They harness these capabilities to help students achieve more through a one-to-one learning experience, give isolated populations access to needed government services, provide the elderly with high-quality health care in their homes, support entrepreneurs to see their ideas quickly come to fruition, get commuters home sooner, and give city employees a real-time, one-city view so they can do their jobs better.

Following are some common areas where city leaders can work with citizens and businesses to drive improvements.

- **Transform** operations and infrastructure by improving city functions with innovative technology solutions; leveraging the power of cloud computing to reduce costs and increase efficiencies; empowering employees with enterprise-grade devices and apps; and enabling innovation with modern solutions and a big data platform.

- **Engage** citizens and businesses by delivering personalized services and apps with a people-centric approach, enabling real-time dialogue via social media; and spurring city app development and economic growth with open data initiatives.

- **Accelerate** innovation and opportunity through programs and partnerships that empower youth with 21st-century learning and personal development opportunities; expand digital inclusion with access and skills training; and nurture new businesses and innovators with resources and support to help cities compete in the global marketplace.

Through a people-first approach and strategic partnerships, cities can enable sustainable cycles of innovation, opportunity and progress for years to come. The result is a city that can compete on the world stage as a premier destination where people can realize their full potential.

New with Less

Given today's economic climate, it is no longer enough to do more with less. Laura Ipsen, a long-time Smart City advocate and vice president for Microsoft's Worldwide Public Sector organization, suggests city leaders should instead begin thinking about doing "new with less" to deliver both economic and social opportunities to citizens, because, at their core, cities are about people.[vi]

Many city leaders are taking a people-first approach to innovation that empowers government, businesses, and citizens to shape their cities' future. People-first means harnessing all of the ideas, energy and expertise of a city's people as they create a healthier, safer, more sustainable place to live. Cities must combine the power of innovation with breakthrough ideas to connect governments, businesses and citizens with city services through innovation that increases efficiencies, reduces costs and fosters a more sustainable life for all.

One sure way to improve city services is to identify opportunities to serve citizens as "one city" across eight critical functions: energy and water; buildings, infrastructure, and planning; transportation; public safety and justice; tourism, recreation, and culture; education; health and social services; and government administration. Many of the services expected by citizens require an "one city" approach. New technologies make it easier than ever to bring that vision to reality. Forward-looking cities work within their means to build on existing investments and incorporate innovations at their own pace—creating an innovation model that works for today and sustains tomorrow. For instance:

Mobility—Through mobile devices such as sensors, smartphones and tablets, cities can reach citizens anywhere, on any screen through the device of their choice. Citizen-centric apps enable people to engage directly and interact with their city governments for services that make life safer and more convenient. Enterprise-grade mobile devices also give employees remote access to systems from any location, improving productivity and responsiveness. These same mobile devices can give many employees access to critical, real-time information never before available.

Cloud—Through flexible cloud offerings, cities can choose public, private or hybrid clouds that protect data sources with the privacy, security and control that is needed in effective cross-departmental collaboration and resource sharing. The scalability and cost-effectiveness of cloud services drive cities' fiscal responsibility. They reduce costs without cutting essential services, and increase worker productivity by supporting mobility efforts.

Social—Through social media such as Twitter, Facebook, Skype and Yammer, cities can open two-way dialogues with citizens and businesses to better understand their needs. Cities also can better protect citizens from safety issues through mobile alerts and social channels.

Big Data—Through data and analytics, city leaders can gain vital, real-time insights from multiple streams, such as traffic cameras, social media and other public channels, to make more accurate decisions, achieve greater efficiencies, and improve preparation, prevention and response activities in emergency situations.

Open Data—The volume of information available in some cities has made their citizens some of the most informed and empowered people in history. Companies like Socrata are helping leaders in some of the largest U.S. cities—Chicago, New York and San Francisco—unlock data, transform the way citizens get answers to basic questions about government operations, and drive entrepreneurs to use the data to apps that spur the local economy and improve citizen services.

> *"Open Data is crucial because it unlocks the potential of New York City's rich data and transforms it into API-enabled, reusable resources necessary for fostering a successful innovation ecosystem. And for those without developer expertise there is easy-to-use search and data visualization. This [Socrata] platform enables us to produce a more user-centric experience of government. It further democratizes the exchange of information and services. It empowers citizens to collaboratively create solutions. It's no longer about consumption only, but the co-creation of government services. If someone wants to build a better app, it's all out there. That is a core concept of the Open Data platform."*
>
> **– Rachel Sterne, New York City Chief Digital Officer**

Cities are already on their journey toward modernizing. Working together, citizens, businesses and city leaders can make the most of existing investments and find the right combination of solutions, partnerships and social programs needed to accelerate innovation and create sustainable cities.

City Challenges

Formidable challenges confront city leaders today and can negate some of the very elements that make cities attractive. While these challenges are not new, their scale and intensity are unprecedented. Addressing these issues in the face of financial constraints, expectations of rapid return on investments, and administrative complexity can be even more difficult. Within individual city domains, the stark challenges and rising citizen expectations include:

Energy and Water—As populations and commercial activities expand, resource-related issues also increase. Both human and economic health can suffer from a lack of safe, adequate energy and from polluted water.

Buildings, Infrastructure, Planning—Buildings consume more than 40 percent of all energy and generate 33 percent of carbon emissions worldwide.[v] Reducing energy consumption and costs is a top economic and environmental priority. For instance, the City of Seattle is engaged in a smart buildings project premised on the adoption of IT-driven energy solutions, which can typically be implemented with less disruption to employees than traditional building retrofits.

> *"Seattle, with its deep legacy of energy conservation and transformative software, is positioned to lead the broader adoption of IT-enabled energy efficiency. We see enormous environmental and economic value in the intersection of advanced data gathering and analytics with building energy systems that will unlock a new wave of energy savings. "We developed a smart buildings project to address two barriers to broad market adoption of IT-driven energy solutions: the need to demonstrate that a new technology will indeed drive efficiency, and address the challenge of integrating new smart buildings technology into the already complex "system of systems" of buildings—including lighting, heating and cooling, and access controls. We aim to reduce energy consumption between 10 percent and 25 percent in the project buildings, and if we can demonstrate that IT-enabled energy efficiency technology can perform well in Seattle—a low-cost energy environment, with a deep expertise in green building—we can share the value of these technologies in markets throughout the world."*
>
> **– Steve Johnson, Director, Seattle Office of Economic Development**

Transportation—Cities with a major rise in their human and vehicle populations experience strains on their roads and public transportation networks, increased pollution, wasted energy and rising commute times.

Public Safety and Justice—Increasingly dense urban environments present hazards to public safety, including petty crime, homicides and mass-scale terrorism. Additionally, threats from natural disasters are real and unpredictable.

Tourism, Recreation, and Culture—Entertainment, culture and recreation not only help attract and retain a vibrant city population, they also draw business owners and tourists who can drive economic activity and enhance a city's reputation.

Education—Increasing access to higher quality, diverse forms of education is expected. Yet most cities struggle to provide affordable education that fosters a highly skilled, creative and employable population.

Health and Social Services—Access to timely, affordable, high-quality health services is a key public concern. Non-communicable diseases present challenging new needs, while the potential outbreak of communicable diseases rises.

Government Administration—Citizens and businesses want virtually all city services to be accessible electronically, but also for their city government to increase transparency and accessibility while protecting privacy and security.

Beyond optimizing operations within individual city domains, city employees frequently need to address issues that affect multiple functions of the city in real time. Citizens and businesses want a city that identifies them once and aggregates services and information across the city in a "one-stop" way, while still preserving and protecting privacy. In addition, cities looking to do "new with less" seek ways to optimize, standardize and sustain an underlying innovation platform that all city functions can use.

Transform Operations & Infrastructure

The reality of transformation through information technology often falls short of the promise. However, transformation does not and should not always start from scratch. Transforming IT is an evolution, not a revolution; new solutions should build upon and work with a city's existing and potentially diverse investments.

Enable new capabilities with flexible cloud services. By capitalizing on the opportunity of cloud computing, cities can reduce costs, increase efficiency and productivity, and engage people in new and innovative ways. Innovative city leaders realize these benefits while preserving precious budget dollars and staff resources for other citizen-focused needs and priorities.

City employees, citizens, and businesses expect to connect with city services using technology. Internally, employees expect to be able to access line-of-business applications and other work content from nearly anywhere, on virtually any device they choose, at any time—whether it's the middle of the business day or 3 a.m. on a holiday. Externally, citizens and businesses expect convenient, instantly responsive ways to access city services online. Both internally and externally, people expect their interactions to be smarter, more automated and more contextual. Cloud services make it possible to deliver the kind of experiences that people expect without the level of investment and management that would be required with a traditional infrastructure.

When news broke that Charlotte, N.C., would hold the U.S. 2012 Democratic National Convention, the city knew that it was time to replace its manual processes for event permitting, especially when considering the challenges that such a large influx of people would bring. Charlotte tailored an event-permitting solution to meet the demands of hosting the convention. A cloud-based solution automates event requests and back-end approval workflows, offering detailed reporting, and enabling mobile workforce management of event evaluations and approvals.

Choice and flexibility are key to cloud adoption now and in the future. It should be up to city leaders to decide what services and assets to deploy in the cloud and when, so that they have they can balance control and flexibility with cost and agility. City leaders should consider cloud providers that will support a move to the cloud at a pace they choose.

Innovate with modern solutions. Accommodating the dynamic scale and reach of modern-style apps requires a modern platform. Cities have to reap all the benefits of scale, speed and agility while protecting existing investments. City leaders must take advantage of the cloud on their terms, without fear of lock-in, and with a consistent and comprehensive range of offerings.

Interconnected computing environments, enabling interoperability between products from different vendors, is more important than ever. City leaders should select products that support interoperability, allow for the connection of systems across a multi-vendor environment, and allow data sharing—in accordance with distinct security and privacy policies and laws.

Innovate with big data. Data is an asset. There isn't a city in the world that isn't swimming in data, but the challenge is to use that valuable resource, combined with the wealth of data available from outside the city, in a meaningful way. Cities need solutions that enable data to flow across an infrastructure—sensors, meters, machines, systems, devices, social media channels and public data markets—and can turn that valuable data into information and insight that people and machines can act upon. A viable big data solution offers the best end-to-end platform to manage any data, of any size, from any source, with industry-leading database services. City solutions should deliver a holistic, citywide view and give employees new intelligence that supports better historical trend and pattern analysis, richer predictive modeling, and more effective real-time decisions. The goal is to help a city optimize its resources, break through departmental silos and provide better services for less.

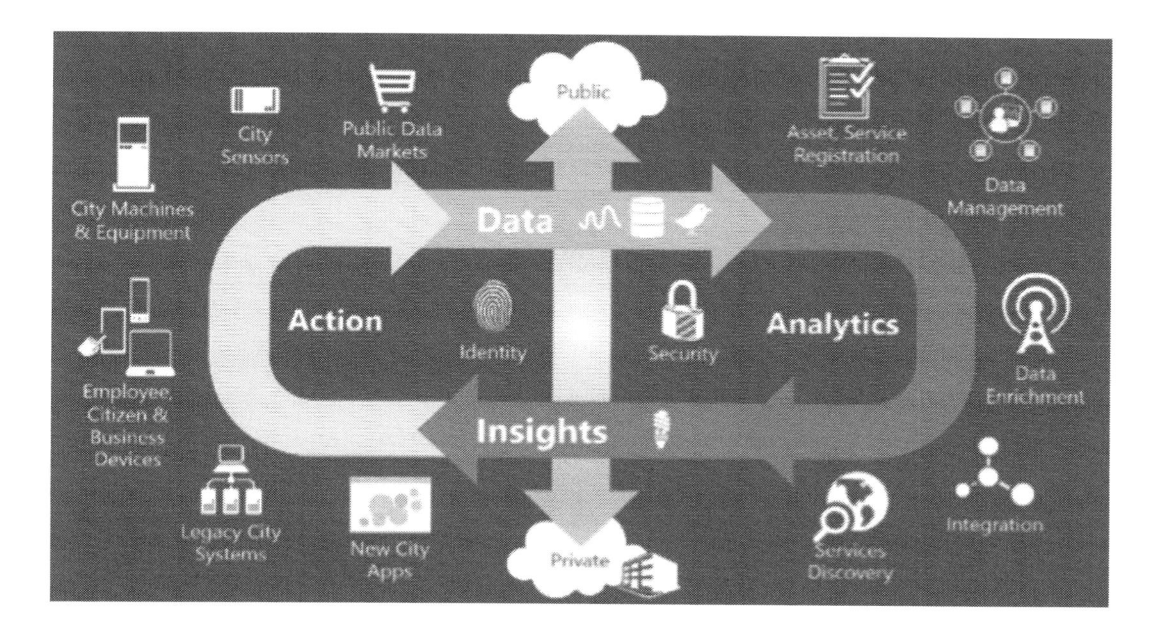

Empower city employees with enterprise-grade devices and apps. Giving employees the ability to stay connected through a mobile device to their department, team members and constituents from virtually anywhere at any time means citizen service does not need to stop the minute they leave the building.

Employees will have strong opinions about which devices they want to use. Let them choose. By using the proper back-end tools, IT managers can make it possible—and easy—to manage and use a mix of devices that run on Android, Apple and Windows operating systems in a city environment. *With proper management and enterprise-grade devices,* city employees can take advantage of powerful analysis tools and sync their case files, reports, models, pictures and settings right from their PCs, tablets, smart phones and other devices, without compromising security, privacy or compliance.

Engage Citizens and Businesses

Whether inspired by a pothole in the street, the need for a permit, frustration over the speed of business development or the desire to contribute, constituents are demanding greater access to and interaction with government. These rising expectations underscore the importance of providing rich, personalized experiences that result in better-served, more engaged citizens and businesses. Giving the public a straightforward way to engage quickly pays off in a variety of ways, including increased visibility into constituents' needs and positive perceptions of city government.

Deliver personalized services and apps with a citizen-centric approach. Most citizens would prefer to engage with "one" city, not a series of disconnected agencies and processes. With emerging identity management capabilities, cities no longer have to ask citizens to identify themselves to multiple departments to access records, submit permits, enroll in school, pay their taxes, and share their health data and access care across different hospitals. Instead, they can engage in a streamlined, "one-stop" experience with their city through personalized hubs that maintain and protect their identities.

In addition to facilitating information access, making technology tools more intuitive can improve the experience of citizens and businesses. People already use gestures and speech to interact with their phones, tablets, PCs, and other connected devices. Such natural ways of interacting with technologies make it easier to learn how to operate them and, in essence, allow people to further personalize how they engage with their communities via their devices.

While technology makes it relatively easy for citizens to use their devices, city leaders must be ever mindful of the need to meet government accessibility requirements. Some citizens do not have the ability to use hands or arms, they have hearing loss, or have speech or cognitive challenges. For many citizens who have particular accessibility requirements, the chance to personalize their devices to meet individual needs not only makes computer use possible, it improves their ability to participate in public discourse, exercise their right to vote, and take advantage of city services and educational opportunities.

Enable real-time dialogue with citizens via social media. Citizens want to make their voices heard; city governments want to hear them more clearly. Cities can encourage deeper civic engagement and participation by making the most of mobility and social media communications channels. City leaders must look for ways to integrate familiar social tools into their city's applications, which can become accessible on many different devices so that city employees can easily share ideas and collaborate with citizens and businesses, regardless of location.

Accelerate Innovation & Opportunity

Innovation is an essential catalyst for economic growth and competitiveness. However, fully harnessing the power of innovation for a prosperous, competitive city requires more than technology itself. It requires efficient infrastructure, effective institutions and the creativity of every city's most important resource—its human capital. City governments can contribute to the sustained economic and social well-being of their communities by attracting talent, helping more people develop useful skills and expanding technology access to those who otherwise would not be part of the digital society. For instance, in December 2012, Mayor Michael Nutter created the Office of Urban Economics, only the second of its kind in the nation. The office serves as an internal innovation hub, connecting city departments and agencies with outsiders to help "create, support or pilot small-scale projects to work toward solutions for civic problems."[vi]

Adopt a broad-based partnership approach. Effective city leaders enter into public-private partnerships to leverage the best that others have to offer and to accelerate progress in addressing their city improvement goals. They know that self-sustaining cycles of innovation that involve whole institutions and individual citizens can provide unique opportunities. Around the country, these partnerships have helped millions of city residents shape a brighter future for themselves and their local communities.

Empower youth with 21st-century learning and new opportunities. Many city leaders already emphasize access to education for all students as a cornerstone of long-term growth and competitiveness. Yet getting technology into the hands of young people is not enough. City leaders must support transformative learning and help students build the skills needed for the future. Government officials, school leaders and educators can consider new approaches to teaching and using technology to help students develop 21st-century skills. Local accredited academic institutions also can draw on support from many technology companies that provide digital curriculum and certifications to provide students with skills necessary to acquire technical certification for today's rapidly evolving workplace.

Expand digital inclusion with access and skills training. One of the best ways to ensure that all citizens—not just students—have basic technology access and literacy is through creative partnerships with technology companies. Many of these partnerships support governments' efforts to achieve digital-access goals, from promoting education reform to developing a 21st-century workforce. U.S. companies understand the importance of empowering individuals to create economic opportunities, build IT skills, enhance education outcomes, and sustain their local language and culture. In addition, some businesses often provide online, multilingual classes, including free software and support. Cities can use these to teach and assess basic computer concepts and skills. City leaders should contact their technology partners to determine what community programs they can offer. These programs help citizens develop new social and economic opportunities for themselves, their families and their communities.

Nurture new businesses and innovators with resources and support. Cities can help their local technology innovators and entrepreneurs turn ideas into thriving local small and medium-sized enterprises by introducing them to valuable programs and partnerships. Just as many companies offer digital literacy classes, these same companies have programs to support entrepreneurs—often at no charge. Advancing the technical knowledge of a city's citizen base is critical to its long-term economic health and competitiveness. That's why many companies provide free access to designer and developer tools for high school and college students and educators, as well as entrepreneurs of all ages.

Where to Start?

Innovating at the scale of a city requires incremental steps and a commitment to the journey. However, city leaders can minimize planning cycles and expense by building on what others—both in the public and private sectors—have learned in advancing program improvements here in the United States and around the word.

- Articulate your long-term goals. Assess a city's current position relative to those goals to reveal development gaps.
- Prioritize investments. Priorities are unique to every city, driven by specific development gaps as well as by cultural, geographic, political, partnership, staffing and other forces.
- Identify cross-domain dependencies. Maximizing value within any domain—whether public safety, transportation or physical infrastructure—requires consideration and understanding of key dependencies across other domain areas.
- Take into consideration stakeholders from the public and private sectors.
- Plan ahead for the accessibility requirements that affect not only the built environment, but also information and communication systems. A proactive approach will ensure full participation by all citizens.
- Embed governance into plans with transparency and measurement tools, such as a city indicator dashboard and other business intelligence, analytical and visualization tools.

- Investigate the range of available solutions and programs that make it possible to optimize a city's existing technology assets and human resources.
- Take a systematic approach to transformation. Select one of the top priorities and tackle it with the confidence that the return on foundational investment will be enhanced by subsequent projects.

By adopting a people-first approach and strategic partnerships, cities can enable self-sustaining cycles of innovation, opportunity, and progress for years to come. Imagine what's next for your city.

KIM NELSON *is the Executive Director of State and Local Government Solutions for Microsoft where she and a team of experts in the areas of Health and Human Services, Justice and Public Safety, and eGovernment work with customers and partners to create and deliver repeatable solutions that reduce risk, cost and time to implement. She is also the United States Lead for the Microsoft CityNext Program, an effort to help cities around the world accelerate innovation and address some of the most pressing problems facing cities today, while building a foundation for a sustainable future. Prior to joining Microsoft in 2001, Kim Nelson spent 26 years in government, where she served in a number of capacities including executive level positions in the Pennsylvania Department of Environmental Protection and, most recently, as Assistant Administrator in the US Environmental Protection Agency. She can be reached at kimnels@microsoft.com.*

ENDNOTES

[i] United Nations, Department of Economic and Social Affairs, Population Division, World Urbanization Prospects: The 2011 Revision. http://esa.un.org/unpd/wup/CD-ROM/Urban-Rural-Population.htm.

[ii] Urban world: Mapping the economic power of cities. McKinsey Global Institute. March 2011.

[iii] United Nations, Rio+20, Sustainable Cities. http://www.un.org/en/sustainablefuture/cities.shtml.

[iv] Laura Ipsen, speaking at the Microsoft Worldwide Partner Conference, New Orleans, LA July 2013.

[v] United Nations Environment Programme. Buildings and Climate Change: Summary for Decision-Makers, 2009. http://www.scribd.com/doc/43780964/Buildings-and-Climate-Change-a-Summary-for-Decision-Makers-UNEP-2009.

[vi] City of Philadelphia, Mayor Michael A. Nutter Executive Order No. 5-12, formally creating the Mayor's Office of New Urban Mechanics. December 10, 2012.

24

Evolving into a Smart City: Riyadh, Saudi Arabia

Abdulaziz N. Aldusari

Saudi Arabia has adopted a long-term development strategy that shifts its focus to develop a knowledge society. In line with this, King Saud University (KSU) in Riyadh has launched the Riyadh Techno Valley (RTV) project to strengthen its efforts to develop a knowledge society in Saudi Arabia.

KSU, as a core of the Northwest district of Riyadh, had an initiative to adopt the comprehensive idea of a Riyadh Knowledge Corridor (RKC) in the Prince Turki Alawal Road area. KSU took part in setting up new Riyadh's Smart City nodes (Smart Riyadh—NWD), and the focal point of it is the RTV project, which will play a central role with other developments in the district, such as King Abdulaziz city for science and technology, Saudi Standards, Information Technology & Communication complex, King-Abdulaziz-and-his-Companions-Foundation-for-Giftedness-and-Creativity, and the King Abdullah Financial Center. This new urban center (Smart Riyadh—NWD) will be added to the four urban centers that were suggested by the Alriyadh Development Authority (ADA) strategical plan as shown in Figure 1.

RTV reflects many issues and principals toward evolving the Northwest district in Riyadh as Smart City. The new urban design of the RTV Development Plan is to "build communities, create destinations." This promotes a sense of place and belonging for knowledge tenants. The RTV plan aims to achieve one or more of the RTV objectives by designing RTV as a smart, intelligent community that fosters an environment of innovation.

RTV aims to build a live, work and play community by having a state-of-the-art "smart" infrastructure that eases the contribution between all research and business development centers within the RTV campus—which will lead to a better quality of life. at the RTV project also strives to deliver a leading/smart campus and environment to enhance research and development. Efficient operation, maintenance and service delivery, in addition to smart/dynamic/cost-effective administration, are among the many aspects of the required design.

RTV should have a smart infrastructure converged solution to deliver all functions and services in the most efficient and effective way. The intended smart solution will cover transport, security and safety, smart building, smart waste management, smart residential housing, a smart grid that will connect to solar renewable energy, smart health and smart education.

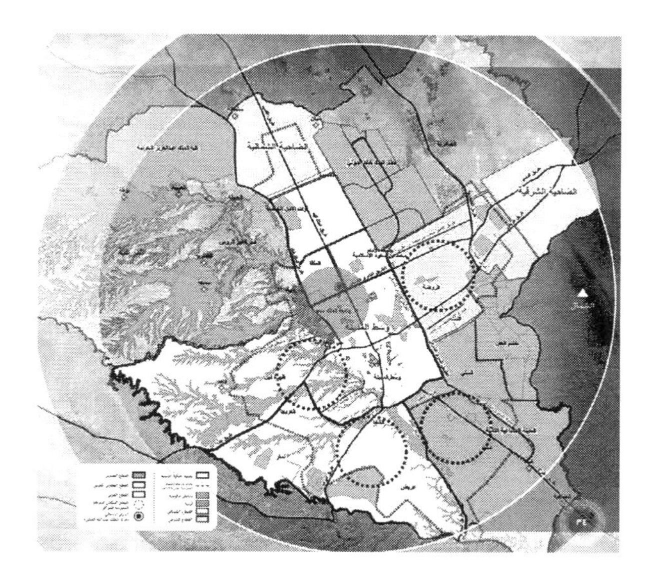

Figure 1. *Riyadh Strategic Plan Showing the New Urban Center (Smart Riyadh—NWD).*

Additionally, Riyadh's strategical plan as shown in Figure 2 (see next page) has two new residential satellites in the north (sultana) and the in the east (Alwasee). The newly proposed urban center Smart Riyadh—NWD will have a residential community, because the main concept of this center is to be a new urban development with mix land use.

Riyadh Knowledge Corridor (RKC) Core Area for Smart Riyadh-NWD

The Riyadh Knowledge Corridor Project is a modern tool structured around a connected group of pioneering knowledge and innovation outlets, whose connection is provided by the vision and objectives of building a knowledge-based society. Because Riyadh City includes a number of economic and knowledge entities capable of efficiently contributing to building such a society, King Saud University proposed the Riyadh Knowledge Corridor Program as a link between educational, research, economic,

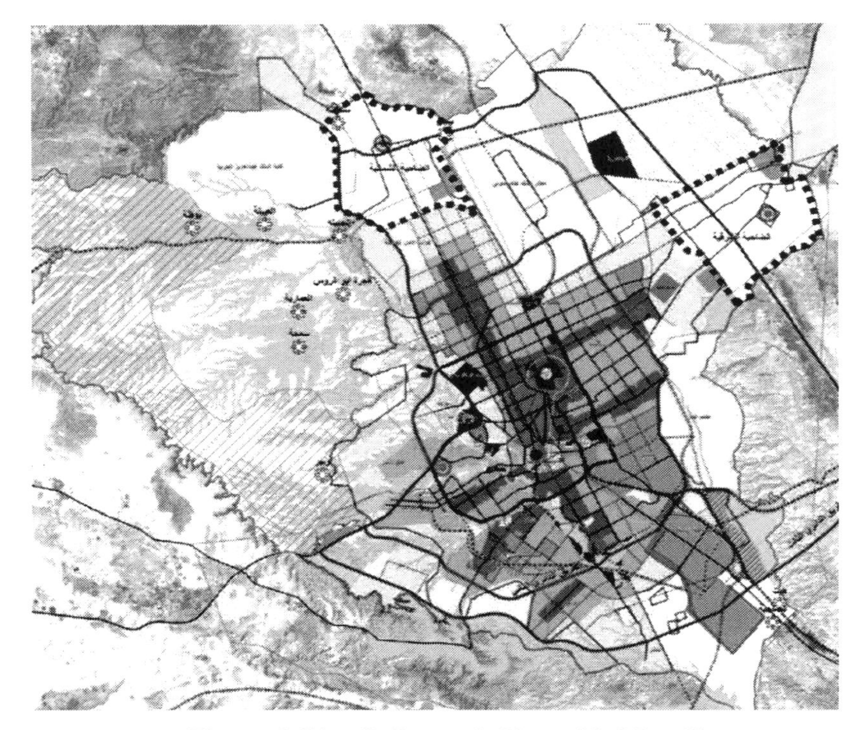

Figure 2. *Riyadh Strategic Plan with 2 Satellites.*

Figure 3. *Riyadh Knowledge Corridor (RKC) in the Northwest District of Riyadh.*

intellectual and knowledge entities in a way that enhances interaction and communication in a smart way.

The objectives for RKC is to:

- Create a smart zone of attraction with high-tech new urbanism for different sections of Riyadh society.
- Encourage knowledge industries and reinforce their competitive potential.
- Encourage genuine partnerships in sources of knowledge and innovation.
- Facilitate access to information and supporting actions. Offer opportunities and exceptional functionality for knowledge generation.

The RKC caters to many knowledge and innovative institutions that are located along its main arterial road (Prince Turki AlAwal) such as KSU, RTV, KACST, ITCC, KAFD, etc.

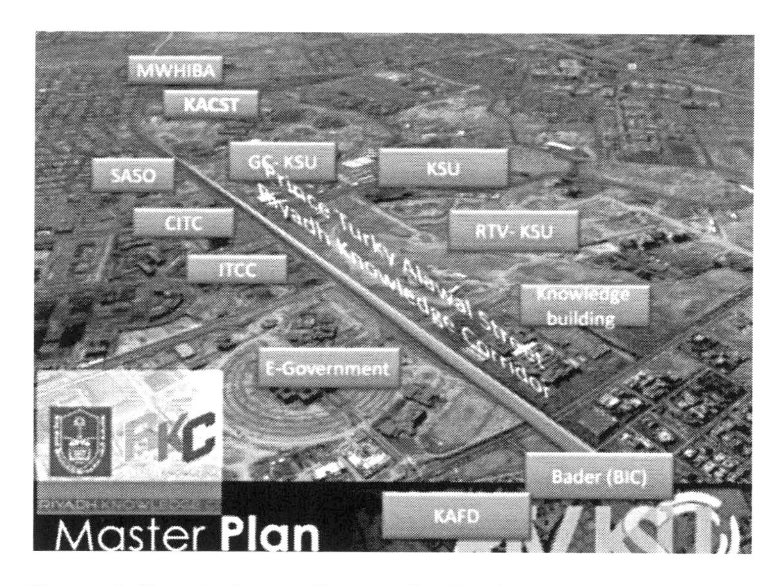

Figure 4. *Knowledge and Innovative Institutions Located Along RKC.*

Riyadh Techno Valley—Anchor for Smart Riyadh—NWD

RTV Strategy

Riyadh Technology Valley was established to achieve the vision of kingdom leadership to enter the "knowledge-based economy," which means "to convert knowledge into economic value" through the conversion of technical inventions to innovations and new products for trading and investing economically in the market. It also aims to deliver a leading/outstanding smart campus and environment to enhance research and development; efficient operation, maintenance,and service delivery; and smart/dynamic/cost-effective administration.

Vision

Leadership in research and business development, as well as technology transfer.

Mission

To establish an ecosystem that attracts research and business development (R&BD) centers toward creating a competitive knowledge-based economy to achieve sustainable development.

The Strategic Plan for KSU

During the past three years, KSU adopted a2030 strategical plandirecting the research university to focus more on applied research, which will bridge the gaps between the university and industry, and provide commercial benefits from the academic research. KSU also is moving toward building a knowledge society on a macro and micro scale by adopting innovations and entrepreneurial programs.

The Kingdom's Development Plans Toward a Knowledge-Based Economy

Consistent with the its development plans , the Kindom plans to build a national basis of science and technology, capable of innovation and renewal, in line with the trend toward a knowledge-based economy. The Kingdom calls for the establishment of "science and technology parks" at universities and research centers to direct attention to the promotion of co-financing and joint research programs between industry and academic sector institutions. These parks also will establish business incubators to transform research results into industrial and commercial application. Thus, the KSU Council passed in 2009 a resolution approving the establishment of RTV at KSU.

Riyadh Techno Valley a 4th Generation Science Park

The concept of brain circulation was adopted in RTV to exchange innovative business ideas and turn them into commercial realities. Exchanging the knowledge globally using the long-distance tools such as internet, video conferencing and satellite technologies are supported by reliable smart infrastructure in RTV.

Research and Business Development

The goal of R&BD activities in RTV are to provide the best environment for the transfer and habitat of technologies toward an ecosystem. This ecosystem should berelevant for the creation and establishment of new technologies to achieve a knowledge-based society.

Technology and Effective Knowledge Management

The use of technologies that provide easy access to users and managers would enhance knowledge management (KM) processes. To improve the productivity at science parks, smart software web-based application tools would make it easy to find information in a short time. In addition, the web-based application developed at RTV would improve tproductivity by executing a smart search that is based on user-profile, storing information more effectively, communicating effectively with other parties, and accessing information securely. Furthermore, it maximizes knowledge sharing and transfer of technologies. The new approach uses the concept of geographic information systems (GIS) within the platform of wireless technologies. The goal is to develop an interactive smart context-aware university GIS that enhances information sharing, communication and dissemination within the KSU campus and RKC area, with the intent to create an information-intensive ecosystem supporting knowledge creativity and innovation in a multi-disciplinary environment.

An Effective Ecosystem for a Knowledge-Based Economy

To establish an ecosystem for a knowledge-based economy (KBE) at science parks, a proper model describing the role of each party and the interaction among them needs to be structured. The innovation opportunities at the universities would be enhanced with the right collaboration and partnership between private research companies and government research institutions nationally and internationally. This can be accomplished by establishing a science park ecosystemthat coordinates and synchronizes its stakeholders, university research sectors, as well as external private research companies and its tenants.

The initiatives associated with innovation would have a great effect on the national economy once an ecosystem and effective knowledge management have been deployed Choosing the right model for the ecosystem plays an important role in maximizing the interaction among all stakeholders who can contribute to the creation of products to boost KBE.

RTV—Ecosystem

Smart Web-Based Application

Web-based database application, if implemented properly, enables users to access stored information securely anywhere, at any time, whether they are stationary in the office or mobile. Thus, using this technology can improve productivity at the workplace because it reduces the delay when accessing information, allow users to interact with others in real-time, and reduces processing time at the work environment. Three web-based smart database applications have been proposed in RTV to enhance the knowledge creation and storage, optimize the knowledge sharing and smart search, and improve the productivity for processing projects and interacting with all staff and tenants at the science parks and campus.

RTV Master Plan

Each aspect of the RTV master plan is designed to achieve one or more of the RTV objectives. Outlined below are the major planning guidelines and how each contributes to the overall RTV vision.

With the overall vision to create a science park that fosters an environment of innovation and collaboration between knowledge-based institutions and industrial partners, the RTV planning team designed an infill development plan inside the KSU campus for RTV. The total area planed for RTV was 1.7 million square meters within the KSU area, which encompasses 9 million square meters.

The following major development clusters have been adopted to generate a vibrant mixed-use knowledge R&BD center. The magnitude of each component was based on benchmarking similar target developments, while keeping in mind current possible stakeholder requirements and KSU potential.

The following are the technology clusters adopted in the RTV master plan based on the Stanford Research Institute (SRI) feasibility study:

- Bio Cluster (Biotechnology)—Composed of R&BD in the fields of pharmacology, environment technology, and food science.
- CheM Cluster (Chemical Technology and Materials)—Composed of R&BD in the fields of petrochemical, materials, chemical materials and energy.
- ICT Cluster (Information & Communication Technologies)—Composed of R&BD in the areas of information and communications technology and information security.

- The Tech Nucleus Cluster (catalytic core and the central research area)—The catalytic heart of the science park, which houses the incubators and the Centre for Entrepreneurs, the Office of Support Services of Operations Research and Intellectual Property, laboratories to serve the local market, as well as KSU and governmental centers for research and development.

Each technological cluster will jointly incorporate a science village, which will serve as the educational and recreational mixed-use core of the project. This zone will cater to workers in the science park, in addition to visitors from within and outside Riyadh.

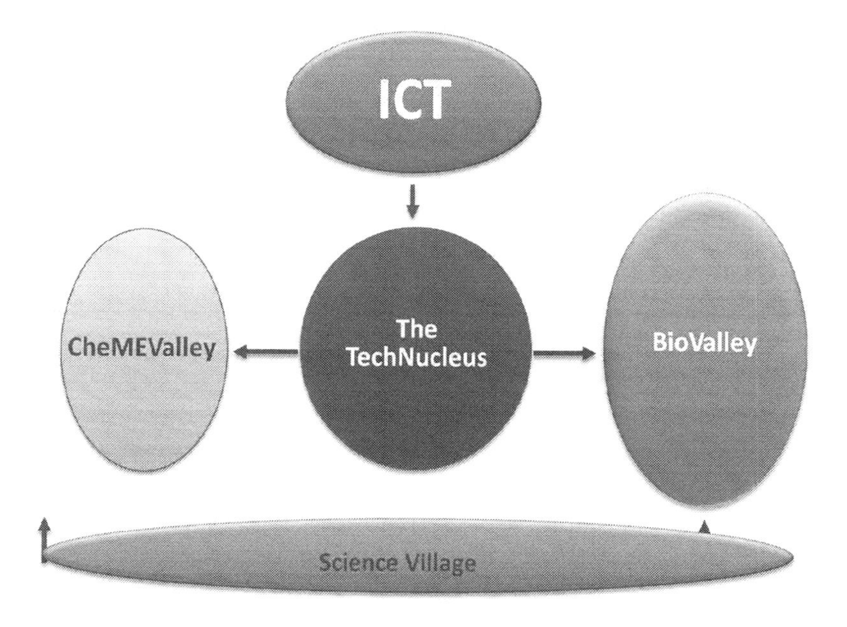

Figure 5. *Technology Clusters Adopted in RTV Master Plan (SRI).*

Central to RTV is the idea of the science village, a highly densified central district of research, business, education, entertainment and lifestyle that acts as catalyst for development. Development will grow in layers from this catalyst core, suggesting a radial expansion to the master plan. This center of gravity acts as a cohesive core to the development but can serve as a focal point, which can extend to accommodate future growth. The Stanford Research Institute Study suggested RTV comprise four development clusters: TechNucleus, Bio Valley, CheM Valley, ICT Valley—that would support the science village and mixed density residential clusters.

Each development cluster is arranged along a tech/knowledge boulevard and ends with a science village. This corridor is important because it sets a precedent for the environment of the park and the highly visible internal axis defining each cluster, and is reflected in the surrounding densities. The building heights of the developments in the park should accentuate the importance of this catalytic core.

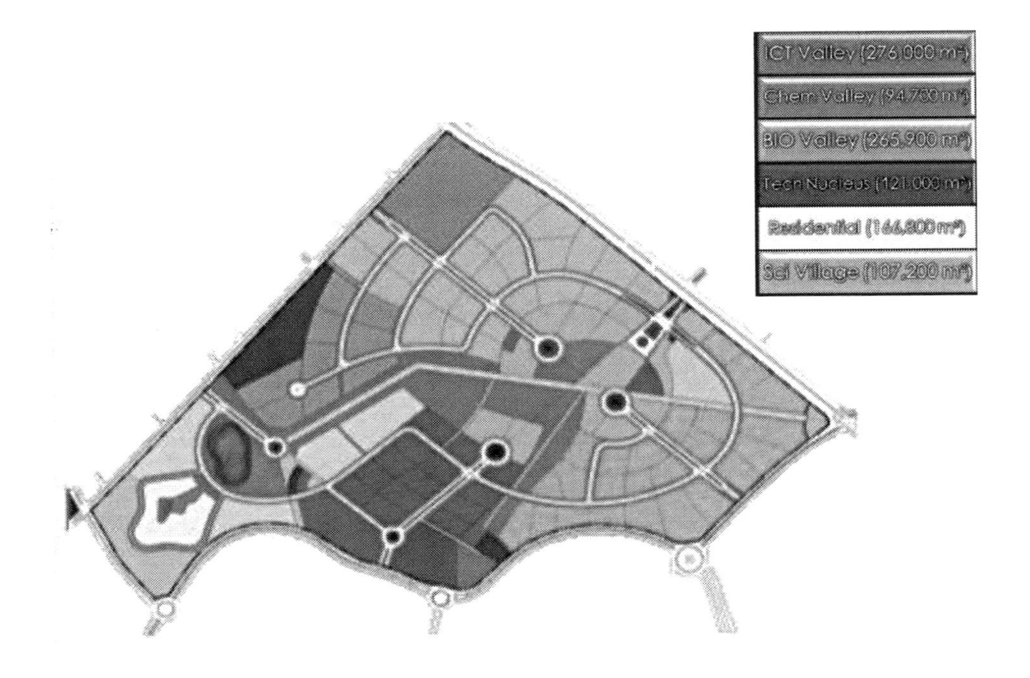

Figure 6. *The RTV Master Plan by Jurong International.*

RTV Projects:

- King Abdullah Institute for Nanotechnology
- Prince Sultan Advanced Technology Institute
- RTV Main Building (Innovation Tower)
- National Diabetes Center
- SABIC Plastics Applications Development Center
- Researchers Housing Towers
- RTV Smart Infrastructure
- Sustainable Agriculture Center

Riyadh Techno Valley Projects (Anchor to Smart Riyadh—NWD)

Main Building of Riyadh Techno Valley (Innovation Tower)

Located on anland area about 24,700 square meters and building area about 9,600 square meetings, the building has been divided into two towers. The eastern tower comprises 10 floors, and the west tower comprises five floors. The two towers are connected through the main lobby and by linking bridges. The RTV adopted the application of open spaces and smart officesto ease re-division of office space and to keep pace with the valley's expansion.

Half of the office area is allocated to meeting rooms, training rooms and workshops because of the importance of communication, participation and debate in the research and development, innovation and technology transfer.

In addition, the RTV building applies sustainability, green and smart building standards, such as:

- Energy-saving systems;
- Power-saving lamps;
- Self-lighting control systems;
- Presence detectors and motion detectors;
- Lighting intensity and energy-saving glass;
- A double-skin façade to protect the building from external climatic factors;
- Water conservation systems;
- Irrigation systems; and
- Parking spaces designed with solarpPanels to create a renewable energy source for the RTV building.

King Abdullah Institute for NANO Technology

Located on a land area of about 12,000 square meters and building area of 8,000 square meters, the idea behind the King Abdullah Institute for NANO technologybuilding design was inspired by the concept of nanotechnology and its components (core and rotation of electrons and protons). The circular shape of the design signifies the movement of electrons and protons around the nucleus. A structured ball was put in the center to represent the core, which functions as the main hall for conferences, meeting and training rooms. The building takes into account the architectural design of the project using state-of-the-art architectural materials to create a more sophisticated look and visual language that will reflect the intended design concept of the building. The project is the architectural language, and the idea is distinct architectural monument.

Prince Sultan Advanced Technology Institute

Located on a land area of about 22,815 square meters and building area of 13,000 square meters, the Prince Sultan Advanced Technology Institute aims to provide a tender knowledge of scientific and technical detail that seeks to rehabilitate national capacity sessions and private graduate programs. The goal is for them to conduct basic and applied research in areas of concern to national security and support its functions by adopting a culture cooperation that contributes to activating knowledge while enhancing efficiency.

National Diabetes Center

Located on a land area of 20,000 square meters, the mission of the National Diabetes Center is to provide organized, advanced and high-quality health care for patients with diabetes using the latest equipment and techniques. This will be reflected positively on the development of medical care for patients with diabetes, regionally, nationally and globally. The project consists of several departments (clinical department, community services department, research department, clinics, 80 hypnosis rooms, and management and services).

SABIC Plastic Applications Development Center

Located on a land area of about 100,000 square meters and building area of 42,000 square meters, the center will be equipped with the latest equipment to provide the best-available technology to integrate the remaining 15 SABIC technical centers inside and outside the Kingdom. This will allow the center to be one of the leading centers in building the knowledge-based economy and actively contribute to the resettlement of technology in the Kingdom by establishing a link between scientists and researchers in universities with manufacturers in the plastic industry. The project is also considered a LEED-certified building because of the green building standards that were applied in the project.

RTV—Science Village

The RTV science village is the dynamic center of gravity, providing a variety and intensity of activities that act as a unifying element for the various innovative clusters. An optimal mix of uses within RTV is critical for social, cultural,and economic vitality to encourage lively interactions.

The science village is the visual junction of the various district boulevards. It is directly accessed by the main landscaped RTV gateway along prince Turki Alawal street, and it is a car-free environment with an integrated people-mover system that connects the science village to the entire RTV.

The science village is a lifestyle center with various scales of commercial, retail, food and beverage, cafes, entertainment, health club, and cultural and lifestyle amenities. Science-themed education facilities such as a science and technology library, science museum, planetarium, business hotel, shopping plaza and serviced apartments support after work-hour activites. In the joint meeting area where the public from different parts of the world and RTV scientists can exchange ideas, innovation and knowledge awareness build a knowledge society.

Smart Infrastructure and Services for RTV (Core Facilities of Smart City)

The project contains the state of-the -rt main infrastructure (electricity, water, irrigation, drainage, sewer and telecom). RTV realized the important of using smart technology to increase the productivity of existing infrastructure, whichis why a smart service profile was integrated. Such services will increase the productivity not only for infrastructure, but also for people living and working in RTV. Smart infrastructure is the application of communications technologies to infrastructure to make better, more efficient use of resources. Smart infrastructure can be used to enhance the transport, energy, lifestyle, communications and water sectors.

Buildings and facilities are connected to a central command and control center through a state-of-the-art communications network. Interconnectivity between buildings and the command and control center shall use an optical fiber cabling system as a primary means of communication. Alternate and backup systems shall use the optical fiber cabling system (redundant and geographically diversified routes). Additionally, the systems use other means of communication, such as wired and wireless networks to further enhance availability/reliability/security. The optical fiber system is capable of supporting ultra-high-speed communications (terra bit), including TDM and DWDM networking and applications.

With the global trend in almost all technologies and applications using packet-based communications (wwired or Wireless); and wherever available/possible, all proposed systems shall be network based (or IP based).

The system will provide a single, integrated communications infrastructure for all systems and services, or separate infrastructure for building management and safety/security applications. The system will include (as a minimum) and not limited to the following:

- Smart Command and Control Center
- Graphical Information Systems (and GIS based Applications/ Services)
- Smart/Intelligent Building Management System (BMS)
- Smart Utilities Monitoring & Management System(s)
- Smart Facilities Monitoring & Management System(s)
- Smart Campus Security Monitoring & Management System
- Smart Office/Home Security Monitoring & Management System
- Smart Road/Traffic/Parking Monitoring and Management System.
- Smart Operations and Maintenance Services/System (including call center)
- Smart Safety Systems (fire/flood/gas/smoke detection and fighting, etc.)
- Smart Public Address & Broadcast (including warning systems)
- Smart Access Control & Security System (including fences, gates, visitor, etc.)
- Smart Surveillance and CCTV System (including recording and archival system)
- Smart Asset Management and Inventory Management System
- Smart Asset Monitoring/Tracking System
- Main Communication Center (including services provider termination areas)
- Smart/Modular Main Communication Room (data center)
- "Research" High-Performance Computing Facility (including visualization)
- Smart Simulation and Visualization Facility (with connectivity to lab facility)
- Local Area Network (LAN), Wireless LAN (WLAN) (including outdoor network)
- Advanced Data Security and Data Leakage Prevention Solution
- Intranet (branches, remote access, NREN, etc.)
- Extranet (companies, factories, etc.)
- Internet Access
- Web Publishing and Portal Services
- Smart IP Telephony (including audio/video and IPT applications)

- Smart Integrated Unified Messaging (voice mail, email, fax)
- Smart Audio/Video and Tele-Presence Solution (including multi-party)
- Smart Collaboration Systems/Services/Tools
- Digital Media & Signage Systems
- Smart Lab and Smart Library
- IPTV and VOD System
- Community/Social Networking "Quad Play" Services

Expected Benefits from Smart Services in RTV

- Benefit for RTV and Other Developers:
    - RTV and other developers can expect a higher asset value and occupancy rate because of smart community service.
- Benefits for RTV and Other Property Managers:
    - RTV and other property managers can not only save operational costs, but also pursue additional revenue opportunities by smart community service.
    - Saving operational costs through integration (energy saving costs of system operation and human resources).
    - Faster and more efficient management with standardized facility management process.
- Benefits for End-Users

    Businesses:
    - Comfortable and safe working environment.
    - Ready for office automation and enterprise solutions.
    - Home Residences:
    - Convenient and sSafe living environment.
    - Community social networking.

    Retailers:
    - Advertisement throughout the whole RTV community.
    - Customer loyalty with smart card membership and mileage service.

    Visitors:
    - Convenient access to real-time community information customized for various purposes (business, social, shopping and leisure).

DR. ABDULAZIZ ALDUSARI *a professor from King Saud University College of Architecture and Planning. He received his doctorate degree in Urban and regional Planning from the University of Florida, USA. Over the years his work and contributions gain recognition in the architecture field particularly his work on Environmental Planning, Urban Planning Sustainability and promoting eco-tourism development. He also held in the past several pivotal positions and currently now the Chairman of the Board for the Saudi Umran Society at the same time Chief Executive Officer for the Riyadh Techno Valley science park.*

25

Smart Cities of South Africa: A Case Study

Silma Koekemoer

The turn of the last century moved the world from an agricultural to an industrial era, and now we are moving from an industrial era to a technology era. Technology is driving change, and those who resist or change too slowly will drop into the abyss of irrelevance and technology extinction (Chang 2013:18).

There is a distinction between a smart city and a living city, according to scholar R. Moyser 2013.. He contends that living cities prioritize "solutions and initiatives that go beyond technology," broadly grouped as:

- Governance and growth;
- Society and community;
- Environment and natural resources; and
- Urban development and infrastructure.

On the other hand, he says smart cities have "resources and technology that interoperate in real time across city functions and are linked to end-users to provide one holistic service," including technology, mobility, society, growth and the environment in the definition.

Social discussions referring to smart cities tend to include aspects such as smart grids, smart meters, technology-based infrastructure used to provide services, electricity and water, as well as Internet-enabled, broadband, wireless and digital offerings. (Hire, 2013)

However, consider a definition for smart cities that provides a framework for evaluation, comparing cities and developing strategies along which to improve delivery. Under this framework, smart cities are defined by their innovation and their ability to solve problems using information communication technologies (ICTs) to improve delivery, quality and capacity. This includes investments in human and social capital, traditional (transport) and modern (ICT) communication infrastructure fuelling sustainable economic development and a high quality of life, wise management of natural resources, and participatory and active engagement. This measurement of smart cities, aligned with traditional regional and neoclassical theories of urban growth and development, include:

- Smart economy;
- Smart mobility;
- Smart environment;
- Smart people;
- Smart living; and
- Smart governance.

There is limited empirical knowledge regarding smart cities within the design, planning and policy fields because it is a relatively new concept with varying meanings. Similarly, no consensus exists amongst academics on the characteristics, conceptual frameworks, sustainability or policy informatics. Therefore, it is helpful to use Desouza's (2012) definition: "A *smart city is livable, resilient, sustainable and designed through open and collaborative governance*:

- A smart city is resilient in that it possesses the capacity, desire and opportunity for sensing, responding to, recovering and learning from natural and manmade disasters.
- A smart city takes a sustainable approach to the management of its economic, social and ecological resources to ensure that they have vitality into the future.
- A smart city infuses information for automated and human, individual and collective, decision-making on optimal allocation of resources, design of systems and processes, and citizen engagement.
- A smart city enables intelligent decision-making by leveraging information via technology, platforms, processes and policies across its environments, infrastructures, systems, resources and citizens.
- A smart city operates as a seamlessly integrated platform where information links the various infrastructures, systems, organizations, and citizens' goals and values.
- A smart city engages citizens in the planning and design of public spaces and governs use of public resources through open and collaborative governance platforms that generate and leverage collective intelligence."

Opportunities in South Africa

South Africa boasts one of the world's most progressive constitutions, which enjoys high acclaim and is the supreme law of the country. The country is governed by national, provincial and local spheres of government that are distinctive, interdependent and interrelated, and were established in terms of this act.

"The local sphere of government consists of municipalities, which must be established for the whole of the territory of the Republic" and their executive and legislative authority vests in the Municipal Council, (Constitution, 1996). The municipalities "function as a fully-fledged level of government in its own right, and are the closest to the citizens of the country." (Alberts, 2011).

The objectives of local government are articulated in the constitution as being:

- To provide democratic and accountable government for local communities;
- To ensure the provision of services to communities in a sustainable manner;
- To promote social and economic development;
- To promote a safe and healthy environment; and
- To encourage the involvement of communities and community organizations in the matters of local government.

"To accommodate the needs and realities of different population densities and levels, and the nature of economic activities of different regions in the country, the constitution makes provision for a stratified structure of local government." (Alberts, 2011) The specific municipal structures are specified in the Municipal Structures Act, Act 117 of 1998, being:

- Category A metropolitan municipalities;
- Category B local municipalities; and
- Category C district municipalities.

Local government consists of eight metropolitan municipalities, 44 district municipalities and 226 local municipalities, (278 municipalities) with 60 municipal entities.

A category A municipality is characterized by high population density; extensive development together with an intense movement of people, goods and services; a center of economic activity consisting of multiple business and industrial areas; a single area for which integrated development planning is desirable and with social and economic linkages between the constituent units.

Table 1. *Category A municipalities.*

Municipality	Location	Area (km²)	2011 Population	Operational/Capital Budget (2013/ 2014) ZAR 000
Buffalo City (BC)	East London	2,536	755,200	4,412,637 879,841
City of Cape Town (COCT)	Cape Town	2,460	3,740,026	26,308,008 5,416,684
City of eThekwini (COE)	Durban	2,292	3,442,361	24,976,074 5,466,767
City of Johannesburg (COJ)	Johannesburg	1,645	4,434,827	33,950,929 7,595,073
City of Tshwane (COT)	Pretoria	6,345	2,921,488	21,646,976 4,345,256
Ekurhuleni Metropolitan Municipality (EMM)	Kempton Park	1,924	3,178,470	24,763,937 2,908,933
Mangaung Metropolitan municipality (MMM)	Bloemfontein	6,284	747,431	5,368,473 865,989
Nelson Mandela Bay (NMB)	Port Elizabeth	1,959	1,152,115	7,659,812 1,135,283

SOURCE: HTTP://EN.WIKIPEDIA.ORG & PRIMARY RESEARCH

The functions and responsibilities of municipalities are well-defined and clearly articulated in the constitution, namely:

- Electricity;
- Water;
- Sewage and sanitation;
- Refuse removal;
- Strom water management;
- Firefighting services,
- Health services;
- Land use and management;
- Roads;
- Public transport;
- Street/informal trading;
- Abattoirs and fresh produce markets;
- Parks and recreational facilities;
- Library services; and
- Local tourism.

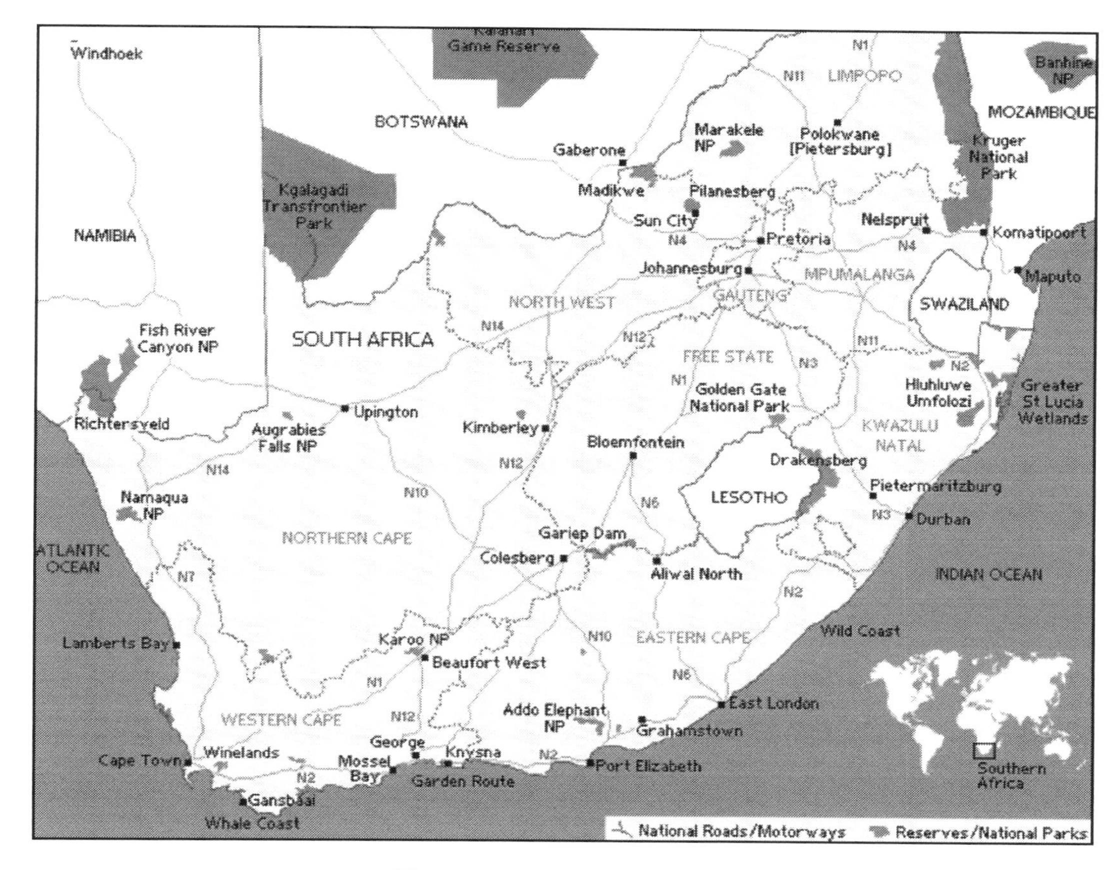

Figure 1. *Map of South Africa.*

SOURCE: HTTP://WWW.GOOGLE.CO.ZA

Since gaining political control of the country in 1994, and in an attempt to achieve the Millennium Development Goals, government has set specific minimum standard and service-delivery targets for municipalities in the country. These can be summarized as follows:

Table 2. *Minimum standards for basic services.*

Service	2014 target
Water	All households to have access to clean piped water within 200 m from the household.
Sanitation	All households to have access to a ventilated pit latrine on site.
Electricity	All households to be connected to the national grid.
Refuse removal	All households to have access to a weekly removal service.
Housing	All existing informal settlements to be formalized with land-use plans for economic and social facilities and with provision of permanent basic municipal services.
Other services	Standards for access to all other services must be clearly defined, planned and where possible, implemented.

SOURCE: SHAI & MHEMHE, 2010

While steady progress has been made toward significant social and economic development, service delivery protests have been escalating since 2004. This is partly due to expectations that were created by the national government that the local government cannot fulfill, placing a burden on them. "Persisting apartheid-era spatial segregation patterns require large subsidies, and poor households face disproportionate cost to access opportunities. At the same time, the current pace of urban population growth is outstripping economic growth, and the urban economic growth rate has failed to deliver required jobs." (Nagooroo, 2011)

Service Delivery

Across the globe, there is increasing focus on sustainable development. Most cities are severely hampered by the huge investment requirements and limited public funding.

"The critical role of cities on the African continent to ensure sustainable natural environments is illustrated by a research report by the Economic Intelligence Unit, based in Germany." (Coetzer, 2012) This report indicates that the number of urban residents in Africa has more than doubled in the past two decades, that there will be more urban residents in Africa than any other continent within the next decade, and that by 2035, more than half the residents of Africa will reside in urban areas. South African cities' performance in the African Green Cities Index can be summarized as:

Table 3. *South African cities' performance.*

Category	Below average	Average	Above average	Well above average
Overall		COT	COCT, COE, COJ	
Energy/electricity		COCT, COE, COJ, COT		
Transport			COCT, COE, COJ, COT	
Water		COJ, COT	COCT, COE	
Air quality			COCT, COE, COJ, COT	
Land use		COT	COE, COJ	COCT
Waste		COJ	COE, COCT	
Sanitation	COT	COCT, COJ	COE	
Environmental governance			COCT, COE, COJ, COT	

List of Acronyms:

BC	Buffalo City	EMM	Ekurhuleni Metropolitan Municipality
COCT	City of Cape Town	IMFO	Institute of municipal Finance Officers
COE	City of eThekwini	MMM	Mangaung Metropolitan Municipality
COJ	City of Johannesburg	NMB	Nelson Mandela Bay
COT	City of Tshwane		

SOURCE: COETZER, 2012

Transport

"South Africa is one of the leading economies in sub-Saharan Africa, and provides a vital transport corridor serving South Africa and a large number of land-locked countries within the Southern African Development Community," according to Davis (2011:48). Transport logistics play an important role in the economy of the region, with transport costs directly affecting the cost of goods and the competitive position of the region. Additionally, green logistics is increasing in importance as part of the national response to climate change. South Africa's public transport sector "was given a huge boost when the country hosted the 2010 FIFA Soccer World Cup and the government called upon municipalities and other role players to put in place integrated transport systems that would not only serve the soccer spectacle, but would remain as legacy projects afterward." (Terblanche, 2011)

The combined passenger and freight transport service in the country consumes approximately 27 percent of the country's delivered energy, 78 percent liquid fuel and 1.6 percent electricity, while also being the fastest growing emitter of harmful carbon emissions. The high cost of imported petroleum products and the uncertainty regarding sustainable sources of fossil fuels after 2030 have necessitated a strategy renewal of the industry. This strategy includes key elements like:

- Kilometer per liter of fuel achieved;
- Average kilometer life of tires;
- Percentage of tires re-used;
- Liters of waste lubricant oil generated;
- Optimal use of vehicle load space; and
- Percentage of kilometers run "empty."

Gauteng is geographically the smallest province in the country, occupying less than 2 percent of the country's land mass. It represents the fourth-largest economy on the continent and therefore needs to maintain transport infrastructure to attract investors to the region. The province is home to three category A metropolitan municipalities and two category C districts. The department of Transport, on its official website, states that "an effective transport system has a significant impact on both the economic and social fabric of the country. It influences the economy in many ways, through its impact on the efficiency of business operations and labor mobility and, for its citizens, the attractiveness of South Africa as a place in which to live and prosper."

Gauteng has led the way in transport, spending more than ZAR38 billion up to March 2013 on new roads and maintenance projects across the province. The Gauteng Freeway Improvement Project, reaching far beyond a mere sporting event, will benefit the whole country, raising international competitiveness significantly. Financing these upgrades remains a contentious issue, however. E-toll proposals are being met with passionate resistance due to the far-reaching financial impact on consumers. (Heyns, 2012)

Except for the Gautrain, commuters do not have access to cost-effective, reliable and safe alternative forms of public transport. The Gautrain is available in Gauteng only, connecting commuters with the OR Tambo International Airport, Johannesburg city center and Pretoria central business district, and carries up to 50 000 passengers per week along an 80 kilometer rail. In context, "South Africa operates a rail network of 20,000 kilometers, of which only 30ilometerskm of the Gautrain are suitable for a rapid rail system." (Coetzer, 2010) The introduction of the Gautrain has made a significant impact on the socio-economic development in the province, providing 94,800 direct, indirect and induced jobs, but also inspiring a new lifestyle, with residents and businesses relocating closer to the service and people opting to use the service for leisure purposes, too. Additionally, Gautrain has introduced state-of-the-art contactless ticketing to the country. (Gautrain, 2010)

According to Terblanche (2011:18), "The city of Johannesburg was the first to introduce a Bus Rapid Transit (BRT) system in terms of the government's Public Transport Strategy. The BRT program is the road-based component of the strategy and is designed to move large numbers of people to all parts of a city quickly and safely in dedicated bus lanes similar to railway systems. This project was the single biggest investment by the South African government in reducing greenhouse gas emissions in public transport. It is estimated that the BRT will reduce emissions by approximately 382 thousand tons by 2013 and 1.6 million tons by 2030." The BRT system transports 40,000 people per day across 950 trips, using 121 buses. The system was awarded a Sustainable Transport Award by the Institute for Transportation and Development Policy in New York.

Water

In our lifetime, communities will wage wars over water considering that we live on a planet with finite resources, which are under pressure from growing human populations, accelerating socio-economic development and increasing waste. (Carter 2010: 57). To rectify this situation, we need to invest resources, technology and leadership in a scientifically supported strategic approach.

"Increasing water scarcity and flood events will have profound social, economic and political consequences with impacts on food, energy, trade, the environment and international relations, as water-scarce nations search for ways to ensure their long-term growth and sustainability." South Africa is a water-scarce country, and demand is set to increase by 52 percent within the next 30 years because of leakage from aging and poorly maintained infrastructure. Demand is forecast to exceed supply by an estimated 17 percent. (Staff reporter, 2012) Water and sanitation infrastructure represent major assets with a long lifespan for which there are few shortcuts available to ensure sustainable management. The Department of Water has confirmed that a concerted effort is required to conserve water, manage demand, reuse/recycle and desalinate seawater to address the situation.

Some of the key challenges affecting South Africa's water supply remain pollution, poor quality and scarcity of the resource, and poor sanitation and service delivery from municipalities. Dams and rivers in the country are subject to excessive nutrients, which has shifted the attention to the use of groundwater and aquifers. (Meyer, 2011)

"Groundwater is more diffuse than surface water, and geo-hydrological processes in one part of a catchment may have little if any bearing on the geohydrology in another part of the same catchment," which makes groundwater quality aspects particularly difficult to address. (Van Vuuren, 2009) "A looming pollution crises more than half a century in the making" is threatening Gauteng with acid mine drainage polluting water resources. The effluent, as corrosive as battery acid and acutely toxic, according to the CEO of the Federation for a Sustainable Environment, also affects the soil and neural development of fetus, leading to mental retardation, cancer, cognitive problems and skin lesions. (Heyns, 2010) Similar challenges exist for estuaries, distinct and valuable environmental assets where the continual mixing of fresh and salt water generates unique ecosystems. The management of environmental flow to these water bodies supports the intrinsic, ecological, social and economic value thereof. The pressure on our aquatic ecosystems are enormous, and there is no doubt that there will have to be trade-offs to balance socio-economic development with environmental protection. A pertinent question is how to achieve this balance to ensure maximum conservation benefit at the lowest possible social and economic cost? (Van Vuren, 2009:94)

The Minister of Agriculture, Forestry and Fisheries reports that, "global warming has already significantly affected marine ecosystems. Greenhouse gas emissions are warming the planet, affecting the global carbon cycle and changing the chemical composition of the ocean." Additionally these ecosystems are disrupted by overfishing and climate change. Vulnerability is not only determined by degree of change, but also the sensitivity and adaptive capacity of individuals and fisheries. Appropriate responses could include "adaptation in the face of resource fluctuations that involve diversifying livelihoods in order to maintain a fishery based source of income, and adaptation that involves completely exiting fisheries for a different source of income." (Joemat-Pettersson, 2011)

The city of eThekwini manages its water resources and conservation with a future perspective. The municipality has developed municipal adaptation plans for the water, disaster management and health sectors. In addition, the city is doing work in the area of community adaptation, focusing on issues such as food and water security. Ecosystem-based adaptation is an underutilized and critical component of any response to climate change. Hence, the municipality is developing projects that demonstrate how improving ecological integrity improves a city's ability to deal with climate change. Further, it is critical that environmental challenges are addressed in ways that seek opportunities for social upliftment and that contribute to the broader green economy goals of the country. (Heyns, 2011)

Specific strategies and activities that are included in water management across the metropolitan area include:

- Use of appropriate technology;
- A combination of maintenance and expansion of the infrastructure;
- Scientific support from external consultants on request;
- Efficient management structure;
- Committed and skilled staff; and
- Adequate funding.

The municipality manages 400 reservoirs and 14,000 kilometers (km) of pipeline to deliver drinking water to residents. The department also manages 450 million liters of waste water daily that is transported through 4,000 km of sewers and 300 pump stations to 27 treatment works, before being returned to the environment. The city of eThekwini has achieved Blue Drop certification for the high quality drinking water, meeting all microbiological and chemical compliance standards. The municipality also has achieved Green Drop certification for waste management, which covers management of wastewater from the source, in the sewer network, treatment at the wastewater works and finally discharge to the receiving environment. (city of eThekwini website)

The Durban Metropolitan Open Space System (D'MOSS) program, launched in the 1980s, endeavors to conserve aquatic and terrestrial life while providing ecosystem products and services to residents. The program, in response to pollution, extinction of species, and inapt development in sensitive areas due to increasing migration to cities, creates sustainable jobs, biodiversity preservation and provides socio-economic benefits such as improved education, food security and community livelihoods. "Ecologically, it enhances biodiversity, water quality, river-flow regulation, flood mitigation, sediment control, visual amenity and fire risk reduction." (Ntsondwe, 2012)

Land Use

"The complex fabric of the human settlements debate provides for an array of immense opportunities for local authorities, the private sector and households, as there are no single sets of rules and courses of action aligned to each point of the debate," according to Muller, 2012. Urbanization is taking place at a much faster rate in the country than anywhere else in the world. There is an estimated 56 percent of the population already living in and around cities and towns, which is reflected in the more than 2,700 informal settlements in the country. Population growth needs to remain under the economic growth rate with a concerted effort at ensuring that poor people do not spend their disposable income on transport alone, have access to acceptable forms of housing and cost effective renewable energy technology to effectively resolve the current housing crisis.

The Gauteng Member of the Executive Committee for Local Government and Housing reaffirmed the department's key programs, saying that "housing remains the backbone of service delivery as it is delivered with many services including running water, sanitation, roads, electricity and many more. Housing delivers security, comfort and sustainable livelihood" and therefore, the department intends to prioritize mixed housing developments, eradicate informal settlements, provide alternative forms of tenure through urban renewal programs and focus on the 20 top priority townships across the country. (Mmemezi, H, 2011)

The city of Cape Town boasts the lowest unemployment rate and the highest health and education standards in the country, with a gross domestic product per capita 40 percent higher than the national average. Its coastal location fosters a climate for exploring, and its biotechnical and information technology incubators further boost early-stage entrepreneurial activities. (Timm, 2010) Considered a beautiful city, locals "divide Cape Town into curtains—The Botox Curtain stretches from Bantry Bay to Llandudno along the Atlantic strip, the Snoek Curtain from Simon's Town to Muizenberg on the Indian Ocean side, while the Lentil Curtain denotes Noordhoek and Kommetjie's bohemian lifestyles." (Hurry, 2012)

The city is "implementing strategies to address a housing backlog of some 400,000 families within an in-migration environment in excess of 16 000 new households being formed each year. This challenge, mixed with the geography of Cape Town, its bulk infrastructure status, employment levels and the complex land ownership scenario ensure the absolute need for the city of Cape Town's integrated human settlements and urbanization strategies to engage with all spheres of government." (Muller) The city firmly believes that one size does not fit all, and while it never was the intention, has come to believe that construction of rows of low cost housing without adequate community facilities creates an environment that is financially and socially unsustainable and insufficient. The city recognizes the rights of all, including the poor, and therefore continues to plan ahead for their land and housing needs, constantly updating their understanding of sustainable land use.

The Cape Town Community Housing Co. was established in 1999 and mandated to provide affordable housing in three segments: social housing for families with income ranging from ZAR 1,500 to ZAR 7,000 per month, subsidy housing to families with monthly income between ZAR 3,000 and ZAR 3,500 who qualify for the government's institutional housing subsidy, and gap housing in the income bracket ZAR 7,000 to ZAR 15,000 per month. The company acts as developer, implementer, and project manager. Services to clients include consumer workshops to empower new homeowners in their role. Topics covered address many aspects of home ownership, such as understanding the repayment system, household maintenance and applying for and consuming municipal services. Included in the mandate is to redress spatial planning and development, ensuring close proximity to places of work, clinics, schools and opportunities for economic development.

Lessons learned from completed projects include a mutually beneficial relationship between public and private sector. Given the complex geography and the availability of and cost of suitable land with access to bulk infrastructure, facilities and employment opportunities, owners of privately held land who are willing to form beneficial partnerships with the city have created cooperative agreements to access this land where the respective objectives of the parties are met.

The supply chain process for land owned by the municipality is clearly defined, but in the case of privately held land, a fair and equitable process needs to be followed. However, the benefits outweigh the risks and provision of appropriate project and financial oversight, and the reduction in cost for the beneficiary supports the municipal objective of delivering housing to the community. (Muller)

Technology

"ICT in South Africa has found itself behind the curve both globally and compared to the rest of Africa. The country has lost its status as the continental leader in internet and broadband connectivity. Pricing of services and equipment remains a significant barrier to the expanded use of ICT Policy constraints, weaknesses in institutional arrangements, conflicting policies between responsible departments, regulatory failure and limited competition have all contributed to this fact. Regardless, for those who do have access, ICT will continue to transform economic and social activities, as well as how individuals and communities communicate and function in our country." (Chetty 2012)

Municipalities are increasingly facing demands for higher quality and cost-effective services. To remain relevant, deliver on political mandates and meet these demands, easy access has become key. "Most municipalities in South Africa are struggling to make this a reality due to inefficiencies in their business technology, processes and practices. It has been found that many of the problems being experienced can be attributed directly to their continued use of disparate legacy, or inherited, information technology applications; a lack of these different applications being integrated; many of these applications no longer being supported; the multiple databases being used resulting in municipalities having no single view of data, citizens or households; a lack of standard financial practices and non-standard payrolls and human resources applications; and inconsistent and inaccurate utility billing services." (Venter, 2009)

Three of the five metropolitan cities being reviewed have gone quite far down the technology renewal route, and the city of Cape Town has been internationally recognized as a leader.

The Information Systems and Technology (IS&T) Department deploys a three-pronged strategy to maximize the use of IT to improve services to citizens. This support organization aims to be a catalyst for the transformation of public service and it will enable the city of Cape Town to become a more efficient and effective local authority. (Stelzner, accessed 19 Oct. 2013)

The strategy, also known as the Smart City Strategy, aims to:

- Improve the administration's efficiency;
- Improve services to citizens and businesses; and
- Enable social and economic development.

"This will be realized by using IT to assist in changing the way local government operates—thereby transforming the relationship between government and citizens, government and business, business and citizens, and citizens themselves. This ambitious objective is to completely change the way in which society and local government interacts and collaborates to enhance the quality of life and economic opportunities of all citizens.

This vision of an enabling local authority that uses IT to implement these changes can only be realized if the administration deploys integrated IT-enabled business processes to render its services to citizens. For this reason the IS&T Department will continue to maintain, enhance and implement new IT systems that improve the efficiency of the administration while enabling line departments to extend their service offering to their stakeholders." (Stelzner, 2013)

The IS&T Department offers 72 unique services across 11 service categories, focused on technology, processes and people, strategically aligned to the city Integrated Development Plan:

- Maintaining and strengthening the IT core;
- Enhancing and extending the ICT footprint; and
- Innovation and transformation of business processes.

Woods (2010) summarizes the challenges faced by government with reference to ICT and service delivery, and provides suggestions for addressing these, which support the city strategy. He starts with shifting the focus to the citizen, developing a customer-centric approach to ICT that will make the life of the citizen easier and deliver services more efficiently. He further suggests benchmarking, internally evaluating progress internally, as well as against other cities. Finally, Woods draws attention to the King III report on corporate governance, providing a new focus on IT governance and IT risk management.

Smart cities are innovative and imaginative about how to make the most of ICT to deliver services to citizens. They draw on insight gained from the past, use a systematic process of thinking, interpret available data, innovate through the use of analytics and constantly communicate with their stakeholders. Technology can be put to creative use, but only humans have the capacity to make it happen. (Fortuin, 2011)

The IBM report, "A Vision for Smarter Cities," (Dirks and Keely, U.K.) articulates the way forward with the introduction statement: "An urbanizing world means cities are gaining greater control over their development, economically and politically. Cities are also being empowered technologically, as the core systems on which they are based become instrumented and interconnected, enabling new levels of intelligence. In parallel, cities face a range of challenges and threats to their sustainability across all their core systems that they need to address holistically. To seize opportunities and build sustainable prosperity, cities need to become smarter."

The report continues by stating that becoming smarter is a journey not an overnight transition, and the authors urge administrators to engage in developing an integrated city planning framework, leveraging the city's core competencies. "Cities are based on a number of different systems central to their operation and development. Smart cities know how to transform their systems and optimize use of largely finite resources" to deliver on their mandate.

The Minister of Finance, speaking at the 2012 Annual Conference of the Institute of Municipal Finance Officers, said that "Local government is at the coalface of delivery of public services and the success or failure of municipalities in delivering services, shapes public opinions about government, both at administrative and political level. More importantly, the success or failure of local government determines whether millions of poor and marginalized people live in decent conditions, have a dignified life, and are able to enjoy a happy and secure family life."

SILMA KOEKEMOER *is an independent management consultant with extensive public and private sector experience, including finance, risk management and technology. An associate member of the Institute of Municipal Finance Officers in South Africa, she gained recognition for her development of a "Municipal ICT Blueprint," which she presented at regional, national and international conferences. She holds a MBA degree from the Potchefstroom Business School, North West University and lectures at Milpark Business School in South Africa).*

REFERENCES

1. Alberts, L. 2011: *Overview of Local Government in SA*. Service Leadership in Local Government Issue 39. Cape Media, Cape Town, South Africa. Sept/Oct 2011.
2. Carpenter, S. 2010: *Leadership in the New World*. The Wits Business School Journal Issue 20. Contact Media (Pty) Ltd, Randburg, South Africa.
3. Chang, D. 2013: *Death By Digital: A Survivor's Guide*. Sawubona. Ndalo Media, Bryanston, South Africa. July 2013.
4. Chetty, L. 2012: *The Promise of Technology in South Africa*. Acumen Issue 2. Gordon Institute of Business. Fourth Quarter 2012.
5. City of eThekwini official website: http://www.ethekwini.gov.za. Accessed on 07/10/2013.
6. Coetzer, P. 2010: *Transformation of Transport*. Service Leadership in Local Government Issue 33. Cape Media, Cape Town, South Africa. Sept/Oct 2010.
7. Coetzer, P. 2011: *Much Achieved, Much Still To Be Done*. Service Leadership in Local Government Issue 40. Cape Media, Cape Town, South Africa. Nov/Dec 2011.
8. Coetzer, P. 2012: *Green, Green Growth of Home*. Service Leadership in Local Government Issue 43. Cape Media, Cape Town, South Africa. May/June 2012.
9. *Constitution of the Republic of South Africa*. 1996. http://www.gov.za. Access on 05/10/2013.
10. Davis, S. 2011: *Is SA on the Road to a Logistics Crisis*? The Wits Business School Journal Issue 26. Contact Media (Pty) Ltd, Randburg, South Africa.

11. Desouza, K. 2012: *What is a Smart City*? http://kevindesouza.net/category/arizona-state-university/. Accessed on 05/10/2013.

12. Dirks, S. & Keeling, M. Unknown: *A Vision for Smarter Cities*. IBM Report.

13. Fortuin, O. 2011: *How Technology Can Make the World Work Better*. The Wits Business School Journal Issue 26. Contact Media (Pty) Ltd, Randburg, South Africa.

14. *Gautrain—Freedon, Convenience and Comfort for the Upwardly Mobile*. IMFO Volume 10 number 3. The Institute of Municipal Finance Officers, Kempton Park, South Africa. Autumn 2010.

15. Heyns, F. 2010: *Pollution Crisis Looms from Old Mines*.Service Leadership in Local Government Issue 32. Cape Media, Cape Town, South Africa. July/Aug. 2010.

16. Heyns, F. 2011: *Climate Change Not Merely an Environmental Issue*. Service Leadership in Local Government Issue 39. Cape Media, Cape Town, South Africa. Sept/Oct 2011.

17. Heyns, F. 2012: *Taking Its Toll*. Service Leadership in Local Government Issue 42. Cape Media, Cape Town, South Africa. March/April 2012.

18. Hire, C. 2013: *Smart Cities is a Vendor/City Term Commonly Used to Refer to the Creation of Knowledge Infrastructure*. http://www.innovation-cities.com. Accessed on 05/10/2013.

19. Hurry, C. 2012: *A Tale of Two Cities*. Acumen Issue 2. Gordon Institute of Business Science, Johannesburg, South Africa. Fourth quarter 2012.

20. Joemat-Pettersson, T. 2011: *Fisheries in a Time of Climate Change*. Service Leadership in Local Government Issue 40. Cape Media, Cape Town, South Africa. Nov/Dec 2011.

21. Lazaroiu, G.C & Roscia, M. 2013: *Definition Methodology for the Smart Cities Model*. http://www.sciencedirect.com. Accessed 05/10/2013.

22. Meyer, S. 2011: *Worldwide Water Crises Loming*. Service Leadership in Local Government Issue 38. Cape Media, Cape Town, South Africa. July/Aug. 2011.

23. Mmemezi, H. 2011: *Beyond Brick and Mortar*. Service Leadership in Local Government Issue 40. Cape Media, Cape Town, South Africa. Nov./Dec. 2011.

24. Moyser, R. 2013: *Defining and Benchmarking Smart Cities*. http://www.burohappold.com. Accessed on 05/10/2013.

25. *Municipal Structures Act*, Act 117 of 1998. http://www.gov.za. Accessed on 05/10/2013.

26. Ntsondwe, K. 2012: *Biodiversity on Top in Durban*. Service Leadership in Local Government Issue 44. Cape Media, Cape Town, South Africa. July/Aug. 2012.

27. Shai, J & Mhemhe, M. 2012: *Service Delivery in South Africa—Are We There Yet?* IMFO Volume 10 number 4. The Institute of Municipal Finance Officers, Kempton Park, South Africa. Winter 2010.

28. Staff reporter, 2012: *SA Leading the Waterways*. Service Leadership in Local Government Issue 42. Cape Media, Cape Town, South Africa. March/April 2012.

29. Stelzner, A. 2013: *Information Systems and Technology Department Business Plan and Strategic Development and Business Implementation Plan* 2010/2011. http://www.capetown.gov.za. Accessed on 19/10/2013.
30. Terblanche, S. 2011: *Greening the Transport Sector*. Service Leadership in Local Government Issue 40. Cape Media, Cape Town, South Africa. Nov/Dec 2011.
31. Timm, S. 2010: *Cape a Springboard to Success*. The Wits Business School Journal Issue 20. Contact Media (Pty) Ltd, Randburg, South Africa.
32. Van vuuren, L. 2009: Service Leadership in Local Government Issue 26. Cape Media, Cape Town, South Africa. July/Aug. 2009.
33. Venter, H. 2009: *Service Excellence Through Integrated Technology*. Service Leadership in Local Government Issue 26. Cape Media, Cape Town, South Africa. July/Aug 2009.
34. Woods, S. 2010: *Under-Utilisation of IT for Service Delivery*. Service Leadership in Local Government Issue 33. Cape Media, Cape Town, South Africa. Sept/Oct 2010.

26

Smart City Service Creation and the Living Lab Approach: Testimony from the EPIC Project

Wim Vanobberghen and Senja Van Der Graaf

The aim of the EPIC project was to examine the needs, requirements and added value of a pan-European smart city delivery platform for leading information communication technology (ICT) companies, specialist subject matter experts (SMEs), Living Labs and established and future smart cities. The objective, therefore, was to explore the implications of a cloud platform paradigm as the basis for a pan-European service delivery platform to enable a more holistic approach in making European cities smarter.

To ensure that the platform is best-suited for the deployment of new smart city services, one important task of the EPIC project was to create different smart city services that each posed different requirements and aspects of the smart city concept. Secondly, in creating these services, the EPIC project was interested in benefiting from the Living Lab approach, which is associated with open innovation and user involvement in early stages of product or service development.

The Living Lab methodology developed for the EPIC project generated three services in three pilot cities: a relocation service in Brussels,Belgium), an urban planning service in Issy-les-Moulineaux,France, and a smart environment service in Manchester,United Kingdom.

Focus, in particular, on the aspect of smart city service development and design in the context of Living Lab research. Drawing on the experiences encountered and the user tests results, the relocation service pilot serves as a case study to: 1) Present other European cities with a hands-on experience of how the EPIC project carried out its Living Labs, guiding user tests of smart city services; 2) illustrate the benefit of this approach by presenting the most important test results and lessons learned on the level of design, smart city value and sustainability; and, 3) based on concrete experiences, provide some lessons about daily Living Lab management, especially focussing on the engagement and management of end-users.

The Philosophy of the Living Lab Approach

First, consider the Living Lab approach with open innovation and user involvement paradigms underpinning technological development. Historically, innovation has been viewed as a linear process, driven and controlled by the industrial developers of products for the marketplace. Today, innovation is increasingly seen as a catalyst for growth and competitiveness. It has been enthusiastically promoted at regional, national and international levels, and included in new policy formulation. The linear concept has evolved more toward a network model involving partners supporting innovation, often focused on cycles of innovation activity.

The greatest shift in how to consider innovation can be detected in what has been termed "open innovation." This concept postulates that companies should have an open attitude toward ideas stemming from outside the boundaries of the firm. Innovation can only thrive when a company uses a network of partnerships beyond its traditional internal resources (Chesbrough, 2008).[i]

The idea of open innovation has converged with a greater acknowledgment of the role of the user in the development process. Living Labs build specifically on this trend, believing that gaining insight into the user and the usage context is one of the critical determinants in successfull product development processes (Eriksson, Niitamo, Kulkki, & Hribernik, 2006).

Living Labs can be defined as a form of open innovation. Yet its activities distinguish themselves from other approaches (such as usability research) by confronting the user with technology (e.g., a prototype or a proof of concept) early on in the innovation process, within their natural environment, and by regarding the user as the co-producer of technology (Ballon et al., 2005, Veekman et al., 2013). Therefore, Living Labs create an innovation environment—a kind of research laboratory—bringing together all relevant stakeholders (research centres, public institutions and organizations, companies) and users. The goal is to develop a research methodology that allows participants to grasp and understand user reactions from their real livese toward the new technology, thereby enabling co-creation with the development team.[ii] The Living Lab approach is getting momentum in Europe, as shown by the creation and successive expansion of the *'European Network of Living Labs'* (ENOLL—www.openlivinglabs.eu).

With this Living Lab approach in mind, EPIC has sought, at the end of the project, to ensure that its pilots would be able to provide user-friendly smart city services that citizens, businesses and city visitors would want to use and potentially be willing to pay for.

Relocation Pilot's Objectives

The relocation service (RS) application is a pilot study that aims to assist professionals and their families in their temporary relocation to the city of Brussels. In its envisioned form, the application focuses on helping expatriate users to:

- Get to know the different areas of the city and help to decide which areas are preferable to live in (guided by language settings).
- Find available housing for sale or for rent within these preferred areas.
- Evaluate individual properties based on a multimedia description of the property and its neighborhood.
- Discover various point of interests (e.g. educational, public transport facilities) around these properties.
- Discover and engage with institutions, organizations and facilities targeted at the integration and support of incoming and existing citizens of the smart city. This includes making sure the user knows what administrative tasks need to be fulfilled to move to the city, where family members can be enrolled in education and more.

These objectives are met by offering a web-based component and a mobile application (iPhone). The web application provides a feature-rich interface that can be used by incoming citizens in preparation for their move to Brussels. These functionalities are extended by an Internet-enabled mobile application that supports incoming citizens when actually "on the move" in Brussels.

For example, preferences and searches made in the Web-based component are reflected in the mobile application as it guides users to preferred properties and points of interest around them. The application also allows users to add their 'favorites' and feedback to the properties and places visited during their actual property search in Brussels. This information is stored online, so it can be used in both the web as mobile components.[iii] Against this backdrop, the smart city objectives are the following:

For citizens (expats):

- **Smart Living:** Find potential interesting property in a more efficient way.
- **Smart Mobility:** Plan one's relocation activities in a more efficient way.
- **Smart Governance:** smoothen the "move and settling-in" process by engaging with local authorities in a more efficient way.

Moreover, the service also can benefit:

City Administrations/Institutions:

- **Smart Governance:** By being able to generate anonymous aggregated data about expats from the service and, hence, develop better policies to meet an expat's requirements.

Businesses:

- **Smart Economy:** Local SMEs and businesses providing services to expats can generate aggregated anonymous statistical data from the service and, hence, better adopt and develop services in line with their needs and demands

EPIC—Living Lab Operations [iv]

None of the pilots were launched and tested in a pre-existing institutional Living Lab with a specific user panel at its disposal. Hence, the Relocation Pilot had to create its own Living Lab environment in the city community to engage end-users with a real-life interest in the topic that could provide reliable feedback.

The most important steps in the execution of the Living lab operations throughout the test period encompasses the following elements:

- The iterative development strategy;
- The recruitment and selection of testers and their participation; and
- The methodology for user feedback collection and evaluation.

Iterative development strategy

Since one characteristic of a Living Lab is to allow for iterative development, a deployment and development strategy consisting of three phases was developed with each phase having a concrete purpose (see Figure 1, next page).

Figure 1. *Iterative Pilot Deployment Strategy.*

1. A **closed group** with a limited number of technically skilled people that had to test whether from an end-user point of view the services were technically working;
2. A broader **open group** focused on the experience and acceptance of the services by end-users within their everyday life context;
3. A **stakeholders evaluation phase** that consisted of an evaluation of the final version of the pilots by relevant actors (businesses, public institutions) in the pilot city that could have an interest in using the service or aspects of the service from their operations point of view.

The closed and open group consisted of multiple test cycles. Each time a new feature(s) was added, tested by the end-user and, based on the analysis of the test results and feedback, the previous version was redesigned or improved.

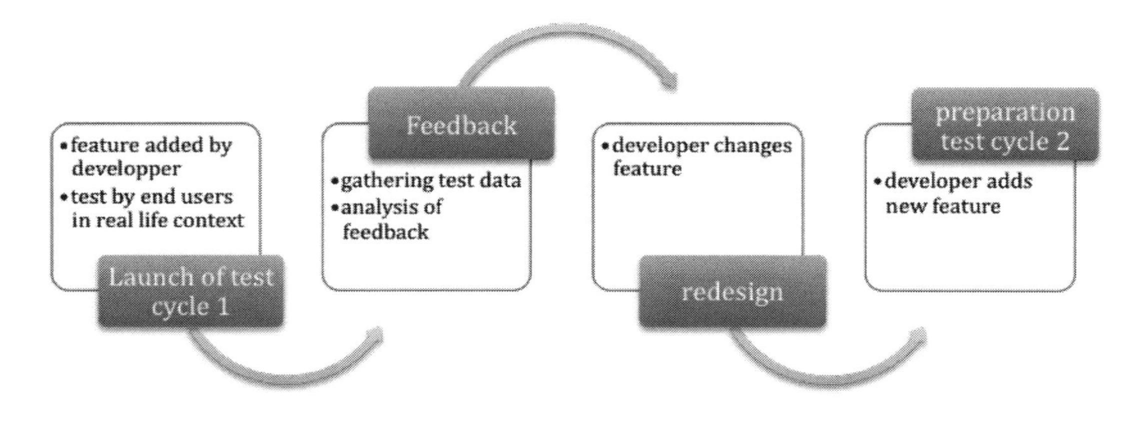

Figure 2. *Test cycle.*

User Test Recruitment and Participation

In line with the aim of the closed group, a limited group of testers, characterized by some basic technical skills was recruited in the local city community. As Figure 3 shows, test users in the open group were selected and recruited in accordance with the user type and roles based on the developed pilot scenarios that guided the testing cycles.

RELOCATION END USER RECRUITMENT			
User type	**User role**	**Target population**	**Participation in test**
EU—nationals relocating to Brussels for professional reasons	Find interesting property to live in Brussels and explore neighborhoods	• EU-nationals living abroad Brussels and having an interest in moving to Brussels; • EU-nationals working and living in Brussels since max 2 years; • Belgian people living outside Brussels;	• One time experience testers • Advisory board • Advisory board

Figure 3. *Selection of user testers and participation.*

Since it became clear that to engage EU-nationals residing outside Belgium in all cycles of the open group was difficult, project organizers decided to reduce their participation to one cycle, as well as to recruit a new test group tailored for each cycle. Besides these "one time experience users, an expat advisory group was created, consisting of non-Belgians that had moved to Brussels in the past two years. This group complimented a small group of Belgians living and working outside Brussels. From the former group, organizers sought to take advantage of their fresh memory of their relocation experience, while from the latter group it was assumed that similar relocating issues would occur to non-Belgians if they would relocate to Brussels. The advisory group, which participated in multiple test cycles, could thus balance results from the testers that only participated in one stage of the development process.

The recruited users tested the application within their real-life context and, apart from the communication of the start and end of a test cycle, no restrictions about use was imposed. Figure 4 (see next page) summarizes how many users the Relocation Service managed to engage (recruit + start survey after test) during the entire iterative development process for the 3 services.

Closed	Number of cycles	Participants	Total
Relocation web	2	Technical skilled	169
Relocation mob	1	Technical skilled	32
Open	**Number of Cycles**	**Participants**	**Total**
Relocation web	3	One time experience expats + Advisory expat group:	340
Relocation mobile and integration web/mobile	1	One time experience + Advisory expat group: Mobile only: Integration web and mobile	29 6 23
Evaluation	**Number of Cycles**	**Participants**	**Total**
Relocation (web and mobile)	1	Public institutions Business Education institutions	15

Figure 4. *Test User Participation Numbers.*

Methodology for User Testing and Evaluation

To learn about the user experience and acceptance of the EPIC solution, quantitative and qualitative feedback was collected during all test phases, deploying the following methods:

Method	Aim	Deployment
Questionnaire	Quantitative feedback/ Qualitative feedback in open question	Closed + open
Interview	Qualitative feedback	Evaluation
Focus group/demonstrations	Qualitative feedback	Evaluation
Participant observation	Qualitative feedback	Open group mobile
Data Logs	Quantitative feedback on usage	Closed and open

Figure 5. *Data Capture Methods.*

Each of the methods was selected to elicit a particular kind of data and enabled a full end-to-end analysis of the pilot services. Questionnaires allowed project organizers to gather quantitative feedback from a large number of end-users in a timely fashion about user experience and acceptance. It also provided qualitative feedback by means of open questions, where testers could express the negative aspects, positive aspects and recommendations for design purposes. Questions were asked that researched their background and the use context. Interviews and focus groups were allowed in the evaluation phase to gain a deeper understanding of meaningful themes, practices and relationships from the interviewee's point of view. Participant observation for the mobile component of the relocation pilot allowed organizers to get a close view on usage and its meaning while expats were actually "on the move" in Brussels to find a place to live. Data logs yielded broader insights into use patterns (time and scenario) of the pilots, as well as helped to detect access and error information.

To evaluate the feedback gathered by these methods, the following measures were identified:

Experience context	
Usability/acceptance	Perceived Ease of Use
	Perceived Usefulness
	Content
	Attitude
	Intention
	User Profile (context research)

Figure 6. *Measures for User Exxperience and Participation.*

Test Results from the Living Lab Approach

The user test results taught us that the benefits of the Living Lab approach were threefold:

1. Identify good design solutions
2. Realistically assess the concrete value of the pilot within smart city objectives, and
3. Identify crucial points for guaranteeing the sustainability of the pilot in the long run.

Learning for Current and Future Design Solutions

The closed phase with technical skilled testers made sure the pilot service was working well from the end user's perspective. Bugs, safety issues, access issues, as well as other minor technical problems that \in a linear development track would only have been discovered when "going to market", were now detected at an early stage.

The open group test in the broader expat community allowed organizers to identify quickly which implemented design options were desired by end-users, needed to be improved or were deemed to be of lesser or no importance and could be removed.

Figure 7 summarizes the main design lessons learned and implemented throughout the iterative relocation service test.

Design Lessons
Point of Interest: – Categorization (Public Transport, Everyday Utilities, Education ...) and hierarchic classification within category (e.g., public transport: underground—bus—tram—taxi) – Selection of relevant categories of points of interest in the property search selection criteria as being the most commonly sought when exploring the neighborhood around a property (public transport, everyday utilities, health care facilities, educational facilities)
Improved navigation options/functionalities between the different pilot tabs and pages (e.g., go from icon of house on map straight to details house instead of having to go to the list of returned properties first)
A clear use of icons for houses and points of interest that improve navigation and understanding of information displayed on the web application
Living in Brussels page on the web application that provides general background information and interesting web links about different aspects related to organize the settling in Brussels (e.g., explanation of public transport in Brussels, school system in Belgium, social security and health care organization)
Save favorite property: Insert extra button for confirming the selection

Figure 7. *Implemented Design Based on User Feedback.*

In addition to receiving end-user feedback on the planned and implemented features, users also provided suggestions about solutions that they deemed necessary to incorporate to improve the value of the pilot from their use-context.

Future Design Options
Interface/look and feel of web 2.0 way for web
Orientation in the city for both web and mobile: search on address , make environments more meaningful by displaying known landmarks on the map (European Quarter, Atomium, Grand Place).
Enrich points of interest with a relevant web address so that more information can be retrieved (e.g. opening hours of supermarket)
Provide interaction with fellow expats via a forum, via testimonies about neighborhoods or ratings by other expats
Individual rating systems to facilitate the selection ofa property to look for at the end of the search
Sharing of personal ratings of a property, points of interest or neighborhood with other users

Figure 8. *Future Improvements of the Three Pilots.*

Although thesuggestions could not realized within the context of the EPIC project, they were nonetheless valuable ideas for cities that offer the relocation service to increase its attractiveness.

These design-related results clearly show that a Living Lab is a useful approach and tool for generating many ideas resulting from people's real-life situations (using the service) from the start of the development process. It thus provides developers with the opportunity to incorporate these ideas already in the early stages of development, and to identify already potential future development tracks that are likely to increase the use value of the prototype.

User Experience and Acceptance: The Smart City Value of Each Pilot

The project is interested in creating smart city services that citizens, businesses and visitors would like to use and are possibly willing to pay for. The best way to assess the impact of the Living Lab approach for reaching this target is during the final open group's test cycle.

Here, the testers are offered the latest version, consisting of validated features and redesigned features from the previous cycles, as well as the latest new features. In addition, stakeholders in the evaluation phase were offered the same solutions and provided feedback based on their experiences in their daily professional context.

Figure 9 summarizes the evaluation on the different measures identified for analyzing user experience and acceptance for the relocation pilot.

Relocation	
Measure	Feedback (end users and stakeholders)
Ease of use	Simple design, intuitive, easy to learn
Usefulness	Combination of property data and points of interest. Web and mobile very useful
Look and feel	Outdated for web; very good for mobile
Content quality	Rich information, covering various aspects of the relocation process
Acceptance	Satisfied with amount of time to find property on pilot, essential application a city should offer
Intention to use	End-users: definitely, although improvements needed (like look and feel and new design features) to increase use value Stakeholders: improvements on level of design and look and feel needed before advising to use to their customers/clients

Figure 9. *User Experience and Acceptance Relocation.*

The relocation pilot was evaluated as an easy-to-use, intuitive tool with a simple design underpinning the property search. Users also showed a positive attitude and satisfaction with the time it took to complete a search and find the appropriate information they were interested in. Its major appeal lies in its innovative character of combining (private) property data and (public) points of interest that were seen as a necessary and welcome improvement in house-hunting in an unknown town. Several expats testified that such a service was something they wish existed in their current city, and deemed it a necessary service a city should offer.

Participant observation with the mobile application also taught project organizers that users found this device particularly useful because it allowed them to explore neighborhoods they passed through and would normally not visit. They also clearly expressed an intention to use such an application if they move to Brussels.

A significant part of the evaluation highlighted that some necessary improvements on the level of look and feel, as well implementation of extra features were deemed necessary to increase the immediate use value. The major objection lies in the look and feel of the web application due to the constraints of the platform on which it was deployed.

Stakeholders expressed similar opinions as expats. Although from a more operational point of view, they would still require a more robust finalization of the pilot before advising their clients to use it. Also, they saw the potential of a payment model with a basic, free service and a payment-model for additional services.

In terms of the pilot's contribution to smart city objectives, the stakeholder evaluation highlighted that the application would contribute to smart living by giving a means to expats to plan and execute their relocation process in a more efficient way. In other words, it would smooth a process that often is accompanied by a lot of uncertainty and, consequently, stress.

Governmental institutions acknowledged that the application could provide them with interesting, anonymously aggregated data about expat behavior, needs and preferences when relocating to the city, allowing them to develop policy that is better suited for the particular population.

Finally, businesses stated that the data would also be beneficial in allowing them to streamline their business offers to newcomers to the city.

The results of the user experience, acceptance of the three pilots and the stakeholders evaluation of smart city objectives indicate that the Living Lab approach can contribute to the creation of smart city services. Users not only expressed that the pilots provide essential, innovative smart technical solutions that their city should offer, but they also expressed their willingness to use the applications.

Guaranteeing Pilot Sustainability

The third benefit for EPIC in adopting a Living Lab approach was to identify crucial issues to sustain the projects beyond the conclusion of the EPIC project. For relocation, the main concerns were the reliability, actuality, sensitivity and maintenance of the data provided.

On the one hand, testers of the mobile application indicated that some points of interest no longer existed. On the other hand, community information needed to be handled with care. Organizers decided not to include information such as air and noise pollution because they were measured years ago.

Moreover, there is also the sensitivity issue tosome data: While some testers asked to incorporate crime statistics and statistics about demographic composition of neighborhoods, pilot develolpers deliberately chose not to add that information to avoid stigmatization of certain areas.

Finally, the Living Lab results made it clear that open data often needs remodelling: They are collected and organized within the logic of the institutions that gather them and often need adaptation to the specific end-user. Working out such strategies onmaintenance and sensitivity are thus crucial to sustain the service. While within the EPIC context this was solved by not publishing some data, it is clear that for future development tracks, it will require some creative co-design thinking to find answers to these challenges.

Living Lab Management: 4 Lessons Learned[vi]

Executing a Living Lab approach is an ongoing process that brings along challenges regarding the daily operation of the innovation environment and the execution of the tests. Four major lessons were learned for engaging and managing end-users that allow increasing their impact on the development process.

1. ***User Test Numbers: Go for Quality Instead of Quantity.*** In a project like EPIC, a pre-defined user number tends to be defined to reach. The three pilots did not reach that set number. Nonetheless, a relative solid number of users was recruited, providing valid insights and test results. Although some delay in technical delivery, leading to a postponement of a test cycle and hence user drop out, is a part of the explanation for this situation, developers belived that the pre-defined user numbers were not realistic.The analysis of the feedback indicated that after a certain number of users, feedback became quite similar. Although one common criticism of the Living Lab approach is indeed to extend results of small scale tests so that they can be generalized, based on the EPIC experience, organizers believe simply raising the number of testers to a level that seems more plausible for large-scale research, is not the way forward in smart city service development, especially when the research starts from the initial prototype phase.

2. ***Manage testers' expectations.*** In contrast to more traditional test settings where an almost finished prototype is presented to testers, involving potential future end-users at an early stage of prototype creation demands that users are aware of the objectives of the experiment and the state of the prototype they are going to be confronted with. Users are not used to working with prototypes and might have too big expectations. Developers learned in EPIC that managing end-user expectations in a iterative development track is a crucial factor in avoiding drop-out, and also in generating valid end-user feedback that is not influenced by feelings such as disappointment.

3. ***Manage the end user influence during the test cycles.*** While users could influence the shape of the pilot, they certainly did not all share the same view. Not all users are the same and have the same requirements and needs. In the case of relocation, project organizers identified, for example, expats moving alone or with their spouse/partner and/or children. What is thus worthwhile for one category might not be useful or important for the other. Management of end -ser influence on any project is therefore important.

   It is important to investigate which kind of feedback came from which kind of testers, and define in advance within which parameters you will take their suggestions into account within the project.

   In EPIC's case, developers defined that a feature should certainly be revised or redesigned if more than 30 percent of the testers within the different profiles provided negative feedback.

   Secondly, within a project, you cannot implement all users' feedback. Developers therefore, opted to focus on redesigning functionalities that were part of its iteration plan. However, as seen in the discussion of the design lessons, users provided much more useful feedback. Therefore, a third lesson is that managing end-user influence requires transparent communication (via a newsletter, updating the project website, etc.) with the testers, explaining why some suggestions were retained and others not and indicating what future plans are in this context.

4. ***Think about ways to sustain a Living Lab community in the long-run.*** In the EPIC project, developers seemed to have slightly underestimated the importance of post-test phase communication to testers and stakeholders, resulting in a lack of awareness about the pilot results beyond the "close EPIC community" created for test purposes. As a result, the continuation of work was endangered beyond EPIC,

especially with an eye toward implementing future design lessons users provided.

The lack of a real strategy for maintaining theuser community after the duration of the project means awareness creation in the local community should be repeated to assure co-creation. Moreover, if the relocation service makes it to the market, developers may have missed out on an opportunity to have a group of end -sers at their disposal who could be recruited to "evangelize" other citizens, SMEs or local authorities to buy, adopt and use the solution and improve it based on their feedback.

Conclusion

This chapter provided an overview of the use of the Living Lab approach as set out and analyzed for the EPIC project. It pointed out the purpose and importance of directly engaging users, via an iterative approach in three phases, gradually broadening the number and user type of participants, in testing the service within their everyday lives.

In particular, the test results highlighted the benefits of a Living Lab approach in the ideation, creation and development of smart city services. Within the confinements of the EPIC project, this approach allowed organizers to identify from the early stages of prototype development to the final test phase, the technical and design issues that needed to be improved, redesigned or removed. It also helped to detect a series of new features that end-users, or at least some, would like to see implemented to increase the use and market value of the services.

The discussion of user experience and acceptance showed that engaging end-users from the early development phases could lead to the development of smart city services that various user and stakeholder groups evaluated as being "easy -o-use" services, essential for cities to incorporate and supported by a "willingness to use" it in the near future. Moreover, the Living Lab approach identified crucial aspects concerning the sustainability of the value of the service. Lastly, in applying the Living Lab approach to smart city service design, the EPIC experience gave developers the opportunity to learn and share four important Living Lab management lessons that are important to increase the impact of users on the development path, potentially facilitating success in the delivery of user-validated smart city services.

WIM VANOBBERGHEN, *Researcher IBBT-SMIT,* ***SHENJA VAN DER GRAAF,*** *Senior director, R&D, ICT, iMinds-SMIT; at Vrije-Universiteit Brussels.*

Acknowledgment

EPIC is a joint effort; hence, gratitude goes to the entire EPIC consortium. In particular, thanks goes to Pieter Ballon (iMinds-iLab.o, iMinds-SMIT, Vrije Universiteit Brussel) for his input and guidance throughout the project, as well as to Hugo Kerschot (IS-Practice) for his continuous support. We also thank WP7-partners Issy Media and Manchester Digital Development Agency.

BIBLIOGRAPHY

1. CHESBROUGH (H.), *Open innovation: the new imperative for creating and profiting from technology*, Boston, Harvard Business School, 2003.
2. ALMIRALL (S.) & WAREHAM (J.), *Living labs and open innovation: roles and applicability* IN: Ejov. *The electronical journal for virtual organisations and networks*, 10, Special issue on Living Labs, August 2008.
3. BALLON (P.), PIERSON (J.) & DELAERE (S.), *Test and experimentation platforms for broadband innovation: examining European practice*, in: Conference Proceedings of 16th European Regional Conference by the International Telecommunications Society (ITS), Porto, Portugal, 4-6 September, 2005
4. BERGVALL-KAREBORN (B.)—STAHLBROST (A.), *Living Lab: an open and citizen centric approach for innovation* in: *International Journal of Innovation and Regional Development*, 2009, 1, 4, pp. 356-370
5. FEUERSTEIN (K.), HESMER (A.), HRIBERNIK (K.A.), THOBEN (K.-D.), SCHUMACHER (J.), *Living Labs: a new development opportunity* in: SCHUMACHER (J.), NIITAMO (V.-P.) (eds.), *European Living Labs—A new approach for human centric regional innovation*, 2008
6. FOLSTAD (A.), *Living Labs for innovation and development of information and communication technology: a literature review* in: *Ejov. The electronical journal for virtual organisations and networks*, 10, special issue on Living Labs, August 2008.
7. MULVENNA (M.), BERGVALL-KAREBORN (B.), WALLACE (J.), GALBRAITH (B.) & MARTIN (S.) *Living Labs as Engagement Models for Innovation*. in: *Proceedings eChallenges-2010*. (Eds: Cunningham, Paul and Cunningham, Miriam), IIMC International Information Management Corporation,, pp. 1-11
8. VEECKMAN (C.), SCHUURMAN (D.), LEMINEN (S.), LIEVENS (B.) & WESTERLUND (M.), Characteristics and their outcomes in Flemish Living Labs: A Flemish-Finnish case study, paper presented at The XXIV ISPIM Conference—Innovating in Global Markets: Challenges for Sustainable Growth, Helsinki (Finland), 16-19 June 2013.

[i] CHESBROUGH (H.), *Open innovation: the new imperative for creating and profiting from technology*, Boston, Harvard Business School, 2003.

[ii] Literature on Living Labs, both from an applied as theoretical viewpoint, is, as this field is growing in importance, nowadays growing but did not result yet in some consolidation of viewpoints. Nonetheless, a basic introduction to the method can be found in the following articles: ALMIRALL (S.) & WAREHAM (J.), *Living labs and open innovation: roles and applicability* in: *Ejov. The electronical journal for virtual organisations and networks, 10*, Special issue on Living Labs, August 2008–BALLON (P.), PIERSON (J.) & DELAERE (S.), *Test and experimentation platforms for broadband innovation: examining european practice*, in: *Conference Proceedings of 16th European Regional Conference by the International Telecommunications Society (ITS)*, Porto, Portugal, 4-6 September, 2005–BERGVALL-KAREBORN (B.)–STAHLBROST (A.), *Living Lab: an open and citizen centric approach for innovation* in: *International Journal of Innovation and Regional Development*, 2009, 1, 4, pp. 356-370–MULVENNA (M.), BERGVALL-KAREBORN (B.), WALLACE (J.), GALBRAITH (B.) & MARTIN (S.), *Living Labs as Engagement Models for Innovation* in: *Proceedings eChallenges-2010*. (Eds: Cunningham, Paul and Cunningham, Miriam), IIMC International Information Management Corporation,, pp. 1-11—FEUERSTEIN (K.), HESMER (A.), HRIBERNIK (K.A.), THOBEN (K.-D.), SCHUMACHER (J.), *Living Labs: a new development opportunity* in: SCHUMACHER (J.), NIITAMO (V.-P.) (eds.), *European Living Labs—A new approach for human centric regional innovation*, 2008–FOLSTAD (A.), *Living Labs for innovation and development of information and communication technology: a literature review* in: *Ejov. The electronical journal for virtual organisations and networks*, 10, special issue on Living Labs, August 2008.

[iii] The information on properties available in Brussels comes from multiple data sources made available through the Internet. Instead of interacting with these data sources directly and individually, all of the information needed is brought together and made accessible to the web and mobile components to one single, custom-built set of web services hosted on the EPIC platform.

[iv] The operationalisation of the Living Lab approach in EPIC is discussed in detail in deliverables D7.1: *'Pilot operations plan'* and D7.2 *'Report on 3 pilots'*, published on the EPIC website: http://www.epic-cities.eu/outcomes/additional.

[v] The test results are discussed in deliverable D7.3 *'Pilot Evaluation Report'*, published on the EPIC website: http://www.epic-cities.eu/outcomes/deliverable.

[vi] The management lessons are discussed in deliverable D7.2 *'Report on 3 pilots'*, published on the EPIC website: http://www.epic-cities.eu/outcomes/additional.

27

Smart City Indicators: Types, Uses, Issues and Standards

Gordon Falconer

Smart cities are very fashionable in urban and city circles, with intense focus on the concept from government, private sector and academia on sustainable or eco cities. Seemingly, every week another smart cities conference is announced or takes place somewhere in the world; it would be quite possible to be a full time speaker on smart cities. While not clearly defined, smart cities generally include a significant element of technology and information communication technology (ICT) to enable efficiencies and improve quality of life. Smart cities also are generally accepted as being highly sustainable and are inclusive of existing cities where eco activities are planned or still being developed.

Much of the focus on smart cities has centered around discussions on what are smart cities, how they should affect people's lives for the better and, in particular, upon the new technologies that offer the promise of doing more with less. Alongside these themes of smart cities is a perceived and, in some cases, mandatory requirement to assess and measure smart cities with an empathies on peer comparison. Multitudes of city indices have emerged to attempt to address this requirement over the years, many of which actually pre-date the current smart city discussions. Among these are the Mercer Quality of Living rankings, which have found favor with human resources managers for international relocation reference as well as the Greg Clark's "The Business of Cities."

When discussing smart cities, it is important to understand the types of city indices, how they are used, or should be used, and inherent issues that may affect the insights they provide, given their seemingly constant proliferation and focus.

Characteristics of City Indicators

The number of city indices around the world—Smart Cities, Liveable Cities, Global Cities, Green Cities, Innovative Cities, etc.—are almost too numerous to detail. Nevertheless, it is important to understand their characteristics to establish a form of typology that identifies broad characteristics rather than a data set and area of focus. Many of the indices will show parts of the defined characteristics below:

1. Annual or "Snapshots"

Most indices tend to be assessed and published annually, making them an annual "snapshot" in many ways. It is clear, however, that most are of a city's performance based on available data at a city level or a country level, taken at a single point in time on an annual basis.

2. Index Focus

Every index tends to have a particular focus area or theme (e.g. sustainability, innovation) and can be effectively broken into three main broad forms in focus and in use:

a. ***Citywide*** (e.g. Mercer Liveability Index, Monocle)

b. ***Sector Specific*** (e.g. U.S. News Top 10 Cities for Public Transport)

c. ***Narrow Sector Specific*** (e.g. Number of Bicycle Racks within The Copenhagen Bicycle Friendly City Index 2013)

The focus area of the index tends to determine whether the index is a high level "30,000" feet high view or a more detailed and specific index. It is difficult for any citywide index to be of great value to a sector-specific city project, which may not be in the areas covered by the index.

3. Qualitative and Quantitative data

Most organizations compile indices using a mixture of quantitative and qualitative indicators, with the weighting of each varying depending upon the methodology and data sets being used. Many indices do not publish in detail their methodology, although they will indicate the data sets used often.

4. Methodology

Every city index has a different methodology that generally comprise a variety of data sources. Each index uses various primary and secondary data sets within different city sectors to derive their results, which reflects the index focus and conclusions being sought. Most of these use publically available primary data or carry out their own direct primary or secondary research, which is still based on available public data but is aggregated or dissected to suit the index's purposes. All of this data is then weighted and scored, which yields an overall ranking; which is a key part of all of these indices.

Obviously, the cost to create and maintain any city index is determined by its focus area and methodology. However, it is safe to say that many indices are extremely expensive to maintain.

At a broad level we have further broken city indices data set types into the following (not exhaustive but simply illustrative):

- Economic performance based (financial, business etc.);
- Technology based (broadband speed, open data, etc.);
- Urban Form based (transport, infrastructure, power, water, etc.);
- Innovation based (knowledge, creativity, entrepreneurs, etc.);
- Environmental (sustainability, quality of water, etc.); and
- Quality of Life (happiness, safety, music events, etc.)

5. Aggregated Indices or "Indices of Indices"

Some indices use other indices in their data sets to derive their results. These indices are fast, cheap and simple compared to the larger indices because they use other primary research upon which to base their conclusions.

6. Research Houses and Sponsors

Established and reputable research organizations prepare many indices on behalf of sponsor organizations or directly for themselves to build thought leadership and credibility. Following are a few of the standard research type companies involved in research directly:

- ***Research companies***—Such as IDC, EIU, Forester, etc. tend to do a large amount of the "leg work" in researching indices.
- ***Real Estate/Engineering/Architectural Groups***—Specialist service companies/consultants, such as JLL, Knight Frank, ARUP, WSP and AECOM compile some types of city index data, but they tend to do so within specific sectors and often on behalf of direct clients, although some publish an index.
- ***Management Consultants***—Such as McKinsey, PWC, AT Kearney, etc., are active in researching and publishing city indices on multiple bases, and often for direct clients.
- ***NGOs/Think Tanks***—Many non-governmental organizations (NGOs) such as the World Bank, United Nations, ADB and Brookings prepare and research urban indices, some of which cross into the city space. The indices researched by the groups often tend to be prepared to promote the capabilities of the group preparing the study or are on behalf of a sponsor company.

Many of the sponsor companies generally seek to promote a particular line of thinking and to establish thought leadership and business credibility in the particular area of the index they are sponsoring (e.g.

Siemens Green City Index prepared by the Economist Intelligence Unit aligns with Siemens' focus on sustainability).

Types of index-sponsoring companies include:

- ***Private Sector Companies***—Heavily involved with sponsoring the publication of indices such as Siemens, IBM, etc.
- ***Universities***—Both sponsor research and develop it, although they are less involved with annual published indices and often use them at the qualitative end of the market and for direct clients.
- ***Governments***—Tend to be less directly involved but will often sponsor one-off city research using existing city index research houses.

Indices Sources and Examples

There is a bewildering array of city indicators, and it is imperative to understand their focus area and what methodology was used to compile them. In many instances, cities use indices as a form of advertising/public relations if they rank highly in them. Following are links to a selection of city indices:

- EIU—Liveable Cities
  http://www.eiu.com/site_info.asp?info_name=The_Global_Liveability_Report
- Siemens Green City
  http://www.siemens.com/entry/cc/en/greencityindex.htm
- European Smart Cities
  http://www.smart-cities.eu/
- Global Power City Index
  http://www.mori-m-foundation.or.jp/english/research/project/6/pdf/GPCI2011_English.pdf
- GSMA Smart City Index
  http://smartcitiesindex.gsma.com/
- Greg Clark—The Business of Cities—100 City Indexes Researched
  http://www.scribd.com/doc/60551428/The-Business-of-Cities-Greg-Clark-Main-Paper-June-2011
- Global City Indicators Facility (GCIF)
  http://www.cityindicators.org/

City Indicator Use

Among the most misunderstood and also rarely discussed issues surrounding city indices is in relation to their actual use and impact, and what unique insight is gleaned from them.

Adopting a cynical view, one could say many of the indices are not for real city usage, but rather to enable the index's sponsor to establish credibility and relevance. Many new indices simply tell us what we already know, especially given the plethora of the existing indices.

Many indices are published as part of an attempt by some companies or groups to establish relevance without really understanding whether the index will provide tangible value to users.

So many questions that tend to be left unanswered with city indices. Who is going to use the index and how is it going to provide insight to the user? Will the index provide a city with a relevant starting point or baseline? Will the index be of sufficient granularity to make a meaningful comparison for another city?

To help answer some of these questions, define a usage typology to examine the way any type of city index is used within a city. Commonly, city indices tend to be used in three main ways that reflect and map to the three defined "focus areas."

1. ***City Specific***—Citywide indices often tend to be used by cities for quick and simple benchmarking against other cities. In addition, cities like to use indices for external marketing, particularly if they have secured a high ranking.

2. ***Sector Specific***—These indices tend be sponsored by companies with a vested interest in selling into these industry sectors (e.g. IBM with its Commuter Pain City Index) and then are used by cities that are planning sector-specific reviews.

3. ***Narrow Sector Specific***—This is where consultants or engineers tend to use narrow sector-specific indices at a project level. If, for example, a city is planning an upgrade of its water treatment and water distribution network, then the relevant information tends to include items such as water use per person per liter per day, etc. Different measures will be relevant to different sectors of the city. Here, the measures tend to be more about "metrics" and not about "indices," as a metric is required at this granular level not a high-level index.

In other words, if a city index is to benefit a city, how will it be used? One way to answer this is to examine how cities set visions, develop programs and define projects to improve the city. To be relevant, any city index must assist a city with establishing its starting point when planning new initiatives. Of particular note here is the work done by the Smart City Stakeholders Platform (an European Union initiative) and the Covenant of Mayors (an EU initiative) to assist cities with planning for new projects. Both groups have prepared, "smart city integrated action plans" and "sustainable energy action plans" via a template approach.

Before cities can plan and evaluate a new initiative, they need to establish a baseline as was mentioned for the Covenant of Mayors. Generally, a city baseline is used to indicate where a city project is relative to other surveyed cities (which provide the benchmarks for comparison) and serves as a starting point to identify areas for improvement." A baseline can include a number of components, such as:

- Baseline Year (e.g. 2010, which is used for EU Covenant of Mayors Energy reductions); and
- Baseline Indicator (e.g. 400 liters of water per day per person usage).

At this stage, it is important to clarify the difference between a "baseline" and other concept such as "benchmarks" because they will affect the choice of appropriate indicators for assessing impacts and eventually assess the degree of success of the project.

Figure 1, which is a hypothetical diagram, outlines and describes how a baseline is used and compares it to other concepts.

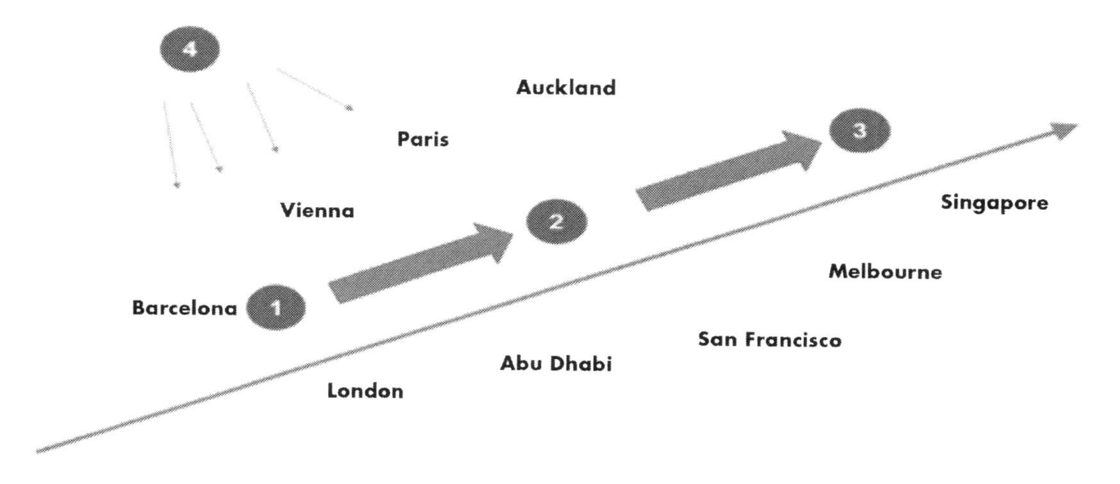

Figure 1. *(hypothetical diagram).*

1. ***Baseline Indicator***—Establishes where a city project or city program is relative to other surveyed cities (which provide the "benchmarks for comparison), but this is a starting point to identify areas for improvement. Various wide-ranging city indicators (e.g. smart city indices, quality of life, etc.) and vertical area indicators (e.g. water usage per day per person) are

available to assist in identifying the baseline for a given vertical area or for the city as a whole.

2. ***Target***—Cities need to set up policies, programs and projects to move from position 1 to position 2, the target, thus improving their performance in a given area (e.g. energy consumption). This target is unique to the particular city. Comparing the target with other benchmarks provides an understanding of how the project is improving the city's performance relative to its peers. The target figure is commonly determined by engineers or consultants based on the anticipated result of a proposed project or initiative.

3. ***Aspirational***—Where a city can aspire to go to by way of further focus and projects. This is a "stretch" target point to aim for, and many cities will adopt these aspirational targets to "shoot for the moon."

4. ***Benchmarks***—Other city scores, for whatever indicator is being measured, are the benchmarks by which the "baseline" location is ascertained. In the example, this could be liters of water consumed by the city per person per day, and shows the city's position relative to other cities.

Different projects will require access to different information or indicators, which are relevant to their particular sector. Often, setting a baseline is simple, while other times it is complex. And, in many cases, a cross-sector project may require multiple baselines. For example, a transport initiative may have a baseline indicator initially based upon walking time to the nearest bus stop. However, the project may affect the consumption of greenhouse gas emissions and thus, another baseline indicator would be relevant when establishing the baselines of the project and its value case.

Conversely, setting a baseline for water use will often use easily obtainable information such as water consumption per person per day, which is easily available, whereas identifying a baseline for "innovation" is less easily defined and requires definition, assumptions and a methodology.

After identifying the baseline, the city needs to compare its baseline against other cities by using benchmark data. Some of these indices are wide-ranging, and many are sector specific. Many of these indices will be suitable for a city when choosing a benchmark set for comparison. Each index uses various data sets to derive their results, and each index reflects the nature of the information and conclusions being sought. Most of these indexes use publically available primary data or carry out their own direct research, which still is based on available public data but is aggregated or dissected to suit the purposes of the index being prepared.

If a city uses a published index, it is important that it understands the methodology used to establish the index and thus why it is relevant and meaningful for a specific case.

An example for how a city uses a baseline in an urban assessment would include EU Planning initiatives. Again, the Covenant of Mayor signatories aim to meet and exceed the European Union 20 percent Co2 reduction objective by 2020 by Sustainable Energy action Plans SEAPs; this process requires a baseline to be established.

Using Indices, Metrics or Standards

Many indices such as World Bank Global City Indicator Forum (GCIF), Mercer Liveability Index, EIU European Green City Index, Sustain Lane (US), MasterCard Worldwide Centre's of Commerce Index, etc., have different definitions and categories, and seek to portray different perspectives of cities. In most cases, the aim of these high-level indices is to establish rankings or scorecards.

However, for a city to use any city index for a purpose other than marketing, it needs to be related to, and relevant for, the program or project being assessed and planned. Accordingly, different cities need different city indicators that match their plans. For example, if a city's new smart city initiatives focus on financial priorities, then the Green City Index would not be appropriate. Similarly, if a city's objectives focus on sustainability then the MasterCard Index is equally inappropriate.

Some index creators hope there will be only one set of city indicators required globally, but because cities are so complex and their priorities and objectives so very different, cities will naturally gravitate toward the city index (or metrics) whose methodology most closely matches their aspirations to enable benchmarking and comparisons.

Metrics is another term that is often used interchangeably with indicators, although the meaning of metrics is more associated with quantitative assessment used for measurement and comparison, or to track project performance. In practice, metrics tends to be a more granular way to measure and compare. Any smart water project, for example, will use specific metrics to establish its baseline and set targets; it may never need to consult city indices.

There is a move toward international standards for smart cities, with the International Standards Organization (ISO) having initiated standardization activities in the field of smart cities. ISO standardization objectives are to build certification rules. Certification standards are purportedly non-binding, which means cities or countries are able to use the recommendations and standards as they wish. In addition, the European Committee for Standardization (CEN), is about to start smart city standardization work at a European level. CEN rules for smart cities intend to build on ISO certification work.

The role and function, however, of smart city standards is unclear in relation to indices. In fact, one can argue that a smart city standard is almost akin to a city index. The issue is complicated by the constant interchange of targets and benchmarks.

Will a smart city standard be used as a target, or will it be confused with a benchmark? And of what level of granularity will it be? Above all, when a city is planning new initiatives, will any smart city standard really help, or will it be of no use at all?

Regardless of the answers are, there will be continued focus on standards, metrics and indices in the discussion of smart cities.

City Indicator Issues

Given that there are so many city indices with different focus areas and different methodologies, it is not surprising that there are a myriad of issues that need to be highlighted:

- ***High Level***—Much data is collated at a high level and not granular enough.
- ***Data Ownership***—Resistance from some data providers in a city's ecosystem to provide data in granular format, partly due to privacy issues and regulatory frameworks.
- ***Cultural***—Massive variations in relationships to data across countries.
- ***Municipal Boundaries***—Vast differences in data comparisons due to the different urban forms, as some cities are mainly residential while others are mainly commercial.
- ***Varied Data Sources/Formats***—Data is from multiple agencies and individual corporations with little uniformity between them, which is exacerbated across countries.
- ***Different Perspectives of a City***—Different indices methodologies view the same cities but by different lenses, meaning cities can have different rankings in various indices.
- ***Data Format***—Most indices are "batch" driven, which is time consuming to collate.
- ***Regional Data***—Much city data is country wide or regionally based, and then adjusted for ...
- ***Typology & Taxonomy***—No standard typology or taxonomy for cities for data reporting;
- ***Data Ownership***—Cities don't own most of the data generated within a city and thus have no access to it, so much is missed; and
- ***Engineering Versus Economic Data***—Causes varied results when two different types of data sets are mixed. Conclusion

Clearly, there are many issues to be aware of when using city indicators. Among them:

- City indices are, mostly, extremely complex;
- They are time consuming to collate and create;
- They require significant resources such as a team;
- They are often extremely expensive to fund annually;
- New indices or standards would need to strongly differentiate themselves from so many others.

Indices, standards, metrics and use is confusing; and the basis and the methodology of various city indicator sets vary widely, with many differences in quantitative and qualitative approaches and methodologies. Many of the indices have different definitions and categories and seek to portray very different perspectives of cities. All of them, of course, have their place and if used well, can provide valuable insights.

Yet with the new city indices appearing disappearing, along with the looming onrush of smart city standards, there is potential for more confusion rather than clarity. It's time to start drawing a line in the sand and be clear about what cities need to progress and become smarter, and how indices and standards will help them achieve that goal.

Moreover, it is crucial to highlight questions regarding how city indices are actually used, who uses them and what value they add. Rather than rushing toward creating more indices and standards, review what's available and what the cities and the users of the information really need and want.

GORDON FALCONER *is a smart city expert advisor, city consultant, global thought leader in cities and technology clusters, property and infrastructure developer, city developer, and property asessor/chartered surveyor/appraiser. He has worked on cities and city-scale projects globally as a trusted advisor to public and private sectors, NGOs, government leaders, theWorld Bank and European Commission. In Singapore, he is an advisor to government agencies and research and development panels. In the United Kingdom, he is an advisory board member for University College London's City Leaders program. Falconer also is formerly a director of urban innovation for Cisco IBSG, and has more than 20 years of experience in urban property development, project valuations/feasibility, property/infrastructure financial structuring, and property portfolio asset management. He formerly was head of strategy and real estate for Masdar city in Abu Dhabi in the United Arab Emirates, one of the world's most innovative sustainable and smart city projects.*

Printed in Great Britain
by Amazon.co.uk, Ltd.,
Marston Gate.